Our
Family's Book
of ACTS
To Love & Serve the LORD

To Elena —
Believe in miracles!!
Genie

GENIE SUMMERS

"It has seemed good to me to publish the signs and wonders which the most high God has accomplished in my regard.

"How great are his signs, how mighty his wonders; his kingdom is an everlasting kingdom, and his dominion endures through all generations."

Daniel 3:100 NAB

ISBN 978-0-615-45595-2

Acknowledgements

This book has been written in little chunks of time over the span of a decade or more. Mainly, I want to thank Frank, my *knight in shining armor*, for standing firm and not allowing me to drop this project. His insistence on accuracy and attention to grammar was essential. I want to thank my fabulous family for living our book of Acts. So many FMC missionaries have contributed what they thought was a small thing but really made a big difference. I am truly grateful for all the people and places in the book. They have made our story possible. I thank my Dad, who encouraged me and prayed over my manuscript from his sickbed. I thank Beau for his earlier insights and editing of the entire book. Mary painstakingly edited several chapters of the second draft. I thank David and Vicki Fruge who lent me their camp, which is a perfect writer's haven. I thank Elizabeth Hollier for proofreading and editing. I thank John Paul for his work and cover design. Jill T. Summers has done the *final corrections*. Sarah's book, ***Eat Raw Omelets,*** inspired me to finish mine, and that really was the catalyst. Thank you, Sarah. Without the technical computer assistance from James Franke, this work would not have made it to press.

Thank You Jesus, thank You Holy Spirit, and thank you, God My Father for all the miracles and especially the miracle of finishing this work.

"But they went forth and preached everywhere, while the Lord worked with them and confirmed the word through accompanying signs."

Mk 16:20 NAB

Wedding Day
May 11,1963

Florida, Passed the Bar Exam! 1966

Family Missions Company
Big Woods Mission
Abbeville, Louisiana 2007

Speaking in New York
September, 2011

iv

About the Author:

Genie Summers

Genie Summers is co-founder and a director of Family Missions Company. FMC trains and sends Catholic Lay Evangelists proclaiming the Gospel and serving the poor across the globe. Genie, with an English degree from the University of Louisiana at Lafayette, is a teacher, playwright, and published author. Since 1970, she has been published in both the Christian and the secular press. Her first book, ***Go! You Are Sent,*** *is* volume one of the testimony of her faith journey. Genie and her family's life and work have been noticed in the media, both television and radio. She has been engaged in conference speaking both in the USA and abroad, and is fluent in Spanish.

Frank and Genie, have been married forty-nine years, are parents of seven children: Beau, Sarah Granger, Susanna VanVickle, Mary Magdalen Hindelang, Simon-Peter, Joseph and John Paul. They have sixteen precious grandchildren, with one more on the way. Genie is explicitly Pro-Life. While respecting all Christians, Genie's ministry has centered in the renewal of her Catholic brothers and sisters at home and abroad.

"So they stayed for a considerable period, speaking out boldly for the Lord, who confirmed the word about his grace by granting signs and wonders to occur through their hands."
Acts 14:3   NAB

Prologue Note:

Go! You Are Sent is the first volume of our testimony. It recounts an incredible odyssey of Faith. Jesus scooped us up, saved our marriage and propelled us into an awesome adventure with Him. We sold and gave away all, and set out as lay Catholic missionaries to evangelize and serve God's children to the ends of the Earth. In the first book, miracles of our own personal transformation and miracles in our ministry jumped off the pages. It has been thirty-six years since we started this journey and miracles still punctuate our lives.

This volume, **Our Family's Book of Acts**: *To Love and Serve* **the Lord** covers lots more years.

We were on fire with the Holy Spirit. Our family set out to be doers of the Word, not hearers only. We did. But The Lord propelled us, taught us to love and serve, and confirmed His Word with Signs and Wonders. This book **is** Our Family's Book of Acts; each chapter extols the greatness of our God in our lives. But, I hope, that, like the book of Acts in the Bible, reading the whole makes truths sink in about our faith, about miracles signs and wonders that the Lord bestowed on us. He never failed to confirm His Word as we preached and shared. It was always His work. We were simply His family of lay missionaries.

Going to the ends of the Earth was our call. Telling the dwellers in those far off places about our friend, Jesus, was our joy. He revealed to us His beautiful bride, the Church. And He showed us, His "family in mission", to His bride. We were blown by the wind of His Spirit, we found ourselves searching in our souls for *our place* in Christendom. Jesus chose *us* and sent *us*. Was he choosing and sending other families and laity? Where were the others like us? Aren't we as laity all called to "evangelize and sanctify the world?" (Vat II. "Decree on the Apostolate of the Laity) Were we, the Summers family, a special species of Catholic that is called to Mission?

We are convinced that others are being called. We begged to be led to them; we set out on a mission, to find that community, organization, or Church family that would say, "Yay! Go for the Gold, Lay Missionaries."

Starting in 1973, God trained us for twenty-three years

in His own roving school of Missionary Evangelism. Then He brought us home. We returned to Abbeville, Louisiana empowered by the display of great signs and mighty works that we saw and experienced. Miracles were our spiritual vitamin regime. Jesus used them to keep us preaching and praying and living the Gospel.

Frank and I have seven children and sixteen grandchildren (and one on the way), and thousands of spiritual "children." We have founded and formed Family Missions Company, an apostolate of Lay Missionaries, families and singles. FMC gives lay Catholic missionary evangelists a home, and sends them out t*o love and serve, to live their own book of Acts.*

At Big Woods Mission (our Central Base), we notice that our prayers have been answered. Our mission work was little understood at first. But, now we can feel a tsunami of grace rolling onto the shores of Catholicism and it is rearranging the Church. One of its principal waves is *vibrant, vital mission*.

The entire planet was preparing for a catastrophic end of the world, Y2K, the year, 2000. As I waited for that year in prayer, I asked God,

"Lord Jesus, tell me how I should prepare for the new millennium."

I heard Him say to me:

"This is the millennium of mission. This is the firing gun, the starting gate of those bearers of hope who will reach the un-reached with the Gospel. Be passionate. The Good News is ready to run. Shout it from the housetops; tell them that I, Jesus, am the same, yesterday, today, and forever. I am the Son of the Father, and the Sender of the Holy Spirit. I am the Way, the Truth and the Life! Genie, let's Go into the new millennium. I will continue confirm your call to the missions with signs and wonders!"

It is good to sing praises unto the Lord…. Sing to the Lord with thanksgiving. Sing praise on the harp to our God. *Psalm 147*

Our family is always singing: before meals; to enter into prayer; and often in spontaneous praise. The Lord inhabits the praises of His people.

To My Children

Beau, Sarah, Susanna, Mary Magdalen,
Simon-Peter, Joseph, and John Paul

You Are the Sunshine Of My Life!

Back (Left to Right) Joseph, Beau and John Paul
Front, Susanna, Sarah, Mary, and Simon-Peter

Artist M. Wayne Broussard's depiction the Summers family carrying our cross, beckoned on by the Lord Jesus.

We answered His call to go into all the world, and preach the Gospel to every creature!

From the Great Wall of China to Amazonia

Received by Papal Nuncios, cardinals, bishops, laity, clergy, singles, families, and apostolates in His Name.

Table of Contents

Chapter One

News From Home – An Open Door

"Pops, we're still in Virginia. It is freezing over here. You wouldn't believe the icicle that is in my friend's shower. It starts at the showerhead and touches the floor." Beau practically shouted into the phone, gesturing from ceiling to floor. It was obvious that he missed his grandfather.

"Are you having any fun there?" my daddy asked.

"I am having fun. I just milked some goats. Did you ever milk a goat?"

Beau listened intently, and then responded laughingly, "Pops, I don't believe you. You *never* milked a *bear*!" Beau grinned and shook his head; his Pops was always ready with a funny answer.

Beau motioned to me, "Mom, Mamaw wants to talk to you."

Mom asked me, "Where are you? I haven't heard from y'all in a while?"

"Hey, Mom. We're still in Virginia in Brown's Cove, house sitting for Jim and Cathy. Today we are with our friend, John Findley. This place is idyllic – a great old stone farmhouse sitting on a hill framed by glorious fall colors. You would grab your paintbrushes if you saw how spectacular the leaves are. "

"Not over here, most of summer is still hanging on. We're outside, eating barbeque in shorts and t-shirts."

"What's new in Abbeville?" I asked, not prepared for the answer she would give.

I was glued to the phone as Mom informed me about the latest happenings in our Christian circle back in Abbeville. She told me that our friends the Listis and the Bernards were making

1

decisions that had electrified our hometown. The Bernards and the Listis, our Abba Prayer Community friends, were seriously committing themselves to building a Christian community.

"The Listis sold their house in Mt. Carmel Heights. They are selling everything too, just like you and Frank did."

"Wow, Mom. That is a crazy surprise. We will have to keep them in our prayers."

"Where will they be moving?" I eagerly inquired.

"I think they have already started working on that old abandoned rectory. You know, the place where you studied Latin that summer, Our Lady of Lourdes rectory. It needs cleaning up and painting on the inside. I don't know much else about it. I told 'Pete' (Kay Listi's mom), 'Don't worry, Pete. It isn't too bad having kids that are religious *nuts'*." She laughed teasingly.

"Thanks, Mom," I retorted, also teasing, "It's good to have you on our side."

"I *pray* for you, you know that!" she said. "I hope you are happy."

As I hung up, Frank was waiting to hear what Mom had told me about the Listis. I enthusiastically reported all the details. "It seems more radical when someone else does it."

I couldn't squelch my surprise and pleasure.

He just smiled, cleared his throat and said, "Let's begin our Bible study. Where did we leave off last week?"

Our weekly Bible study with John Findley during our Virginia sojourn had been a source of strength and ministry for all of us.

Only a few years back, Frank and I had come so close to divorce. Now, as we ended our Bible study and supper with songs of praise and worship, all was right in our family. Frank's full voice always soothes me and anchors my soul. Peace swept over me as I nursed Sarah and watched Frank play. Just three years before, Jesus had stepped in and saved us knowing what a great adventure He had planned for us.

The Lord moved into our hearts and lives with amazing power when we first turned our lives over to Him. So much has happened since. We even looked different physically. Frank grew a beard, wore simple clothes. I let my hair grow longer and wore longer skirts. Frank was over six feet tall, and I am only five feet tall. Frank is blond with hazel eyes, and wears simple glasses. I have dark brown hair and dark brown eyes. Beau, at twelve, still dressed like a kid, and had a full head of extra blonde hair and strong good looks. He had not hit his growing spurt yet, but he looked like he would soon shoot up, strong and tall. Our beautiful baby, Sarah, delighted us with her big, steel blue eyes, porcelain skin and blonde hair. She had full lips and a dimple in her chin, just like mine.

"Can you believe it, Frank?" I whispered after Beau and Sarah were asleep.

"Believe what?" he replied.

"After so much searching for just the right community, the Abba Prayer Community in Abbeville is going to gel after all. All those months we prayed, before we left for mission…it's finally happening." I explained.

"Tell me again exactly what your mother told you. The Listis and the Bernards are ready to move into a live-in Christian community?"

"Exactly. They are already fixing up the old Lourdes rectory. It is happening."

"Well, that could be what we have been waiting to hear. I have been expecting God to indicate when and where we will be on our next mission. Latin America isn't open yet. Jim and Kathy have been great hosts, but it is time for us to move on."

"I've been asking the Lord to speak to us soon." I answered.

"Maybe this news is His guidance to go back to Abbeville for a season." Frank said.

"We begged God to build a Catholic covenant community and waited months and months. We thought His answer to that prayer was, '*NO!*' Apparently *His* answer was really – '*Not yet.*' Is now the time? Has Catholic community arrived in Abbeville at last?" I asked.

That night as I lay down on our bedroll and cuddled next to Frank, I closed the day with prayer, "Jesus, we are yours. Thank you for the privilege we have enjoyed as your servants in Tonga, Samoa – so many places. If it is truly Your will, allow us to go home for a season. Let us participate as fully as we can in the work You are doing there."

Soon after, we left the icicles in Virginia. In early November, we arrived in Louisiana by train to experience the tail end of a lazy summer that had not yet retired. The Atchafalaya Basin's sultry swamp showed few signs of fall. The trip had taken about a week from Charlottesville to New Orleans. We stopped briefly at the Summers' home in Uptown New Orleans, borrowed a car, and headed out to Cajun Country. We loved the drive over the Basin. It was so pristine; some said there were places in the vast waterways that man still had never seen. Tall, straight cypress trees hovered over the stretches of idyllic scenery. The "knees" dotted the smooth surface, looking like miniature sentinels dutifully standing their ground. The skies were incredibly blue, Spanish Moss swayed in the breeze. Yep, we were home; home in God's country.

"The basin is healthy right now. The water is so clear." Frank commented as we drove along.

"A beautiful white egret over there, and look there's a great blue heron." I joined in.

"Did your Mom say she was cooking jambalaya or sauce piquant?"

"I think she said jambalaya, and teal ducks. Dad and the boys had a great teal season this September."

Beau and baby Sarah were asleep in the back of the car. It wouldn't be long now. Abbeville was about fifty miles away.

"We'll be home for awhile. I'm fine with Abbeville being our mission post for now." I mused as we drove along.

"Mission life is the best life for us – not because the life we renounced wasn't great. Mission is the best life, paradoxically, because in renunciation of our old life, our old life is redeemed. God calls us to love and appreciate the faith, culture and family back home as a gift from God," Frank commented.

We had been missionaries for two years now, and had been to the ends of the Earth – it is amazing the love God has for His children tucked away at the ends of the Earth. There the Lord had used us, trained us, tried us, and cemented our desire to serve Him full time. And now, He was sending us back, directing us clearly through His word. Frank had heard the Lord in his prayer time speak clearly to him, "Frank, now is the time for you to support the work that I, Myself, am doing."

"Do you want to recite the Rosary? We have enough time to finish one before we get there." Frank suggested.

"Sure, let's remember to pray for a place to live next to the old rectory that the Listis and the Bernard's are renovating." I answered.

Frank began, "Lord Jesus, we lift up this Rosary in gratitude for all the miracles, signs, and wonders you have performed in our mission life so far. We wait to hear from you. We will serve wherever You place us. Please be with us in our time at home. Help us to be blessing to those who wait for us. Sweet Mother Mary, enfold us in your mantle, let your humble 'Yes' always guide us in imitation of your Divine Son. Holy Spirit inflame us with zeal. In the name of the Father, the Son and the Holy Spirit...."

As we left the basin bridge behind, we were once again in the *heart* of our Cajun culture – truly a subculture. How can we describe our captivating region – old-world charm, genteel ways, tantalizing cuisine, a rich deposit of faith, an art of turning marshland into productive, well groomed farmland, a respect for life, a mystical music that spins a melodic spell and tells yarns of a people, ultra-sincere hospitality, a love of creation, and an easy "family-first" fidelity. Acadiana speaks two languages. I remember my great-grandmother was visiting in Kansas City once when my uncle's friends teased her about her French accent. She answered, "I speak two languages. How many do you speak?"

Kisinoaks, my old home, spread its green lawns out to us; so many things on the estate were evergreen. The gentle brown bayou rippled with a cool north wind. Across the bayou and in the woods the trees were donning their fall hues. Fall rarely arrives in Louisiana before November. Sometimes it barely arrives at all. The big colonial house looked whiter than ever and the shutters a deeper green – a jewel in the perfect setting.

We woke Beau and Sarah, and started unpacking our meager belongings. We sounded the horn and a steady flow of Gremillion's (my brothers and sister, nieces and nephews) emerged from the house. Mama's jambalaya and the aroma of teal ducks stewing beckoned us inside. It was good to be there. We had been so itinerant, like St. Francis of Assisi, like St. Paul, in these first two years of mission. What a two years it had been, a roving, missionary "boot camp." And we had seen His power at work.

Daddy asked Frank, "How long do you think you will be here this time?"

Mama chimed in, "I wish you all would decide to come back permanently".

"It's amazing how God has led us. We are home for a while, but He hasn't showed me how long. We'll just trust and see." Frank answered.

"I'd like to find a small place, perhaps with two bedrooms." I said hopefully.

"Let's at least stay a week here at Kisinoaks. I've been lonesome!" Beau added.

"Sure, we'll stay for awhile. Maybe soon we can find a place near where Vince and Kay and the Bernard's are. We want to be as near to them as we can." Frank said.

I replied, "I do too. Let's go early tomorrow morning after prayer and scout it out."

After a scrumptious meal and a rare but wonderful time of prayer and praise with the Gremillions, we went upstairs to the bedroom I used as a girl. Even though I had been gone from home for thirteen years, the room was still a prissy pink. My flounce bedspread was still on my brass bed. Sarah's portable bed fit perfectly in front of the balcony door. We slept in total peace.

The next morning we headed out to Our Lady of Lourdes rectory, which was being transformed into the home where community was to be built. "Look Dad, that must be the house. The Listi's and the Bernard's are out in the yard."

Our brothers and sisters looked up from their work. Welcoming smiles reached out to us. Suddenly, almost instantly, we were united in Jesus. The call of the Gospel to "give everything and hold nothing back" was real. It was real for the Summers', it was real for the Listi's, it was real for the Bernard's.

"You have an extra paintbrush?" Frank asked just before Vince gave him a big bear hug.

"When did you get in?" Kay and Judy asked in unison.

"Yesterday" I replied. "We drove by here as soon as we

got back, but y'all had finished for the day. When do you think you'll be moving in?" I asked Kay.

"Donnie's lumberyard just has to put in the kitchen floor, so it should be just a few days. Do you want to see the house? It's plenty big enough for two families."

My eyes welled up with tears as I walked around the old rectory. It was simple. It was spacious. It was perfect for the beginning of community. Already, religious art and symbols of surrender to the Gospel adorned the walls. The Holy Spirit was living there even before they moved in. I could feel Him.

Vince was being offered the old Elizabeth Seton convent a block away, to house a ministry to the poor in Abbeville. The new ministry was called the Christian Service Center. Red Bernard continued his work as an electrician, but also became the youth minister for the parish.

Almost three years before, several families gathered weekly to seek God's help for building a covenant community modeled on the Book of Acts. Nothing materialized. The call in the heart of the Listis and Bernards just would not go away. Now with the help and blessing of Monsignor Mouton, the pastor at St. Mary Magdalen, the door was being opened. The Listis and the Bernards put their faith into action and walked through that door, hoping other families would soon follow. They had begged Jesus to name their community. Jesus answered. In prayer, they received a name – The Open Door Community. God's word had inspired them with the beautiful quote from Revelation 3:8: *"I know your works, behold, I have set before you an open door, which no one is able to shut."*

From the outset, the Summers family shared goals and hopes in common with the members of Open Door. We had outlined essentials for our life; their essentials matched ours. The main difference was that we desired to live our call in the foreign missions, and they felt the call to be "in mission" to those in Abbeville. We became associate members, because we would move about. Open Door was our spiritual home.

Compared to the Alleluia Community in Augusta, Georgia and Word of God Community in Ann Arbor, Abbeville's effort was a small beginning, but, nevertheless, a great beginning. We lived so simply. Our family's material needs were met by a small mineral royalties check or an

7

occasional donation from those who wanted to applaud and uphold us as lay Catholics in mission. When we talked at conferences, people always slipped a little something into our pockets.

In time, the Lord Jesus used us all to build these humble beginnings into the Family Life Community. Today, thirty-four years later, Abbeville's spiritual fiber is strengthened by the "Yes!" of that first community.

Frank, Beau and I had prayed and searched for a house to rent near the community. The phone rang while I was at Kisinoaks one day. It was Frank calling from the Center.

"*Right across* the street from the Christian Service Center? A rent house? Really, Frank?" I could hardly contain my excitement.

"Don't get too excited until you see it. It's spacious, but it is very poor and basic. The greatest thing about it is that it's a block away from the Open Door Community home. We'll be able to share in all of the community life."

The day we moved in, Beau made friends with our new neighbors, Ronnie Meaux and his twins named Ronald and Donald. Pops, my Dad, brought us a swing for our porch. Sarah was learning to scoot around in her walker and the large rooms were perfect for us. We were so happy!

When the Lord begins a work, there is a glory upon it that ignites those who participate. Open Door Community was like the first Christian community – the one Luke describes in the *Acts of the Apostles*. The Open Door Community did indeed have its door open to all who came. We loved Jesus in the least of our brothers. One of the regular visitors at the kitchen door of the old rectory (turned community home) was Sarge. He came by often. We smiled as we heard his familiar:

"I have ulcers. The only thing I can eat are cheese and jelly sandwiches. And I just can't wait, or my ulcers will get worse."

Another regular was the deaf mute named Murphy, who came on his bicycle every evening; we served him a take home plate. He would use sign language to say "Thank you from my aged father and me."

We had our meals in common as a community. After our common meals, lunch and dinner, Vince, using his head coach voice, called out the clean-up duty roster. He sounded like an announcer at a football game calling out the line-up. We laughed and joked as we worked together. Even chore time was fun as good-natured banter filled the kitchen. Since we chose not to have a television, we always had some news of the work God had done in or through us for others, rather than watching the news each evening.

I believe we were a sign to those who came into contact with us. We learned God's ways as married couples and as parents by reading, studying, praying, and most of all, by exerting all of our strength. We women of the Open Door Community were fully engaged in God's service. Only, our service was done in our homes.

"Frank, I am so happy with all the time I get to spend in community activities with Kay and Judy. Andrea, John, and Pam are such a gift to Sarah." I said one evening.

"You are really enjoying our sweet Sarah, aren't you?'

"All those years, I didn't have a baby. What was I thinking? This is a joy that engulfs me. My favorite part of the day is when we swing on the porch together." I turned from Frank to Sarah as she looked up from nursing.

"You are a little charmer, my Sarah. Your hair is as soft as a blooming mimosa."

Sarah smiled up at me.

In my heart, I was filled to overflowing with gratitude for Open Door and the life we lived for Jesus.

Frank, Sarah, and Mary Magdalen is in the back pack. We were in mission in Malaybalay, Bukidnon, Philippines. Kaamulan Festival of Tribal Peoples. 1982

Two mission hearts and lives united as one:
Kevin J. Granger and Sarah Summers Granger.
This was our whole family on February 2, 2009.
Eight have been added since. One more is on the way.

Chapter Two

Christian Service Center

The old Seton Convent was a perfect place to receive the constant stream of those in need. Located in a fringe neighborhood, it was accessible to all of Abbeville. Holy lives had been lived there when Mother Seton's nuns gave their lives in service of the poor. The convent's efficiently planned small spaces exuded a fragrance of sacrifice. There was a chapel, small offices, a kitchen, storerooms, and a simple living room. The Christian Service Center, directed by Vince Listi, was a sacred space. Frank was delighted to be a volunteer, to surrender his time to answer God's call to serve the poor. Most of those in need believed that their principal need was for financial help. An enormous variety of emergencies gripped them in helplessness and in panic.

Vince and Frank's constant refrain to the endless stream of needy brothers and sisters challenged them to come to a new perspective, "We can help you overcome this emergency. We can give you clothes or money now, but *only Jesus* can continue to supply all your needs in the future. The greatest need is to know Jesus!"

Vince and Frank would pray and counsel them for the worry and problems that brought them to the center in the first place. After prayer, they would counsel them. "You must first 'repent, reform your lives, and believe the good news.' And it is good news. Jesus loves you and is waiting to show you his love."

Conversions abounded as hearts of the clients witnessed these strong men of God laying down their lives in the service of

11

the poor. The Center became a haven for those who found Jesus. They came back, volunteering themselves using the newfound grace they had received to give back to others. Every day the whole operation shut down mid-morning for a prayer meeting with the staff and the needy. It lasted an hour. Frank played the music. Vince and Frank gave teachings. Early on, Frank's song, *Walking with Jesus,* became the theme song of the center.

They interceded for the needs of those who came for help, praying for the spread of God's Kingdom on Earth, and for donations of food, clothes, furniture and other basics that the poor lacked. God answered their prayers. Volunteers prayed specifically, "Lord Jesus, please send a good mattress for old Mr. Campbell. Please send a good stove for Miss Crissy." When the exact specific things they had prayed for were brought in by donors, their shouts of joy reached me in my kitchen all the way across the street.

Besides prayer for physical healing and spiritual counseling, the Christian Service Center connected the poor with all the services offered by the government and other volunteer organizations in the region. There was no public transportation in Abbeville. People needing rides to the doctor, or during other emergencies, would be picked up by volunteer drivers from the center. Clothes, food and furniture were given out. Jim Grant, a former Peace Corps volunteer, baked and distributed bread there. God's people found the Christian Service Center to be a lively, bubbling, fountain of grace.

One afternoon, Frank and I were sitting on the porch when I said, "Babe, I feel like true missionaries right here. I guess God will call us back to foreign missions soon."

"Genie, I'm surprised at how happy I am to be in evangelistic outreach to these neighborhoods and housing projects. The marginalized and 'un-churched' are easier to reach when someone meets them where they live."

"We really are becoming a part of this area." I added.

"I love working at the Christian Service Center's house prayer groups. Every week, I marvel at their faith. One of our small groups has felt inspired to pray fervently and diligently that "Son of Sam", that scary serial killer, will be converted. That takes faith! Their faith is so bold and simple," Frank explained.

God answered the prayers of not only our small house prayer group but also of many others. David Berkowitz, also known as Son of Sam, *was converted* and has spent the remainder of his life ministering to others. He has a ministry called "Forgiven for Life." He has even been interviewed by Focus on the Family. He is reaching out to others with the Gospel.

For those associated with the Christian Service Center, prayer was the work of the Lord, and *nothing* was too big for their faith.

One day a friend called Frank at the center. He made an urgent plea. "Please help my former worker, Al. He's not married in the church and now he's dying of heart trouble."

Al's house was three or four blocks from the center. It was a rent house, badly in need of repair; the porch was giving way. From the outside, it was a sad little house. Frank knocked, and a young woman in her early twenties answered the door. He thought that her husband would be young, too.

"How strange for a young man to be dying of the complications of a heart attack," he thought.

Susan, Al's young wife, ushered him into the second room of their two-room house. Al was not young; he was completely grey. His hair was grey and his skin had that grey pallor of death. Susan was pregnant.

"Nelson called me at the Christian Service Center," Frank began, "He's worried about you and he asked me to come here and pray for your healing. Would you like for me to pray with you?"

"Okay," Al replied reluctantly.

Frank started talking to him about the Lord, and the saving, healing power of Jesus. He spoke to him of the hope we find when we rely on God; when we call on the power of the Holy Spirit to fill us, heal us and renew us.

"You need a new heart, Al," Frank said with compassion, "That's the business the Lord Jesus is in – the new heart business. He can heal you and give you a whole new life!"

Al kept talking about the faith that his mother had. He didn't make any clear profession of faith in Jesus, but he opened his

13

heart to the prayer Frank prayed for healing. A few days later, Frank was shocked when Al came walking into the Christian Service Center.

"I came by to tell you that the Lord healed me! I want to serve him."

He was healed and needed a job to support his wife and coming baby. Fervent petitions went up. A job was created for him; several pharmacies got together and hired him as a deliveryman. He and Susan were instructed and married in the Church. Plumbers and carpenters offered their services to fix up his house. The new heart and the new life that Jesus promised became a reality for Al and his wife.

Many of the people who came to the center were in need of temporary shelter. Our home was the answer for those in need. We usually had someone staying with us. Quite a few had mental problems. Once, we had a bad experience with a young man who was hallucinating from LSD flashbacks. After the cops hunted him down in our backyard, Beau (now thirteen) prayed, "Dear Lord, please, *'puhleese'*, don't send us any more crazy people."

And Jesus said, "Yes!" He didn't send any more people suffering from mental illness to Alphonse Street.

Jesus' enemies called him a winebibber and a glutton, as well as friend of tax collectors and prostitutes. The Christian Service Center dealt frequently with hard working people who had been hurled into hard times. Transients, motorcycle gang members, prostitutes, the disabled – both physically and mentally - rape victims and others from all walks of life who found themselves in need came to us for help.

Community life and service at the Christian Service Center was an important formation for our family – Frank, Beau, Sarah and me. Beau entered Mt. Carmel Elementary in seventh grade. Beau was persecuted at school. The other kids teased him for professing boldly that he believed in Jesus. I recently visited with a woman who was a year behind Beau in school. Tears streamed down my face as she related the suffering he had endured from those who teased him while at Mt. Carmel Elementary. Part of his difficulty stemmed from changing his position as one of the more financially and socially privileged students to one of the least privileged and the poorest – a hard transition in a same small community. God was faithful; he had other things he wanted to teach Beau.

He found many new outlets for the energies of a bright thirteen year old. He endured and came back stronger. Beau started a lawn mowing business with his neighborhood friends. He came bursting into the house one day. "Mom, Ronald and Donald can't believe how many rich people I know. And the rich want to pay us for mowing their big lawns. They think I have 'connections'."

Beau learned trick cycling, aggressive street basketball and developed passionate friendships in that neighborhood. He read avidly, and had a full life. Living for a while in a lower middle class neighborhood in America gave him a perspective that years of school could not have given him.

My contribution to community life was the weekday lunch meal. Everyday I cooked for the staff of the center, the poor that happened to be there at lunch, and the community. Frank washed all the dishes.

We had a huge dining room. The meal was served buffet style in the kitchen. On an average day eighteen to twenty people came for lunch. Marc André was a Christian who hailed from Montreal. He found the Lord in a movement of Catholic young people called the Apostles of Jesus through Mary. Marc and his family were staying with us while they worked on their bus turned mobile home. One day we served tuna casserole with noodles. We sang joyfully to the Lord before every meal.

Frank prayed "Jesus, thank you for your provision. You always feed us from your abundance. Please bless our food and our fellowship, feed your poor, give us all we need, Lord, send us every good blessing. Bless us, oh Lord, and these Thy gifts...."

Marc Andre came in late for lunch one Friday. About twenty of us had already gone ahead of him. When he finally got to the huge magnalite pot of tuna casserole, there was only a couple of tablespoons left.

He served the meager serving and thought to himself, "Oh, well, I'll fill up on bread and butter."

After a few minutes, he was still hungry, and went into the kitchen to try to find something else to eat. He happened to glance into the pot that he himself had emptied. In utter astonishment, he caught his breath.

"This pot is half full of tuna casserole! It was empty a few minutes ago!" He praised God in his charming French accent, returned to the table, and sat down to eat.

Others then also went back for another serving. The Lord had *multiplied the food*. There were several witnesses. We were reminded of the scripture, "*The poor are filled with every good thing*!"

Sarah was almost a year old during our first time in the Open Door Community. One morning in May, we strolled down our front walk, heading for the local corner grocery store. We didn't have a car. Beau whizzed by on his bike and flashed me a smile. My freshly washed sheets, flapping in the wind, caught my eye as I left our house behind. It was one of those days of wonder and peace when, as my friend Kay says, "God is in His heaven and all is right with the world." We felt so settled, so truly at home.

Returning from shopping, I put the groceries down and was pulling the stroller up our front steps onto the porch. The mailman Jimmy came sauntering up. With Sarah on my hip, I crossed the street to the Christian Service Center to tell Frank that we had some interesting mail. He walked back across the street with me so that we could read our letters aloud together. Mail, for the missionary, means a great deal. It's a social occasion! We sat on the swing and read. Father Jim, whom we met the year before, from South America, was very interested in our offer to serve in "El Camino" Community in Colombia, the Diocese of San Gil.

His beautiful letter:
Dear Frank, Genie, Beau and Sarah,

El Camino community serves young people who live and work on the community farm. They grow as Christians and have an opportunity to receive a secondary education. Volunteers have come for short periods. We would be interested in your offer to give a longer time to the mission.

I will be in Ann Arbor, Michigan next summer to visit with my cousin. If you want to further discuss your interest in El Camino, would it be possible for you to meet me there?

Your Servant in Christ,
Fr. Jim Mitchell

"Wow, Sugar, I had almost given up on hearing from Fr. Jim. Last year when we were in Ann Arbor, we didn't expect to wait this long for a response. Are you up for another trip to Ann Arbor?" Frank replied.

"Has it been a whole year since we were in Ann Arbor?" I queried, "Well, it would be fun to see the Wilds again, but we don't have a car."

We shared the news with Beau, who responded, "Daddy, I bet we could use Paw Paw's red farm truck, to go to Ann Arbor."

"That's a thought; maybe we could make a camping trip out of it – less expensive."

"Yes," I said, "My father has a camper top out in the woods that he's not even using. I wonder if it would fit on the red truck?"

And it did – the camper fit perfectly on the truck! God was providing. We saw His hand at work.

What was first planned to be a *two-week trip* was turning into a *two-month trip*. Frank's sister, Susan, lived in Truckee, California. She begged us to go out there and visit her before our appointment with Father Jim in Michigan. The Wilds would receive us at Word of God Community in Ann Arbor; we had an open invitation. On the way to California, we could visit our old friends in El Paso, and Phoenix. Marc Andre' and his family were back in Montreal and they, too, had been very anxious to have a visit from us. We could head to Montreal from Ann Arbor. Jim, Frank's brother, and his wife Kathy were in Virginia. John Finley, our friend from Virginia asked us to attend his wedding; the timing – God's timing – was perfect. John's wedding ceremony was in South Carolina, about mid-way from Virginia to the Alleluia Community. We loved Alleluia, and they loved us. Jesus had connected the dots. A mission trip that criss-crossed the USA and Canada was taking shape.

Sarah, my little joy bundle, was a great traveler. She and I rode in the camper part of the truck most of the time. Beau and Frank, riding up front, had the chance to spend some quality time together. Moving about always made us "gel". Something special, a special grace was at work in our lives as we went forth.

"Go forth" is the direction missionaries should find easiest to follow. Once we got our guidance, once we were moving as the Lord directed, it felt right. We were at peace with this mission-camping trip. Countless evangelization conditions were just waiting for us when we arrived on the scene.

On one leg of our journey, we were hoping to get to a campground south of Reno in Arizona before nightfall, so we could set up before dark. We had a flat tire that delayed us and were worried about the route and the lack of alternative camping spots. After the flat, it was obvious that we didn't have enough daylight hours left.

I prayed. "Lord Jesus, please take us into your care. Help us to find our campground and set up without any major problems."

We did arrive at our campground before dark. We had traveled eight hours worth of miles, but only seven hours had passed on the clock.

"This is not possible," Beau said.

We did and redid the math. There is no way we could have traveled 520 miles, driving 60mph, and arrived in seven hours. Frank did not speed because of the mountain driving. It should have taken us eight hours. God multiplied our minutes, just as in the past when He had multiplied our food. That day, He stretched out the hours.

"Someone *up there* has done some careful planning." I said as we told that story at our next speaking engagement. "The Lord is not bound by the laws of nature. He made the laws!"

After our two-month trek, evangelizing and sharing with Christian Communities, we came back to our basic house in Abbeville. It was a pretty humble place, but we were glad to sleep in beds every night, instead of living in the back of the pick up truck.

"Our time with Fr. Jim was all that we hoped it would

be. But the most exciting event is that Fr. Jim has invited us to Colombia." Frank commented once we were home. "He gave me some advice on working on our visas."

We began to work right away on our visa applications to Colombia. Frank volunteered full time at the Christian Service Center. We gave some "Life in the Spirit Seminars." I did the children's ministry.

Beau went back to Mt. Carmel, while we waited on news of our visas. The endless teasing and agonizing persecution he got in seventh grade, got much worse in eighth. He wore a wooden cross – that was a no-no. We had decided to live in poverty. Since Mt. Carmel Elementary had not yet adopted a uniform for all boys who attended, Beau's clothes were clean, but not the "IN" clothes. Now thirteen and in eighth grade, this harassment was a big deal. His views on the Christian life were strong and clear. He had made his own commitment to Jesus, but on occasion, the torment and persecution at school was more that he could take, and he retaliated. We understood, but Beau struggled with his inability to handle the situation. After he had been at school for three weeks of eighth grade, he began to leave his cross at home. I knew he didn't love Jesus less; but I did see that it meant that the situation at school was getting rough. Beau's difficulties struck straight at our hearts but it also coincided with our increasing desire to serve again in foreign missions.

"What does God want, Frank?" I asked worriedly.

"Let's have a family retreat. We always hear God when we do." He replied confidently.

"I'll take having the reading for Morning Prayer." Beau grinned, "I won't have to go to school."

"Okay with me," I agreed. "This is an important decision and we need the Lord to speak through each of us."

The family retreat is something we do every time a major decision comes up. We set aside a certain number of days for the retreat, we assign each member of the family the task of seeking an inspired reading, a reading to be brought to either our morning, noon or night prayer sessions, and we open ourselves to the charismatic gifts of the Holy Spirit for direction and guidance. We even listen for comments from our toddlers; Jesus can and does speak through them. We go on about our lives, but

19

schedule three family prayer times daily instead of one. At this time, we have our antennae up for the leading of the Holy Spirit in every day circumstances.

"Remember y'all, openness and expectancy is the attitude for our retreat." Frank said.

"The Lord knows very well that, we as missionaries can't be at the right place at the right time if He, Himself, doesn't reveal the plan. We NEED to hear wisdom and direction, right now." I said.

"If the Lord is calling, He will make the way and prepare a place for us. He always does." Beau added.

In our retreat, we heard the Lord say again, as He has so many times, "Go!"

We had been open and we were ready to obey His prompting. "Going" always means, "leaving"!! The greatest difficulty about our participation in Open Door was the mixed emotions we came up against every time the Lord called us away again. On one hand, our brothers and sisters were truly rejoicing with us. They had prayed with us for an opportunity to go forth in Jesus, in His Name to all the Nations, but when the time came to leave, it was just plain hard.

Chapter Three

The Center of His Will

Mesa country near Amarillo, Texas was in the full throes of fall. All the trees had donned their coats of many colors. The crisp air was invigorating, and wild turkeys pranced about at the edge of the rocks. Damascus Ranch was a temporary home to our dear friends, the Disciples of the Lord Jesus Christ. As we drove up the drive, spotted the big barn and the nestled buildings busy with people, we knew that this could be the perfect waiting spot. Surely our Colombian visas wouldn't be delayed much longer. These nuns, along with families and lay singles were in search of a contemplative, spirit-filled work life. The call to community was reverberating through the church, and the aspirants to community life were living a lifestyle and a calling. The Disciples of the Lord Jesus Christ were a newly formed order of sisters, and they embraced our family and eased our sadness at leaving the Open Door Community.

The week of our departure from Louisiana, we spoke with Mother John Marie by phone. She had suggested to us, "Come, be with us. Wait on your visas over here. We are building our new facility to be named Prayer Town Emmanuel. Your family can participate in our prayers and projects and I know you will love Damascus Ranch."

"We won't be in the way, Sister? We have a one year old." I asked.

"No, not at all. We have some families out here right now and lots of kids."

Sarah loved the place. She wore long gingham dresses and chased after the domestic geese. She reminded everyone of the little "Goose Girl" by Pissarro. Beau and Frank got into the swing of things and were blessed by the manual labor. We had a new home away from home.

"We have been trying to get our visas to go to Colombia. When I called the consulate in New Orleans, they told me that the delay is due to a lack of information from the government in

Colombia," Frank announced a few days after we arrived.

"All this is taking such a long time. I wonder how we can move the hand of God to get this process moving quickly?" I responded.

"Let's hear from God. I want to ask Him why this is taking so long. How about another family retreat, only this time let's reinforce it with fasting," Frank said.

Beau joined in the total fast and I went on bread and water because I was still nursing Sarah. On the second night of our fast and retreat, we were at Mass in the underground chapel. A former tornado shelter now sheltered the King of Kings in the tabernacle. It was a beautiful, and moving celebration. The priest talked about his recent experiences in Mexico. Our hearts were burning within us as he shared his mission stories. After Mass, we went up to the celebrant.

"Father, we're lay missionaries; we'd like to serve in Mexico or South America. It's been a long time since we applied for our visas to go to Colombia. Do you have any suggestions?" Frank asked.

"Do you speak Spanish?" he responded without hesitation.

"No, we don't, but Father Jim told us he thought we'd learn as we went along – a sort of sink or swim proposition," I said.

"I think you ought to learn Spanish first," he answered.

Sister John Marie was standing nearby and confirmed the priest's suggestion. "I believe the Lord is saying that your family ought to go to Cuernavaca to study Spanish. I have a friend, Sister Antoinette; she works with Monsignor Carlos Talavera of the Justicia and Alabanza (Justice and Praise) Community in Mexico City. I'll give you her number and you can call her tomorrow. She'll help you with the details."

The Lord had answered our prayer! Our fast and retreat had brought us an answer. "This is it Frank! I know in the Spirit it is!" I said. "The Lord wants us to go into Mexico to study Spanish."

The Sisters knew several Christians in Mexico City, who they assured us, would be there for us because we were missionaries. It would be great to learn the language as we waited for those elusive visas. We decided to travel to Mexico City by train.

El Paso was our first destination, after which we could board the train in Juarez right across the border. So often when we are ready to go, we meet the opposition of our familiar enemy. Satan opposes missionary work with a determined ferocity. We were rarely surprised by the almost insurmountable obstacles we faced as we moved in God's plan. And we were attacked again as we planned to leave Damascus Ranch.

I was in the community trailer, packed and waiting to make some final phone calls. We had previously made arrangements to be on a bus to El Paso the following morning. I happened to glance out of the window and saw Frank in excruciating pain. I threw open the door, "What happened? Can you stand up?"

"Can you help me up the stairs?" he replied. "I was fixing a tire on the sister's Volkswagen bus and stepped on the tire tool. I have totally wrenched my back. I half shuffled and half crawled all the way over here."

"You look like you are in pain. Let me get you some aspirin."

Back rubs, heating pads, and aspirin didn't help; the pain pressed on relentlessly. He could barely straighten up. The whole community began praying in earnest, and we called Open Door for an extra prayer boost. Sister John Marie came to visit him as soon as she heard about his injury. She convinced Frank to let her call one of their supporters from Amarillo, who was a chiropractor. Even though it was late at night, the doctor came.

He examined Frank, asking him to stretch out flat on the couch. With a flying leap and a jerk of Frank's knee, the doctor made the adjustment – instant relief! We praised God for His mercy! The soreness was still there, however. We burst into prayer, "Thank you, Lord, for the relief. Please, Jesus, help Frank to endure the nine hour bus trip to El Paso tomorrow morning."

Contrary to our fears, Frank got continually better all the way to El Paso. The Lord granted us the victory over Satan's attack.

Father Rick Thomas's ministry welcomed us back. Altura House, a Jesuit residence in El Paso, was our home for about a week while we made arrangements to enter Mexico by train. We needed visas, and Sarah needed some booster shots. Although it was great to be back in El Paso, our sights were set on Mexico and learning our new language.

"Why don't we get some lightweight back packs?" Frank suggested.

"Do you think a couple of back packs would hold everything we have been packing in the Tonga mat?" I asked.

"Are we going to give up the Tongan mat – our bed-roll and our luggage? We've had it since we left Nuku'alofa and the islands." Beau commented.

"The mat does have sentimental value, Beau. It is a symbol of the islands and our first mission in the South Pacific." I said, ruffling his hair. "But, now our family is getting bigger and we need some supplies for Sarah."

"That's right, son. You can come with me to pick out the backpacks in the morning. I also want to go by to talk to Father Rick about language school. He might have some good ideas," Frank said.

We were a bit apprehensive about the train trip to Mexico City taking two days, because we didn't speak any Spanish. As Frank waited outside Father Rick Thomas's office at Our Lady's youth center, he heard the song, "Be not afraid" playing over the public address system. *"You shall cross the barren desert, but you shall not die of thirst - You shall wander far in safety - though you do not know the way. You shall speak your words to foreign men and they will understand. You shall see the face of God and live. Be not afraid. I go before you always. Come follow Me and I will give you rest."* The lyrics dissipated Frank's fears. The Lord was calling us to follow Him; why should we be afraid?

A Christian television talk show heard that we were in town and invited our whole family to appear on its program. They wanted us to witness about our call as lay missionaries in the Catholic Church. The appearance was scheduled the night before our train left from Juarez.

On the way out of the door, little Sarah screamed out in pain. "My hand! My hand!"

We couldn't see what in the world was wrong, but she was suffering terribly. "It looks like a sprain, or a dislocation to

24

me. I hope it isn't anything too serious." I said as I held her close.

We anointed her with holy oil and pleaded with the Lord to heal her so we could make it to the television station, but she was inconsolable. "Go on, Frank. You and Beau will do a great job. If she doesn't get better soon, I'll ask Father Rick's secretary to take us to the doctor."

Even though she was only eighteen months old, she kept her arm completely immobile for the remainder of the night.

"Frank, I'm worried about taking that train ride tomorrow. Suppose this happens again and we can't find anyone to help us?" I said when they got home from the television station.

"Babe, this is an attack of the enemy. We need to find the victory of Jesus. If the devil can run us off now, he can keep us running. Let's pray."

We sat on the bed; Beau sat on the neatly packed new backpacks. Turning to the Lord in prayer, Frank closed his eyes. "Father, in the name of your Son, Jesus, and by the power of His blood, we come to you for the victory in the spiritual battle we are fighting. Please heal our Sarah, and send your angels to defend and protect us in the rest of this trip. We want to bring your Gospel to the nations, but without your constant help we can do nothing. We love you, Lord. Send your Holy Spirit upon us to refresh and strengthen us, so that tomorrow we can go forth confident and effective witnesses to your power. Amen."

Sarah woke up healed, and we were on our way. The train was much more pleasant than we expected. Seeing the beauty of the interior of Mexico aroused in us so much excitement about our new mission.

Sister Antoinette and Msgr. Talavera's group took good care of us in Mexico City. They met many American leaders in the Charismatic Renewal, Spirit-filled servants of the Lord. They were particularly excited about our presence, "It is most impressive to see a whole family giving up everything to be lay apostles. We want to help in any way we can!"

The bus ride from Mexico City to Cuernavaca, where our language school was located, took us even deeper into unfamiliar surroundings. I was praying that we could quickly settle into our new surroundings, but there were some hurdles we'd have to get over - entering language school and finding housing. Sr. Antoinette had given us the name of I.D.E.A.L., a language school that suited our needs. From the bus station, we got in a taxi, showed him the address, and arrived at the school. Cuernavaca, noted for its wonderful climate, is called the City of Eternal Spring. Even in mid-December, it was sunny and pleasant.

Like almost every other house, the *Instituto De Estudios Americanas Latinas* (I.D.E.A.L.) had bright magenta bougainvillea plant draped in profusion over the high walled fences. Beau and I walked with Sarah in the lovely garden while Frank registered and spoke with the owner-operator.

Emilio, the director, said, "We love missionaries. My wife was a papal volunteer," he offered. "We just had some Maryknoll priests here."

We felt comforted by that and enjoyed a mid-afternoon snack as Frank discussed the details with us. Language school cost fifty dollars a week per person, and it was very intense – five hours of non-stop study daily. We discussed our options. We simply couldn't afford for all three of us to attend; it was too expensive, so I suggested, "You and Beau go then, Frank. I can't leave Sarah that long anyway. I'll just ask the Lord to give me the gift of Spanish!"

Beau and Frank signed up. Hurdle number one conquered. Hurdle number two was finding a place to stay for the six-week period. Our new friends in Mexico City had been trying to prepare us for the worst-case scenario. "Cuernavaca is a vacation resort. People in Mexico City often go there to escape the cold of December. It is so crowded during the Christmas holidays there. You are traveling at a bad time. It'll take a miracle for you to find a place to stay," they had said with foreboding.

We had been traveling from Samoa to New Mexico two years ago at Christmas. The Lord had his hand upon us then; surely he wouldn't forsake us this time. Joseph and Mary had been traveling at Christmas – a very good model for families trusting the Lord. Frank later admitted amusedly, "On the whole bus ride I had my eye out for a stable or a barn if we couldn't find a house."

Emilio's wife, a former papal volunteer, was vigorously

26

trying to find housing for us. "We know a lot of people who accept boarders, but Christmas time is the most difficult of all. Let me see what I can do."

My heart sank. I wondered if we made a mistake coming at this time of year. She left us on the sofa, while she went to begin telephoning different houses. "Oh, Lord Jesus, you are our only hope. We have been asking you to prepare a place for us. Please let us find the place you have already prepared," was Beau's prayer.

It resounded in my heart. The cost of even a few days in a hotel would throw us into a serious economic crisis.

"No one has space available," she reported.

"No room at the Inn", I thought.

"There is one more possibility," she offered, "My neighbor right across the street sometimes takes in students. She's a widow and has two teenage daughters. Her rooms don't have a private bath, and the house isn't luxurious, but certainly is adequate if you can live without a private bath. I'll go across the street with you to check it out. She doesn't speak a word of English. That'll help you learn Spanish faster." She said.

At this point, a roof over our head was a lot more important than a private bath. The widow and Frank came to an agreement, one room for the four of us, with board. The price and location were very good and we would trust God for the rest. The guys started language school the next day and I started my own language study at home. The widow, Lucha, talked constantly, and I was determined to learn as much as I could. I bought a small pad of paper and wrote down every new word I learned, disregarding spelling for the time being. While we struggled with a new language and culture, we endured occasional chills or dusty blasts from the windows in our crowded little room and often had long waits for the bathroom. Lucha couldn't figure us out. Our commitment to the Lord was an obstacle for her.

She told me one day "It's easy for you to be peaceful, you have a husband. It upsets me the way you walk around here totally peaceful, and I'm struggling."

I was totally stumped. I was trying to witness to her in my humble Spanish. I had hoped by quietly praying for her, I could win her friendship. There was a lot of tension between us.

The name "Lucha" literally means "fight" or "struggle" in Spanish and it seemed fitting somehow. Life at Lucha's house was a sacrifice. She obviously wanted to save money and our food supply was meager at best, but we learned to fill up on tortillas. On the positive side, we were across the street from the language school, and close enough to the center of Cuernavaca to learn the rest of Mexican culture as well.

After one particularly frustrating morning, feeling hungry and having waited an extended time for the bathroom, I decided to sing praise songs to the Lord as a defense against the enemy. A mighty flow of God's grace went through me, melting away all my hurt, pain, and anxiety. Joy swelled up in my heart; I was being set free. I sang while I washed on the scrub-board; I sang hanging out the clothes; I sang in the shower; I sang in my room mopping the floor. I couldn't stop praising the Lord; His nearness filled my being and encouraged me.

Lucha knocked on my door and demanded, "Would you please stop singing, you're disturbing my daughter who wants to study for an exam!" I was incredulous; how could she say *that*? Her daughter was constantly seated at the table with the *radio blaring so loud it could be heard across the street.*

Instantly, the Lord reminded me that my struggle at that time was not against "flesh and blood but with the principalities, with the powers, with the world rulers of this present darkness, with evil spirits in the heavens." (Eph 6:12). When that scripture came to me in prayer, I claimed its strength: "The struggle is *not* with flesh and blood, the struggle is *not* with flesh and blood!" I repeated to myself. "How can I be so foolish as to let this poor woman cause me so much grief?" It was the devil who was trying to torment me. He was arming her with things to use against me to rob me of my courage.

Lucha, however, was standing at my door with arms folded, scowling. She was unsuspecting of Satan's evil designs. Again, I mulled it over in my mind, "How can she believe that my singing disturbs her daughter who listens to the radio with the volume up full blast? What do I do, Lord?"

Then it happened, a mystical, spiritual moment of truth. It was as though spiritual scales fell from my eyes, and instead of seeing the widow actually standing there; it was the devil actually standing there. Satan, in his hideousness, reeking of

28

stench, was confronting me with an evil boldness. A second or two later, the devil disappeared and it was the widow again. After the devil vanished, his devious tactics were exposed. I saw her with a whole new set of eyes. She *desperately needed* my understanding and love. We defeat the enemy by overcoming *evil* with *good.* How much I regretted that this revelation came to me with only one week left to work on it. I wanted to make things right. I knew Jesus wanted to love her and her little family through me.

We had spent Christmas with them. They had not had a single celebration of any kind since their father died three years before. We had contributed a turkey to Christmas dinner and bought them gifts. Anita, the thirteen year old, invited Beau to help her arrange their manger scene. Lucha had protested, but Anita prevailed.

As our two families gathered around the manger scene on Christmas Eve, Lucha put her arm around Anita and said, "This is our first really joyful occasion in forever."

Frank and Beau found the school very intense. Beau learned fast; however, Frank was struggling along. He had studied a week or so longer than Beau to finish his final studies. Beau and Sarah and I spent some time practicing vocabulary in the house and the town. We used some techniques from the school. Learning a new language is an exhausting proposition.

In retrospect, six weeks wasn't all a struggle. It was a joy attending Mass in Cuernavaca at a church dedicated to Santa Catalina. Worship was so easy in this impressive glass building in a walled garden. Father Onesimo, the pastor, was filled with the Holy Spirit. The language of love was easy to understand.

We also worshipped the Lord at the nearby Benedictine monastery and enjoyed the fellowship of the monks. Cuernavaca's quaint charm was captured in both of these Holy places. We attended prayer meetings and conversed haltingly with our new friends. We learned the essentials of shopping in a food market, riding public transportation, and took some preliminary steps into ministry in Spanish.

The time in Cuernavaca was drawing to a close and we were much more in tune with Mexican realities after a full eight weeks of walking with Jesus, carrying our cross than when we boarded that train in Juarez. We wrote Monsignor Carlos

Talavera offering to work in the apostolates of the Secreteriado Social there in Mexico City.

Much to our joy, he wrote back quickly, "You are most welcome. We will be happy to use you to work among the poor in our Diocese. Will Rodriquez, our lay evangelist, will be waiting for you in Mexico City; he'll help you get started in your ministry."

Now that we were leaving and a victory had been won in a fierce spiritual battle, it was easier to focus on the wonderful things the Lord had done for us in Cuernavaca. Language school had ended. We were all communicating in our limited Spanish. I was speaking the most Spanish, Beau next, and then Frank. He, however, could read the Gospels in Spanish. I was in our room at Lucha's, packing and getting us ready to take the early bus to Mexico City the next day. Our neighbor across the street came to say that there was a phone call for us. I stayed at the widow's house while Beau and Frank went to answer the call, which seemed to take an eternity. The minute they walked in, I knew something was wrong, terribly wrong.

"Who was it?" I asked anxiously, "What's wrong?"

"Let's close the door," Frank answered solemnly. My heart dropped; I was weak. I had hoped he'd reply, "Nothing's wrong, don't worry".

I looked at Beau and he dropped his eyes, he wouldn't look at me. This was serious! Frank closed the door. "It was Bruce. He called to say that your brother Jed is in Oschner hospital undergoing brain surgery. He became unconscious this afternoon. They're pretty sure it's a blood clot. There are no guarantees; he may not even make it through the surgery. If he does survive the emergency surgery, they can't promise anything – blindness, loss of mental faculties and paralysis are all possible prognoses. Your mom and dad are on their way to New Orleans. Bruce promised to call us early tomorrow morning with another report, or sooner if they know anything."

"This can't be happening," I thought, "not Jed; he's so young, only twenty-three years old."

Piercing pain gripped my heart. My godchild, my baby brother, my Jed! He lived with our family in London for over a year. He had a wonderful wife, Susan, and a promising career and life ahead of him. We have always maintained a close relationship. This news was almost unbearable. I began to sob out my prayer from the inmost part of my being. "Save him, Lord. Please help us, Lord. Protect my Mama and Daddy on the highway! Be with Bruce, Brian and Rachel, too. Help Susan, Lord!"

Frank held me in his arms; Beau was crying, too. Thank God little Sarah was asleep. "Let's pray together," Frank suggested, and he took out his guitar. I began, at last, to feel the presence of the Lord. After we closed our prayer, Frank looked at me and asked, "What do you think the Lord wants us to do?"

"Well, it seems obvious to me that he wants us to go home and be with my family. We're almost all packed; we can get that early bus to Mexico City and fly to New Orleans tomorrow. Later, we can come back to Mexico City. It's not like we've actually started any work, no one is depending on us right now. *I want to go home!*"

"Me too, Daddy. I think we ought to go to be with Uncle Jed and Mamaw and Pops," Beau insisted.

I felt like I was barely holding on inside. All I knew was that I desperately needed to be in touch with Jesus. Lucha, the widow, knocked on the door. She had heard the crying; she was sincerely concerned. Our tragedy broke down barriers. I was grateful that she and her daughters wanted to join with us in prayer for my brother. We said a rosary, sang songs of victory, re-read psalms of deliverance and offered up heartfelt and fervent petitions. At the end of the prayers, when we were alone again, we still had to make a decision of whether to go back home or continue on mission. What did God want? We had completed this period of training and began to plan for our new work. Suddenly, we were faced by such a compelling and urgent need at home.

"I don't hear Jesus telling us to go home," Frank shared. My head was swimming. I had all but stopped crying. I was newly pregnant with our third child and weaning Sarah from the breast. Frank's words stabbed at my heart. I could hardly believe what he was saying. He could see that I was struck to the core.

The first hours were, by far, the worst, however. As promised, we received a call with the latest news. I was relieved to hear that Jed survived surgery. Rachel, my sister, had called the Open Door community to ask them for prayers. Bruce reported, "Lots of people are praying for Jed. I'm praying harder than I ever have."

The operation lasted six hours; the neurosurgeons removed a blood clot the size of an egg from the right side of his brain. They then probed the brain for hours trying to find the cause, and never could. The doctors told Mom and Dad that Jed would have died had he not been brought to the hospital so soon; he had gotten some of the finest care available in very quick order because his wife worked at the hospital – had this occurred under other circumstances, he would not have had much chance of survival. Another factor in the amazing outcome was that they lived near the hospital. The doctors said that Jed suffered from a cerebral hemorrhage. I prayed with Bruce on the phone, "Give us a miracle, Lord. Let all the best that can happen, happen. Don't let us lose him; we love him so much."

"Why don't we finish packing and pray for clear guidance about what we should do," Frank said after the latest news. He came to me and I rested my head on his chest. Putting the last few things into the suitcase, I kept begging the Lord to let us go home. After the last suitcase was closed, Frank called us together again.

"How do y'all feel after praying about it?"

"I still think we should go home." I answered. Beau agreed. His uncle Jed was like a brother to him and obviously, still not out of the woods yet.

"I feel differently. I hear the Lord saying that we should go to Mexico City. I feel like He's going to hear our prayers for Jed, and that He wants us to offer up our new work in thanksgiving to Him for Jed's healing."

I threw myself across the bed. I was screaming inside. A million thoughts flooded my mind. "What if Frank isn't hearing the Lord; what if it's just that he wants to go to Mexico City more than he cares about how I'm feeling? What if Jed dies and I won't be able to see him one more time? What if my family misreads our motives and thinks we're calloused and uncaring? If I insist that we go, would that be a sin? If we were there to actually lay hands on Jed, would that make a difference?"

I cried some more.

Finally I got control and began to pray, "Lord Jesus, the

noise in my heart and soul is so loud, and I cannot trust myself to hear You. I don't hear You telling us what to do. I do know for certain that the place for me to be right now is in the center of Your will. I can't let anything stop me from being at least one person in the family who is offering all. You know my greatest hope is that all my brothers and sister, my parents, and all my loved ones go to be with You in heaven. If Jed is more prepared to meet you *now,* than later, take him into Your heart. If this is his only chance to be with You forever, then I give him to You on behalf of our family. If You can still use him here on earth, and then please heal him and let him live. I would prefer if You heal him, Lord, but I completely surrender him into Your hands."

The next morning early, I was at the neighbor's waiting for a call from Bruce. Bruce and I cried on the phone. He reported, "He made it through the surgery and through the night."

I kept saying, "Praise you, Lord, Praise you, Lord."

Bruce filled me in on some details. Jed had been struck down with a horrible headache that was so painful he asked his wife to drive. Once at home, he went to bed and later vomited, finally losing consciousness. Susan immediately called the hospital. How vital and providential it seemed that Susan had quick medical instincts. They lived close to the hospital – a boon in the light of such an unforeseen and terrible attack on the brain. By the time they got him into the emergency room, Jed's whole body was fibrillating so much that he was flying off the stretcher. It took three orderlies to hold him down.

Susan's dad, who later joined her at the hospital, overheard the doctor scolding the nurses about something. The doctor shouted, "Get in here right away, I've got a twenty-three year old man dying of a brain hemorrhage."

A priest was called and Jed had been given Last Rites, the Sacrament of the Anointing of the Sick. I was relieved that in the crisis, the family took Jed's faith into account. He was taken to the hospital just in time; the neurosurgeons just *happened* to be in the hospital on another call. The operating room *was* available, which was seldom the case. Bruce said, "The doctors are being very cautious. The odds for a full recovery are slim. He will probably be in intensive care for six-weeks and in the hospital for three months."

"What do you think; have you seen him?" I asked.

"A couple of good signs – Jed's brain had popped back out to fill the head cavity after the clot was removed. They are saying that's very good. One nurse told us that he moved one of his legs in the recovery room which is also a good sign."

I hated to hang up the telephone. I wanted to cling to Bruce's voice. It was hard to tell him that we weren't coming home. "I'll call you from Mexico City as soon as I know where we can be reached by phone. In the meantime, let's keep praying." We prayed together on the phone. It was good to pray with Bruce.

"Please tell Jed I love him the next time you see him."

"Sure will!"

"I love you, Bruce."

"I love you, too, Genie."

The ache in my heart went down to the marrow of my bones. On the way back to my room I was already praying from my heart. "I want to be where **You** want me to be, so that I can offer You the prayers of an obedient servant. I don't want to do **my** will. If I submit to Frank's discernment in this, I know I will be in the center of Your will, and that my prayers will be more effective. Look on my suffering, and heal Jed please, Lord!"

That night was spent between waking, and dozing, and crying and praying. The next day's news was better yet. "Praise the Lord, he made it through the night" was becoming a standard in our family and, in days not weeks, Jed was out of intensive care. In weeks, he was out of the hospital. In just one month, he was back in law school. He graduated *magna cum laude* from law school. He made a full recovery. At first he suffered from a little short-term memory loss, but his law school buddies coached him faithfully and he didn't even lose a semester. The doctors had to admit that it was a miracle. There was no other way to explain Jed's beautiful, rapid recovery. When he went back for his check ups, they greeted him with the name "miracle boy".

The center of God's will is a good spot to sit in when you need to intercede for someone you love. The transition to Mexico City and Jed's crises changed me forever. I knew that I never want to be anywhere else but the center of God's will.

In Cuernavaca, we took leave of Lucha and the girls.

During those difficult months that were spent in their home, they had grown to love us. We took a taxi to the bus station. In less than two hours we were in Mexico City. That night, at one of the Justicia and Alabanza prayer meetings, Monsignor Talavera announced that some guests needed housing. To his surprise, it was the Auxiliary Bishop's own eighty-two year old mother who offered to house us. The Lord had selected the perfect place for us to be, considering the trials we were undergoing. Senora Talavera was a widow, a living saint. She was so peaceful, warm and welcoming. Her house was clean and spacious, but most of all it was permeated by the presence of God. Our Spanish was still very limited and she was a patient teacher, full of love and support. It was a time of healing and rest. She had a telephone and I was able to keep up with Jed's remarkable progress.

Mexico City is so big it's hard to fathom. The Charismatic Community of Justica and Alabanza was alive with the Holy Spirit. Monsignor Carlos Talavera was solicitous of our needs. Sister Antionette, who worked with him, took us under her wing and introduced us to the work among the poor of the *Secretariado Social* (The Social Apostolate of the Archdiocese of Mexico City). It was exciting to see the spiritual dimension of the prayer community in operation. Monsignor Talavera assigned Frank to work with Will Rodriquez, a lay evangelist who worked full time among the poor. Will was a little older than we were and he had a recognized gift of prophecy in the prayer community. He lived in a "colonia" of Mexico City called the Cuchilla del Tesoro, which means the "wedge of treasure." We decided that we would live there, and asked the Lord to find a place.

Shortly an apartment became available; as poor as it was, this was the place. We had no furnishings. The word spread among God's people and soon we had everything we absolutely needed, and nothing more. This little apartment next to the International Airport was our home for the next five months. The "treasure" in the "wedge of treasure" was not the physical surroundings; it was the happy Mexican people. Frank accompanied Will to several different prayer groups in the poor barrios of Mexico City. At first his Spanish was so limited that he mainly played the guitar, listened attentively to the sharing of

God's Word, joining with Will and others in praying for the sick. The sick were healed in numbers and God confirmed our mission with signs and wonders. We were invited to join with the regional prayer groups that were having a day of recollection at the oldest church in Mexico City, San Augustin. We brought our lunch and we tagged along with Will, his brother-in-law Benito, and their family.

We went to the leaders' meeting where Will introduced us. He briefly told them our testimony of conversion and the call to mission. After the leaders meeting, we broke for lunch. Frank, Beau, Sarah, myself, and the "church ladies" from La Cuchilla were eating tacos on the lawn of the old church. Since we had been living in Cuchilla del Tesora for only about three weeks, we were so excited over the fact that we seemed to be understanding at least the gist of the talks given in Spanish.

While we were still having lunch, Will came up to find Frank at our spot on the lawn. "Francisco", which means Frank in Spanish, "the leaders want you to give the principal address this afternoon. It's the last talk before the closing Mass."

Frank laughed, "Will, I can barely say 'good afternoon', I don't think I could give a talk in Spanish."

Will smiled, "The leaders and I think the Lord wants you to give the talk. If the Lord wants you to do it, then you can do it."

Frank looked at me and said, "I think this is crazy. I can hardly say anything in Spanish, but I feel like I'd better at least pray about it." He turned to Will, "I'll pray about it for a little while." Beau and I stayed behind while Frank went off alone into a corner of the garden to pray.

As he poured out his heart and his excuses to the Lord, he felt that the Lord wasn't accepting any of his excuses. "Frank," the Lord said, "What do you think I sent you to Mexico for? You're here to proclaim my Word. Now that you have the opportunity, I want you to accept it."

Frank felt very humbled. He said, "Yes, Lord, I'll do it, for your sake, but you'll have to help me!"

Will was confident and happy that Frank accepted the invitation even if the talk might be very short. Frank had a new Spanish New Testament. He chose the first letter of St. John, Chapter 1 about living and walking in the light. This reading had meant so much to us when we first began to walk with the Lord. He knew Jesus had led him to that reading. The church was packed with about five hundred people. It had been a beautiful day. The praising, singing and teaching had gone very well. The immense power of the Holy Spirit was definitely present, and Frank remembers feeling incredibly nervous as Will introduced him to the church full of people. Will was giving a rousing introduction to the missionary who had sacrificed so much to come to Mexico.

"Now the people here today are going to be blessed with the chance to hear a message from Francisco Summers, missionary from Louisiana."

"Lord," Frank thought, "I'm going to read the reading and then you will have to give me a few words to say." Frank got up and read the reading, and he began very simply, "Brothers and Sisters, Jesus wants us to live in the light. Jesus wants us to walk in the light. In God there is no darkness at all…"

He preached for forty-five minutes. He spoke in very humble, broken Spanish but it didn't seem to matter to the audience at all. They were attentive. After a few minutes, Frank became aware that he was preaching, not in his own power, but in the power of the Holy Spirit. The Lord had a message for this group of His faithful followers, and He had chosen Frank to speak it to them.

After Mass, many, many brothers and sisters came up to tell Frank that, as he proclaimed God's Word, it touched them deeply. Frank had been given a supernatural gift of preaching in Spanish! From that moment on, he would share the Word in small groups, as well as follow in Spanish, almost anything that pertained to talking about the kingdom of God.

One of the poorest barrios in Mexico City was San Lazaro. San Lazaro's houses were centered round a low-lying area. It was filled with fetid water, which had garbage floating in it, and gave off a putrid odor. Beau accompanied Frank to a prayer meeting there.

"Mom, you and Sarah better not go to that place; you might get sick. I felt sick the whole time I was there when I went with Dad."

The people of San Lazaro were sorely tried by the fetid water and the lack of potable water for drinking. They had tried unsuccessfully to obtain the government's help with their water problems. The first time Frank attended their prayer gathering, God promised them "living water." The living water was the Lord's Word spoken in prophetic utterance. Within weeks, they found themselves praising God that the government had, at last, met their need for potable water. They praised Him for at last draining and leveling the low spot filled with filth, and at last connecting them to the city's water system! God helps his poor when they unite in prayer. Prayer is faster than government red tape.

Our family's mere presence in the quite poor barrio of Cuhilla del Tesoro generated a lot of interest. One storekeeper asked me, "Why would a nice family of North Americans come to a place like this? Our streets are full of holes and rocks; we have no trees; and the airplanes make so much noise that you can't carry on a conversation. Why don't you go back to the United States or find a prettier part of Mexico to live in?"

What a perfect opening he had given me. "Sharing the love of God with the people of the Cuchilla is why we're here! For us, it is more important to be where God wants us to be than to have a lot of beauty and comfort. The consolation of knowing that we are where the Lord wants us to be is sufficient."

There was a prayer meeting in the Cuchilla, and one in an adjoining colonia named "Siete M," which was a large housing project for government employees. After only five months, Frank was ministering on his own without Will. He led meetings in our colonia, and in the government projects. Beau, and many of the other youths, liked to accompany Frank. Day and night people came to request that we go into their homes and hold a prayer meeting to pray for a sick relative or friend. People began to come to us from farther and farther away in the city.

With God doing so much healing of others in our midst, I could not believe it when, suddenly Beau was struck with appendicitis. Why didn't He heal Beau miraculously of his appendicitis attack? For about a day and a half Beau had been complaining of a stomachache. At first, we weren't too worried; however, when he lost his appetite, which for Beau is something serious, we paid attention. He felt bloated and the pain moved to his lower right side. We asked our friends, Will and Benito, to give us all a ride to the doctor. When the doctor told us that it was definitely his appendix, I panicked.

Frank's grandmother died of a ruptured appendix, Frank's mother almost died of a ruptured appendix. I had been operated on at seventeen for appendicitis. I knew we didn't want to take any chances. We had to go to the hospital. I really wanted the Lord to heal Beau on the spot, to show the world how well he takes care of his missionaries. I kept expecting Beau to jump up any minute saying, "The pain is gone, I'm healed."

The religious sister-nurse who admitted us into the hospital examined him, too. "It's his appendix, and it seems pretty bad; I'll call the surgeon right away." I hadn't expected us to have to face an operation on this mission and I was still waiting for that instant healing. Finally, I had to realize, and admit to myself, that he was definitely going to have surgery. Then came the hard part – I had to surrender Beau to the Lord again. We all prayed together before surgery, praising God that it was a Catholic hospital. As they wheeled Beau into the operating room, Frank had the Lord's peace. I went down to see our friends who were waiting with Sarah at the street level. By the time I got back upstairs, they had Beau in the recovery room. I could not believe it was over so quickly. Beau stayed in the hospital in a private room for five days and came home feeling great. The whole cost, everything included, was one hundred and ten dollars. The Lord does take care of his missionaries. Sometimes, the way he does it is to show us that He's in charge. If He wants to heal us through the ministry of the medical profession, He will, and He will provide financially for their services.

A funny language mix-up happened while Beau was in the hospital. One reason hospitals in developing nations are more economical, is that they don't *supply* everything and don't *charge* you for everything. You bring your own towels, toiletries, toilet paper, and soap, etc. Beau wanted a bath on the day after his surgery, but we didn't know we had to supply our own soap. Frank went to the nurses' station to ask them if they had any soap. The problem was that the word for <u>soap</u> in Spanish is *"jabon."* The word for <u>ham</u> is *"jamon"* and Frank asked the nurse if they had any *jamon* (ham).

He said in Spanish, "Do you have any ham we could have? My son, in room 215, really needs some." The nurse looked completely puzzled, and replied in Spanish, "No sir, I'm sorry we don't have any *jamon* (ham*)."* Frank was surprised, thinking to himself, "What kind of hospital doesn't have soap?" So he asked the nurse insistently in Spanish, "This whole hospital has **no** ham (*jamon)*?" he was still asking for ham, but really trying to mean, "soap." Again the nurse looked quizzically at him and said, "I am really sorry, Sir, we don't have any ham!"

Seeing the disappointment in his face, she gestured that he should wait in Beau's room and she would be back. From the room, Frank watched her descend the main stairway, go out of the front of the hospital and walk down the street. It was about five minutes later, she appeared at the door to Beau's room. She knocked, smiled and handed Frank a small plate of ham. It was only then that Frank realized his mistake. He smiled back at her, thanked her very much and closed the door. Frank and Beau laughed so hard, they worried that Beau would pop his stitches. And, they enjoyed the ham.

We have always fed the poor who share our lives; it wasn't any different in the Cuchilla. Angelica, a little ten-year-old neighbor, came over every day to talk to me, to play with Sarah, to have a meal, and to take the plate scrapings to the animals at her house. Eva was a nineteen-year-old girl who came to stay with us for two weeks. Unfortunately, Angelica and Eva didn't get along very well. They vied for my attention and squabbled over Sarah.

One day I was preparing a meal for company. We were having hamburgers on French bread and potato salad, which was really a splurge for us; we hadn't had hamburgers in a long time. I was getting ready to make the patties and asked my little friend, "Angelica, are you going to eat with us?"

"No," she said pouting at Eva, "I'm going to eat at my house today."

Ordinarily, I would have tried to solve their relationship problem, but we were running late with the meal. "Okay, then we'll see you tomorrow," I told her.

Angelica scuffed her shoes out of the door, twisting her neck to see if Eva noticed. Turning to Eva, I said, "If she's not staying, we'll only need ten patties." We made the ten patties and cooked them. We counted them again as we put them on a platter. I told Eva, "Call the guests to the table; we'll eat in a few minutes."

Next thing I knew, Angelica was back in my kitchen. She had gotten over her pouting and was asking to join us for dinner. "I am going to eat with you; I already told my mother. She likes it when I eat here," she announced happily.

Eva heaved a big sigh and rolled her eyes in disgust, "What are we going to do now? Everyone is here; it's time to eat and we only have ten patties?"

"I'll eat a potato salad sandwich." I told her "It doesn't matter. Go ahead and get ready to serve, let's put the patties in the bread and put some potato salad in a piece of bread for me."

When she got out the last bread, she gasped in shock, "There's an extra hamburger patty! There are eleven hamburgers! We only made ten hamburgers and now there are eleven!!"

"Check again!" I said, "Maybe you missed one. Maybe there's a bun without a hamburger," I told her.

She checked and exclaimed, "God gave us another hamburger. You won't have to eat a potato salad sandwich."

The witness of the multiplication of the hamburgers ran through our ministry. God's Word was again confirmed by signs and wonders.

Our six-month Mexican tourist visas were expiring and our first Latin American mission was drawing to a close. We had to leave Mexico to renew our visas. If we had had a vehicle, perhaps we would have left the apartment furnished, gone home on a short visit, and then returned. We hadn't received any clear guidance about the future. We were still hoping to go to the El Camino Community in Colombia. I was five months pregnant. I was hoping to be settled somewhere when the baby was born.

The day before we left, we attended a going away party the people planned for us in the colonia, Siete M. The brothers and sisters from the Cuchilla were also invited. It was a great celebration with lots of food, laughter, singing, reminiscing, sharing and prayer.

Frank squeezed my hand under the table. "It's been fruitful, hasn't it? Look at all these people; the change in their lives shows in the glow on their faces."

After the festivities, people began to ask for prayers for

healing -- long lines of people. Sarah and I left after an hour of praying, but Frank and Beau prayed for three hours without stopping. We left early the next morning. It wasn't until our *next* visit that we were told of the full impact of that healing prayer service. God granted many healings and miracles that afternoon of our going away party.

One nun declares that her religious vocation was a direct result of that afternoon's prayer. One family, our close friends, had a child who hardly talked. Medical doctors said that little Manuel was retarded. He was a happy little fellow. Being their first child, his parents were anxious for him to start school. Manuel had some preliminary tests at the local primary school, which showed that he would have to be enrolled in a program for special children. The final test to determine his placement level in a special school for the retarded was scheduled for the morning after that prayer session. Frank and Beau prayed over him, his mother joining them, too, in tearful supplication. The next day, the psychologist said to Manuel's parents "There must have been some kind of mistake. This child tests at a normal level, he is above average for his age group." The next year when we visited, he was doing brilliantly in the first grade.

A marvelous grace is at work when the Lord calls us to leave. He ties up loose ends; people who hesitated, come to Jesus thinking, "I should've done it before now. The missionaries are leaving; maybe I won't get another chance." Others think, "This is my last chance to get healed."

Our job is to be faithful; to be in the center of His will. We must answer His call to go. He does the rest.

"When you hearken to **the voice of the Lord, your God, all these blessings will come upon you** *and overwhelm you. May you be blessed in the city, and blessed in the country! Blessed be the fruit of your womb...May you be blessed in your coming in and blessed in your going out! The Lord will beat down before you the enemies that rise up against you; though they come out against you from* **one** *direction, they will flee before you in* **seven**. *The Lord will affirm His blessing upon you...so that when all nations of the earth see you bearing the name of the Lord, they will stand in awe of you." (Dt. 28:2-3)*

Chapter Four

Heavenly Bells in the High Andes

Another train station, another tearful departure – Mexico was no longer some strange land to us. In these months, we had learned its language; we had been accepted and loved by its people; we had been greatly enriched by the Mexican culture and ways. Relaxing on the train, I had more time to focus on my coming newborn. Sarah really needed a sister to play with and that's what we were hoping for. We remembered that while we were in Brown's Cove, Virginia, we had decided that when the Lord sent us another girl, we would call her Susanna, inspired by the story in the book of Daniel. That birth was still four months away, but Susanna was snug inside my womb, being loved by us.

"Where will we be, I wonder?" I asked Frank as I rubbed my belly. "We've moved around so much, but, I know I will get that nesting instinct when it is time for the baby."

"Remember what the Lord showed us in Tonga? We must make our home in His Word. Let's take one day at a time."

"As hard as it was to leave, I'm happy with this train ride where we can be alone for a change. Look, Sarah is asleep already."

Frank took out his guitar and began to play. We sang "Lead us on, oh Lord, lead us on. Lead us where we dare not go. Lead us on, oh Lord, lead us on. Be with us as we face new days."

Part of the new day the Lord had for us, was a new place for us to stay in Abbeville. When we were home between missions, Vince had arranged for us to live in the abandoned St. Elizabeth Seton School. The school was on the premises of Open Door community. We were used to poverty, so the fact that the school had no privacy, no hot water, no showers, and no toilets in the living quarters was only a minor problem. In the middle of the night, if we had to use the bathroom, we used a camping toilet hidden by a cane screen. This toilet had to be emptied daily in the bathrooms outside. Going out into the elements, carrying a toilet bucket to be emptied each day was a mission sacrifice I could easily make. Only because we were in the USA did it seem more sacrificial. The Seton School, as it was nicknamed, afforded us the opportunity to maintain our commitment to gospel poverty. In all of its humility, it soon became home.

"It is so great to be back," Frank said as he sat down with Red and Vince.

"It seems like you never left," Red commented. "The youth group is meeting this week. Maybe y'all can give a teaching."

Beau broke in to the conversation, "Red, am I old enough to be in the youth group? I just talked to the twins and they told me to ask you?"

"Sure, Beau, how old are you now?"

"I'll be fourteen next month."

"Kay, can you believe Beau is almost fourteen?" I asked.

"Fourteen going on twenty-one," she teased.

Vince asked Frank, "You will be coming back to the Center?"

"The Christian Service Center is a godsend for me. Where else can I participate daily in the fruitful evangelistic work among the poor?" Frank replied. "What's happening in parish ministry?"

Early on, Monsignor Mouton realized that he had hit upon a treasure with the spiritual energy generated by the community of two full-time lay families, and an additional one when we were home from our missionary work abroad. He promoted the active role of the laity, and soon there were three hundred of the faithful in the parish involved in some kind of committed service. So, besides work at the Center, we were constantly invited to participate in the evangelistic outreaches of the parish. Slowly, through evangelism, more families and singles were woven into the fabric of life at Open Door.

Shortly after we arrived in Abbeville, we received a letter from Father Jim Mitchell at El Camino.

Dear Summers Family,

Congratulations on your language study and your recent mission to Mexico. If those long-term visas haven't arrived yet, you should just to come over to Colombia on tourist visas. Tourist visas are good for three months. Those three months would give us time to work on your long-term visas from here. There is a chance that you could possibly exit at the border between Colombia and Venezuela and renew your papers when the three months are up.

Looking forward to seeing you in Colombia,

Fr. Jim Mitchell

This whole process of going to Colombia had taken almost two years and now I was six months pregnant.

"Frank, should we take the risk of the possibility of being asked to leave Colombia around my due date? Maybe we should wait the three months, and then go. We've waited this long, three or four more months won't hurt."

Frank's response was quick, "The big question is, 'What does the Lord want us to do?'"

We started another family retreat.

Again the Lord's answer was "Go! Go forth trusting me! Go now!"

Three weeks later, tourist visas in hand, we boarded a jet bound for Miami. Again we experienced opposition to our new mission. The devil does not like mission, and the primary focus of spiritual attack came upon Sarah. The afternoon before our flight, she came down with fever and hives. The doctor couldn't guess at what caused the hives and put her on antibiotics and Benadryl.

We had other worries, too. Father Jim had asked us to bring hand-farming implements like shovels, hoes and ground axes. Not too many tourists go to Colombia with shovels and things; suppose the government decided not to let us in? We could turn around and go back, but that would be a terrible disappointment! Father Jim had given us some names of people we could contact if he couldn't be there to meet us. Now with Sarah sick, I was concerned about arriving and not being met at the airport. It was going to be a long day; we had a four-hour layover in Miami.

Once we were in motion and on our way – worries and fears seem to diminish. Our long awaited mission to Colombia was really happening. Beau, at fourteen, loved to explore the airport. We had our family prayers in one of the more deserted waiting rooms, and then, armed with God's grace, really began to enjoy our trip. We arrived in Bogotá at about ten o'clock at night. I was so happy to see Father Jim's smiling face peering over the airport fence!

But Frank did have to explain the farming implements. The Columbian officials hemmed and hawed, but they let us in anyway. I thought we would spend what was left of the night in Bogotá, and go on to El Camino in the morning. Father Jim informed us that we still had some errands to run, and then we would continue the five-hour drive to Cité, a tiny village in the beautiful Andes Mountains. It was already 11:00 pm and we had been up since 5 am. Although it was July, the night air in the Andes was chilly. I couldn't help but worry about Beau, with several Columbian boys, in the back of the pickup truck that had an open canvas cover. The cold air blew through there. After a while they were all huddled together for warmth, away from the central area that held the cargo.

Up front, in the cab of the pickup, we were getting better acquainted with Father Jim. He hadn't heard that I was pregnant and we all prayed together for Sarah's healing. She fell into a peaceful sleep. I was terribly sleepy; we had been awake for almost twenty-four hours. The mountain roads didn't have embankments and very few road markers. It was foggy, and moisture gathered on the windshield.

As the night wore on, I became less and less comfortable. The winding roads were incredibly steep. Father Jim suffered from strabismus, and amblyopia, commonly known as "lazy-eye". I had no idea how much his driving might be affected by this, and pretty soon his head was nodding with sleepiness.

He pulled over to the side of the road, "Frank, can you drive awhile? I'm falling asleep, and in this drizzling rain, that could be dangerous."

"Okay," Frank said eagerly, "I'll be glad to." The side of the road was terrifying. When Frank opened the car door to take over the driving, he had inches to walk around the truck. Right past the inches of ground was a terrifying, precipitous, sheer drop.

I had been bombarding heaven with prayers for our safety, and now Frank was going to drive. I gave his hand a desperate squeeze before we took off again. Frank was bound to be sleepy, too. He wasn't used to the mountains, or the truck, and visibility was only a short distance ahead. I prayed, "Lord Jesus, give me peace! I love you, Lord. I know I'm always telling you that I would do anything for you, but this is not what I had in mind."

I wanted to keep talking to Frank so that he would stay awake, but finally exhaustion took over and I dozed off, hugging Sarah close to my heart.

It was still pitch dark and drizzling lightly when we pulled to a stop in front of a Colombian farmhouse.

"What do you think, boys, it looks like it's been raining a lot, should we chance getting the truck stuck in the mud on the road, or should we just climb the hill up to the community house?" Father Jim asked the young men in the back.

"Leave the truck here," they chorused. "We can carry everything."

Everyone grabbed supplies and our luggage; Frank carried Sarah and I carried a light bag. Beau carried one of our backpacks. We crossed barbed wired fences, groped our way through muddy fields, and kept climbing up and up and up a hill. We crossed a stream and a road and kept climbing. We skirted animals in the fields and almost brushed the horns of a cow, in the dark. Finally, in the distance, further up the hill, lights twinkled in the fog.

"There's El Camino!" my young companion, Norberto, told me proudly. "There's your new home."

Somehow those words consoled my heart; we were almost there. The young men banged on the wooden doors. Even in the foggy night, the building showed some character. A tall bell tower, topped by a huge cross, was its most important feature. Accentuated by bay windows, trimmed in wrought iron, the monastery-like brick construction was very attractive. After a good long time of knocking, the doors flung open wide. The light of the entrance hall shone on several sleepy, but happy young people. They extended to us warm embraces of welcome. Our family was escorted to a room at the end of the long hall.

Getting here had been an adventure, to say the least. Before we turned in for the night, we asked for a drink of water. Instead of drinking glasses, Miguel and Norberto handed us plastic bowls, *margarine bowls,* full of water! Beau and I looked at each other. Because we were experienced travelers, we could readily avoid showing too much surprise. An amused flicker of a smile that passed between us said it all. We had used that same smile for many similar occasions in the missionary life.

"This must be some kind of initiation test," I thought to myself.

I looked around for Father Jim. I wanted to ask if the water was safe to drink. Ernesto, who seemed to have an air of responsibility, guessed what I was thinking.

"We boil our water here. Father Jim is very insistent about that. Don't worry. It's safe."

I was so thirsty and the water tasted very good, even out of a bowl. The next day, I learned those bowls were for real. They served as coffee mugs and drinking glasses. The call to missions is a call to flexibility; in a day or two the bowls began to look like a good idea. They could be stacked, washed and dried very easily in the communal kitchen. Overall, life in El Camino seemed to make pretty good, functional sense. Thank the Lord; we had a spacious room. A triple bunk bed occupied one wall; Beau slept on top and Sarah on the bottom. An old, green, iron double bed leaned along the other wall. They offered it with great flourish. It had been acquired just for us. We thanked them profusely and they left us alone to settle in for the remaining few hours of night.

Turning back the covers, I discovered that the mattress looked like a topographical map of Colorado, but when I stretched out on the bed that night, a four-poster bed in Buckingham palace wouldn't have felt better. Before we shut our bleary eyes, we thanked and praised God for our new home, our new mission, and our safe journey.

The wake-up bell rang. The few hours' sleep had made

an enormous difference. Sarah, with her big blue eyes and bouncing blonde hair, was on top of us and then she was snuggling under the covers.

"Wake up, wake up, rise and shine." At two years old, she spoke fluent Spanish and impeccable English.

Her enthusiasm was contagious and soon we were all awake. I walked over to the bay window, which had no windowpanes, totally open to the outdoors. The freshly made curtains had been closed to help keep out the cold night air. When I opened the curtains, the scenery almost took my breath away.

"Oh, wow! It is gorgeous, y'all. Get up! Come quickly! Look! It's so beautiful."

The same hill that had seemed so threatening in the dark last night was the centerpiece of a picture perfect, stunning landscape. Dark green, taller mountains stood in the distance; bright green hills closer up were dotted with scattered farm houses; fields, fruit trees, and gigantic sunflowers dancing gaily in the breeze.

"Jesus, you continually impress me," I said. "Praise you dear Lord, for this beauty. Praise you for the Holy Spirit I feel in this place. No wonder You brought me here at night. You wanted to surprise me in the morning."

He delights to give us His good gifts. The view from El Camino was one of those good gifts I'll never forget. Maybe it was like that for Mary and Joseph. I'd like to think that after the mysteries of Christmas night, the sun dawned on a spectacular view from the stable door.

El Camino was a community in formation. Those who had been there for a few years could relate the stories of the glorious beginning, when everything was just getting off the ground – stories of sacrifice and the moving of the Spirit. The house was still under construction; community members were doing the majority of the work themselves. Donations came in from the States. The food was supplied by their own subsistence farming efforts. Vegetable growing, with large fields of corn and beans, were the principal crops. When we were there, their effort at raising animals was in the developmental stage. Our diet was basically vegetarian, not for philosophical reasons, but out of necessity.

Cooking and cleaning were undertaken as teamwork. Single and married ladies did the cooking except on Sunday. It was a challenge to feed forty hard-working people on vegetables everyday, and keep them going. The community, as well as us, learned about organic farming and intensive agriculture. El Camino was trying to create new patterns of prosperity in a subsistence world. These were ideas that the counterculture in the developed world had explored in the sixties, and they have become more current today. In those days, however, it was our faith in Christ and our desire to share Christian love that made it all possible and pleasant.

Our little family was at its slimmest during our stay there and it was impossible for Beau to gain weight. Frank and Beau had both evangelistic responsibilities and a small garden nearby. He and Frank worked with the *asedon*, which was a primitive hoe on a long handle, in their own parcel of land. It was real, hard, physical labor.

"Son, I can see your bones. It is good thing you are building some muscle." I said one day when he took off his sweaty T-shirt.

"Mom, there really isn't much food here. The only time I feel full is when Dionera (his girlfriend near the town) feeds me eggs and sausage. The boys and I stop on the way back from every errand to eat corn, fruits, and snacks. All of us are skinny!"

To an American eye, the three meals a day at El Camino were extremely light. Since the diet was so meager, the few "extras" like eggs, milk and special treats were scarce.

Most of the community members were young high school students walking into a deeper commitment of faith. Many of them had been rescued from being forced into drug traffic, or the violence that goes along with refusing to be a part of that traffic. We had a large stereo system with speakers scattered all over the farm. The youth loved it. It was great when Christian music flowed out to all of us while we were washing clothes, working the farm, or feeding the animals – not so great when Father Jim left and they played Elvis non-stop.

Each morning, a wake-up bell called us to ready ourselves for a Spirit-filled time of praise and worship; either at Mass, a para-liturgy, or a prayer meeting. We were equipped for the day with the power and presence of the Holy Spirit, and the chapel was always open for adoration. We had breakfast in a common dining area, then the students left for school, and the adults went out to their various assignments. Beau and Frank had a patch of land to farm, and Sarah accompanied me in my duties in the kitchen. Many times during the day, we shared with other members of the community the marvels that God had done for us. It was a place where we were free to break into songs of praise. In the evenings after supper, small teams would go out into the mountains to evangelize in the *veredas*. On Saturday evenings we had a charismatic Mass in the village. Sunday morning found us again in the village at a Mass for the entire parish; the children were taken out during the homily for Catechism and Bible instruction. Sunday afternoons, too, found the teams evangelizing.

One Saturday evening Mass, a very short *campesino* (Colombian farmer) made his way to the front of the church, and he was swaying and reeling, but not to the music, he was drunk. He came back the next morning for Mass, obviously drinking, but not drunk. Later, at home at the community, we prayed for this man. The next Saturday he showed up again for the Mass, showing no signs of being intoxicated. He became a faithful regular of the prayer meetings and Masses. He never said very much, but always listened to the Word of God with rapt attention. After a particularly beautiful Sunday Mass, I had to cross through the side chapel where the sanctuary was. This little man, obviously chiseled by life, was kneeling before the Blessed Sacrament. He didn't even notice when several children traipsed through. I was stopped in my tracks by an overwhelmingly strong, beautiful smell. It was a heavenly perfume flowing out from God's humble son, which was a sign to me of the holiness of humility. I've experienced this gift from time to time. The Lord allows me to smell the fragrance of holiness. I knelt behind the campesino for a few minutes in the presence of God before I had to get up to go for Sarah at a nearby house.

After having coffee with the Nunez family who had taken care of Sarah during Mass, I walked back through the chapel to meet up with Frank and Beau. The man was still there. He still didn't look up. Again, I smelled that wonderful smell, so did little Sarah.

51

I heard the Lord tell me, "You're going to be surprised at how many of the last are going to be first, and how many of the first will be last at the banquet in heaven. Never underestimate the power of true repentance. These little ones at the `ends of the earth' are worthy of hearing the Gospel. That's why you've come."

Another one of the least brothers that I remember from Colombia was Don Carlos. "*Don*" is Spanish for "Sir" and it took more than age to earn that distinction in Andean Colombia. He lived in a settlement called *La Palma Baja,* which means "the low palm." It was about an hour away on horseback.

He would appear on his old horse, his body like a gnarled tree weathered by the storms of life, in his work clothes, with rags around his machete. Still, he possessed a kind of nobility that our family fondly recalls. He was absolutely one of the poorest men I've ever known. He would donate one or two mornings a week to work on the community farm and he displayed many years of using hand tools when he worked. He was almost faster than a modern motorized tiller. His clothes were so patched that you couldn't tell where the patches ended and the clothes began.

Frank, Beau, Pablo Pinzon, Sarah, Miguel Barriga and I went up to *La Palma Alta,* the high palm, one day. On the way up to La Palma Alta, we passed Don Carlos's house. It was a very small hut. The land he farmed was not level at all. I guess that's why he was so poor. I was seven months pregnant, and the two-hour climb straight up the hill was a real challenge. I felt even more inadequate when I saw a woman twice my age walking up the hill carrying a huge load of firewood on her head. She passed me up like I was standing still. The climb seemed to take forever.

One of our favorite songs in Spanish is entitled "*Mas alla del Sol*" meaning "beyond the sun," and it talks about the beautiful life we'll have when we get to heaven.

Sarah asked, after about an hour and a half of climbing, "Where in the world are we going anyway - *mas alla del sol* (on the other side of the sun)?" We all laughed.

We finally reached our destination, a small settlement on the top of a mountain. The vegetation and the view were awesome, the people, simple and poor. In their poverty, they rushed around and prepared something for us to eat while we waited for the villagers to gather for the prayer meeting. The meeting was held outside. Frank gave our testimony and shared a short teaching from the Bible. While I was giving my part of the testimony, I noticed a poor old man, sitting on a fencepost, far away from the rest of the people.

He seemed so interested and attentive, that I wondered why he didn't come any closer. We closed the meeting and I was hugging the children and shaking the hands of the adults on the way out. I smiled and offered my hand to the man on the fence post; he kept his hands under his jacket.

I moved my hand closer to him and said, "God Bless You!"

He nodded his head in acknowledgment, but did not offer his hand.

I felt the Lord urge me to persist with my hand outstretched. "Jesus Christ loves you and I do too," I said softly.

Finally, he reached out his hand and tears filled his eyes. "*Gracias, gracias*", he said.

I was very touched when I saw his hands; they were nothing but nubs, eaten away by leprosy. As I shook the nubs, I felt the love of Jesus flow through me toward Jesus's brother, who had to live on the fringe of life. This is one of the privileges of being sent to love and serve.

The birth of our baby approached while we were settled there in El Camino. We had seen the signs and wonders that God promises. Father Raphael Herrera Garcia of the *Minuto de Dios* community in Bogotá had been instrumental in getting through the red tape in the government offices for our long-term visas. Our bathroom in the community house was finally installed; Frank and Beau had painted our room. Some ladies from the nearby city of Barbosa had bought me a "Moses" basket for my coming baby. My nesting instinct was kicking in and I was in love already with the babe in my womb.

One day while bringing coffee to Fr. Jim, he told me, "When I was in the Amazon Jungle, I did a c-section on a woman. Her baby had died in the womb and she was getting sick. She was not able to deliver the baby."

He took a book off of his shelf. "Using this medical textbook, I performed the surgery and the lady survived."

When I told Frank about the conversation, I said, "Maybe he wants me to feel better, but it isn't working, I'm scared. What if he decides to do a c-section on me?"

We were living in mountains, miles from the nearest town with a hospital. One of the doctors in town was providing my pre-natal care; however, I was hoping to have the baby at El Camino with a mid-wife. By God's providence, one of the ladies in the community was a mid-wife. She had delivered over a thousand babies. There were some things, though, that were disconcerting. Father Jim wanted to be present at the baby's birth. I refused insistently, but he jokingly insisted. He had been present at Sandra's birth, a one-year-old toddler, in the community. I was worried about getting into a difficult part of labor and having Father Jim deciding to operate. On the other hand, he had the jeep, and if I got into trouble it would be impossible to get into town in the middle of the night if he wasn't there. I didn't know how to pray into it. I just put the whole thing into the hands of the Lord and trusted His providence and help.

Sylvia was a forty-year-old single lady in the community, who had a quiet and gentle spirit. Everyone recognized that she was experienced and operated in the gifts of the Holy Spirit. She came up to me on the morning of September 20, 1978; she grabbed my hands and was bubbling over with joy.

"Your baby's going to be born today. I'm so happy. I'm so happy for all of us," she told me, all smiles.

"How do you know? My date isn't until the 26th," I answered.

"This morning, I was awakened by the most beautiful sounds; bells were ringing and ringing. At first, I thought they were tolling our church bells in Cite´, but they were too glorious – hundreds of beautiful bells ringing in a melody! I was filled with joy, extraordinary joy. I told the Lord, 'Thank you Lord, for letting me hear these heavenly bells; but why are these bells ringing?'"

Tears ran down her face, she was so visibly moved.

I hugged her. "That's great, Sylvia, what did the Lord say to you?"

The Lord said, "These bells are ringing because a new

citizen of the kingdom of heaven is going to be born today. The baby of Francisco and Maria will be born today!"

Sylvia shared this with me right after morning prayers, and most of the morning I had no sign whatever of the eminence of our baby's coming. Wednesday was my day off from the kitchen, so I took my dirty clothes down the hill to wash them by hand. The washboard basin was in a very awkward position for a nine-month pregnant lady. While I was out there, Pablo, the livestock man, came to me with a washtub full of chickens.

"These chickens need to be dressed and cleaned for sale. Please, help me wash the chickens with blue detergent and water. The merchant needs them washed and wrapped by early afternoon."

I had never heard of, and didn't even believe in, washing chickens with detergent, but he sounded so desperate that I gave in. Washing chickens in the hot sun wasn't any easier than washing my dirty clothes; it was harder. The thought of heavenly bells had slipped my mind as I washed chickens, and looked down at the pile of dirty clothes that still would need washing after the chickens were done.

Suddenly, Beau came up to me like a knight in shining armor. "Mom, I'll finish washing those chickens. You look so hot and tired. I'll wash the clothes too. Father Jim decided not to take me along with him on his trip, so I have the rest of the day free."

I was so grateful. As I walked up the hill to the house I began to think of those bells again. Father Jim was going on a four-day trip. Now *wouldn't* be a good time for the baby to be born. I walked into the office where Frank was working and shared with him what Sylvia had said.

"I am so tired; I found it really hard to wash the laundry and helping Pablo with his chickens, but Beau came to my rescue."

He held me in his arms, "Go, lie down and rest. I'll be praying for you."

I did. I went straight to bed. I was about to doze off when I heard Father Jim and some kids driving off in the jeep. I said a quick prayer for their journey. Without warning, I had a strange sensation and I realized that my amniotic sac had ruptured. This was a sure sign of eminent childbirth. I was so excited. Fatigue dissipated immediately. I called out to Frank and he came right away.

"Frank, the baby *IS* going to be born today! A new citizen of the kingdom of heaven is going to be born today!"

"Thank you, Jesus, that the time has come," Frank said. "Babe, I'm going to find the mid-wife. I want to make sure she will be at hand."

About one o'clock in the afternoon, my labor started in earnest. Everyone in the community was praying. Frank played the guitar and we prayed the rosary to pass the hours as the time got closer and closer. Community members, one by one, stuck their heads in our room, to say a quick prayer.

All seemed to be going very well, until about nine o'clock at night. A thunderstorm came up and we had a total blackout – no electricity. Often these blackouts lasted all night. We hadn't prepared for this eventuality. Frank looked all over for candles.

"I can only find a couple of very small candle stubs, they won't give much light and won't last long," he said.

Frank went from room to room asking the people," "Wake up and pray that the lights come back on soon."

Miguel ventured out in the midst of the storm to the village below to get votive candles from the church. I was touched and blessed by this gesture, and a little bit worried about him in the storm. Twenty minutes and several hard contractions later, the lights came back on. Simultaneous, spontaneous shouts of praise went up all over the house. Forty-five minutes later Susanna Maria was born!

I held her, nursed her, and cried with joy. God was so good. She was healthy and beautiful. Her skin was flawless and she had my dimple in her chin. We didn't have a scale, so Pablo went for the chicken scale. We put a baby blanket in and weighed her, eight pounds and four ounces. Frank and Beau "ooohed and aaahed", over the latest addition to our little family. We were now a family of five missionaries!

Before the baby was born, I had bought material for a baptismal dress. Elena, one of the young girls in the community had promised to make it for me. October 8th is the feast of Saint Susanna. We planned the baptism for that day. Frank and I had a little money saved and we invited all the people of the barrios (villages or marginal neighborhoods on the outskirts of the town) and the village that we knew to share in our joy and participate with us in her Baptismal Mass and a meal afterward. We even bought meat and I made a jambalaya.

The day of the baptism, Elena still hadn't finished the dress. Just an hour before mass, she confessed sadly, "The dress won't be ready until tomorrow."

I cried. I wanted Susanna to wear white. The only white she had was a little Carter's knit nightgown. It was on old hand-me-down that had a stain near the collar. She did have a little loose knit sweater that was almost white, and a white blanket.

"This will have to do. I thank you Lord, for our poverty. I know that the whiteness of her baptism will outshine the sun," I prayed sincerely, but I was still so disappointed.

Beau and Frank were already dressed and waiting in the chapel. I bathed and dressed Sarah and myself. The stained nightgown looked really old next to the white blanket. I had a lump in my throat, as I was about to dress her. Someone knocked gently at the door. It was one of the supporters of the community from the village. She walked in and handed me a package. We had about five minutes left before Mass. I felt so rushed that I almost didn't open the package.

My friend insisted, "Open it now."

I removed the wrapping paper carefully, to save the paper. The box fell open and out dropped a frilly white dress! Jesus wanted Susanna to have a white baptismal dress after all. I dressed her and scooped her up into my arms. When Mass began that evening, the heavenly bells were ringing loudly in my heart. Susanna's godparents are my sister, Rachel, and Vince Listi. Of course, they couldn't be present in person, so we needed someone to stand in proxy for them. Father Jim suggested that we ask the entire community and poor in attendance that beautiful night to stand in proxy. The memory of all those humble believers filing by and making the sign of the cross on her lily-white forehead is seared in my memory forever. Especially when Don Carlos, in his patched clothes, made the sign of the cross, his hand trembled from emotion. His eyes were moist with tears. Our littlest missionary was already touching hearts.

One morning when the baby was almost a month old,

Frank and Beau came to me.

Beau said, "We want to participate in more evangelism. We just talked to Father Jim. He doesn't have any more opportunities around here. But he told us that we might want to explore the possibility of ministry in Florian, a parish he once worked in, deeper in the jungle,"

Frank said. "Father said we could go soon to visit if you feel up to it."

We boarded a rural bus, traveled for hours deeper into the jungle, amazed at the lush vegetation and praying for the natives that would intermittently emerge from the bush. Florian had no priest and it had a big empty rectory. We loved it and wheels began to turn in our minds about how we might minister effectively there.

"We could still be members of the Community, and get together with y'all from time to time. It seems to be the perfect place for us," I said when we reported back to Father Jim.

"I'll present your proposal to the Bishop," Father said. "I'll be seeing him this week."

"I pray the Bishop will say yes," Frank said as we gathered in our room later that evening.

Much to our regret, the Lord slammed that door shut! The Bishop said to Father Jim, "I am not at peace about an American family living in Florian. It is a center of guerilla activity. Don't you remember, Jim, the adjacent building to the rectory has bullet holes from a past machine gun volley."

Father Jim reluctantly agreed, "I guess there is suspicion of foreigners, not to mention the many armed political factions."

Father Jim and other community members went on their annual retreat right after the Bishop said no. Our family stayed home at El Camino to seek the Lord. We had our own retreat in their absence. We had barely started our retreat when we heard God's clear guidance. We were sitting under a palm tree looking out on the impressive view.

Frank opened his Jerusalem Bible. "This is what I received in prayer, earlier this morning. I didn't want to hear it as God's Word but it really is. I know his voice:

Alleluia!
Give thanks to Yahweh, for he is good,
His love is everlasting;

let these be the words of Yahweh's redeemed,
those he has redeemed from the oppressor's clutches,
*by bringing them home **from foreign countries**.*

Ps107; 1-3

"That's like the reading I got in Isaiah, Dad, here in Chapter 43 it says *'Bring back my sons from afar, and my daughters from the ends of the earth,'"* Beau said excitedly.

The Lord was calling us to go back home. We wouldn't worry about the ramifications; we would obey. We had prayed and waited two years to get to Colombia. We had hoped it would be our permanent home.

Obviously, what God wanted from us was for us to be a missionary "SWAT" team, not a family of missionary settlers. Again, leaving was pretty tough. At our going away Mass from El Camino, Arturo, the only other married male in the community, gave Frank a very large, wooden "pectoral" cross. He had carved it to send as a gift from the community to the new Pope, John Paul I, but that Pope had died after only thirty days in office. The cross was already packaged for mailing, but it had been returned to Auturo un-mailed.

"Frank, I think the Lord wants you to have this cross," he said with a grin.

Frank took off a smaller wooden cross and put on the larger one.

"I guess the Lord wants me to be an even bolder witness for Him. Thank you, Arturo."

We flew out of Bogota, Colombia on December 12, the feast of Our Lady of Guadalupe. I felt Our Lady's love and protection. "Thank you, dear Mother, for your prayers for us. Help us to have many more chances to share about your son, Jesus, with our Latin American brothers and sisters."

Romans 12:16 tells us to make *real* friends with the poor. Susanna easily lives this verse with her sunny disposition, and her genuine love for all of God's children.

Michael and Susanna VanVickle in General Cepeda, Coahuila, Mexico. It was a beautiful missionary wedding. Susanna and Mike spent their first years in mission. They are a beautiful witness to their faith, and raising a Catholic, Christian family. They support FMC, Pro-Life work, Blue Knights, and Enthronement of the Sacred Hearts.

60

Chapter Five

San Pedro

The Blessed Mother must have immediately brought my prayer to Jesus, because shortly after we arrived in Abbeville, we received a letter from Monsignor Carlos Talavera, Auxiliary Bishop of Mexico City.

Dear Frank and Genie,

I am inviting you and the children to join with others from all over Latin America at a Charismatic House of Prayer in Puebla, Mexico. John Paul II will be visiting Mexico and the Latin American Bishops are having a conference, which the Pope will attend in Puebla. Let us know and we will enroll you in the prayer house registry.

Carlos Talavera, +

Auxiliary Bishop of Mexico City

The invitation to be on the international prayer team interceding for the Puebla Conference and the visit with Pope John Paul II was quite an honor. Our immediate response was "Yes, Lord. We will go."

"But how will we get there?" we asked ourselves. We had just spent our precious funds on plane tickets home from Colombia. We couldn't afford another set of airline tickets. We would need to drive to Puebla. It was not much farther south than Mexico City, but we didn't have a vehicle.

Heaven had to hear our fervent prayers for the funds for a new mode of transportation!

The Lord provided the funds for us to buy a used green Dodge "carry-van." Frank quickly adapted it into living quarters for the five of us. We carried a camping stove, portable toilet, dishes, catalytic heater and the bare essentials in clothes. In mid-January we were on our way. For a week, we lived in the van on the street in front of our old apartment in the Cuchilla del Tesoro during the Pope's visit to Mexico City. Frank and Beau were privileged to see him twice during his time there. They welcomed him upon his arrival at the airport, and they were in the crowd of twelve million people at the Basilica of the Virgin of Guadalupe. They waited for hours in the hot sun. Frank said that the order in the vast crowd was amazing. At communion, two priests came out, each carrying a ciborium of hosts consecrated by the Pope. Frank prayed, and one priest came right over to him. This special Eucharist humbled him. Leaving the Basilica after the Mass, the Pope was carried out into the crowd, on his chair, to bless them.

Frank prayed, "Lord Jesus, please allow the blessing of this Holy Servant of Yours to fall upon us and our life in mission." John Paul II was blessing the crowd with the sign of the cross made in large sweeping motions.

Then for a moment, his eyes met Frank's and he made a very small individual sign of the cross directed especially at him. "Thank you, Jesus" Frank said, his eyes brimming.

A week later, we were participating in the prayer house in Puebla. Hundreds of turned-on Christians at the prayer house from all over Mexico, Latin America, North America and around the world supported the Pope's visit and the Bishops' conference.

The attending priests were being housed in a beautiful mansion; it was a couple of blocks from the prayer house. We were allowed to live in the truck on the grounds of the mansion and to use the bathroom facilities, so for us, it was great. Puebla is a beautiful old city with three hundred sixty-five churches, one for every day of the year. Sarah, with her little blond ponytails was the darling of the week.

At two and a half, she was already an evangelist. She was fond of gathering a crowd of people at a fountain in the middle of the courtyard, she would say in perfect Spanish, "Turn to number 3 in your songbooks, we will sing 'Pasa por Aqui.'"

Song 3 wasn't "Pasa por Aqui", but everyone went along anyway. She was just a toddler, and the "missionary" in her was showing strongly! Susanna melted every heart and people stood in line to hold her. Beau was participating as an adult, and his insights and gifts were a major contribution.

The clergy and leaders in Mexico had never seen, or conceived of, a family in missionary evangelization. Frank, our wonderful children and myself exemplified the plan of our Lord to call and send out lay evangelists who could renew the Church in a season of crisis. The crisis that perplexed the Church was the lack of priestly vocations and the lack of women embracing religious life.

Some of our friends in the clergy told us, "Maybe the Lord is leaving space for the gap in 'vocations' to be filled by lay apostles."

Pope John Paul II's pope mobile passed by on the street outside the home where we were parked. As he drew near, there was such jubilation, such unity and such joy. It made me think of the Second Coming of Jesus. Sarah was on Beau's shoulders. When he neared our corner, she shouted, *"There's my Pope, there's my Pope!!"*

When Jesus comes, we will each shout, "There's my Jesus!" As every knee bows, and every tongue proclaims His Lordship, He will be there for each and there for all. Division will melt away, and we will be one!

At the prayer house, Father Victor Cervantes and Father Alejandro Burciaga took a special interest in our ministry and in our life and call. One afternoon at the mansion, Father Victor came out to visit us on the grounds. His eyes always twinkled; you could tell he was taken by our simple accommodations in the van.

"Come, you can work full time as missionaries with me. My parish is named San Pedro (St. Peter's) in the Diocese of Cuatitlan. It's not too far from Mexico City. The town was formerly named San Pedro Atzcapotzaltongo. Everyone still calls it San Pedro, but its new name is Villa Nikolas Romero. I want you to show my congregation that laity must be living the Word, they need to embrace the apostolate."

"Thanks Father, that's really one of our hopes, to inspire others to evangelize." Frank said. "We are limited by a six months visa, so we should have five more months on this one."

I was really attracted to Father's humility and sincerity. "I'm happy to hear Frank accept this offer, Father, we'll be there as soon as possible."

We arrived in "San Pedro" on the feast of the chair of St. Peter – another God-incidence.

Father Victor welcomed us warmly and allowed us to live in our truck in an enclosed garden of the rectory while we tried to find more adequate housing. Eventually, we moved into a warehouse, it was a wing of the rectory. We lived a full and happy life for several months in that humble place, surrounded by boxes and banners that were no longer in use. We killed eleven scorpions in our living quarters; that was pretty frightening because we slept on gymnastic mats on the floor at night.

Our Mexican friends were astonished that we, Americans, could live so simply. One of my new friends, Sofia, who had a really nice house, said to me. "Explain this living, why are you doing this?"

"God led us to this place to share His love and His son Jesus with everyone. I can cook on my camping stove, we finally have a toilet and a shower, we don't need a fridge, and we live right across the street from the market. All of our basic needs are met." I explained. "We find real joy, not in things, but in each other and our mission".

"I wish I could do that, but I need a real bed at night. I can't sleep on a mat on the floor," she responded.

"If Jesus wanted you to sleep on a mat on the floor, He would give you the grace to do it." I answered confidently smiling. She half-heartedly smiled back. But I knew it was true, He could and would give her the grace if she asked for it.

Frank and Beau walked everywhere (we could not afford gasoline on a daily basis). Sometimes it was miles over hill and dale to small chapels. Daily, they were giving Life in the Spirit seminars - preaching the good news about Jesus Christ, His Salvation, and the empowering of the Holy Spirit. These people were hungry for the Word of God, and the ministry really took off. Many people were converted, and lives were changed. One of the brightest spots in our entire missionary career was the working relationship we enjoyed in San Pedro with Father Victor. He inspired us by his untiring service. He was on call for his parishioners from early morning 'till late at night. He was only one priest, and he had twenty thousand Catholics in his pastoral care. I prayed with women, for the sick at healing sessions, and was wife and mom. I evangelized at women's functions, and held weekly women's groups in nearby villages.

Beau, at fourteen years of age, was given a significant role in the leadership of the youth community. In a short time, the numbers grew to over a hundred youth at the assembly. A core of about thirty, who were giving of themselves in ministry, met weekly. The group also interacted with a more secular music ministry; youth followed Beau into direct ministry to the poor and remote villages. Lalo, Lula, Anabelle, Pilar and others became some of the closest associations Beau had ever formed. His friends came to our warehouse apartment to play with his sweet and delightful sisters, Sarah and Susanna, whom they regarded as living dolls.

Beau recalls, "This was a time, too, of great strain because of the lack of reliable resources to support the ministry. My friends brought their friends to me. Many were facing struggles with teen pregnancy, alcoholism, drugs, abortion, and gangs in their milder forms. I kept most of those secrets to myself for years. I begged the kids to contact certain adults for help, but I felt I could not tell the adults myself. As I earned trust and made friends; I also experienced some of the normal struggles of youthful rebellion, which were much highlighted by our position as ministers and missionaries. San Pedro stayed in my prayers for years."

Beau, the girls and I all developed a close relationship with the fascinating, elderly parents of Father Victor. They were a rich source of stories and lore about Mexico. In San Pedro, we were all deeply enmeshed in the life of the local community.

Up until the time Frank began preaching in the barrios, Father Victor made his rounds to those same places, but he would encounter only a handful of people attending Mass. He made monthly visits to the barrio chapels, but few showed up. However, once Frank began his evangelism, there were always eighty to a hundred in attendance at the barrio chapels each week. Simultaneously, the prayer group in San Pedro swelled and flourished. Several people were joining Frank in his outreaches. God was moving! His Spirit was upon us.

One evening I was walking Susanna, singing her to sleep in the church proper, while the Parish prayer meeting filled the adjacent church hall. She had finally dozed off and I was about to rejoin the prayer meeting. Then, I noticed a man at the back of church. He was dressed all in white, with mussed hair. He was slumped over the front of a pew. I thought he was drunk and began to pray that the singing from the hall would minister to him. Later that night, I was up late writing. That same man was sitting at the kitchen table with Father Victor, whose kitchen was visible across the courtyard from mine.

The man was obviously not drunk – they seemed to be

enjoying their conversation very much. As I saw them saying goodnight, I heard the Lord tell me, "This man is going to be the answer to your prayer for a strong male companion for Frank in his ministry."

The next morning early, Father Victor brought Eloy Garcia over to meet us.

"Welcome, Eloy, what brings you here?" Frank asked.

"I am about to retire from government service. I have taken off walking to the mountains near Mexico City, searching for a greater meaning in my life. Father Victor, here, thinks your family might be part of the answer to my searching."

"What else is the Lord going to do? I am in suspense. I have given Eloy a room near the school," Father Victor chimed in happily.

To everyone, it seemed totally providential that our family and Eloy should end up in the same rectory at the same time. Eloy, who was an engineer, told us his own tale. "I had walked for two days and was trying to rest for the night under a tree in the countryside. Suddenly, I was surrounded by barking, snarling, dogs. Their owners were not far behind. The owners were very threatening and told me to go back to town, and when I got to town, I was interrogated by the police." Eloy recounted, raising his heavy, bushy eyebrows.

He continued with his story, "And, of course, because I had taken off from home with *nothing*, I had no ID. God helped me to convince them that I was a professional. But it really unnerved me. After my ordeal with the police, I took refuge in the church, where I rested and prayed during the prayer meeting. When it was over, Father Victor spotted me sitting in the back of church, brought me to his rectory, gave me supper, a gymnastic mat and an empty room to sleep in."

"What an adventure. Well we are glad you're here," I remarked.

Frank and Eloy had an instant respect for, and rapport with, one another. After Frank shared his testimony with Eloy, he was so moved that he decided to stay and work with us. He felt that our ministry and mission answered his quest for more of the Spirit. "I had intended to leave my family for a longer journey at a greater risk. I know my wife, Soccoro, will be relieved if I continue my prayer and spiritual quest nearer my home. She and my daughters will be able to visit me here." He laughed a soft, full laugh; "She'll be thrilled to be able to reach me by phone."

Financially, Eloy had left them very secure by Mexican standards. His family had tried to understand his seeking a spiritual reawakening. Eloy lived a Christian community life with us, and he grew by leaps and bounds in his walk with the Lord. "He who seeks, finds."

Many future missions would find us blessed by the visits of our good brother, Eloy. He has used his retirement to serve the Lord full time, fruitfully in evangelization in Mexico City.

At one of the poor barrios, La Libertad, where Frank ministered, a childless older couple, Pepe and Lucita came every Wednesday to hear the Word of God. Frank and Eloy gave the Life in the Spirit seminar. The talk on repentance was always followed the next week by a renewal Mass. Father Victor went to the barrio and heard confessions for hours. The majority of the people went to Communion for the first time in many, many years.

Pepe and Lucita received the Sacraments, and rejoiced that night in their glorious reconciliation with their heavenly Father. The next morning, Pepe was knocked off the side of the road by a hit and run vehicle. He was killed instantly. He had pushed a popsicle cart all of his life and was dearly loved by generations of children. At his funeral there were countless stories of the generosity of this loving man. He never refused a plea from a little child to let him have the popsicles at a lower price. The popsicle vendor was even known to give them away at times, which cost him money out of his own pocket.

In a gesture of their gratitude, the children of this village gathered money together for an offering to the widow, crying sadly as they presented it to her. When Frank and I came to Lucita to make a contribution toward the casket, (the poor can hardly afford to die), she embraced us. "*Graçias, Graçias*, I thank you with all of my heart. Pepe was so happy last night; He was prepared and ready for his death. He died forgiven of his sins and filled with the Holy Spirit." Frank was humbly grateful that he had been able to play a part in this man's journey home.

One morning at about 9:30, I had just come in from the market when my friend, Maria, came into the house. She was a member of the ladies group I led once a week in a village about five miles away. To get to the meeting, my two little girls and I had to walk across a footbridge (which I nicknamed my "purgatory" because I was terrified each time I crossed it). The footbridge spanned about a hundred yards, was about fifty feet high and only a foot a half wide.

This morning, when my friend arrived, I was pressed for time because Frank went to three prayer meetings in one day. He would go to one in the morning and have just enough time to stop for lunch, then head out walking several more miles into the countryside, get back just in time for supper, and head out again for a prayer meeting at night. Maria was practically in tears; she wanted me to go to her village, San Ildefonso, to witness to her sister who was very distraught.

"My sister, Lety's, husband has left her for another woman. She has four small children and no means of support. Lety's oldest child was born with a birth defect - his feet begin right below his knees. He has no lower legs, only feet where his legs should be. He has already outgrown the prosthesis his father got for him earlier. Now, he can hardly walk." Maria sniffled and continued. "They have no money for a larger pair." (Our family hurriedly solicited funds and received those funds from the USA for his new prosthetic legs.) "All of these things have Lety very sad. Can you come to her? She needs you!"

"What about lunch, Maria? I have to cook for Eloy, Frank and Beau so they can be on their way again by two o'clock? It'll take two hours for us to go to San Ildelfonso and back, there's no way I can do it," I said. She looked so miserably downcast; I decided to ask the Lord about it. I closed my eyes and prayed. "Lord, should I go?"

There was the instant response, "Yes, go."

I said out loud, "I'll go. The Lord wants me to go with you. I don't know how I will feed Frank, Beau and Eloy. I guess the Lord will have to send angels to cook my lunch while I am away."

I packed Susanna in my kangaroo pouch and tugged Sarah along side me. We hadn't reached the bus stop yet, when we met Lula, an older girl from the youth group. She begged me to take Sarah to her house for a couple of hours, and Sarah climbed readily into her arms. Well, my burden was lighter, but

68

my mind was still on the uncooked lunch at the house. Suddenly, I heard someone calling my name; it was another good friend, Rosa.

"Stop, stop" Rosa called, "I was just about to go to your house and invite you to come to our house for lunch, one of my sons is having a birthday and we want your family to join. Earlier this morning, I talked to Frank, Beau and Eloy, and they've agreed to be at my house at one o'clock."

I don't know whose face showed the most shock, Maria's or mine. "The angels *ARE* cooking my lunch," I laughed, "but these are the flesh and blood kind of angels, their names are Rosa and Edwina. Praise God! Thank you, Rosa."

"I'm making my special *sopes,* your favorite," she said proudly.

"We'll be there." I said to Rosa. "Can you phone Lula to bring Sarah to your house for lunch?" She nodded, hugged me and scurried off. Maria, Susanna and I now happily boarded the bus.

Lety and her four children lived in one room made of cinderblock. It was immaculately clean, however, and had bright airy windows. Her little boy with the disfigured legs was beautiful but he looked deeply troubled by their family problems. She confided in me the details of her problem.

I told her, "A broken marriage is never 100% the fault of one partner. It takes two to make a marriage work, and it takes two to make it fail. One partner may be only ten per cent at fault, but that ten per cent is 100% wrong. That 10% needs to be corrected!" I said to her as she listened intently.

She was so in need of truth. She cried.

Maria and I hugged her, and rubbed her shoulders.

I continued, "Are you walking in the Lord's ways? Do you know Him as your friend and Savior? Only He can save your marriage. If you go to confession and become reconciled to God, if you pray with faith, if you determine to live your marriage according to God's plan, He WILL save your marriage."

"Can you pray here in our house with us, right now? I know I can't do anymore than I have done, only the Lord can do something, that's why I allowed Maria to go for you," She remarked.

"Lety, don't lose hope. Holiness is an irresistible perfume! Jesus promised to be where there are two or more of you. Pray with your children, build a peaceful life here. You and the kids will be happier." We talked a long time and then we prayed. I felt the power of God come down.

"Your husband will be back. When he comes, use the opportunity to do the things we talked about," I told her as I walked out of the door.

Three or four days later, Lety was at my door. She came in, sat down and started crying, "Carlos did come back, but he was drinking, he spent the night and the next morning he hit me and walked out. I was so surprised to see him and the children were too."

"Well, God is hearing you. At least he did come back," I said.

"I have been to confession and the children and I are praying every day. I'm reading the Bible my sister lent me. I do feel much more at peace but it hurts me so much when he leaves."

I encouraged her, "You did very well. He'll be back, just remain faithful to Jesus and Jesus will remain faithful to you. I know it hurts you, but you can offer up that pain for the Lord to change his heart." We prayed together and she left cheered up and with a promise to see me at the prayer meeting that night.

The next week she was back. "My husband came home again, this time he wasn't drinking very much at all. He was happy, we talked and laughed, he spent the night and played with the children. But the next morning, he got angry and he hit me again, only he hit very softly - it didn't hurt - then he left." I encouraged her to keep on praying and trusting in Jesus.

Finally her husband came back for good. She came to tell me that he was back, but he wouldn't allow her to go to any prayer meetings, only to Mass on Sunday. I told her to submit for now and to trust the Lord to finish His work.

One morning a handsome young man knocked on our door. It was Carlos, Lety's husband. He said, "I came to see if you and Frank could come pray for my mother, she's dying. Prayers have changed Lety's and my life so much, I think maybe prayers can help my mother."

Frank, Beau and I went that very afternoon. I was so

surprised to see how well furnished and how big his mother's house was. Carlos' mom was lying in bed breathing oxygen through a tube in her nose. She was blind from diabetes. She was ashen in color, and near death.

Frank and I evangelized her and she accepted the Lord with an open heart. She agreed to have Father Victor come to hear her confession; this lady had *never* made a confession as an adult.

Two weeks later, Maria, Lety, her sister, Carlos, her husband, *AND his mother* were at the parish prayer meeting praising the Lord and giving testimony of the Lord's greatness.

After the meeting, the young couple invited Frank and me to be the Godparents of their two-year-old daughter who had never been baptized. At the baptism, Maria bubbled with excitement about all the work the Lord had done in Lety's life. "Their conversion really shows us and everybody else how God forgives sinners," Maria said to me, "because Carlos's mother was the town abortionist for fifteen years, that's how she made all that money!"

One day Frank was walking alone through the town plaza carrying his guitar and his Bible. He was on the way to our friend Catalina's house to meet those who would accompany him to the Morning Prayer meeting. Turning to the side, he saw two uniformed men with weapons drawn running full speed across the plaza in his direction. He looked around to see whom they might be chasing and astoundingly enough, they ran up and pointed their guns at him. "Come with us, you're under arrest," they barked.

He could not believe this was really happening, and began to silently implore the help of the Lord. He was brought into the police station, and into one of the back rooms where an officer and a woman were seated. "Yes, that's him! That's the man!" she yelled and pointed.

Frank's mind was boggled.

The horror stories of Americans in Mexican jails came rushing into his consciousness. We had a ministry to that same jail in San Pedro, and he knew that something scary was happening to him. The woman accused Frank of coming to her house in the middle of the night and asking for a place to stay. She said that when she refused to let him in, he forced his way

71

in. The accusation was so absurd that Frank could not believe it. The wing of the rectory we lived in was enclosed by two separate gates, both locked at night. There was no going in or coming out without the key. He could easily prove the accusation false, BUT would he be given the opportunity? And why was he being accused? Frank realized that the devil was putting this woman up to making false accusations.

"Lord, Jesus," he screamed within, "Come, Lord, with protection and victory."

Praise God, several of the influential people we had been evangelizing had seen the arrest in the plaza. Word spread rapidly that the police had taken "Hermano Francisco (Brother Frank)" to jail. Soon a small crowd had gathered outside the police station, protesting this police action and defending Frank's innocence. We learned later that the woman, the accuser, was the sister of the local judge. She was also a Jehovah's Witness. She was concerned about the great response of the people to our presence and ministry. The judge's sister had been very vocal in her strong opposition to our work in evangelization.

The townspeople were adamant in Frank's defense. A small crowd of them forced their way into the Police Chief's office, saying, "This is a good man. He is being falsely accused."

The police reluctantly let Frank go. They warned him, however, "if we catch you outside at night after 10:00 pm., we'll put you in jail without asking questions."

I knew nothing about this whole incident the entire time it was actually happening. I was at home attending to my girls. It was Thursday, the only day of the week when Father Victor was out for the whole day. Satan must have planned it that way. Fr. Victor was not there to come to Frank's aid. Frank came home directly from the jail. I was surprised to see him walk in a little early.

"Why are you back so soon, didn't anyone show up for the meeting?"

Then I saw how pale he looked." Are you sick, what's wrong?" I asked, very concerned.

He plopped down on the sofa, letting his guitar and Bible bag fall roughly to the ground. "Come sit down, sugar, we've got to talk." He explained the whole episode, finishing the statement, "We need to pray about what to do."

"You can pray about it if you want to," I said in true panic, "I'm going to start packing. I think we should get out of here as quickly as we can. This is nothing to fool around with."

"Hold on, Genie, we can't just pack up and leave without talking to Father Victor, that's surely not what the Lord would have us do."

I burst into tears, I was really, really scared. "Father Victor won't be back 'till late this evening. I don't know if I can put it out of mind for that long. Where's Beau? I don't know where he went. As soon as he gets back, I want us to pray together." I said between sobs.

Father Victor came home late that evening and he was shocked to hear about the trouble we had been through. He was not a bit afraid. "I will talk to the officials in the morning. We will get this whole thing straightened out. This is ridiculous!"

"But, Father, our visas expire at the end of next month, shouldn't we just leave now to avoid any hassle?" I asked, still hoping he would agree.

"There is absolutely no reason for you to leave now, Frank will be fine. Besides, I still want you to give that course on lay evangelism. Relax, trust, Smile!"

Smiling was the last thing I wanted to do. After a lot of prayer, I relaxed a little and enjoyed our last weeks in San Pedro.

A few weeks later, the Church bells pealed all day long on the parish's feast day. The Bishop came to celebrate the feast of St. Peter and St. Paul. He thanked us for our ministry. When we look back on our time at San Pedro today, it is as an indication of the kinds of roles lay missionary evangelists can fulfill in the Church where so much needs to be done. We hope we have gained wisdom without losing the willingness we had then – a willingness to get muddy in the Lord's service.

Gaudencio Cardinal Rosales, Cardinal of the Philippines, and Genie after lunch at the Cardinal's Palace in Manila. In March 2012, FMC installed the Alvarez missionary family on Camiguin Island. En route to the island, Cardinal Rosales hosted us in Manila and invited us to lunch. He and I had a great reunion remembering our work together in Malaybalay during his Episcopate. He encouraged the Alvarezes to continue the mission of Frank and Genie and family.

Our family rejoiced when Frank was honored with a medal. He received the Diocese of Lafayette Bishop's Service Award Spring of 2005

Bishop Michael Jarrel, Diocese of Lafayette, Celebrating Mass at FMC's Home Base

April 2011.
Bishop Cornelius Sim, Genie (left), and Gerry Yee at Starbucks in Singapore. Bishop Sim had visited our family in mission before he ever entered seminary.

Chapter Six

Storms, Surprises and Saltillo

St. Paul and his evangelization team moved around a lot!

In our last few weeks in San Pedro, we had been corresponding with an evangelistic group in New York City. We left our dear Fr. Victor, and looked forward to a brief stop in Abbeville to visit Open Door.

Then we headed to an entirely different world - maybe we would finally find a missionary community in New York City. An evangelistic group invited us up to explore missions.

The Summers family now had many connections in the Body of Christ; they were all important to the work God was doing in and through us. We were living in the green truck again. Beau had an upper bunk that was about twenty inches wide, with about an eighteen-inch clearance.

Laughingly, he remarked, "Maybe the Lord is preparing me for concentration camp."

Frank and I both slept on one twin bed mattress and the little girls both slept in an area about one yard square. Equipped with a lot of love and enthusiasm, and not too much in the way of material goods, we spent the next six months going where the Spirit led us. Our first destination was New York City. A lay missionary, who had served in South America, invited us to visit and discuss formation of a lay missionary community. On our way, we stopped in at the Alleluia Community, in Augusta, Georgia. We drove into Faith Village; the place was almost deserted. Finally, we found someone who told us the whole community was attending a general assembly at another location.

Rushing to their school where the prayer meeting was being held, we praised God that, by His providence, we would be able to worship with them at their General Community Gathering.

Dr. Kevin Murrell, one of the elders of the community, was leading the meeting. We sat down at the very back so we wouldn't disturb anyone.

After a few minutes, Kevin spotted us, "Frank, come up here and talk about what God has been doing in your mission. You may have a word from the Lord for us."

"Thanks, Kevin. It really is a blessing to be able to report to all of you. We appreciate your constant openness, love and support. I wish all missionaries had communities that wanted to hear their reports," Frank began. It was true; we were honored by the mutual respect we had for the Lord's call for them and for us. Every visit with them empowered us to continue our work.

Years before, we had lived in New York City while Frank did post-graduate studies in Law at Columbia University. This time, we stayed with families in Brooklyn who were trying to build a community, and to combine this effort with support of the foreign missions. Our luggage was barely down and into the house, when someone threw a rock through a side window of our van and stole a few of our belongings.

Our inaccurate first thought was, "Oh well, we might have expected as much, in New York!"

What we didn't expect was how generous God's people were in Brooklyn. Early the next morning, someone came over and said, "I have a garage around the block, you can park your van in safety." The next knock on the door was a lady in their community saying, "We collected from the brothers and sisters in the Charismatic Renewal enough money to pay for your window. So relax, enjoy the time you have with us."

Beau revisited the Empire State building with one of the Coffey boys (our host family). They played sandlot baseball on a real Brooklyn sandlot. There was also an aspect of pilgrimage in the trip. We had read the *Catholic Worker* newspaper and *Penny a Copy* by Dorothy Day. In times past, we had corresponded with Dorothy Day, co-foundress of the Catholic Worker movement. Frank and Beau visited the Catholic Worker's ministry of Dorothy Day in the Bowery. She herself was too ill to receive them, but it still inspired us all to touch the place where her work had begun. New York City may be one of the places where sin abounds; however, God never abandons His people, and where sin abounds, grace abounds more.

The Brooklyn families' readiness to form a lay missionary community was barely in the preliminary stages. The missionary community we sought was not waiting for us there, but we loved our visit there and were happy to know God's servants were active in New York.

Heading south once more, we stopped in Charlottesville, Virginia. It was great to see our friends in Browns Cove. We participated in a Christian coffee house ministry, and gave our testimony in a group that met in St. Thomas Aquinas Parish. Our time in Virginia the year before had borne good fruit.

Campgrounds are good places to minister, too. Our family enjoys camping. We have often found that, if we pray, God leads us to people whom he has pre-arranged for us to meet. They are our divine appointments. Seldom have we left a campground without having an opportunity made especially for us to bear witness to Jesus Christ. Our children are great evangelizers and it seems that a campground puts them in a very effective setting! We camped in Florida while we waited out Hurricane Frederick, which was battering Mobile and other areas on the Gulf Coast. It must have been some storm.

As we drove along I-10 through Mobile back to New Orleans, I said, "I am astonished at this destruction."

Frank prayed, "Lord, tell us if we can give more than just our prayers to help the hurricane victims."

At Frank's parents' home in New Orleans, the network news announced that food, clothing, and other goods were being shipped to Mobile from all over the country. The Archdiocese of New Orleans was involved in the relief efforts.

"Good Morning, we would like to volunteer to help Frederick victims in Mobile. Whom should we contact?" Frank inquired.

The Archdiocesan office was very helpful. "Here's the number of Father Tom Weise. He's director of Social Services for the Diocese of Mobile."

Frank called Fr. Tom, "Sure, Frank, we can use all the help we can get. Come right away!" he said.

The urgent need for help was at the temporary receiving and distribution center where all the goods were being shipped for hurricane relief. Frank and Beau were put in charge of the warehouse where truckloads of goods were received and redistributed to centers throughout the disaster area.

"Genie, this is a big job. They really need us here in Mobile. You would be so proud of Beau. It's a lot of work," Frank said as he reported home from the first day of relief work.

"I'm also proud of his dad," I said, rubbing his beard.

The first couple of days in Mobile, we lived in the van in the parking lot of a newly constructed nursing home. We knew we were better off than many of the hurricane victims in our meager surroundings, but one morning, the director and leader of the Little Sisters of the Poor, came to the back door of the van where I was cooking on my camping stove.

"Please move into the nursing home. We hate to see your family living in the parking lot, and Fr. Tom says your husband and son are like a miracle for Mobile."

"Thanks Sister, it is a little hard for the girls not to have a place to walk around," I answered with enthusiasm. "Our family is used to living in our van, though. It hasn't been bad compared to the people who have lost everything."

Sister persisted, "We have a room and bath. Actually it is one of our guest suites. Our home has a big generator, so we have electricity. That will be nice for the baby."

Frank and Beau worked almost eighteen hours each day, so when they got back that day, Sarah and Susanna and I were already at home in the nursing home. They were happy to have a hot shower and comfortable bed after their long days.

Those old folks were so delighted to see my two precious little girls. We ministered God's love and healing all day long, everyday. Susanna celebrated her first birthday there. I had planned to have a party at Kisinoaks with her cousins and the Listis and the Bernards. The Lord had other plans. We serenaded her early in the morning, and then had a party. It was a small, simple celebration. The nuns put a candle in a square of white cake, but I'll never forget the look on her little face, and on theirs, as the elderly sang "Happy Birthday" to her. Being free to go where the Spirit leads us has rewarded us with so many priceless moments.

78

Back in Abbeville, after our hurricane relief efforts in Mobile, we were settling in for a stay in our schoolroom apartment at Open Door when Beau came home from an errand, looking kind of shaky.

"What's the matter?" I asked him.

"Mom, I was riding my bike and I just got stopped by a police officer." (Beau was fifteen, and school in Louisiana was compulsory until you were sixteen.) He told me, "You have to be in school."

I explained to him, "We are missionaries. We don't know how long we will be here in Abbeville."

"The officer was pretty tough on me; he told me that he could even take me into the station. This time, he gave me a warning, but to be sure to come home and talk to y'all about it. According to him, 'You are subject to the law just like anyone else.'"

When Frank got back from the Christian Service Center, we told him what had happened, and we took our predicament directly to the Lord.

Frank prayed, "Lord Jesus, you know that as your servants we want to give a good witness to the world around us; we don't want to be breaking the law. And Lord, you know that we don't want to put Beau back into the school system, so please provide for your Christian people some acceptable alternative to the school system, especially for your missionaries."

I added, "We don't know how long you want us here, and we haven't heard where you want us to go next. Please give us your clear guidance and direction. We love you, Lord, and are willing to go where you will lead us. Amen."

"Go west!" was the short and instant answer Frank got. "The Lord just told me that we should go west. Do either of you have any sense of what the Lord is saying?" he asked.

Trusting in the guidance that Frank received, we called the Disciples of the Lord Jesus Christ, in Texas. The Sisters generously agreed to receive us on another short visit while we sought the Lord's direction for our next mission. It would be fun to share with them some of the Spanish songs we had learned since last we saw them. The sisters had recently moved from Damascus Ranch into Prayer Town Emmanuel, their long awaited ministry site. They housed us in a cute little travel trailer with a nice view. Prayer Town Emmanuel was just that, a place steeped in prayer. The Lord continued to speak to us, "Trust in Me, I affirm your call. Confidence and patience are what you need, and then you will see My glory!"

"What is next, Lord?" Frank asked.

Beau heard God say, "Keep going west until I open the door for your next mission!"

From Prayer Town we traveled to Phoenix; that was west. Friends in Phoenix suggested we visit a famous ministry, which ministers to Hispanics in California. That was really west! We found a neat little campground right in the middle of Los Angeles. The fall was crisp and pretty all around us; Beau played Frisbee with a camping neighbor, while I cooked up a delicious Mexican lunch on our camp-stove. The girls entertained themselves on a nearby jungle gym. The first night we were at the campground, we just rested, prayed and sang. The sun rose the next day on us, a seemingly peaceful, well-ordered missionary family. Frank went to use a payphone for an appointment with the director of the evangelization ministry which we had contacted while we were in Phoenix.

When Frank came back he said, "I am going to meet with Marilyn, the director. You and the children will wait for me here in the campground."

I was caught completely off-guard. "Are you saying your plan is that the children and I will have to stay in the campground, without any shelter, while you drive off in the truck, to meet the director for lunch?" I asked, in shock. I felt that was unreasonable.

"There is a shelter nearby, and I shouldn't be more than two or three hours." This was before cell phones, and that truck contained all we had in the world.

"Frank, this is Los Angeles; what makes you think we will be safe here? I don't think your plan takes us into consideration." The devil – that roaring lion – was waiting to pounce and jumped right in and caused wounds in our relationship.

I asked myself, "Why can't he see how unreasonable this plan is?"

I don't remember exactly how the argument escalated, but soon I was nowhere near anything that looked like submission and respect for my husband. Frank, in turn, was certainly not cherishing me with love and honor. In fact, we were yelling at each other so loudly that other campers turned around to look at us. Beau admonished us, but to no avail – he was so upset, he ran across the campground. He found a payphone, called Vince and Kay at Open Door, and told them that we needed prayer *desperately,* right now!

Later they told me they had dropped everything and prayed! Those prayers must have been effective, because by the time he got back from the phone, only the tailwinds of the storm were beating away at us.

However, the plan changed and we all met with the director and toured the facility. Our whole little family went to lunch. I was still so hurt and angry inside, I could hardly converse. I did hear bits of her testimony, though. She and her ex-husband had served the Lord together several years before; her marriage had been annulled since. God had redeemed her life and was using her effectively in this Hispanic ministry and as a speaker nationally.

At the same time, I was staring a strong truth right in the face: serving Jesus does not immunize us from our own failures or the attack of the enemy against our marriages. We must work out our salvation with fear and trembling. Without the overpowering grace of God and my 100% response to it, earlier that day, I could have walked away from Frank and, consequently, the Lord. I knew I had to repent. No disagreement was worth the shattering of our marriage, our ministry, and probably our whole lives. I repented, and asked forgiveness. Frank forgave me and asked my forgiveness, too. We were reconciled and took our injuries and heartaches to the Lord. I knew that Jesus is a healer, but the lingering pain of the morning was still there. My insides were tender and sore. The temptation to say, "This life is too hard; I don't even like you right now," was breathing down my neck.

Back at the campground that night, Beau's friend that he played Frisbee with earlier, a very nice young man, came over for dinner. He sat up with us in the van till the early morning. We talked and shared with him about the Lord and about His saving power. It was then that he made a decision for Jesus Christ. Witnessing to Beau's Frisbee friend, and the oneness we experienced as we led him to Jesus, was the healing balm we needed. Our story is our story; no one else has lived it but Frank and me. Jesus saved us back at the beginning and He is still saving us now. The next morning, the sun rose on a stronger mission team.

At the Hispanic ministry, it had been suggested that we contact Father Alejandro Burciaga, whom we had met while in Puebla. He was ministering in Tijuana, Mexico at that time. Tijuana was several hours away, so right after family prayers; we drove out of the campground and headed for the border. A thrill ran through me as we drove into Mexico. We found the church. The Missionaries of the Holy Spirit, Father Burciaga's religious order, were pastoring it. When we first arrived, Frank and Beau went inside, while I stayed in the van with the little girls.

A little while later, Beau came out. "Mom, Father Burciaga wants you and the girls to come in and see him, but please don't be put off by how rich his office is."

I was frankly surprised that the priest of such a poor looking parish would have a "rich" office. I was trying to prepare myself as I walked along the dusty parking lot. I almost burst out laughing when I entered what was the simplest, poorest church office I'd seen yet. Three metal folding chairs and a simple desk surrounded by packing boxes, gave the room an air of stark poverty. Beau glanced teasingly at me, as I shook Father's hand.

Father Alejandro smiled, "Welcome ladies. It's good to see you. Jesus loves you. How have you been since Puebla?" His presence lit up the whole room and when he looked into my eyes the way Jesus would, he conveyed the joy of his priestly vocation.

"Thank you, Father Alejandro. We are doing great. It's amazing that the Lord has brought us together again."

"You are right. I think it is the Lord. I told Frank and Beau that I am inviting you to come and work with me," he responded.

"I love you, Father 'Jandro'" Susanna said as she crawled up on his lap sensing the love he exuded.

"My problem is that I am winding up my assignment in Tijuana and being transferred to Saltillo, Mexico. I suggested to Frank, that we meet in Saltillo, about a week after I get settled in my new community. That would be about December 12th, about six weeks from now."

"We have gone as far west as we can go and I am sure this is what the Lord was indicating when He said to go west," Beau said as we walked out of the office across the parking lot. He liked Fr. Burciaga.

"Our new mission is going to be in Saltillo, Mexico, working with Father Alejandro Burciaga. Thank God that we were willing to accept guidance to 'go west!'" I said, as I loaded the little girls into the van to drive back over the border to San Diego.

The more immediate question before us was what to do with the four to five weeks we had until we got to Saltillo. Frank's sister, Susan, still lived in Truckee and his sister, Missy, lived in Kirkwood, a ski resort about an hour away from Susan's. "Why not visit them and then we can make a spiritual pilgrimage to Junipero Serra's California Missions?" Frank suggested.

Visiting the entire chain of 21 California Missions was a sizable undertaking. We were about to embark on a very blessed pilgrimage. We embraced the poverty of our situation. The climate was great, and compared to the cells of the early monks that we saw in each and every mission, our van was comfy. Our campsites were the parking lots of the California missions themselves. We visited all but two. San Diego Alcala was the very first one built by Fr. Junipero Serra on July 16, 1769. (I revisited a few years ago, it is still a beautiful Holy place.) While we were driving through the city, it was time for lunch. We had stopped at a Laundromat to wash our clothes. Then we were going to head north.

"I'm really hungry, Mom" Sarah said.

"Me too, me too, me too." Susanna chimed in.

"Frank, we better find a park or someplace to cook lunch, preferably a place where the girls can run around a little." I said.

"Look in our guidebook, there must be a park or a visitor center around here." Frank answered.

"There's a sign to a park, next exit, thank you, Jesus!" Beau proclaimed.

We pulled into the park, got out of the van near the picnic tables. Next I put our sturdy green-checkered tablecloth on the picnic table.

"I've got the camping stove for you, Mom," Beau said.

"Okay son, I've got the groceries." I smiled.

It was a lovely, quiet space. It was mid-week so we were almost the only ones there. As I began chopping the onion, the girls were climbing up onto the table.

"Hey, Babe. There is a playground over there. Beau and I would probably be more help if we took the girls to the swings," Frank suggested.

"Sounds like a good plan," I agreed, busying myself with food prep.

They took off in the direction of the playground. Motherhood and caring for little ones, especially travelling in a step van, had become a serious prayer concern of mine. I loved the Lord and was willing to serve Him in whatever capacity He called me. I had begun to think about the Blessed Virgin Mary a lot. All the years of not practicing our Faith had put my relationship with the Mother of God on a back burner. I wanted to have a relationship. I loved Jesus so much and the more I read scripture, the more I knew that "all generations will call her blessed." I had been praying for the Lord to reveal to me how to be faithful to Him, and at the same time have a relationship with His mother. Hadn't He told John as He died on the cross, "Here is your mother?" And although these meditations had been part of my personal prayer in recent weeks, I was singing a praise song as I pumped pressure into the camping stove and lit the fire. I wasn't thinking about our Blessed Mother.

Suddenly, surprisingly, out of the corner of my eye, I noticed a lady standing about four feet from the picnic table. She was a little taller than me, but her coloring was close to mine. She had rich dark brown hair, bright brown eyes and olive skin. She had a toddler with her. He had medium length curly brown hair and was hanging on to her skirt facing her. The back of his head was facing me. She wore a long skirt and a veil. (But I wore long skirts in those days, so that wasn't that odd to me.)

The first thought that popped into my head as I turned to her was, "**I know her, she's a friend of mine.**" I had a deep, immeasurable feeling of familiarity, and nostalgia at the same time. I smiled at her, about to ask, "What are you doing, here? I'm sorry that I don't remember your name."

Then the toddler lifted up his arms for her to pick him up. She looked so lovingly into his beautiful little face and raised him up to her hips. It was a scene I had seen hundreds of time with my mom and my friends, and a totally natural action I myself did dozens of times a day.

She smiled at me. I couldn't speak. It was the most beautiful smile I have ever seen.

I wanted to run to her and hug her, but she completely disappeared. She vanished. She was really there, and then she was really gone. Everything I just described took place in a matter of about a minute. And I knew it was our Blessed Mother.

I wished Frank and Beau would hurry back so that I could tell them. I wondered, "What is she trying to tell me? Why did Jesus allow His mother to visit me in a park where I was cooking on a camping stove?"

The visit had a huge impact on me, but I knew in my heart it was a visit for me, to tell me something. And although I have shared this story at retreats and talks, I still know the Blessed Mother wanted me to know an important truth and had come from heaven to show me.

I continued cooking, and then I knew what she was telling me. She wanted me to know she was familiar to me already. She was like my friends, like the other moms I knew. She loved and cared for Jesus like all other human moms had done throughout the ages. She liked me, because she likes moms and motherhood. She loved her little boy, and they were "attached at the hip", like any other mom and child that age. I felt like her appearance to me in the park that day was telling me that she was easy to relate to. The intangible, ethereal relationship I thought I needed to find was not the kind of relationship she wanted. She wanted to be real to me – a real mom, a real friend, and a real contact with her Son, Jesus.

Her clothing was not the traditional blue and white, although her veil was cream colored. Her clothing was a muted red and muted green. She looked like an ordinary woman. She wanted me to know she was easy to reach. (Just recently – 2010- - a statue of Our Lady of the Bayous has come to mean a lot to me. Mary in that image is clothed exactly the way Mary was clothed when I saw her in the park in San Diego.)

Frank and Beau got back with the giggling, hungry girls.

I fed the family first, we sang a praise song around the table, and enjoyed our meal. I waited until we washed up from lunch, and I told Frank and Beau what had happened. The girls overheard, and Sarah wanted me to show her the exact spot where the Blessed Mother stood. They had not seen anything, but the whole family felt blessed by her visitation and the message I received from that wonderful event.

November 13 is my birthday. Again our celebration was very simple, but I remember that I asked the Lord, "Jesus, give me the gift that You know I most need." To my surprise, the gift I most needed was the conception of our fourth child. She was my belated birthday present.

After the pilgrimage and visits with Frank's sisters, we entered Mexico. The Disciples of the Lord Jesus Christ had given us the name of Father Felipe Flores who lived in Escobedo, outside the city of Monterrey. We were ten days early for our appointment with Father Burciaga, so we drove over to Father Felipe's church. He remembered us from the Prayer House in Puebla. He received us with great enthusiasm and immediately tried to convince us to stay and work with him in the Charismatic Renewal Office of the Diocese of Monterrey, where he was serving. During the course of our stay with Father Felipe, he was scheduled to go to a Charismatic Conference in San Louis Potosi. It was just what we needed – an opportunity to praise Jesus again with five thousand brothers and sisters!

San Louis Potosi is an antique, classy, intriguing city. The conference itself was in a lovely venue. I instantly felt the blessed assurance of the presence of the Holy Spirit. At one point, we were all singing in tongues in the conference, when suddenly, gently but insistently, I felt that I was praying in a different prayer language than I ordinarily prayed in. All around me the prayer in tongues came together in the same prayer language; all five thousand of us were singing the exact same thing. There is no earthly explanation for that.

It was very, very beautiful, and the power and majesty of the Holy Spirit descended on that auditorium. Weeping broke out sporadically; some of the weeping sounded like a release of joy; other weeping sounded like God's children were experiencing healing; a strong man behind me was crying, "I need you Lord Jesus. Forgive me, Lord Jesus. Please forgive

86

me, Lord. I am a sinner."

If the whole story were ever told of the Charismatic Renewal of the sixties, seventies and eighties, it would have to be seen as one of the great movements to sweep the world in our time. Life giving faith was breathed into the Church. A change of mission and hope resulted from that work of God.

Saltillo, about an hour west of Monterrey, is a lovely, cosmopolitan, bustling city high in the mountains. Father Burciaga's community ministered at the Sanctuary of Our Lady of Guadalupe, a beautiful, gothic church in the center of the city. We arrived on the 12th of December, which is the *feast day* of the Virgin of Guadalupe, and which is all of Mexico's principal feast of the year. As we walked into the church, we found that all the pews had been removed and the church was packed solid with standing worshippers.

The Bishop was celebrating Mass. "In this time, we need evangelization and evangelizers dedicated to the spread of the Gospel," he said in his homily. How encouraging for us to find out after traveling so far, we were definitely needed!

We made our way to the sacristy and found Father Burciaga. He sat down with us and welcomed us to our new mission. Father had been inquiring about the spiritual climate, and gathered that there was little or nothing going on in the renewal in Saltillo. He found a room for us to stay temporarily until we could find a house to rent nearer the Sanctuary.

Father Burciaga said, "We'll talk more later. I am expected to join the Bishop and my fellow priests at the feast day meal."

As we turned to leave, Father Alejandro's superior, Father Lazaro showed up. Father Alejandro introduced us and before we knew it, Father Lazaro grabbed us and invited us to celebrate the most important feast of their church and of all Mexico by eating with the Bishop and several priests. Father Lazaro said, "Those we invited didn't come, there are four places set; we would love to have you. You can meet the Bishop."

So, on our first day in Saltillo, we had a chance to dine with Bishop Francisco Villalobos. As we shared over the meal, he extended a formal welcome to us as evangelists in his diocese, and happily encouraged our work with Father Burciaga. Twenty-five years later, Family Missions Company has sent thousands of God's servants into that diocese and our family has had a long and fruitful relationship with Bishop Villalobos. That surprise meeting with Bishop Villalobos that fateful day has been an enormous blessing.

The first arrangements for our lodging didn't work out, so we were living in our van again on a street behind the sanctuary, combing the neighborhood for a house to rent. We hoped to be in walking distance from the church because we didn't have long-term auto insurance. We planned to park the van and use it as little as possible. Father Burciaga went from door to door, finally finding a single lady who was willing to rent us a room, with rights to the kitchen, for about two weeks, which would at least give us somewhere to be through Christmas. A couple of days after Christmas, the lady told us she needed the room for an elderly aunt who would be coming to live with her. She asked us to vacate the room in two days.

Our ministry was already moving with the Spirit. The first prayer meeting we had was held in a small room behind the church. Father Burciaga, Frank, Beau, Sarah, Susanna, Feliciano, Aldolfo, Eusebio, Esteban, two others and myself were in attendance. (Today Feliciano, Esteban, Eusebio, and Adolfo are priests) We noticed that we were twelve, a significant number. Apart from the prayer meeting, Frank and I were being invited into people's homes for small group ministry and prayer for the sick. Even though we had lots to do for the Lord, if we didn't find adequate living quarters, we would have to leave which was pretty discouraging.

It was cold and windy. Both of the girls were feverish and suffering with bronchitis. Thank God we met a medical doctor. He treated my girls free of charge. I was injecting them with penicillin twice a day, but if we had to sleep in the van in that cold, it would've been dangerous to their health. We had no choice. Without a house to rent; we would have to go back home. I sent Beau to the grocery store to get a few things for the possibility of the returning trip home. Meanwhile, Father Burciaga was praying at a prayer meeting that the Lord would make a way for us to stay. He strongly sensed that the Lord wanted us to remain. At the grocery store, Beau met a lady who told him she knew of a house that was coming up for rent, two blocks behind the sanctuary. They agreed to meet at the grocery store the next day at eleven a.m. to find the rent house. The next morning we had breakfast and vacated our temporary lodgings. We had our family prayer time in the van.

"Lord Jesus," I prayed, "we need a miracle of your provision. We are so happy with the ministry available here. Please find us a house so we can stay in Saltillo and serve You. Supply all of our other needs too, I beg You. Heal the girls, Lord, for our good and for Your glory! Amen."

We parked in front of the grocery store. Our new friend, Graciela, took Frank to the landlady's house at 11:00, but she wasn't there. Someone on the street said they thought the house we wanted was already rented. We were disappointed. "Should we just drive off?" we asked ourselves, dejectedly.

Frank and Beau went to mid-day Mass and came back elated in spirit. Father Burciaga was sure the Lord would provide something, and insisted that we stay! Frank went back to the landlady's house and this time she was there and willing to show us the rent house. "If we hadn't had such a struggle to find a house, any house, I don't think we could see this one as the house for us," I whispered to Frank as she showed us the premises. Beau commented in English, "All the windowpanes are broken. The floor looks like the hill country. The bathroom is outside and the hot water heater doesn't work." But it was walking distance to the sanctuary and we agreed to rent it.

The electricity wouldn't come on and neither would the water. There were two large rooms and a smaller kitchen. It was very dirty. Father Burciaga came by shortly after we agreed to rent the house; he knew how desperate we were to find a place, but he could not believe we were willing to live here. With the wind blowing in through the broken windows, the house was too cold for the girls, so I stayed with them in the van. Every once in a while, I started the engine and ran the heater. Meanwhile, Frank and Beau got in the house with a shovel, broom, mop, and cleansing agents, and borrowed water from next door. A few hours and a lot of elbow grease later, they cleared out the greatest part of the dirt. As they came into the van, hungry and tired, they prayed while they snacked, "Lord, help us to make this house a home."

When they were almost finished, our neighbor came by and turned on the water; someone else turned on the lights.

Later, Father Burciaga's brother-in-law installed panes of glass on all of the windows. The house was ready for us to move in, but we didn't have a stick of furniture; we would have to put our van mattresses on the floor. I was worried about Beau. His paper-thin mattress wouldn't be much good on the cold floor. There was a knock on the door. "Hi, I'm Graciela's husband. She asked me to bring a folding cot." Praise God, Beau wouldn't have to sleep on the floor!

Another knock, "I'm your neighbor around the block. Do you need a table?" Another knock, "These chairs were in my garage, I hope you can use them." The knocking persisted and we couldn't put things in place fast enough. Before we went to bed that night, over forty people had come with blankets, beds, furniture, food, detergent, pillows, sheets, encouragement and prayer. It was a miracle – no doubt about it.

We had never met most of those generous souls and God did grant us marvelous provision! I went outside, I laid hands on the hot water heater, "Lord Jesus, we need a hot water heater and we don't have the money to buy one, can You please heal this one?" I prayed. It worked! I shouted for joy.

Our landlady proclaimed, astonished, "This is the first time it has worked in seven years!"

This poor house became home to us and a gathering place for the people of God. Here they found the peace of Jesus, his love, and healing. Frank played the music for the prayer meeting at the Sanctuary. Father Burciaga and Frank taught and preached. The Word of God spread like wildfire. We gave our testimony everywhere. We fasted and prayed for the renewal in Saltillo. The anointing of the Holy Spirit was upon us all. The Spirit seminars, retreats, and days of renewal kept us busy. The prayer congregation mushroomed. In only six months, there were more than six hundred people attending each week, the same congregation that began with only twelve faithful followers. Soon, there was standing room only and all the children sat on the stairs around the altar. People's lives were changed drastically, and many were delivered from the grip of Satan.

An elderly woman came to us and asked us to pray for her son, Daniel. He and his wife were separated and he was miserable. He wanted to be reconciled, but she would hear nothing of it. We prayed with the mother and suggested she convince Daniel to come to the prayer meeting. About two weeks later, she brought him. Afterwards, he came up for prayer. While we were praying, I had a vision of a double bed made up with fresh new sheets. I kept waiting for a message to come with it, so I could share the vision with Daniel.

The Lord kept saying to me, "Just go ahead and tell him about the double bed and sheets."

Others were saying encouraging words to him. I was reluctant to share what I had seen, because I had no idea what it meant. The prayer finished and I had still not shared my vision. Daniel and his mom walked down the long aisle on their way out of the door, when the Lord told me, "Run over there and catch up with him, NOW!"

So I ran.

"Daniel, while we were praying, I had this vision..." I told him about it.

He was silent for a moment, then he muttered, "Thank you," and walked out.

I felt so dumb. I began to complain to the Lord, "You see, Lord, I made a fool out of myself. I didn't even have a sensible message to give him. I'll be surprised if he ever comes back."

Three nights later, I was bowled over with surprise when Daniel showed up at our house. "Can you help me with my marriage problems? I almost gave up hope, until the other night. You see, as soon as my wife kicked me out of the house, she sold our double bed, and all the sheets. She sleeps in the room with my daughter. If we are ever to be reconciled, we'll have to get a new bed and new sheets. When you shared your vision, the Lord was showing me that there is hope!"

Months later, Daniel and his wife were reconciled, after much prayer, patience and perseverance in his conversion of life.

Another beautiful experience happened when a pair of middle-aged parents came to our home for prayer. Their youngest son, Roberto, only ten years old, needed healing. He had cataracts in both eyes and was almost totally blind. He was no longer in school, unable to read or see the teacher; he couldn't play marbles; he couldn't play any games. He saw shadows and nothing more. His parents had no money for surgery and they were terrified that the boy would lose his eyes if he went to the hospital. They had fallen away from the faith and wondered if God would not answer their prayer.

"How much will you charge to pray for Roberto's healing?" they asked cautiously.

"God's gifts are free, absolutely free," Frank assured them. Jesus was calling them back into His flock, and if they believed, repented, and prayed with faith, they would find God's salvation and healing. We prayed with them.

They did change their lives and return to the church. The boy got a little better and, encouraged, they brought him back for more prayer. We hadn't heard from them for a while, when one night after a prayer meeting, while our house was full of friends, the boy's mother came running into our midst. "He's healed," she shouted, "My boy was blind, but now he can see, he can see! He's back in school and he can see!"

Our housing was poor but our spiritual life was rich. Because we lived so close to the sanctuary, we were able to attend Mass often. There were several Masses a day. We took turns caring for the girls so that we could each go to Mass. Every Mass was preceded by recitation of the rosary. The core group of our prayer community met in our home every Sunday afternoon for vital, rousing praise, worship and fellowship.

I asked the Lord, "God, guide and direct us, Your people. Protect those who are being added to our number day by day. Let them see clearly that Jesus saves us from the futile way of life handed to us by our ancestors. Renew your Catholic Church, Lord. Love us into faithfulness. Amen."

One day, I was walking to the nearby park, pushing little Susanna in an umbrella stroller, with Sarah tagging along beside. I was pregnant and showing! All of a sudden, it hit me, "I really am a new creation, and my old life has passed away. I'm a full-time wife and mother and loving every minute of it. I'm a missionary. I've accepted His call and I'm watching God delight in providing all my needs according to His riches in glory! The race that I've begun is not nearly finished, but by the grace and mercy of God, I am persevering. I am who I am by the call and election of God."

A settling in my soul took place at that moment. My spirits soared and I relished the springtime that was exploding around me in the warm breeze, in the blue skies, and in the flowering plants on the windowsills of the houses. The metamorphosis had taken place; I was free to be me!

Beau, too, was growing into manhood in the Lord. He had a more responsible and serious attitude about his education. He studied American History, reading a college textbook from cover to cover. He studied Biology. He always read voraciously; however, now he was selecting more educational material. He wrote a lot, and copied Psalms to improve his handwriting. He studied the Church documents, and apart from using Scripture in his personal prayer time, he studied the Bible systematically. He also learned the art of conversation, which is not taught in any educational system, sitting at the feet of an economist who was also an amateur astronomer. He integrated his academic life into daily life. And he read extensively in Spanish, trying to apply his new skills as much as possible. He often accompanied Frank and the evangelization teams to the ranchos. His spiritual life and input were an integral part of our life together as a missionary family. Sarah and Susanna were an unadulterated blessing to him. We asked Beau to be the godfather of our fourth child. He looked forward to it with real anticipation. Trials and temptations typical of the teenage years affected Beau, which was normal; yet, he served God without reservation.

The Lord was doing new and exciting things in Frank's life, too. In addition to his work in the Charismatic Renewal at the sanctuary, he was ministering two or three days a week in the ranchos, the small villages scattered in the desert. People in the ranchos were starving for lack of God's Word. Mexico has only one priest for every fifteen thousand Catholics. This is the worst ratio of priests to Catholic people in the world. Ministry by the laity has got to be God's answer for His scattered flock!

Frank's heart was softened more and more as he went forth in the name of Jesus to bring the Gospel to the villages. "What are the ranchos like?" I asked Frank before I had the chance to accompany him.

"The majority are simple goatherds, who work small parcels of government land on which they grow staple crops, like corn and beans. They work by hand, or with oxen, mules or horses. As great as their material needs are, their spiritual needs are greater still."

"Well, what do they need most?" I asked.

He responded, "They are God-fearing and religious, but know very little of the teachings of Jesus or the Catholic catechism. They do not have a personal relationship with Jesus Christ. They know almost nothing of the person and works of the Holy Spirit."

"It sounds like there is a lot of opportunity for our ministry there," I said.

"Sure, Babe. I have been given *carte blanche* by the priests I am working with; I am really happy to have this chance." Frank liked to work with a team; friends accompanied him and brought clothes, food and friendship to the ranchos.

Our family life was also solidified. In trying to live the gospel, we had placed ourselves totally at the disposal of the people to whom we ministered. We were a close-knit family; mission life automatically fosters that. Together, we agreed that we should rarely refuse to accept an invitation. We would drop whatever we were doing to rush out to meet the needs of others. Our door was always open, and we counseled and prayed with the needy at any time, day or night.

After a few months of living in Saltillo, the ministry grew so much, and demanded our time. I began to feel a strain on our family life. Frank saw my distress and decided to protect the good order and harmony of our family. That harmony was the foundation of our life in service to the Lord. He began to guard the children's naptime from intrusion by neighborhood children and noisy visitors. He felt free to announce to the constant stream of locals that it was family time. We were finally able to have our private meals.

One night, after we had an especially crowded week, I was having an especially difficult time coping with a problem. I was in tears. At that moment, Armando, a young man who played music with Frank in the large prayer assembly, came to the door. Six hundred people would be at the church, the music was vital to the quality of worship. Frank was in charge. Armando said to Frank, "Are you ready to go?" I overheard to my great joy, Frank say at the door, "I'm sorry, Armando, please tell Father Burciaga that I can't be there tonight; my wife needs me. It'll be a chance for you to see how well you can do without me." I did need him, and I was so glad he had chosen me and my needs that night.

As our six-month visas were expiring, we came to a familiar crossroads. The Charismatic Renewal at the sanctuary in Saltillo was flourishing. Frank's love for preaching in the ranchos, his urgency to go where others were unwilling or unable to go, were important factors to consider as we decided what to do. We hoped to return to Mexico, after we had time in the States to renew our visas. Father Cardona, from General Cepeda, had invited us to live and work with him. General Cepeda is a small town in the desert with fifty-four ranchos assigned to the parish as mission outreaches.

In another family retreat, we asked the Lord, "Where to now?" We thought the answer would be either Saltillo or General Cepeda.

Much to my surprise, right from the beginning, the Lord began to talk to us about distant nations, about islands, about people far away waiting to hear. At first, I balked at the messages we were receiving in Scripture, prophecies, and visions. I had my heart set on General Cepeda. Being pregnant, I didn't relish the idea of going so far away again. At one of our last prayer sessions, I heard the Lord tell me to turn to the end of Daniel, chapter 3. I knew chapter 3 so well; it was one of our favorite readings, ending (or so I thought) with the beautiful canticle of the three young men in the fiery furnace. I wondered, "What can that canticle have to do with our decision?"

Reluctantly, I opened the Bible. My eyes fell on verses 98 and 99, "... to the nations and peoples of every language, wherever they dwell on earth; abundant peace! It has seemed good to me to tell the signs and wonders which the most high God has accomplished in my regard." That settled it for me; we were going to nations and peoples of every language. This meant more "good-byes," instead of "we'll be back."

Our Saltillo friends were pouring out of our house and lining up down the street as we got in the van to leave for Abbeville. We could see the fruit of our labors. It was abundant. Jesus Himself would have to bring to completion the work He had begun through us at the Sanctuario.

Back in Abbeville, the abandoned schoolrooms became home again. We were fed spiritually by the sweet fellowship with our brothers and sisters in the community. My pregnancy progressed well, and we were all looking forward to our new baby. I felt a need for a time of spiritual refreshment and grace before the birth of our next baby. Frank suggested I make a silent retreat at Our Lady of the Oaks Retreat house in nearby Grand Coteau, Louisiana. He and Beau had just come back from one and found it very refreshing and renewing. Beau, at sixteen, was the youngest retreatant they'd ever had at a men's retreat. Perhaps I would be among the women most advanced in pregnancy to make such a retreat.

At first, the secretary at the retreat house told me that there was no space available. But we prayed. She called me back two days before the retreat started; there had been a cancellation and there was a space available for me. I thanked God, and packed. Our Lady of the Oaks is beautiful; the very ground exudes the grace of the years and years of prayerful reflection that has taken place there. I was worried about having a room too far away from the bathroom facilities. My due date for the baby was only two weeks away. All pregnant women know that a restroom is a must at that stage. When the receptionist directed me to my room, I could hardly believe that it was adjacent to the chapel. It was perfect.

"You can't miss your room; it's the only one that adjoins the chapel," she said.

It was like the Lord had said to me, "This is our time together. I'm going to give you the best. I love you. Just relax and we'll enjoy our nearness to one another." I was overcome with emotion. I put my suitcase down, threw myself on the bed, and cried. It almost seemed too good to be true – two full days and nights with Jesus.

Our retreat master was excellent. The priest in charge of the retreat house was a little nervous; he said they had never had a baby born at Our Lady of the Oaks. He confessed on the last day of the retreat that he had gotten very little sleep thinking that every noise was me getting someone up to help deliver the baby. When we broke our silence at the end of the retreat, one beautiful young woman laughed and said, "You needn't have worried, Father, I'm an obstetrical nurse and I had my eye on her all the time. We would've delivered it just fine."

We had chosen names for our baby. We still liked the

name Simon Peter for a boy, and we had chosen Mary Elizabeth for a girl. I had prayed that our baby could be born on a feast of our Blessed Mother. During the retreat, I woke up at 4:00 a.m. for one of my bathroom trips, but could not go back to sleep. I felt the close companionship of the Holy Spirit. I decided to get up and go to pray in the private meditation chapel. It is a small chapel; Jesus is present in the Blessed Sacrament and there is room for only a single occupant. I brought my Liturgy of the Hours to pray morning prayers.

It was July twenty-second, the feast of St. Mary Magdalen. The antiphons and prayers spoke to me: "Very early in the morning...Mary Magdalen came to the tomb just as the sun was rising saying 'My heart burns within me; I long to see my Lord!'" and in the response, Jesus says to her, "Go to my brothers and say to them: The Lord is risen from the dead."

I began to meditate on the wondrous ministry of Mary Magdalen, the friend of Jesus. She was the first to proclaim the Good News of the resurrection. She had repented and was freed from the bonds of sin, and used that freedom to follow the Lord with all her being. Our church parish was named St. Mary Magdalen. Surely she had been a part of our call and election to proclaim the Good News. I closed the prayer book, sat down and closed my eyes.

Then I heard the Lord speak to me, "Genie, the baby you are carrying is a girl, and I want you to name her Mary Magdalen!" Mary Magdalen! It was a name I would never have chosen in a million years. Yet because I had heard the Lord say it, it sounded beautiful to me. She was one of his best friends and a faithful disciple. Why wouldn't He want the little disciple I was carrying to be named after her? I worried a little that Frank might not like it. I needn't have. He loved it.

Coming back from the retreat, I was spiritually prepared for the birth of our baby. Frank was fully engaged in the Lord's service in Abbeville and the surrounding community. A couple of days before my due date, we were looking at the calendar. "Well, Frank," I said in mock resignation, "I suppose I'll be pregnant forever. There isn't even one tiny space in this schedule for the birth of the baby."

On the fifth of August, the feast of Our Lady of the Snows, I had early signs of labor. That afternoon Frank was scheduled to give a talk in the Life in the Spirit series out in the country. Just as he was leaving, I began to have a few contractions. "Don't stay for coffee," I called to him as he drove out of the driveway.

It was my turn to cook supper for the community. The little girls were napping while I cooked dinner and set the table. Beau was volunteering at the Christian Service Center. After dinner was cooked, I went back to our school apartment to have my prayer time and to rest. The contractions were still not too strong and only at fifteen to twenty minute intervals. There was a light knock on the door. It was Kay.

"Genie, its Dr. Mayeaux's office on the telephone. His nurse says he will have to be out of town for a couple of days beginning tomorrow, and he's wondering what's happening with you. Can you go in to the office for a check-up before five?"

"Wow, that's a very interesting development," I said. The Lord always keeps me praying. "Actually, Kay, I am having contractions. Tell him I'll come in for a check up when Frank gets back. He should be here by 4:30 at the latest."

Kay's expression changed, "Really, do you need me to stick around then? I was going to take advantage of my day off from cooking to run some errands, but if you need me, I'll be happy to stay here."

"No, no, you go on and enjoy your day off. Nothing too big is happening yet, I'm sure I'll be fine 'till Frank gets back. Just stop at the Center and tell Beau to check in with me a little later, in case I need something," I replied confidently.

I heard Kay's car drive off a few minutes later. I lay back down to continue my prayer, when suddenly I had a pretty tough contraction. "What now, Lord, I'm all by myself with these two little girls (Sarah 4 1/2 and Susanna almost 2). I forgot all about how we have been begging you, Jesus, for a speedy delivery for a change."

I heard the Lord say, "Trust me, you're not alone. I am with you."

I tried to concentrate on the scriptures and not the contractions, but I was getting a little nervous. About half an hour later, Frank's cousin, Odile knocked on the door. She was looking for Frank. She had just heard about the Life in the Spirit Seminar, and wanted to participate. "You're a little late. It's 3:30

now, Frank and the team left at 1:30, but it could be that God sent you to me. Could you possibly take me to the doctor? I'm having contractions and I think it would be better not to wait for Frank."

"Sure, I'd be more than happy to, but what about the girls, should we take them, too?" Beau rode up on his bicycle. He kept the girls while Odile drove me to the doctor.

Dr. Mayeaux said, "You are dilating a little already. Why don't I put you in the hospital and induce, we'll have that baby by 7:00 tonight?"

I explained that Frank wouldn't be back in town for another hour or so and that I preferred to let nature take its course. Odile drove me home from the doctor. I felt more at peace knowing that today was the day, and finished packing for the girls and Beau who would be staying at my sister's house while the baby was born. I changed the sheets on the beds; gave the house another quick once over; went on over to the Open Door main house to take a shower; and put together the finishing touches on the dinner.

It was 5:15 and Frank still wasn't back. I couldn't reach him by phone since cell phones were unheard of then. Evidently the hostess of the prayer meeting had taken her phone off the hook. Vince came strolling in after work at the Service Center and asked innocently, "Hi, how's everything?"

"Fine, I guess. I'm in labor and waiting for Frank. He should've been here by now. I hope he didn't forget and stay for coffee."

Vince paled, "Where's Kay?"

"She and the children left earlier to run some errands. She should be back any minute."

About that time I had a really hard contraction. I began to praise Jesus rhythmically, in order to relax through it. I closed my eyes and then felt Vince's hand on my shoulder; he was praying for me. When the contraction was over, I looked up at Vince; he was extremely nervous. He knew I had given birth to Susanna at home, and that I had only reluctantly decided to have this birth in the hospital.

He laughed nervously, "I don't know ANYTHING at all about delivering babies and I don't know why Kay isn't here. She ought to be here. What can be taking Frank so long?"

"Vince, I won't be here for supper. Tell Kay everything is cooked, except I don't think I'll be able to make the salad; the lemonade is already made; and the rolls just need to be browned and..." Another contraction, still harder....

Vince paced and said emphatically, "Don't worry about the salad! We don't need the salad! What we do need is to get you to the hospital!!" Vince was really worried, "Where are they? Kay knows she should be home by now; it's almost time for prayer." There were no cars at Open Door for our use.

I prayed after my contraction, "Lord Jesus, send Frank home quickly, please! I don't want to go to the hospital without him." No sooner that I had prayed the prayer, Frank drove in, followed shortly by Kay.

Beau, who had been popping in and out to check on me, had the suitcases in the driveway. Beau, Vince, Kay, Frank and all the children gathered together to prayerfully place me in Jesus' care for the delivery. We threw the luggage in the truck and went to drop the children off at Rachel's, on the way to the hospital.

My labor had really picked up. We stopped at a corner. I was really having a hard contraction when Frank heard the cry of what he thought was a baby. His face went white! He thought the baby had been born in the truck.

"What's wrong?" I asked worriedly. Looking past me, across the roadside fence into a pasture, Frank spied a goat that had bleated. We still laugh about the fright he got when he confused the goat's cries with a baby's cry.

God granted us the speedy delivery we had prayed for. Our third little girl was born on the stretcher; I never made it to the delivery table. She was beautiful, and she nursed hungrily right away. I noticed she had a dark brown birthmark high on her forehead, a little above where they place the Ashes on Ash Wednesday, (But it was eventually covered when she finally grew hair.) Here she was – my little penitent, my Mary Magdalen. The baby was supposed to "room-in" with me, but she had a little phlegm on her lungs. They convinced me to let her stay in the incubator overnight.

At one o'clock in the morning, just five hours after Mary Magdalen was born, I was watching her through the nursery window. A young couple walked by looking very distressed.

They sat, looking lonely in the waiting room. Their two-week old baby boy was back in the hospital. Doctors were alarmed that he might have meningitis. They had him in isolation. As they shared their deep concern with me, I began to talk with them about the Lord, trying to instill in them faith and hope in the healing power of Jesus. They were Baptists who had grown away from their relationship with the Lord. I encouraged them to remember their personal experiences with Jesus and to decide to repent and be forgiven. I suggested that they go back to church and Scripture reading, and receive a whole new life from the Lord.

"Why not start over right now? Can I pray with you?" I asked.

The husband answered, "I'm ashamed to pray now that I'm in trouble. All this time I've been ignoring the Lord. Isn't it hypocritical to pray now?" he questioned sincerely.

"That's one of Satan's most ridiculous arguments. He's trying to keep you from the God who loves you with such foolish thinking!" I exclaimed. "Don't you love your little son more than ever as you watch him suffer? Don't you long to hold him in your arms, whole and healed? Would it matter to you, would it, if he ignored you? The main thing you care about is his wellbeing and life! That's precisely how your heavenly Father feels about you. He can see your suffering and he longs to hold you in his arms, He longs to comfort and heal you, He wants you both to begin again, and I believe He wants to heal your baby."

They were both crying, tears of release and healing. Soon, I was crying, too. We knelt down and prayed.

I had been offering up my suffering at the separation from my baby. I longed to cuddle her. I'd been offering up her suffering for her; when she was older and needed the grace of her suffering, it would be there. I always ask the Lord to put my children's suffering in His "spiritual bank". They each had their own spiritual savings account earned by their childhood suffering. I knew they would need to draw abundant grace in their youth and other times of need. Already, for my sweet newborn daughter, that suffering was bearing fruit. If Mary Madgalen hadn't been in the incubator, I wouldn't have met this young family. They had come back to Jesus. There was rejoicing in heaven.

Back in the nursery, Mary Magdalen had gotten very pink; I could tell she was out of danger. At sunrise, I went in to nurse her and at 7:30 the nurse rolled her into my room in her little hospital bassinet. She was the very first baby in the history of Abbeville General Hospital to "room in" with her mommy.

Six weeks later, Mary Magdalen and I were waiting in my pediatrician's office. A radiant young woman with a fat, healthy baby turned around from the registration desk and greeted me with a great big smile. She was so changed that I almost didn't recognize her. It was the young mother I prayed with in the hospital. Her son had been quickly healed; it hadn't been meningitis after all. She and her husband were going back to their Baptist church, and they were having a daily family prayer time. Their life had turned around completely. They were planning to teach a Sunday school class as soon as the baby was a little older.

We hugged – a Holy embrace. Just as the baby in that manger changed the course of history, Mary Magdalen from her incubator had already started changing hearts. The mom of that baby boy and I followed Jesus in different churches, but we were sisters. He brought us together. He expected us to love each other and it was easy. We had seen His salvation together.

Mary, a graduate in education, married Chris Hindelang. Chris is a P.A. They have four children. Mary is a full time mom, and a Theresian, and dedicates herself to teaching her children about Jesus. Chris serves on the Board of FMC.

Chapter Seven

The Vision Still Has Its Time

Go to the nations, but which nation? God's directive to "Go to the Nations" was clear to us.

Waiting between missions always was a challenge; we waited to be moved by God's mighty hand. Waiting always made us totally dependent upon God. We certainly had been kept very busy at home. Back in Abbeville, especially at Open Door Community, people were living more committed lives. The joy of ministering at home could sometimes almost distract us from the Lord's clear direction to go forth again to the ends of the earth.

The community had been in a time of crisis. Judy Bernard had been diagnosed with breast cancer. We had seen so much of the Lord's healing, so much of His love, I simply could not understand why He wasn't healing Judy.

Even as they were about to operate on her, I kept waiting for that wonderful phone call telling us, "The mastectomy has been canceled!"

I truly expected that healing would be discovered in the nick of time. But God's ways are not our ways.

This was the beginning for Judy of a seven-year valiant struggle against cancer. Being such a small community, we groped about for the best way to handle Judy's needs. All those knowledgeable about cancer said rest would be essential for her expected recovery period - we hoped she'd find that in community. Judy was so conscientious about her chores in the house, she so desired not to be a burden that we failed to see how much strain the intensity of life and ministry at Open Door was really causing her. Little details about the life-style that had been taken for granted as the way "the Lord would have us do it" became subject to review and revision.

I have often agonized over it. I have asked myself, "How could we have protected her better in her illness? How could we have been more flexible?"

Today, we do not live with the same kind of strictures on our dress, schedule and leisure time as we did in the first decade of our mission life. I know we needed those years to really draw a new direction; it was a painful and flawed process.

Judy had always possessed a wisdom that called for a normalcy and moderation. She knew His way was often somewhere in the middle as we tried to zealously serve the Lord in community. I must thank God for her here, and honor her memory, as she struggled to do the right thing in her life. Judy was able to be there for Mary Magdalen's Baptism, she was her Godmother. As she stood beside Beau at the Baptismal font we saw a legacy there. Indeed, our Mary does in some way continue her gentle and steady spirit. She certainly has that inborn sense of balance. We couldn't have picked a better role model for our little girl. In some mysterious way, Judy's illness was a ministry, liberating us from excessive rigor.

As her illness progressed, I anticipated with joy and sadness visiting and praying with her. Those visits always strengthened me. All who visited Judy came away with more goodness than they were able to bring to her.

Our family's private kitchen in the abandoned school was just a sink and a small cabinet with our camping stove propped on top. Our table was a institutional folding table and folding chairs. We still didn't have an indoor toilet, using a portable one that had to be emptied daily. Living with hardships *was* our comfort zone. We took things in stride. Being holy in the pursuit of living community life was a great challenge.

Frank had written letters of inquiry about Asia, and especially the Philippines, to some mission societies, and to Ralph Martin, with whom we had kept up a correspondence since our friendship began in the South Pacific. Ralph sent us the name of Father Herb Schnieder, in Manila. Frank wrote Father Herb right away. He didn't answer our letter. Later we surmised that the letter might have never reached him. This, too, was part of God's plan. Anyway, we had been working on offers to serve in distant lands. Nothing had come, so we decided to seek the Lord's will in another family retreat. We moved into Frank's parents' summer house there in Abbeville, and began our seeking.

We always carry on our normal activities during family retreats, except for our three prayer sessions. Beau had gotten a job doing legal abstracting with his great-uncle. He had bought himself a Schwinn ten-speed bike and used it for his transportation. He would be arriving any minute from the office. Lunch was ready and Frank and I were waiting for him to come home so we could eat and then have our prayer session. "He should've been here by now, the soup's getting cold." I told Frank.

The phone rang. Frank answered. "Hello," he said normally. Then his voice changed pitch and he asked anxiously, "Where...When?... Is he all right?.... I'm on my way."

He slammed the phone down and grabbed his jacket. "Beau's been hit by a car! He's not conscious! That was Butch Hollier, it happened a few minutes ago, right in front of his house! I'm going over right now!"

I was holding the baby in my arms, but I dropped to my knees and cried out in terror, "Oh Jesus, Help him! Please Lord help him!"

Then I saw that Frank was already rushing out of the door. I wanted desperately to go with him, but the other two little girls were asleep. By the time we woke them and put their jackets on and everything, it would've taken too long. Frank was praying out loud.

I started praying in tongues, I could feel the terror diminishing, and a little more control coming into my being. The telephone nearly slipped out of my hands. I called my sister. It just so happened, that one of my brothers was in her flower shop, buying my Dad a birthday present. It was his birthday. Jed agreed to drive Rachel directly to my house to care for the children; he could drive me to the scene of the accident, or to the hospital. While I waited for them, I continued praying in tongues. I had the sense that I was praying for Beau's head. Without any of the details, I was glad to be able to let the Holy Spirit pray through me for his healing. St. Paul says in his letter to the Corinthians, that "if I pray in a tongue, my spirit is at prayer, but my mind contributes nothing." I certainly was too uninformed to pray through it mentally. It was a prayer of total dependence on God.

Jed and I drove up to the scene of the accident, there was Beau's bike stuck in the radiator of the car. The crowd that had not yet dispersed told us that Frank had taken Beau to the hospital, shaky on his feet, but ambulatory. I praised God that he was alive, after seeing his bike, and the dent Beau had made in the hood of the car!

Beau was on a stretcher in the emergency room. He turned and smiled at me weakly, "Hi, Mom!" I was so relieved; tears started streaming down my face.

"Don't cry, I'm alright. They x-rayed my head and my leg, nothing's broken, I just need a little sewing up, that's all."

He pointed to a short but deep hole in his left leg that would require several stitches. That accident was a sort of casualty stemming from our mission life. Tonga was full of ferocious dogs and Beau had always carried rocks or a stick on his trips from school to defend himself. The Tongan dogs were beastly and had no veterinary care. As a child of three, in Louisiana, he had been savaged by a large dog and had grown wary of such animals. When he heard a canine attack at his heels, and could not retaliate, he was determined to avoid being bitten. On his bike, Beau had been trying to outrun the snapping, barking little dog that belonged to the Hollier family. While looking back at the dog, he swerved into the path of the oncoming car. The driver, seeing what was happening, had been in the process of braking, slowing down, or it could have been much more serious.

That night, our friend, Evelyn Hollier called me, she was concerned for Beau. Evelyn is a registered nurse. She had seen the accident as she turned the corner in front of her house. Beau had hit the car, been thrown forward onto the hood, then upward onto the top of the car, and finally rolled over off the top and landed flat on his back on the sidewalk. By the time she parked her car and went out to meet him in the ditch, he was asking her for prayer in a confused sort of way and was obviously in mild shock.

She had stayed with him until Frank came and prayed

for him with the laying on of hands. After awhile, Beau was helped into the truck.

"Evelyn, we're just counting our blessings, he has a few bruises, some stitches in his leg, and soreness, but other than that he's fine," I said gratefully.

"What about his head?" she asked, "When I got to him on the side of the road, he had a huge bump on his head, what did they say about that?"

I told her about my prayer in tongues, sensing that he needed prayer for his head. "God must have answered that prayer and healed his head, because by the time I got to the hospital, there wasn't even a trace of a bump on his head."

Jesus is a great and mighty King. Beau told us that he had been praying on the way home from work. He had said, "Lord, if you call me home, I'm ready."

"Well, Beau, you might have been ready, but the Lord knows your little mother isn't ready. I don't think I could have been stretched that far. I know I can't handle letting you go just yet."

Beau's accident demonstrated to us very clearly, that our children's lives are in the Lord's hands. Many parents hesitate to answer God's call to the foreign missions because they worry for the safety of their children. At home or abroad, He has his angels watching over them and there is no safer place to be than in the Lord's hands.

We continued the retreat. The Lord was indicating Asia. He was calling us to "Go as far as you can go."

With that guidance, we got out the atlas and tried to figure out how far we could go in the direction of Asia! We might try to visit our friends again in Samoa, Tonga, and Fiji. That sounded wonderful, but there was no way we could have possibly made all these stops. Now we were a family of six and we didn't have the funds.

"The Lord said we should go as far as we can go. It looks like the closest we could get to Asia at this point would be New Zealand. New Zealand is not Asia; it is prosperous. And like Mexico and Tonga it is a *Christian* nation."

Beau piped up, "Not necessarily, I recently heard an NCAA Tournament basketball player say on the radio, that he would be going to New Zealand to spend several years as a

107

Protestant missionary. When the anchorman asked that basketball player, "Why?' He responded, 'Less than five percent of New Zealanders go to church on any given Sunday. Lukewarm Christians need missionaries.'"

"That's so true. Many nations, including our own, want the blessings of a Christian heritage without seriously addressing Christianity itself. But, the culture of Christianity will fade if it isn't supported by true faith. So, we can ask ourselves, 'What is mission?' Mission is serving in New Zealand, as well as China, if that is where God sends *you*," I commented.

"Ewen and Gillian have been so faithful in our friendship over the years that I know that they would be happy to help us find a place to serve," Frank said, and wrote Ewen that same day.

While we had been in Tonga together, Ewen and Gillian had been volunteers with their young family. While there, Ewen had confided in Frank how blessed he felt to be in full time service of the Lord. He was dreading returning to New Zealand to work in his previous secular job as a social worker and probation officer. He longed to be in a position to help troubled young people in a way that was explicitly Christian. Troubled young people need the power of God and his Holy Spirit to be unleashed in their lives. Ewen had a dream of beginning a foster care ministry, that would place troubled and at risk kids into good solid Christian homes.

The Laurensons had remained in Tonga after we left and sent us a letter as they prepared to leave for New Zealand. Once again, they expressed their strong desire to pursue a work in full time service of the Lord. Frank felt inspired to write them a letter exhorting them to be bold and to expect God to work things out to make a life in ministry possible for them.

Later, they told us that it was Frank's letter that gave them the push they needed to begin the Open Home Foundation, a Christian foster care ministry that has spread to many centers all over New Zealand. Ewen answered our letter requesting help in finding work in the Lord's vineyard in New Zealand. He sounded excited, and assured us that they would be delighted to have us stay with them for as long as necessary. The letter continued, "Wellington is a beautiful City, but it is very, very windy. The clouds go whizzing by. You have to be forewarned

108

about the wind."

"Isn't it strange the way Ewen mentions the wind in every letter?" I asked

"It can't be that bad," Frank answered. "We'll see when we get there."

In our excitement, we made plans. Then, we found out about the price of airline tickets. We didn't have enough money to transport all six of us, so we went to the Lord in prayer. Frank prayed, "Lord Jesus, you know where the finances are for our mission to New Zealand. Please release them to us, in your perfect time. Also, please help us with our visas. Help us to wait patiently until you send us, because we're ready to go now! Help us to bring to completion the work we've begun here, bless Open Door in our absence. Fill us with the Holy Spirit, and the 'new zeal' that we will need to go to New Zealand."

A few days later, a check came in the mail. I came running in from the mailbox, "Frank, Frank, our friend Father Martin has sent us a really generous donation. Can you believe it? It is just the amount that we needed to buy the airline tickets!" I shouted.

We danced, we kissed and hugged each other, and called the Laurenson's. We got their invitation in the middle of November, and it wasn't until February 13, 1981 that we headed out on a seventeen-hour flight to New Zealand. Our waiting had made us ready; ready to go again to the ends of the Earth.

Our three little girls were dressed alike as we boarded the jumbo jet, and filed by our fellow passengers. Beau, Frank and I each had one little girl in our arms. As we sat down, I leaned over to Frank, "It's interesting to read the looks on people's faces. Not too many of them like the idea of little children on a long flight. Did you see that guy staring reproachfully at the wooden crosses we all wear around our necks?"

"Don't worry, Genie, we paid for our tickets and our little girls will show them how great kids can be."

About seven hours into the flight, we bumped into some severe turbulence. The big plane shook like it was a toy on a string in the hands of God. Everyone got very quiet and serious, bracing themselves against the brutal bouncing. We bowed our heads in prayer, making the sign of the cross as we began. The

109

turbulence cleared and we continued on our way. After that, I noted a much friendlier atmosphere in the aircraft. A little danger goes a long way in turning our hearts and minds to God and in helping people to accept, and even rejoice in the presence of His servants.

What a joyful reunion we had with Ewen and Gillian in Wellington. After happy embraces, we headed out to their car for the ride home to Johnsonville, a suburb of Wellington. We couldn't help but notice that Ewen's warning about the wind was right on. It was windy! The clouds did fly by, and it took me awhile to adjust. One day as I climbed to the top of a hill outside Wellington, the wind was blowing in my face relentlessly. I thought the view was spectacular, and had come up for my prayer time. "What a bother the wind is," I thought, "I can't read by Bible, the pages keep flipping."

I heard the Lord say to me, "Genie, the wind is your friend. Enjoy it and let it invigorate you."

Wind is a symbol often used for the Holy Spirit. In Jerusalem, the Holy Spirit came "like a Mighty wind." The Jews were satisfied with the religious *status quo* in their lives. They served the living God – what more did they need? They were "His chosen people." Who could preach anything new, anything worth hearing, to them, they were the apple of God's eye! So God sent a mighty wind to them, to get their attention, to shake them out of their complacency so they would listen to the band of men who had followed an executed prisoner, and were now being led by a humble fisherman. These men, these disciples had good news.

Ewen and Gillian were such gracious hosts. We stayed in their house with them for over six weeks and lived a full community life. They had adopted three beautiful children. We had met Ruth and Michael in Tonga. Little Timothy was a darling too. They had a couple of foster children living with them. Their office was in their house, down in the basement. They were praying for new office arrangements. Imagine taking in a family of six for six weeks! They never once complained, to the contrary, they made us feel as though we were a blessing from the Lord.

What we needed was a mighty wind to make the way for our mission. Our friend, Wayne O' Hallaran was trying to describe the character and culture of his fellow countrymen to us one night, "New Zealand has so much going for it; our people are fairly moral, we all play sports. We are interested in art and culture; we have a good standard of living; there are very few cases of real poverty; AND those who wish to go to church Sunday do so. Problems may come, but we console ourselves with our favorite saying, 'She'll be right.' You know, Frank, that's why we have so much trouble believing that we need missionaries, we're so complacent."

Frank replied, "Wayne, Even the Pope has declared that as a Christian people, we need to evangelize and be evangelized. He included himself in the 'we'. The gospel is good news, who doesn't need to hear good news many times over?"

Wayne smiled in agreement, "I know, Frank, I'm convinced, but you'll have to be patient and I think you will see. God will move among His people."

Ewen was leading a home bible-study program. He and Gillian attended from time to time a Charismatic prayer meeting in Khandallah. Through their Christian friends, we were kept busy sharing our testimony and building relationships. We also came to know the beauty of the people, and to begin to discern the greatest spiritual need for God's Word to become alive in their midst. Ewen introduced us to some priests, who considered using us in their parishes or apostolates. Father Jim MacDonnel showed a keen interest in using us in his parish. We met him around the time when we had made an appointment to meet with the Archbishop Tom Williams (he is now a Cardinal). Of course, we prayed and did spiritual warfare for the success of our talk with the Archbishop. We were so surprised to see how young and full of life and energy he was.

He gave us an hour of his valuable time, thanking us for our generous offer to serve, "How could I refuse, the need for evangelization is great in my diocese. Your offer is to work on building communities, evangelization and promoting lay ministry. These are some of the priorities that I've outlined in my pastoral plan. All you have to do is to find a priest to work under, and you have my blessing."

"Thank you, Archbishop. We feel certain the Lord will help us serve your people," Frank said.

He gave us the names of some priests he thought might

be interested, Father Jim MacDonnell from Titahi Bay was first on the list.

We contacted Father Jim again, and he invited us to go to talk things over with him at the rectory of St. Pius X Church, in Titahi Bay. We talked about the possibilities, the programs, and the services our ministry would make available for the Parish. Father thought it would be essential that the Parish approve the invitation he wanted to make to us. On one Sunday he announced to the Parishioners that we would be speaking at all the Masses on the following Sunday. An open forum in the school cafeteria would follow. Parishioners were invited to ask questions and express any negative feedback that they might have. At the very beginning, we made it clear that the Lord had called us to Asia, and that we didn't feel that we could make a very long-term commitment. Our letters of inquiry into Asia were still pending. The congregation was intrigued, open and willing to welcome us. We did assure Father Jim that while we were in Titahi Bay, we would give our all for the building of the Lord's kingdom. Father agreed to help us find housing.

Actually, the Parish had inherited a house. He would have to see if the present tenants were willing to vacate it. In the meantime, he invited us to live in the downstairs of the rectory. The downstairs had three bedrooms, a sitting room, two institutional bathrooms with showers and a laundry room. I borrowed Father's camping stove, and people from the parish brought dishes, utensils, and pots and pans for me to set up a temporary kitchen in the laundry room.

I could see the eagerness to help, the joy the people of St. Pius X had through sharing some item that was extra for them but essential to us. Perhaps that's why Jesus tells his disciples to take nothing for the journey. Arriving empty handed is a good way to make friends quickly. The people that have loaned or given us things are super interested in our work. They really want to get to know us as *missionaries*. They have an investment in the success of our mission.

Living in the rectory had some great advantages, of course. Daily Mass, close relationships with Father Jim and Father Pat McCullough, his associate, and the indisputable sign it was of the approval of the clergy for our ministry. Lots of friends came over, and some faithful church workers took us under their wing. By June, the Parish's house had been vacated.

A lot of prayer and work went into getting it into shape for us. Volunteers helped with the cleaning and getting it clearing out. It was a community building project. Friends washed walls, others put in new carpet in the hall, some scrubbed the bathroom, and others cleaned the yard. We moved into the comfortable old house and began to receive visitors. Our friends, the Pryors, were the leaders of the Charismatic Renewal there. Bob topped off the house restoration with a beautiful gift: he made a nine-foot wooden cross for our front yard!

Frank had devised a program taken from our experience in Latin America, for the building of Christian Communities, in lie with Archbishop Tom Williams' desire was to have his Archdiocese pursue the vision laid out by the important conferences in Medellin and Puebla in Latin America.

"That is truly neat that Archbishop is all for the documents we have been studying so much. I know that this program is going to bear good fruit. I can feel it," I said to Frank as he zealously typed out his outlines.

We set out a three stage program, which began with an initial week-end of evangelization, a series of training sessions on how to form and conduct small house prayer groups, and then actualizing the meetings – couples and singles were expected to meet weekly in their homes. Spontaneous prayer, the mass readings for the upcoming week, and the study of some Christian teachings led participants to spiritual growth and maturity. These small Christian Communities brought swift life and growth to the parish. It was exciting to watch the parishioners grow in their hunger for God's Word, and their fellowship with one another.

Each week, Frank wrote a study and sharing sheet that went out to all the communities. I belonged to a Basic Christian Community of women. We chose the name for ourselves, "Our Lady's Group." It really did make the sharing easier when each person present had the sheet in front of them.

The neighboring town of Tawa invited Frank to present the Basic Christian Community program there. Father Cocharan, the parish priest, was especially in tune with our charism as missionaries. We became real friends and enjoyed his visits to our home.

The parish had a small youth group, but it had not been focusing too much on spiritual life. Beau helped it adopt the form of the Basic Christian Community program, with time for fellowship and fun afterward for the young people's program. The youth really clicked. They were excited about Jesus and what He was doing in their lives. Even their social events began with getting centered in the Lord. A marvelous transformation took place in the lives of some of the youth.

Beau also attended a local high school, Viard College. While he struggled with Math there, (as it was totally unfamiliar to him), he excelled in other subjects and made a good number of friends. Another facet of his education was to spend a great deal of time working for an older cabinet maker, who taught him some of the arts of design and craftsmanship. The man's own sons had moved to Australia. Beau played outdoor sports and hiked with Fr. Pat. He turned seventeen in New Zealand. The youth group, Beau had coaxed into being a Chrisitan Community was called "Maranatha". They gave him a great send off when we left, and several of the young ladies had taken a fancy to him, his missionary calling being part of the attraction.

The most multi-faceted ministry we'd been in until then took place in Titahi Bay. At first, Frank really missed the chance to be preaching regularly. He missed the poor. The nature of "need" there was almost entirely spiritual! The elderly were in need of ministry. Frank gave a weekly teaching in the nursing home, and found it a fertile ground for the Word. Our house became a house of hospitality. While opportunities and invitations to go out in the name of Jesus seemed scarcer in this English speaking land, our home ministry was thriving.

Frank voiced his complaint about preaching opportunities to the Lord. In response he received the reading in Isaiah 60, "Rise up in splendor! Your light has come; the glory of the Lord shines upon.... Raise your eyes and look about, they all gather and come to you: Your sons from afar, and your daughters in the arms of their nurses.... Your gates shall be open constantly... Once you were forsaken and unvisited, now I will make you the pride of the ages, a joy to generation after generation."

In this reading, we heard God say, "I, *Myself*, will bring those to you, whom you can serve in my name!"

114

Over the next three days, we had seventy-two visitors; and in a whole week, we had one hundred twenty-five visitors. The harvest is rich and the laborers are few. The Lord wasn't going to let us sit by idly when we longed to serve Him.

One day, while we were still living in the rectory, we made a connection that would have a central place in our ministry in New Zealand and also be dear to our hearts for years to come. Father asked us to instruct a young couple who was not married in the Church. When they walked in to our sitting room, something special happened. Henry and Sue were Polynesians. Besides needing marriage instructions, Sue had never been baptized into any faith. They were a beautiful couple, eager and willing to hear the Word of the Lord, to learn more about Jesus and His salvation. We developed a deep friendship.

We soon learned that not only was Henry the shot-put champion of New Zealand, he was an awesome guitar player. Frank and Henry began to hold a guitar practice. The Holy Spirit really blessed the music and lots of people wanted to join the newly forming church music group. We had practice once or twice a week at our house. The group was anointed. Beau participated as well. Sarah, Susanna and Mary sat in the doorway trying to sing. A good number of years later we got a cassette tape that Henry and his group had produced. They were widely known in Catholic Christian music and were performing nationwide in New Zealand. I guess that was a fruit of our ministry too. They were still playing beautiful music to the Lord, singing the praises of Jesus.

Music was not the only way that God used the Summers and Smith families together in that work. Henry came from a very large family; they were close to one another. Their father had recently passed away. After his death, several of the brothers had taken to drinking to excess and often got into trouble. Henry's conversion began to be a light to the others, and soon other family members' lives were changing. An Aunt came down from Auckland for Sue's Baptism. I was privileged to be Sue's Godmother, so they all visited with us after the ceremony. Henry's Aunt had an exciting story to share with us:

"I belong to a prayer group in Auckland, you know, miles away in the north of New Zealand. One day, months earlier, I was at my prayer meeting. I had been praying for

115

Henry's family. I was worried about the direction my nephews' lives were taking. Suddenly, one of the ladies at my prayer meeting cried out, '**Your prayers will be answered!**'"

Auntie continued, "I asked her how she could be so sure, and she told me she had seen a vision of a family coming from across the sea to minister to Henry and his family. The man in the vision had a beard."

Auntie was so excited that we, the Summers, were there. "Imagine, it really happened, a family from across the sea came to Titahi Bay. Frank has a beard, and now you are Sue's Godmother! I can't wait to get back and tell my friend that her vision was fulfilled!"

Titahi Bay was a very short distance from the Porrirua National Mental Hospital. A number of the housing projects there function as halfway houses for the former inmates of the mental hospital. The Lord sent to us those who were recuperating from mental disorders. This was a very challenging ministry! By His providence, our house was often filled with our friends from the Basic Christian Communities. As the "well and whole" Christians shared life with the "sick and disturbed" – our home served as a fountain of love and healing for these victims of the cruelest disease of all – mental illness. Frank has the patience of Job, and he could spend hours helping to untangle the knotted threads of those mental patients' lives. One of our "regular" halfway house visitors brought over a new friend. I remember wondering, "How in the world is Frank going to introduce the Lord to this guy?"

When Frank extended his hand for a handshake, the man introduced himself, "Hello, my name is Bob and I'm a manic-depressive with homicidal tendencies!"

Frank never flinched, "Hi, Bob, I'm Frank Summers, I'm a missionary, and I want you to know that Jesus loves you."

The healing in Bob took place very slowly, but the darkness he deeply struggled with made way for light. There is no "lost lamb" that the Good Shepherd can't find and bring home on His shoulders.

Our family prayer time became a regularly scheduled event for many of our visitors. We constantly had the teakettle on, and a cupboard full of home-baked goodies to share with those who needed evangelization, counseling or just plain

116

fellowship. I didn't do all the baking. New Zealand women are the best in the world in the culinary art of home baking. My friends kept us in a constant supply of desserts, cookies and pastries for use in our hospitality ministry. Housekeeping and caring for my family kept me busy. Our very old wringer washer kept breaking down, and I had to spend hours washing clothes and cloth diapers in the bathtub. We had a growing and full ministry, but not a very well structured "job" for Frank in New Zealand. In some sense, for all its blessings, the mission in Titahi Bay had never been a complete fit for what we felt was our call as lay Catholic Evangelists. St. Paul says, in Romans 12, "We, though many, are one body in Christ and individually part of one another. Since we have gifts that differ according to the grace given to us, let us exercise them."

In March, Frank and I had felt we could give a whole year to the ministry in Pius X Parish in Titahi Bay. Frank's gift is preaching the Word of God. He longed to exercise it. He was having very few opportunities to do that in our present ministry. The Basic Christian Community program was getting to be self-sufficient, that's what it was supposed to do. We were training leaders to take over the BCC's and the music ministry.

Almost everywhere we've been, the Lord has made prophetic statements to the Church through our witness. That's why the Lord sends missionaries. Those who come from far away can see the sin and weakness that the local church has grown accustomed to, even where the customs are those of a young and changing country like New Zealand. It is never easy to proclaim a hard word that goes against the practice of the place you're in. Frank had preached in the renewal at the Diocesan level. There was a great deal of opposition when we shared about the roles of men and women; the roles of the laity; the call to Catholics to live unequivocally a pro-life, non-contraceptive married vocation; the strict call to chastity in the normal Christian life; the need for radical repentance; and the daily surrender to Jesus and His Gospel.

One day Beau came home distressed. He was burdened by some bad things that had been said about our family. We recognized it as persecution against the word that had recently gone out. I was cleaning up after supper and Frank was building a fire in the fireplace. I could tell he had been very hurt by

117

Beau's report and the unjust criticism. He finally got the fire blazing and sat dejectedly in front.

Frank's pain and dejection worried me.

I went into the kitchen and prayed, "Lord Jesus, this is so unjust. What should we do?" The Lord answered me, "What did I tell you to do?"

"I don't remember you telling me anything," I responded sincerely.

"What does it say in the scriptures?" He prompted.

I thought a minute, then I said, "Oh yeah! It says we're supposed to rejoice when we are persecuted and dance for joy, because our names are written in heaven."

I walked into the living room and I said, "You know what we're supposed to do, Frank? We're supposed to dance for joy."

"That's the last thing I feel like doing, right now, but that's what God's word says to do. Let's do it!" he said.

And we did. We danced and danced all around the living room, making up verses to songs that said that our names were written in heaven. Soon we were truly happy, laughing and giddy with joy. About that time, Beau came back from an errand. He walked in and looked at us askance, "What in the world is going on here?"

"We're dancing for joy, Son. Do you want to join us?" Frank answered. Beau joined right in and after awhile we all fell into a happy heap on the sofa. The pain was completely gone and we were able to relate to those who had criticized us without any resentment.

In New Zealand, we received some criticism, but never in our ministry have we been more noticed by the press. We were written up in secular and Christian periodicals and newspapers. This was such a "happening" in our lives that the little girls went around with pads and pencils playing interview. We could say with St. Paul, "We are treated as unrecognized and yet acknowledged."

Living in such a beautiful country, made us aware that the beauty of nature that surrounded us enriched our life there. We lived within walking distance of the beach, and often went to sit on the shore, have a picnic, watch the water, and wade. It was too cold to swim most of the time. Beau and Frank also enjoyed hiking in the hills that were dotted with sheep.

Beau was confirmed by Archbishop Williams in New Zealand. An overnight camping retreat was what he and Frank planned to help him prepare for the sacrament. The first thing they did was to find a cave to spend the night in, but it began to rain and the cave got wetter and wetter. Finally, after the rain stopped, they went on the beach to spend the rest of the night. Beau was awakened by Frank's shouts of "Hey, wait a minute, what was that?" They sat up in time to see a penguin waddle away. "That penguin just pecked me on the head." Frank said in surprise. We still marvel at Frank's experience of being attacked by a penguin.

But of all the natural features of Titahi Bay, none is as noticeable as the wind. It was a blessing. We got sick less and germs didn't have a chance; they were blasted away by the wind. Our home had those umbrella type clotheslines, the "brakes" that held it in place while I hung the clothes kept giving way, and the line would go spinning around and around in the wind like a pinwheel. It was frustrating; but I did learn that the wind really is my friend, because those clothes dried *fast*.

We learned a beautiful song in New Zealand, called "Wind, Wind." The first stanza goes like this: "Wind, Wind, blow on me: Wind, Wind set me free, Wind, Wind, my Father sent the Blessed Holy Spirit." I sang that song while I hung the clothes and the Holy Spirit did set me free! Free to go about my duties with a heart of thanksgiving, I was better able to serve those who, at times, I felt inadequate to serve.

One day we were in a time of worship, Frank was asking the Lord to reveal to us the fruits of our ministry in New Zealand. While we prayed, I had a vision of a calibrated thermometer on a Billboard. Under the thermometer was written, "Summers New Zealand Mission." (It was the kind of thermometer that is used for fund-raising drives, where the progress of the drive is periodically colored in until the goal is reached.) In the vision, Frank, looking very small, walked up to the billboard and colored in only a very small amount of the whole thermometer, and stood looking sadly at the rest of the thermometer. Then, still in the vision, I saw the hand of God come down and gently move Frank out of the way. There was a paintbrush in God's hand, and He quickly filled up the whole

119

thermometer, with some color bursting out of the top! God was saying, "No matter how you see it, I am pleased. You have accomplished your mission."

That was a very freeing word for us, because Asia still beckoned. We longed for a more intense ministry of preaching and serving the poor. We spent a good bit of time seeking wisdom on the nature of our next mission. We had been in correspondence with the Philippines. Frank wrote a second letter to Father Herb Schnieder, a Jesuit priest, who was the overall coordinator of the "Ang Ligaya ng Panginoon" (Joy of the Lord) community in Manila. Father Herb had written a beautiful response, telling us that the Lord would surely take into account our willingness to serve the poor in evangelism, and that he would send our letter out to those who might be interested.

Shortly thereafter, we received a letter from Father Pacana, S.J. Bishop Francisco Claver of the Diocese of Malaybalay, Bukidnon had asked him to write us and invite us to work under Fr. Pacana, the Pastor of the Cathedral Parish, San Isidro. Father Pacana's invitation was positive and warm. (Fr. Pacana is now Bishop Pacana, and our missionaries serve under him today.) When we wrote back asking about a time frame, asking when would be the best time for us to come, Father Pacana's answer by return mail was, "Now!"

A year and a half before, Jesus told us that He had prepared a place for us in Asia. We had found the place. The place was Malaybalay, Bukidnon, Philippines. We had never even heard of Bukidnon, much less Malaybalay. That didn't matter, God had heard of Malabalay. Already we felt a happy expectation about the mission to God's people in the Philippines. Our happiness was mixed with sadness, though. We had made so many wonderful friends, brothers and sisters in the Lord, there in New Zealand. We would miss their love and support.

We'd miss Paul and Allie Ell, and their three daughters who were exactly the same age as our daughters. We had seen such healing and growth in their lives. We talked about leaving all of our friends, but as we talked about the Ells, Sarah piped up, "Mom, let's talk about the miracle of the lollipops, that's my favorite miracle."

Sarah's lollipop miracle happened one Friday. The Ells had come over for fish and chips. They were on their way back

120

from a children's birthday party. At the party each little girl had been given a lollipop. Abby, the Ell's baby was too young for candy, and so was our Mary Magdalen. There were three lollipops and six girls, but two of them were babies who could not eat lollipops.

The minute they walked in the door, Tracey told Sarah, "I'm going to give you Abby's lollipop."

Susanna was always at Sarah's heels and asked, "What about me? Is there a lollipop for me?"

Allie Ell, the girls' mom, looked over at me, "Oh dear, Genie, I'm sorry, there are only three lollipops, Tracey shouldn't have offered it. Maybe Tracey or Stacey will give up one of theirs for Susanna."

I tried to make light of it, "No, that's all right, neither of my girls need a lollipop, they can have some cake instead." In no time at all, we had four little girls, crying over the lollipops.

Finally, Sarah said bravely, "Susanna and I can share one."

"That's good," I said, "Give me the bag of lollipops until after supper." Tracey handed me the bag that was battered from tugging and pulling.

"I want the red one, I want the orange, I want the green one...." Their little voices trailed off as they went out to play with the toys. After we said the grace and blessed the food, Sarah intoned, "And please let the lollipop not break, Lord, when we cut it in half."

We all laughed and said, "Amen."

The girls had barely gobbled down their fish and chips, when they were asking for the candy. I reached up on the shelf, then I handed Sarah the bag. She opened it up, and gasped. "Mom, there are four! Look! Tracey, Four. Jesus made us a new lollipop. There's the green one, a red one, the orange one, and a yellow one. I want the yellow one! I want the one Jesus made!"

Allie and I stared at each other incredulously. We had both held the three lollipops in our hands. The rejoicing in our kitchen reached fever pitch. Children and adults were filled with amazement. Beau said, "I'm sure Jesus enjoys multiplying candy for the little girls, as much as he enjoys multiplying food for disciples. Look how happy they are, you can't tell *them* Jesus doesn't multiply food *and* candy."

Father Jim, our pastor at Pius X, was disappointed at first that we weren't going to extend our mission. However, he soon found the Lord's peace and approved of our decision. The parish had a big send-off for us. Pius X was a different parish than it had been almost a year earlier. The Puebla documents call Basic Christian Communities "the hope of the church." People sharing their lives and their Christianity in small groups on a daily basis inject hope into the daily lives of Catholic Christians. Basic Chrisitan Community is an essential supplement to the more formal, yet central, parish celebration of the Eucharist.

At our going away party, the music group was excellent and confident. Beau's friends, Wayne, Michelle, Anne, Peter and all the rest had experienced tremendous growth in their walk with the Lord. Our dear friend, Ian McClean was preparing to join a live-in covenant community. All of our friends had served us so well. This good-bye was one of the hardest yet. All night people came by to help us pack, pray with us and wish us well.

The next morning a large group accompanied us to the airport. Ewen and Gillian, Henry and Sue, and others were all trying to be lighthearted. We were, too, but the grief of parting was smoldering deep in our hearts. We sang and prayed, and bid our good-byes.

Henry said, "Maybe one day, the Lord will need a big guitar player and I'll be a missionary, too."

"Don't say 'no' when He calls," I said. As we were about to board the plane, headed to Australia, Henry pressed a gift into Beau's hand and a gift into Frank's hand.

"Don't open them until you're in the air. I mean it. Wait until you're airbound."

As we taxied down the runway, we waved to our friends, who waved vigorously back at us from an outside deck. Beau first, then Frank and I, burst into tears, not just silent weeping, but real, from the gut, sobbing, as we looked down at the contents of the packages. Henry had given us his most prized possessions. Beau gently, fondly held up the red ribbon on which the Silver Medal hung. "Henry won this at the Brisbane Games," Beau said emotionally.

The stewardess looked at us uncomfortably as we wept. "I'm not ashamed of crying, y'all. I am honored to have such friends. Even if we do without a lot of things in our mission, nothing can equal this awesome feeling. I feel a real, true, joy from having been loved like this!" I said tearfully.

We were traveling from love to love as we went forth through Australia to the Philippines. A Marist, Sr. Mary Joseph, was our friend from Tonga. She had been such an inspiration to us that we wanted to see her again. We wrote her from Titahi Bay, "Sister, we want to visit with you."

We found her in a hospital in Sydney, "It breaks our hearts to see you laid up in this hospital with a stroke." I said as I squeezed her hand.

She was really blessed by the little girls. "I shouldn't complain, I have had a wonderful life. I have been so active in my life, some called me a 'dynamo' for Jesus," she struggled to say. We knew how hard it was for her to be bedridden.

"Let's pray," Frank said, "Lord Jesus, heal your friend, your brave lady. She has faced sharks, wild animals, ministered to lepers, poured out her life bringing healing and hygiene in your name. Now, give her courage as she is facing a more frightening threat, enforced inactivity. Lord, we know that the last mile of a race is the hardest; only seasoned runners can run it and capture the prize. Remember the holiness she worked for on the mission field. Multiply minute by minute, on her sick bed, that holiness. Blessed Mother, Star of the Sea, enfold Sister with your veil. Amen."

A mantle of peace descended on her. She assured us of her prayers. We knew she would win, by her prayers, special graces for our mission in the Philippines.

From Sydney, we rented a car and drove north to Brisbane. We camped out and found a place on the beach. We were amazed by how much some of the countryside reminded us of the southern United States, where we had our own roots. In order to get the economy fares to the Philippines, we had to wait twenty-one days. That gave us a few weeks to spend Australia. We first heard about the Emmanuel Community in Brisbane from Ralph Martin, when we met in 1975 in Fiji. We had corresponded, and the community replied in a letter, "We will be happy to receive you as guests of the community."

Frank went into the offices of Emmanuel and came out smiling, and one of the brothers invited us all to the coffee shop for snacks. A family in the community would be gone on vacation the whole time we needed a place to stay. That family would be happy to let us stay in their home. The house offered to us was right next door to Peter and Marion Shakovskoy and their family. Peter was a coordinator in the community.

Peter and Marion took us into their hearts and lives. We learned the ways of God's people in Emmanuel. They lived in a cluster, where Christians were neighbors by choice. "This is a lot like Alleluia Community, it is so good to see the order, peace, and discipline they live," I commented to Frank one evening. "I think we can take some of their practices for family life with us."

It was in Emmanuel that we first experienced the "Lord's Day Meal." Every Saturday evening, the family celebrates with a special meal. The table is set with its best tableware, and they sit down together to welcome the Day of the Lord, which is Sunday.

Enjoying the goodness of community life, we missed Open Door. "Why can't we have community and mission?" I asked myself.

It was in December of 1981, during our visit to the Emmanuel Community, that Frank first began to pray for the Lord to build a community of missionaries. They would have to be sold out to Jesus; they would have to be called out in His name. They would have to be willing to accept poverty, the poverty of being itinerant, with no place to lay your head. The Lord would have to prepare them.

"Are those missionaries out there, Jesus?" He pleaded.

Jesus answered with a loud, clear voice. We heard Him remind us of one of our favorite scriptures: *"Write down the vision clearly on the tablets, so that one can read it readily. For the vision still has its time, presses on to fulfillment, and will not disappoint; if it delays, wait for it, it will surely come, it will not be late!"* *(Hab 2: 2-3).* Frank recorded his prayer that December day for missionary community in his "Liturgy of the Hours". God would amaze us eventually. He absolutely would finally fulfill the vision. We would just have to wait!

Henry and Beau,
farewell at Wellington,
New Zealand 1981

Chapter Eight

Malaybalay – Mountains and Marvels

Asia! We had landed in Asia. December 20, 1981, our missionary family landed in Manila. We knew the airport would be crowded, but we were not prepared for the veritable sea of faces eagerly eyeing the deplaning passengers. It was the old Manila International Airport, and it was much too small for the amount of air traffic flowing through it. Soldiers with machine guns were an alarming sight to travel weary missionaries; Filipinos returning home were almost unaware of them. If we were going to inculturate, if this was our new culture, we needed to get used to them. While we waited in long lines inside the crowded airport for the immigration and customs check, we began to wonder how we would ever connect with our ride outside in the crush of people.

Our trip from New Zealand and Australia had landed us in the lap of a new continent.

Father Herb had offered us hospitality in the Ang Ligaya Community, until we could be on our way to Malaybalay. Our last note from Ed, a community member said*, "We will have someone from the Community at the airport to pick you up. A wonderful family has offered to be your hosts."*

"Girls, help Mama pray that we don't have to unpack our bags at customs."

"Okay, Mama," Susanna said, immediately folding her little hands.

"Jesus, don't let them stop us in the line, let us get out of the airport soon," Sarah prayed aloud.

The Filipina lady in front of her flashed her a big smile. I'd gotten pretty good at packing by now; all of our clothes were rolled up in backpacks. Even our little girls, Sarah and Susanna carried backpacks, full of toys and books. The customs officer noticed our wooden crosses, was charmed by our family, and let us glide right through without a baggage check.

Outside the door of the airport, hundreds of people pressed against a cyclone fence. All of a sudden, we heard above the roar of the crowd, "Frank Summers, Frank Summers!" Four young men were holding a poster with our name on it. Physically, they looked like their fellow Filipinos, but spiritually they looked very different. The light of Jesus shone through them. Relieved and happy, we got in the van and drove off, praising the Lord. We were seeing our new country for the first time. The girls and Beau were immediately at ease. Our young driver explained, "Tonight is Ang Ligaya's Christmas Celebration, so, we will go there first and then to the home of your hosts."

An open-air auditorium of a Catholic girl's school was the site of the Christmas celebration. "Those native costumes are really authentic," I commented to Frank. "And the fine dancing and performances, are these really just members of the Community?"

The driver was proud of the professionalism of his fellow community members, as he assured me that the festivities were all done by the community.

"We couldn't have possibly had a better introduction to the culture," Frank added.

The Christmas celebration that first night also introduced us to people we would relate to for years to come. The program was followed by a time of fellowship and sharing. We met members of the Ang Ligaya Covenant Community.

Father Herb was there, "Welcome, Frank and Genie, and this must be Beau."

"I'm Sarah, this is Susanna, and our baby is Mary Magdalen," Sarah said, with not a trace of shyness.

"Well, I'm glad to meet you, Sarah. This is your host family, the Gamboas: Larry and Prissy, and Ianee and J.B., their children.

"Well, we hope you have a wonderful time in Manila. Everything is ready for you at our house," Larry offered.

Our early days in Manila would remind us of Mexico, and of the United States, and yet more than anything would make us feel that we really were in Asia, a very new and different part of the world. Beau quickly made several friends among the young single men. It was good to be here.

126

I was tired, but content. When we arrived at Prissy's, I realized how generous the Gamboas were being. The house was decorated for Christmas. They had welcomed our family, strangers, into their home during the holidays. The house was large and we were given our own room with a bath. "Thank you, Lord," I sighed happily, "I always underestimate your provision for us."

The next day, Frank met with Father Herb and the leaders, and we toured the community offices. We were surprised that almost everyone spoke English. Almost everyone in the Philippines speaks at least three languages! English was the language of academics and commerce.

I would never advise anyone to try to do all of your Christmas shopping at a market in Manila on the twenty-third of December. The crowds were horrendous. I came home with the biggest headache in history. And while the markets of Mexico City, and the crowds of New York, were part of my experience, nothing could match these crowds. I had shopped for so little, but it was a big effort. We had a very simple Christmas that year. We made a paper Christmas tree in our room and bought a folding manger scene. A little tinsel, and a lot of love, sufficed for our décor. As usual, the Lord Jesus did His part to make our celebration of His birth special.

We were about to turn in for the night on Christmas Eve, when Sarah, then five, said, "All I want for Christmas is one of those fans like the ladies here use. Those are so pretty, and then I could fan myself when it gets hot." I hugged her and kissed her, "We'll have a very nice Christmas." We said our prayers and the little girls promptly fell asleep. I curled up next to Frank, crying softly. "What's wrong, Babe?" he asked, concerned.

"I just feel bad about Christmas, that's all. I know it's the Spirit that counts, and I want more than anything for our celebration to be Holy, but it was so hard this year, being in a strange place and everything. I could have so easily gotten Sarah one of those fans, if I had known. Now it's too late, everything is closed."

"Once she sees her other things she'll be happy, don't worry, trust the Lord!" Frank kissed me goodnight.

The next morning we sang Happy Birthday to Jesus. We had our prayer time, reading together the Christmas story from the scriptures. The peace of the Lord settled on us, and then we exchanged gifts. Frank was right, the children were happy. A doctor in the community, who had only met us briefly, had sent over some gifts for the children and we opened these last. Sarah's gift was one of those fans she had asked for! She danced around fanning herself gleefully, "You see Mama, I did get one. I asked Jesus for one, and I did get one. Thank you, Lord! Thank you, Lord!"

Our stay in Manila lasted almost three weeks; procuring resident visas took a lot of time. The Lord kept us busy though. We were invited to give our testimony on a television program called "*Sharing in the City*! We sang, "Praise the Name of Jesus," and talked for fifteen minutes. That video was aired twice during Christmas week in a city of five million people. A week in Asia, and we were already sharing the works God had done in our lives with millions in this nation.

We decided to go to the Island of Mindanao by boat. It was cheaper. Boat travel gave a better understanding of this nation of islands. Many Filipinos call their country "the broken rosary" because it is full of so many small islands, like rosary beads, especially in the central Visayas region.

"In some ways," Beau later remarked, "a journey through this area reminds one of the Mediterranean world where Christian missionary efforts began." Small boats on short voyages, and small sea-going fishing vessels passed near our passenger ship many times. Right away, we had chances to share about Jesus. Frank witnessed to a Muslim. The man was seriously interested, "What are you all about? You are the only Americans on this boat, your family is obviously happy and in good order."

"We are 'about' Jesus, about His Gospel; we are missionaries in the Catholic Church."

"What do you believe about Jesus Christ?" he asked pointedly. Frank felt a tremendous amount of grace and was able to witness and dialog with him for several hours. From the moment we set foot in the Philippines we were fully occupied in sharing the Gospel!

Frank celebrated his thirty-ninth birthday on the boat. It was January 9, 1982. The Lord's gift to him was this mission to the Philippines. More than we could ask or imagine was waiting for us. The Filipinos were prepared to hear the Word of the Lord. They were Catholic, by and large, and appreciated our faith. Their country was being torn by strife and injustice. At times, they lived in fear of losing their lives and property. Rumors of guerrilla activity and brewing attacks abounded. In their difficulties, they turned to the Lord.

Back in Manila, at the American Embassy, we had been told they were recommending that Americans NOT travel to Mindanao. The embassy's diplomatic advisory was part of our prayers for guidance. But in prayer, we heard God say, "Go! I am sending you to Mindanao." Once we heard Him clearly, we were not afraid.

A Charismatic Community, *Kahayag Sa Dios,* was based in Cagayan de Oro, the port city closest to Malaybalay. Families from *Kahayag* were waiting on the dock with welcome posters. The Summers family was accepted and loved already. God's world is small and He connects the dots for us. The Lord Jesus was leading us in the path He had chosen. Jun and Alma Messina opened their home to us, not only on that first arrival, but also throughout our entire years of mission there. We marveled, time after time, at their self-sacrificing love. They served us with servants' hearts. Before we went up to Malaybalay, we attended a *Kahayag* assembly in Cagayan. Seeing their commitment and exuberant joy, gave us hope that the same move of the Spirit would happen in Malaybalay.

We met with the Archbishop of the Diocese of Cagayan, Archbishop Cronin and another Bishop from an adjoining Diocese. They invited us to stay and work in their Dioceses but we were in a hurry to arrive at our destination. "Isn't it amazing, Frank, how often we pass through a Diocese and, even though they have never seen us or heard of a missionary family, the Bishops will invite us to work with them?"

"Genie, the need is always so great, and no one ever knows it better than the Bishop," Frank commented after the generous invitation to serve in Cagayan.

Jun took us to the bus station in Cagayan de Oro and helped us board the bus that would bring us to Malaybalay. Public buses, then, were like school buses, but not in as good condition as American school buses. Some of the buses had no window glass. When it rained; wooden slats were pulled up and hooked in place. Malaybalay is about 60 kilometers (forty miles) from Cagayan. We would be climbing all the way. It was pouring down rain as we rolled out of the bus station. The bus was packed to capacity, with people, produce, chickens and pigs. We were only about ten miles out of town, when the bus broke down. I had been enjoying the scenery; the views were magnificent. The girls were riding on our laps. The bus had to turn around and go back to the station. Carrying girls and luggage, we traipsed across the mucky, muddy station to another bus. We spent about half an hour accommodating luggage, people, produce, pigs and chickens and the driver came in and tried to start the bus. Another half-hour of frustration, and by now my little girls were getting a bit restless.

"Why not just get out of the bus and call Jun, he said the roads weren't in good condition, he offered us his home. Couldn't we stay here until everything dries up a little? It's been two hours already and we still aren't on our way," I pleaded with Frank. I felt a little worried because now we would surely be traveling in the dark. Frank wouldn't consider a delay.

"We sent a message to Father Pacana that we'd be arriving today. I don't want them to wait," he explained.

So we unpacked the second bus, traipsed back across the quagmire of a parking lot and got into another bus, and another half-hour of accommodating people, produce, pigs and chickens. We were finally on our way! There was a break in the rain and the scenery was gorgeous. On the inside, I was struggling about taking this trip. I could tell the road wasn't all that good, and we'd been told that there was a very bad spot further up. I just kept saying, "I love you, Jesus. I love you, Lord. Bless our mission, Lord, Give me courage, already it seems hard."

Beau and the girls didn't seem to mind at all. They were at peace. Mary Magdalen, then, was seventeen months old, Susanna was three, and Sarah, five. Beau was seventeen. It started to rain again. This bus had the wooden slats. So we had to close up the windows. The smell of cigarette smoke, and the winding roads made Sarah carsick. We hadn't been able to sit together so we were all praying individually. I looked over at Frank. He had Sarah in her blanket, sleeping on his lap. There was a leak in the roof right above his head and it was dripping slowly on his head. I couldn't help but laugh, I thought, "Some people take their kids to Adventure Land in Disney World, but this is the real thing."

I began to quietly sing praises to the Lord, song after song; I needed to enter His courts, to be near Him. I needed to feel the consoling presence of the Holy Spirit. We did hit that bad spot in the road. A tractor had to tow the bus through the slick, thick mud to the more solid part of the road. ***Eight hours*** after we started in Cagayan, the bus rolled into Malaybalay. It had taken us eight hours to travel forty miles. The Lord had told us to go to the ends of the earth, after the eight-hour bus ride, I felt absolutely certain we were following His directions. People began getting off the bus at one stop after another.

"Where is the station?" I asked the lady who had shared the seat with me.

"I think there's a station at the end of the line."

"Oh, oh, she only *thinks* there is a station at the end of the line. I wonder what that could mean. She *lives* here and she doesn't know *if* there is a station."

The bus ground to a halt at the market on the far edge of town. It was the end of the line. We were the last ones left on the bus except for the driver. There was a little restaurant with benches in front of it - *that* was the station.

We unloaded our luggage, and put the girls on the benches; it was still raining and pitch dark except for one light bulb in the "restaurant". Frank went in to inquire about where we were, and how we could get in touch with Father Pacana. The little waitress didn't speak English. Everything was deserted; there was no traffic. We could tell we were a distance from the center of town.

Frank and Beau bowed their heads, "Lord, we've come to serve you. We're all wet and tired. We're hungry. We need your help. Please send someone to help us, and please Lord, let them speak English!" Beau had asked in faith, and as soon as they finished their prayer, a young boy in a jeep drove up to the house adjoining the bus stop.

"That's the answer to our prayer," Beau said as he dashed over to the jeep. We could hear him ask, "Do you speak English?"

We actually jumped for joy when the boy said, "Yes, I do. Can I help you?" Billy became one of our first friends in

131

Malaybalay. Frank explained to him our plight - that we needed a ride to get to Father Pacana.

He said, "I'd be happy to take you, just let me go and ask my Mom."

Billy drove us to the rectory, and then knocked quite a while at the door. Finally Father Pacana came down. He was all smiles, "Frank, I've been expecting you for weeks. I didn't know you'd arrive tonight." He had not gotten the message we sent from Cagayan. "Let's put your things in my jeep and we'll go check out the rent house we found for you. Let's see if it is ready. If not, don't worry, the landlord's family owns a hotel, and they've offered to put you up there for awhile."

We thanked Billy and got into Father's jeep. The house where we were to live was pitch dark and we knocked, and knocked to no avail. Father brought us to the center of town to the Balbon Hotel. It was more like a rooming house. But we were so warmly welcomed, they asked if we were hungry, and quickly they fixed us a delicious meal. Susanna, Sarah and Beau slept in one room, and Frank and Mary and I slept in another. I was so tired I slept through the entire night, but I woke up early the next morning to check on Susanna. I was heartbroken when I saw her. "Sweet Susanna, you have been eaten up by mosquitoes," I gasped. "I don't think there is a square inch on your body that doesn't have a red welt."

"Sarah and I are pretty eaten up too," Beau said sleepily. They looked so pitiful. The next night we used repellent and mosquito coils and that helped a bit.

The rent house was in good condition and well furnished. Roly, the husband, had been living there alone for a while; his wife was working away.

"It needs cleaning, but it is more than adequate for our needs," I said after our walk through.

"We better buy some mosquito nets, there are no screens," Beau noticed. No screens, no fridge, an outside bathroom, not at all like America, but in Malaybalay, it was a modest house – the place that the Lord had prepared for us. We were grateful.

Malaybalay is in a beautiful plateau surrounded by mountains, covered with lush tropical growth. The bamboo native huts are aesthetically appealing, dotting the landscape and adorning the productive farms. Orchids, Birds of Paradise, Impatiens, Hibiscus, and Night Jasmine grew in wild profusion. Shortly after our arrival, we were invited to a birthday party for the local Prosecuting Attorney along with Father Pacana. The food was magnificent. I can honestly say, Filipinos are the world's best cooks. They have an endless variety of their own dishes, and can imitate anything (spaghetti, caramel custard) and make it better than the original.

Father Pacana introduced us at the Masses the following Sunday, and let Frank tell the people why we had come. His words were met with smiles and nods of assent from the congregation. We met with the Bishop within a few days. Bishop Claver told us he had invited us because the Diocese was in real need of the spiritual renewal. Bishop Francisco Claver is famous for his teachings and writings on the issues of Social Justice. "We have put a great emphasis on the Social Justice aspect of the Gospel here in the Diocese, and I am concerned that the spiritual side of the ministry has suffered," he explained candidly. "Some of our priests are ready to take up arms! That's why I invited you to come, the emphasis on evangelization and renewal in the Holy Spirit will help to balance the situation."

Frank answered, "Thanks for inviting us, Bishop; I think evangelization will make a marked difference. The Word of God is alive and active; it will have a good effect."

"That's a great attitude, as far as I am concerned, the door for your ministry is open wide," Bishop Claver said as he visited with us over coffee and snacks.

Father Pacana took Frank to the newly formed core group of the Charismatic Renewal. He encouraged the leaders to allow Frank to help them in the development of the renewal in the Parish and the Diocese. He was very well received, and soon invitations were coming in from cities and villages for preaching, teaching and testimony.

The vast majority of the Filipinos are Catholic. There wasn't the same kind of division of Church and State that we experienced in the States. The contrary was true. The first important work the Lord called us to do was to give a Life in the Spirit Seminar to High School students, at the public school. Several of the team leaders were teachers, and God did a mighty work. The kids were happy to be praising the Lord, and Jesus filled them with the Holy Spirit. The Lord ignited one hundred forty-four flames, students with ready hearts, to go out and spread the Word to parents and friends, that they had found a Savior and friend in Jesus.

Frank's desire to preach and teach was fulfilled in Malaybalay. He wrote and delivered a variety of evangelization courses: on the spiritual gifts, on prayer, on family life, on Christian Manhood, and on service. Some evangelization teams are still using those course outlines and notes. Life in the Spirit Seminars given by us and others were continually offered in the Church.

The "Heights" group, later renamed, "The Good Shepherd Prayer Community", met in our home weekly. People invited us to come to their homes to begin prayerfully their celebrations of birthdays, anniversaries and other festivities. We often had two or three invitations for the same day. If there had been three or four more families like ourselves to evangelize and pray, there still would not have been enough of us to go around.

We were invited to give our testimony at the Rotary Club. Frank was really anointed, "The world offers nothing in comparison to what Jesus can give." During the question and answer period, there was a fair amount of skepticism and scoffing, but greater was the fruit borne.

As the Word of God took root in Malaybalay, many of the professionals, businessmen, and their wives became very active in the work of the Lord and the renewal of the Church. The sheer scope of our ministry and opportunities to serve the Lord as Lay Catholic Missionary Evangelists was unprecedented; we knew our work there had been ordained by God.

Beau, too, was involved in a lot of youth ministry. He got invited to give teachings and talks at different colleges around the province.

At Christmas time for several years, we had sent out a newsletter, but things were happening so fast that we decided to send out a monthly letter. We were anxious to get out the good news of the marvels and wonders our God was doing. We needed the support and prayers of our friends and loved ones – their partnership with our ministry was essential for the continuing challenge. We prayed one day for a name for our newsletter, and we got the scripture passage in the book of Jonah: "My prayer reached you in your holy temple...I, with resounding praise, will sacrifice to you." We called our newsletter - "*Resounding Praise*".

The Lord used our letter to make us more keenly aware that our mission must be supported by many. Writing it helped us to keep focusing on the awesome majesty of the Lord of Glory. (Now, in 2011 our current Family Missions Company newsletter has evolved to a publication called SERVE. Our friends in all 50 states, 5000 readers, write us and tell us that they enjoy receiving our news. Some say they copy our letter and send it out to their parishes or their Catholic schools. Other Christian publications have picked up articles written by us or our children, and reused them in their periodicals.)

Not many months after we arrived, Bishop Claver was transferred, and Bishop Guadencio Rosales was made the Ordinary of the Diocese. Bishop Rosales was wonderful to us. He spoke boldly in the name of Jesus, and yet was a quiet and gentle man. A follower of Charles de Foucauld, he believed that you should "proclaim the gospel with your life." Our friendship grew, and we enjoyed the mealtimes he spent with us in our home and outings with him to places he thought we would like. The Bishop appointed Frank as the spiritual director for sixteen young men in the minor seminary. Our children thought every family had a Bishop as one of their "*barkados*" – best friends. (Bishop Rosales is now Gaudencio Cardinal Rosales, the Archbishop of Manila, the Prince of the Church for all of the Philippines.)

Malaybalay, we soon discovered, was one of those places God hand selects to be sacred. In the early eighties, Bukidnon was still considered by the sophisticates in Manila as frontier country. They thought we had traveled to the boondocks. They were wrong. God loves the ends of the earth and the distant coastlands.

Our life there was so rich. The Holy Spirit had placed our ministry in Malaybalay, but we found a rich assortment of other works that had landed on the "frontier". We soon visited Nasuli, the Southern Filipino base of the Wycliffe Bible Translators and the Summer Institute of Linguistics. We had hoped for a bamboo house, and our friends suggested we see the

135

nice bamboo houses that some American bible translators occupied. Nasuli was so beautiful, and we counted it a great blessing to come to know and have fellowship with these other missionaries.

Frank met Hart Wiens, the director of the group, at a festival. Hart said, "Frank, why don't you and the family come to our Sunday evening service to share your testimony?"

"We will be there," Frank responded without hesitation.

Many of these SIL missionaries were delighted that the Lord had sent Catholic lay evangelists to the area to work for renewal of the Church. Our personal testimony places so much importance on the scriptures. The purpose of the missionary translators was to bring the scriptures to life in the languages of the peoples of the Philippines. In a way, our individual missions complemented one another. Our girls attended their mission base school once a week. The take-home lesson plans fit our lifestyle perfectly. Actually, the years of our girls study at the mission school in Nasuli set the tone for our future home schooling.

Pat and Joanne Cochraran, logistics administrators for the base, received our girls, Beau, or Frank for a meal once a week when the girls went for their schooling. Nasuli and its people were a place of respite and refreshment for us. Several holidays found us taking advantage of a rental bamboo house on their grounds, overlooking their crystal clear, spring-fed swimming pond.

The diocesan order of nuns, Missionary Congregation of Mary, and the R.V.M. nuns were both growing communities. The Lord really blessed me in my relationship with these holy women. They invited me to give retreats to their novices and even to the professed sisters. Their convent was always available to me, and I often took a few days off to make a private retreat. The quiet solitude of the convent was a good setting. My girls remember vividly the retreats each one of them had with me when I prepared them for their First Holy Communion.

One pretty day, I stood at the curb on the principal plaza, waiting for a motorella, (a mini-cab pulled by a motorcycle). A man next to me grinned at me with a great big grin. That was very unusual! Men rarely spoke to women they didn't know. There was something unique about this man; for one thing, he had a shirt made out of a flour sack and a cowl collar. He was glowing with happiness. "Did I just meet your son at church?" he asked.

"You probably did. I think my son, Beau, was going to the rectory today."

"I was very impressed with him, and I was thinking of coming to your house today, to talk to you and your husband. I'm Father Colombano, I'm a Benedictine."

I responded happily, "Anytime, Father, you can come right now, if you like."

We got on the motorella together. Father Colombano exuded enthusiasm as he laid out the Benedictines' hopes for a new monastery in the area near us. He chatted with Frank over coffee and cake, "Frank, I am so happy about our new monastery. We will build it outside the city, overlooking the countryside. We want to call it the Monastery of the Transfiguration."

"That's wonderful, Father," Frank responded.

"We were so blessed when the Bishop accepted our offer to come to Bukidnon. I love it here already," Father absolutely radiated joy.

The Benedictines would give the area yet another dimension of blessed spirituality. Our family made a donation to assist in the construction of their monastery, and wrote home and invited our supporters to contribute as well.

In March, I was chased by some dogs while walking to early morning Mass. I took a nasty fall and came back to the house feeling wiped out. I did not know that I might be pregnant. All day I had cramping and a little bleeding. I began to think, "If I am pregnant, then I might be threatening a miscarriage, and if I am pregnant, then I really don't want to lose this baby."

I prayed, "Lord, I want to keep and cherish whatever life you give to us. Please don't let me lose the baby."

The cramping stopped. I still am not sure if I was actually pregnant at the time. I was definitely pregnant by April. Frank was very supportive and we rejoiced together in the gift of life. "Each new baby is another rung on my career promotion ladder. After all, if my career is being a wife and mother, then a new baby means that those in High Places have noticed my capabilities. I'm moving up," I said to Frank, once I was sure I

137

was pregnant.

The Lord was changing us from glory to glory by His grace. The demands of the ministry were so challenging that we needed to have our lives in good order. Jesus worked in our hearts, too. We had to be more faithful than ever to our prayer, study, and sacramental life. There was a joyful, rhythmical goodness to our lives. We were able to budget our time and our finances well. Even when the cupboard seemed to be getting bare, our Filipino friends would arrive with gifts of food, we trusted and the Lord provided.

Far from the loved ones we had left back home, our children didn't have cousins, aunts, uncles or grandparents around to cuddle and care for them, but the Lord blessed us with "one hundred times as many" relatives. Close relationships developed with our neighbors and our friends, rapidly. Within a few months of our arrival, Malaybalay, Bukidnon was "home". Our life in this place, known to the world as a "trouble spot", was the most untroubled spot we had experienced in years.

The Ang Ligaya Community hosted a Bible Institute in Manila in the end of April 1982. We sought the Lord together and felt that Frank and Beau should attend. This was a big step for us; we had never been separated for three weeks before. It would mean that the children and I would be left behind on Mindanao (still plagued by guerrilla activity as well as brutal government counter-insurgency strikes). As a family of Americans we felt called to minister Jesus in a land where American involvement was a divisive issue. For better or worse, we lived across the street from the jail. When we first arrived, I felt ill at ease as I passed by the military police that manned the station. The machine guns were an unfamiliar and threatening sight to me.

Shortly after we got there, Beau started a ministry to the prisoners. "Mom, I can bring them soap, toothpaste and detergent. The police let me visit with them a little and evangelize them through the barred window."

"That's great son," I answered.

"I think I am slowly beginning to make friends with the police too," he said. One of the policemen, Melvin, was our next-door neighbor. His little daughter Zorabelle (nicknamed Crackers) was our daughters' best friend. He was into cock fighting and drinking, but was also very kind and constantly shared meals with us. The police even asked us if we would let the prisoners (the trustees) cut our grass and weed our garden for exercise. The prisoners were supervised in our yard by a policeman carrying his automatic weapon. The policemen often helped me carry my groceries into the house. Usually, they were standing outside the station and saw that I was overloaded with bags as I got out of the motorella, and they would rush over to bring my groceries into the house.

In Bukidnon, there was a constant stream of violent incidents involving the New Peoples Army (NPA) – the communist guerrillas that were spotted at times in groups of hundreds in the mountains nearby. One night, while Frank and Beau were still in Manila, I could hear a prisoner being beaten at the police station across the street. His tormentor was accusing him of being a member of the NPA, and he was crying and screaming at the top of his lungs. I could understand enough Visayan to know that he was calling on the mercy of God. It was horrible! I didn't know what to do, so in my bedroom, I cried out to the Lord! Finally, I awakened the young lady who was spending the night with me, and asked her if she could accompany me across the street to talk to the policeman.

She said, "You don't have to come at all, my brother is an investigator for the police. I'll go talk to them." She was gone for a few minutes, and praise be to Jesus, the beating and the screaming stopped. This was the first of many incidents, but because I was alone it seemed to be the scariest. A few nights later, I heard volleys and volleys of machine gun fire in the distance. I was sitting at the dining room table writing to Frank. I wondered if it was the beginning of the threatened massacre. I just went to the Lord in prayer and felt the immediate anointing of the Holy Spirit. I experienced a sublime peace and abandonment; our lives were in God's hands, where could we be safer?

The next morning early I discovered that the gunfire was only a signal that fire-trucks were needed in a certain area of town. There had been a very destructive fire, but no guerrilla activity. After that I never let the gunshots bother me. Frank and Beau were afforded countless opportunities to share the Word of God traveling to and participating in the Bible Institute.

The first leg of the journey was to the island Cebu. At a church in Cebu City, they gave their testimony to a prayer assembly of over two thousand people. In Manila, they became acquainted with those involved in evangelism throughout Asia - they made lasting friends that later opened the way for ministry in other Asian nations.

While Frank and I were apart, the Lord showed us just how much we strengthened one another; the great privilege living our family life was; and how much we were a *team* of missionaries. The girls and I took our afternoon walk down the country lane, which we called the "running road", because the girls could run ahead, out into the open spaces. We petted the calves and moved out of the way of the farmers who passed by riding their "*carabaos*" (water buffalo), headed for home after a hard day's work. We watched the giant fruit bats fly high overhead going out to raid some banana plantation; and we watched the sun go down behind Mt. Kitanglad. Those sunsets were spectacular. Their awesome beauty made us girls left at home lonesome, it wasn't the same without our Frank and Beau.

One morning while the guys were away, we were eating pancakes for breakfast. Sarah looked up at me and started crying. "What's wrong, sweetie?" I asked her.

I noticed that Sarah wasn't eating and asked her why. "I can't eat pancakes without Daddy," was the tearful reply.

I was feeling lonesome too, and I imagined she was too lonely to eat, still I asked her, "Why?"

She answered sincerely, "Because you never let me put enough syrup on them and Daddy always does!"

I had to laugh, she'd discovered another reason why families need to be together, and Sarah got a "Daddy-sized" portion of syrup that day. The girls and I made posters and hung yellow ribbons around our trees, and on our fence to welcome the guys home. Frank had done some thinking, "I made some decisions in Manila. With all the ministry, the food preparation, the care of the children and your current pregnancy, you should have a live-in helper."

"Wow, you did miss me," I teased.

"No, I'm serious, Babe, mission life should be a joy for you, too. You do more work than I could possibly do. You don't have any of the conveniences Americans take for granted, like washing machines, and hot water heaters," Frank continued.

"You're right," I said, "Not to mention, we don't have potable water (we had to boil all of our drinking and cooking water), 'instant foods', fast foods services, a dishwasher, a dryer, adequate closets, or an automobile for shopping, I'm glad God showed you that I really and truly need help."

We struggled at first with the new concept of having live-in helpers, but the enormous difference we soon discovered in my ability to cope, and be joyful in my role, convinced us of the rightness of our decision. We were able to help the families of our household helpers a great deal. There is no greater way to evangelize than to share your life, really live in the same house, with someone. We found our "House girls" coming to real conversion. Today, some of these girls have become evangelizers!

The incidents of torture and violence at the police station were reported. Frank, Beau, and our family continued to be positively involved with both the soldiers and the prisoners. Beau recalled later, "Mom, three men were shot the day I brought you an anniversary cake. I was right there."

A few blocks away, Earl Martin, who was a Mennonite missionary working with the Catholic Diocese, lived with his wife and kids. He had written a book titled *The Other Side* about his work in Vietnam and more or less open sympathy for the North Vietnamese cause. He and Beau often conversed and later corresponded. They both shared and argued a great deal. From that relationship, and his close ties to many conservative pro-American Christians, especially in Manila, Beau developed a series of talks titled "Jesus and Social Justice." He delivered these talks throughout the Diocese and in other parts of the Philippines.

In New Zealand, I had formed a group of women who met in prayer; we had called ourselves Our Lady's Group. In Malaybalay, I formed a group of women who met each week to pray, praise the Lord, and to use the study and sharing sheets Frank had prepared for growth in the Christian life. My friend Tita Mercado brought along her mother, Mrs. Estrada, and we usually had about eight to ten women present. We met in the rectory of the Cathedral parish. We called ourselves, "Our Lady's Group". We began spiritual warfare, and we studied about the Christian's call to serve. Everyone, especially Mrs. Estrada, wanted to respond with an immediate action. The ladies started a fund to buy medicines for indigent patients whose families could not afford medicines. Later it grew into a ministry of bringing cooked food to patients who had no one to provide their food. We also prayed diligently for God to raise men to positions of leadership in the work of the Lord in Bukidnon. We prayed extra hard for the husbands of the members of the group.

The Lord answered our prayers in a most surprising way. Tita was visiting her sister, Annie, in Cagayan de Oro one day and Tita talked to her about a lump in her breast that she had recently discovered. Annie became alarmed and insisted that Tita go directly to the doctor. The doctor was very concerned and scheduled the surgery as soon as her husband, Rudy, could come to be with her. They allowed Rudy to be in the operating room. The doctor began removing the lump and found that it was bigger than he had thought with several other smaller tumors connected to it. He said out loud to Rudy, "This doesn't look good."

Rudy told me later, "Right then and there, I said to the Lord, 'Lord, if you heal Tita, I'm your man!'"

Rudy was a man's man. He was very athletic, and a big man by Filipino standards. The Mercados had a lot of friends in the city, many of them businessmen. We had met most of them at the Rotary Club. Their friends showed real concern for her condition. Tita, with a lot of grace, confidence, and trust, asked us to come together with her family and friends and pray for healing. It was during these prayer meetings specifically that we could see the Lord moving in a powerful way among several couples. Their hearts were opened to hear the Word of the Lord, and to be introduced to the Charismatic renewal, now that Rudy was taking an active role in the prayers. There was some unexplained delay in the return of the results, and everyone was left in prayerful suspense. We had more and more prayer meetings.

Beau said during one of the meetings, "We have to pray not only for Tita to be healed, we have to pray for the lab specimen to be healed, too. Otherwise she might have to have a dangerous and unwanted surgery, and maybe even have to have chemotherapy."

Finally the results came in "negative" – no cancer! The rejoicing and gratitude was wonderful. A thanksgiving prayer meeting was held in the home of Tony and Ligaya Evangelista, who were already our social friends. They were happy and excited to agree to meet weekly, moving about from house to house among their group. Most of these people became involved in the core group and the leadership of the Renewal itself. Tita and Rudy, and Tony and Ligaya's group, now calling themselves the "Vine and the Branches" is still meeting weekly (29 years later).

Hunger to know the Lord, and more about His Word and His ways spread all through the diocese. We were invited to the farthest reaches of the state accessible by road, to teach and preach about Jesus and the powers of His Holy Spirit. We went, responding to the leading of God where others feared to go. In 1982, the parish priest in Kibawe invited us to come and spend a week, to give the annual teachers' retreat for the Catholic elementary and high school teachers. Later, we were to give the Life in the Spirit seminar to the entire parish. In Kibawe, a year before on April 13, 1981, Fr. Godofredo Alingal, Kibawe's Catholic pastor, had been shot to death as an act of political vengeance, shot for defending the rights of the poor farmers in his area. The murder had taken place in his rectory where our family was being housed! The bloodstains still showed in the hallway where he died. We were living in the residence of a modern martyr.

The whole town was still living in fear. Father asked us to assure him that all the sessions take place and finish by early evening. Kibawe's people did not want to be out on the streets late at night. They were usually closed into their houses by nine o'clock pm. At home in Malaybalay, preparing for our outreach to Kibawe, we had asked God for His help, "Jesus, since the violence, we know that the town of Kibawe is in bondage. Defeat their spiritual enemies. Pour out Your Spirit of freedom and love; expel the evil of fear and mistrust. Use our family to heal and restore their trust in you."

Although the first days of the retreat were rough, we could see the fruits of our labors in prayer. Beau worked with the youth, we gave the retreats to the teachers, and conferences to the whole congregation. Sarah, then six, gave her first

143

testimony in a parish church, and even our household helper, Farrah, gave a testimony.

One male teacher came to us with a lot of questions about the repentance talk. He said he thought the American churches were "forging ahead" on the issue of birth control and allowing American Catholics to prevent life in the marriage relationship. He said, "Your teaching, coupled by the fact that you are living what you believe (I was obviously pregnant for our fifth child) has shaken me up quite a bit. I really want a deep personal relationship with the Lord. I have been thinking that I am faithful to the Church. Yet, I always feel there is something keeping me back from receiving the fullness of God in my life." Then his shoulders slumped and he confessed, "My wife has been sterilized, with my consent and approval. What can I do now?"

I told him, "The Lord our God is a merciful God. You need to repent. If the doctors can't reverse the surgery, at least you can reverse your attitude."

Frank continued, "From now on, you can see in little children, the blessing of the Lord. Your change of heart can help others avoid a similar failure."

"Father is hearing confessions right now, take this opportunity and be totally honest!" I encouraged him. He did avail himself of the sacrament of penance, and he looked like a new creation when he came out of the confessional!

Several professors at the University in Musuan invited Beau to put on a week long "Crusade" on campus. A group of faculty wrote me a letter thanking us for lending them our son and declaring that they saw the "Crusade" as an enormous success. He spoke in different dormitories, fraternities and associations. Professors even invited him to preach about the Lord Jesus Christ in their regularly scheduled philosophy and history classes. God moved in wondrous ways and a strong youth group, radically committed, was empowered to carry on the ongoing evangelization. Beau received Christmas and birthday greetings for over 12 years from Marlene Trompeta, one of the youths they had prayed for during that Crusade. She had been healed, through prayer, of an inoperable brain tumor, and had miraculously gone on with her life.

Many older people who became aware of Beau's

ministry were far from seeking the Lord and the Sacraments, but they were being convinced by the repentant spirit they saw in their kids. Their kids' lives were changing. One retreat he gave was for one of the wealthiest families in the region. The Casanova family later became generous benefactors and supporters of his ministry to disadvantaged youth and college students.

During Lent, Liza Barretto, the bank president's secretary, invited us to give our testimony to the workers at a bank, *during banking hours*. All the chairs were rearranged to form an audience for our testimony. It was an unforgettable opportunity. The bank seemed to be the key to several future opportunities in our life and work there. Later, we were invited to give our testimony to the staff in the Governor of the Province of Bukidnon's office. We gave our testimony in the Province Treasurer's office, and in the Province Social Welfare office. As a result, many people in government offices joined the neighborhood Charismatic prayer groups and returned to the sacraments. A prayer group was even formed in the Capital Building.

Frank talked about the Lord with an executive of the bank, Rene Maagad, whenever he went in to do his banking business. Rene kept expressing an interest in the work we did, but hadn't attended any of the courses we gave. He told Frank that he and his neighbors would be interested in forming a small community and knowing more about the Lord. We had a full schedule. There was only one night when we were both available to start yet another group. We strongly felt the Holy Spirit urging us to give the introductory talk to the Life in the Spirit seminar to Rene and his wife and their neighbors. The three couples lived close together, Rene and Mer, Ben and Dada, and Pablo and Ida. Their backyards touched and they had developed a close relationship with each other.

Their houses were about a block and a half from ours. I had often walked in front of Ben and Dada's house, and had the sense that I should pray for the occupants of that particular house. A few months before, Frank had gone to hold a prayer meeting to pray for the healing of Pablo, Ben and Dada's neighbor, shortly after he suffered a stroke. Frank was invited weeks before by our friend, Tita Mercado (Ben's sister), to pray for Ben's daughter Beza, who had a serious illness she just couldn't shake. Beza recuperated, and Pablo made slow steady progress in the healing of the stroke, so the Lord had gone ahead and inserted our prayers and our ministry into the lives of these three families in a variety of ways.

The first evening that we gathered with the small neighborhood group, there were only the three couples, the Maagads, the Estradas and the Modequillos. They were disappointed that other neighbors had not come. Ben belonged to a movement called the Christian Life Communities, sponsored by the Jesuits. Other than that, they had no formal evangelization, although they were all "Sunday" Catholics. The Holy Spirit descended upon us that night, they were surprised by the gift of His presence. The Lord gave them more than they had asked or imagined.

"We would like to do the Life in the Spirit Seminar as a group," Ben announced as we said goodnight.

"Wasn't it great, tonight, Frank?" I asked, later, as we slipped into bed, "The best part for me was around the table this evening, eating Mer's delicious flan, laughing, talking and being friends. The love of God was upon us."

"That's true, tonight was out of the ordinary; something special was happening. It was tangible and it was real."

"Out of all of the things we are doing, tonight was so powerful and inviting, I can't wait to start the Seminar," I said.

As Frank and I took that short walk every Tuesday evening from our house to theirs, we looked forward to the time we would have together. "It is comforting to see them being obedient to the Word as they hear it," Frank said.

"I am so happy to have some deep friendships, and it's so neat that the Estradas and the Maagads have kids the age of ours," I said.

Before this small neighborhood group started, we had made many friends, but we really had missed the community aspect of our lives that we had enjoyed at Open Door. We longed to have friends in a more casual way - people we could be with "in the Lord" but on a social level, too. This was a group where we could bring some kind of structure to our fellowship. We started having Lord's Day Meals together; we ministered in the jail together on Sunday afternoon. We went on picnics together. God was building community. Only He could do it, it was our great joy to be a part of the process. We couldn't get enough of talking about Jesus and singing His praises together. Soon Rene played the guitar, too. We spent many an evening learning new songs. We sang and sang to the Lord. Dada and I were both expecting babies in December. We called our small community "The Servants of the Lord".

Frank formed an evangelization team, to reach out to different villages, and he was accompanied on various occasions by members of the Servants of the Lord and the Vine and the Branches. Frank's teams were a catalyst for the spread of the kingdom of God. Soon others were forming evangelization teams, too. One of the most effective groups was the Jesus in the Mountains team. It was like a tidal wave of evangelization.

As my due date approached, I participated less in the far out-reaches. Still, we always had the poor in and out of our home. Frail, little, and advanced in age, Ben and Tita's mom, Mrs. Estrada came for me almost every day to accompany her in soliciting funds for the indigent patients.

"I've been soliciting funds for years, Christmas is a good time to ask for help, people are more generous," she told me. I was impressed with her work, and people responded generously.

As Christmas approached, Beau, too, was busy soliciting funds for a statewide conference that the poorer youth would be able to attend. The devil put up many obstacles, there was a mix-up in reservations of the hall, funds were slow in coming in, and it looked like the whole conference might have to be called off. That would have been a terrible disappointment to the youth, because Mike Joseph and Gil Galeste had agreed to come down from Manila as guest speakers, and their time was a gift to Bukidnon.

Beau had spent a month in the Brotherhood in the Ang Ligaya Community. When he returned he told me, "I was impressed with the power of their life, their aggressive, adventurous, innovative and dominating focus on Christian manhood. They remind me of the real historical Jesus, He was a man, and he appealed to men."

"Did you get to minister with them?" I asked.

"It was great, I shared at their groups, and I told them about the ministry I was involved in here in Bukidnon. Honestly,

147

I think they were surprised that an eighteen year old could know so much about evangelism. They have never been around a missionary family before. I've been giving testimonies since I was in Samoa."

"So, are they coming to the conference you planned?"

"The Ang Ligaya community feels brave because they have an outreach to Cagayan de Oro, on the dangerous island of Mindanao. The very fact that *I* come and go from Manila and as a young American, and that I preach all over the Province, has them interested. They say they will come."

Beau learned a lot about confident prayer and fasting. He went on a three-day fast, and the floodgates of heaven were opened wide. The Casanovas donated whole meals for all the attendants of the conference; adult leaders pitched in and helped organize the chaperoning and the meals. The example of the Casanovas especially seemed to inspire generosity in others as well. Filipinos of many classes, several regions, and different political backgrounds collaborated in art, drama, and meals. Talks would cover spiritual growth and also justice issues. It has stayed with Beau all these years as a small example of what can be done, through Jesus, in developing nations. The American establishment, and other powerful forces, often consigned certain areas to a future of chaos and decay. But Jesus can mobilize His people for the future of their youth. The logistics for the State Youth Conference squared away, we could relax a little and wait for the coming of our new baby and the celebration of our Savior's birth. Every time Rudy Mercado saw me he said, "That baby's going to be born on **Christmas day**".

My due date was the twentieth. Dada's baby was born first, a beautiful baby girl, Carissa – she was a gift from God, and Frank was her Godfather. Carissa made us all the more ready to receive our little one. For once, I had really shopped ahead for Christmas. Everything was in good order for the blessed event!

Chapter Nine

S.P.E.S. – The Latin Word for Hope

Life had been so good since our friendship with the Servants of the Lord Community. It was our second Christmas in the Philippines. The weather was genuinely fine and the house was decked out in Christmas decor. The girls and I had made our own homemade ornaments AND Frank had made our "homemade" live tree. Real Christmas trees didn't grow in the Philippines then. Most people didn't have them with the exception of the more well off homes, which had artificial ones. Bukidnon, because of its mountains, had tall pine trees that had been planted years ago. The climate was hard on pines and they didn't reproduce. Still, a few community members had managed to cut off some pine tree branches. We tied them together with a rope, secured them in a bucket with some rocks -- the results, a beautiful evergreen tree.

A friend volunteered to be our midwife to attend our home birth. I was hoping to repeat the same wonderful experience that we had had with Susanna's birth. Our midwife was a member of the Good Shepherd Prayer Community. I had been receiving prenatal care from Dr. de la Cerna who was also a member of the Vine and the Branches. She had tried to convince me to have the baby in the hospital, but I was looking forward to having a home birth to welcome our little one right away. I wanted my darling little girls to be nearby and ready to receive their little brother or sister into their lives. We had picked out the names, Simon Peter for a boy, and Joanna Beverley for a girl. During my pregnancy, Beau expressed some foreboding about the delivery and suggested that a hospital might be better, and that I might need some kind of medical care in advance. I didn't think it was necessary; I felt well and had delivered at home before. Advent had been a holy season for us. Along with the Christmas tree we had prepared a more austere tree to decorate with Old Testament themed ornaments during Advent -- a Jesse tree. We made our own Jesse tree symbols, and traced salvation history and the promises of the coming Messiah. Lighting the candles on our Advent wreath, one candle at a time for four weeks, built up our anticipation. Our hearts were prepared to receive Jesus and also to receive our new baby in His name.

Light labor kept me awake most of the night on Christmas Eve. Rudy's prediction was coming true. It looked like our baby was going to be born on Christmas Day. WHAT A GLORIOUS PRIVILEGE! Even though the labor was not too strong, it was consistent. I remembered how fast our Mary Magdalen had been born. I didn't want to miss our early morning procession with baby Jesus, the Happy Birthday Jesus ceremony, and the opening of gifts. I woke the family at about six in the morning. After celebrating our traditional ceremonies, we had a leisurely breakfast. We advised the midwife that labor had started, but advised that we would let her know when it progressed to the point of needing her. Everyone was excited that I'd be giving birth on the Lord's Birthday. Frank went to 10:00 Mass, and took the children to the Baptism of Carissa afterward. It was hard to stay at home and think of all the fun they were having as a community, but I was trying to be at peace to prepare myself for a blessed birth and I was content to be praying. Soon Frank and the children came back with other people. They were downstairs in our living room. He was playing the guitar and singing with them.

Slowly, through the afternoon, my labor increased. The children would come upstairs periodically to look in and give me a kiss. The midwife and her companion kept checking dilation of my cervix. They advised me that I was fully dilated and that I could begin the delivery process, but things didn't go well. Finally, I called for Frank to come upstairs, "I'm not happy with the way things are going. I've been pushing for a while and now I'm worried about the baby. Please send Beau to get Dr. de la Cerna." We didn't have a phone or a car. I don't know how Beau got to town, but he found my doctor at a Christmas party. She and her husband came straight to the house.

The doctor arrived and checked me, "You are almost fully dilated, but not quite. You've been advised to push prematurely. Why don't we go to the hospital? I'll feel better. I think the conditions will be more sanitary, and I'll have more equipment available."

By then, concern for the baby overwhelmed me, "Do

you think my baby is alright?"

"I don't think there are any problems. I can hear the heartbeat, it sounds strong. I just prefer to deliver in the hospital," Dr. de la Cerna said comfortingly.

I loved my doctor as a doctor, but more than that, I loved her as a sister in Christ and as a friend. She had almost retired from delivering babies, but was happy to take me as a patient. I was relieved when she took over. It was a very rough ride to the hospital in a pick up. Frank rode in the back. The simple hospital was teeming with visitors, because it was Christmas night. I walked to the upstairs delivery room, with Frank on one arm and my friend, the midwife, on the other. By now, my labor was incredibly intense, and I had to stop every few steps to breathe through a contraction. Everyone was staring at me, most with pity and concern. "Babe, just be at peace. The Lord is with us," Frank reassured me.

Finally, I reached the delivery room. What I didn't know was the doctor had a deep concern for the safety of the baby. She had secretly prepared the operating room for a Cesarean section!

In the delivery room, the nurse said, "Climb up onto the delivery table." I was shocked. I said to the midwife, who was also a nurse, "That table is unbelievable; it's caked with blood from previous deliveries."

My doctor was out of the room. I looked desperately to the midwife and to Frank, "I cannot get up on that unsanitary sheet. Please ask them to change the sheet."

By now my emotions were at the breaking point and I was on the verge of tears. At home, everything had been made as clean and safe as weeks of preparation could make it and here things were worse than unsanitary.

"We used all of our clean sheets," the nurse answered. "It's been so busy here today."

I clung desperately to Frank and breathed through a contraction that brought with it the urge to push. "Oh God! Jesus please help me, the baby's coming!"

My friend, the midwife, who had worked in OB-GYN at the hospital before, ripped off the soiled sheet and opened a cabinet behind us. "Praise God," she said, "Here are some sterile gowns."

151

I almost cried with gratitude as she covered the table with two sterile doctor's scrub gowns. She and Frank helped me onto the table. Frank prayed in tongues, and then he leaned over me, clutching me with emotion. "Oh Jesus," he pleaded, "Bring the baby quickly!" Frank was aware that the operating room was being prepared.

They hadn't told me about the possible C-section. I had O negative blood. Asians don't have O negative blood. Now that I might have to have a section, Frank was worried that if I needed the surgery and needed blood, there would be none available!

The attending nurse called for the doctor, and my baby boy was delivered. As the doctor held him up, I could see a worried look cross her face. He was bluish and was crying, but very weakly. They thought the weakness was due to aspirated foreign matter, and put him on a table beside me, suctioning his lungs. I was worried, too. I could see him struggling for breath. It seemed to me he was too near an open window and would get chilled without any clothes on. They wheeled me down the hall to a semiprivate room. They were still working on the baby. After about an hour, they brought him to me in my room; he was connected by a tube to a fifty-pound oxygen bottle because the hospital didn't have incubators. He was pale and cold, but sleeping peacefully. It was about nine thirty at night. We looked at him. He was beautiful. I kept piling on the blankets and holding him close to me to warm him with my body, but I couldn't waken him so he could nurse. The doctor came in and told me not to worry; babies who have somewhat traumatic births often don't nurse right away. Putting a diaper on him, I had noticed he had undescended testicles. Again the doctor told me not to worry, this could be a temporary difficulty. I was very tired, and after our many visitors left, Frank and I praised the Lord for the new son He had given us on Christmas Day. We decided to hyphenate the name Simon-Peter, and add the middle name Emmanuel (God is with us) to commemorate his Christmas birth. Simon-Peter Emmanuel Summers – it was a wonderful name.

During my pregnancy, I had noticed less forceful movements of this baby compared to my other babies. Dada's baby in her womb was visibly a lot more active than mine had

152

been. Her stomach would leap and lunge with her baby's movements. I had hoped my baby's inactivity only meant that I was carrying the peaceful baby I was praying for. I awakened several times during the night; still the baby showed no interest in nursing. He was getting pinker and warmer, though, and this encouraged me. We had planned a Christmas lunch the day following Christmas with Hart and Ginny Weins, friends from Nasuli. Instead, they came to see me in the hospital.

The baby had opened his eyes, but was not very active at all. The Weins had a car. They offered to drive the baby and I home from the hospital. Ginny was a registered nurse. She held the baby and noticed his weakness. I was beginning to get worried. He didn't have a rooting reflex when I brushed his cheek with my finger.

"This is the most relaxed baby I've ever seen," I told her, trying to find the positive in our circumstances. When he lay unwrapped on his little back, his legs flopped out like a frog. He had muscle weakness in his neck, but I wanted to believe it was the twenty-four hour recovery from trauma that my doctor had told me it might be.

That night, December 26, 1982, a prayer group, the Good Shepherd Community, had scheduled their Christmas gathering. They came by and invited Frank and Beau to go. Frank, at first, was going to stay at home with the baby and me, but the girls were all in bed asleep. The leader suggested that Frank and Beau attend the prayer meeting; they could thank the Lord for our new son, and ask prayers for his good health. I wanted them to stay home, but I also wanted prayers for our baby.

He still hadn't nursed and the 24 hours were almost up. His little jaw hung open while he was asleep. My beautiful Simon-Peter was really weak. I reluctantly sent them off to the prayer meeting. I began to pray, really pour my heart out to the Lord. I was trying to keep fear and confusion at bay. As I was praying, I had a vision of Jesus's face crowned with thorns, with his lower jaw hanging down, just like Simon's was! I interpreted the vision to mean that this suffering, too, Jesus had taken with Him to the cross. He was in Simon. He was with me.

About an hour after they left for the prayer meeting, I heard a knock on the door downstairs. It was late, and I was puzzled. Who could it be? I went down and opened the door. It was Hart and Ginny Weins, and Dr. Steve Lynip. Steve was a doctor from the U. S. that served the Nasuli base of Wycliffe Bible translators. Steve and his family were friends of ours. I was surprised to find them at our door at that late hour. Because of the guerilla activity, everyone tried not to drive late in the evening on the highways. They could see the surprise in my face as I asked them to come in. Ginny looked straight at me and said, "Genie, when I got home, I couldn't stop thinking about the baby. When I held him, I tested his reflexes, and was pretty alarmed. I talked to Steve about it and he offered to come over this evening and examine the baby."

I could feel my heart sinking. Ginny was expressing out loud all the things I was fearing but unable to admit.

"Thank you for coming," I said, trying not to choke on my tears. "He's upstairs asleep. He's still not showing the slightest interest in nursing."

Once upstairs, I began telling Steve all about the difficulties we had experienced with the delivery and about how my doctor was trying to reassure me that the baby would be all right as soon as he got over what she termed as birth trauma.

"Ginny told me all about that, yet she felt that there was something bigger than that," Steve answered, determinedly. "Let me examine him."

It was like a bad dream; my heart was being stabbed by the reality that was sinking in. I could hardly even speak. Steve undressed the baby, and gave him one of the most thorough examinations I've ever seen done on a baby. He dropped the baby quickly, while still holding on to him; Simon-Peter did not flinch. Steve explained, "He has no Moro reflex. Most babies stretch out their limbs, shiver, and cry when dropped".

Each pronouncement was like a new stabbing pain.

"He has no sucking reflex; he has a high arched palate; he has undescended testicles and extra small genitals; he has total head lag, he can't lift his head at all," Steve laid him on his back and his extremely weak muscles let his little legs flop down. "He's very hypotonic (no muscle tone); there's something here more serious than birth trauma," Steve explained, "It's something genetic or congenital."

"What should we do? How long can he go without

nursing?" I managed to ask, without crying,

"Thirty-six hours. If he's not nursing by tomorrow morning, take him into the Baptist hospital. They have incubators and you'd be more comfortable in a private hospital. I have to fly to Malayasia in a day or two for a health conference, but Ginny will be back to check with you tomorrow," Steve told me. I wrapped the baby up again, and held him close to me. The pain I was experiencing penetrated to my bones, Simon-Peter, our precious baby, so sweet and innocent, with so much to fight against.

"How long will it be until Frank gets back?" I could tell that they hated to leave me alone with the bombshell that had just exploded into my life.

It took every ounce of my strength to answer them, "He shouldn't be too much longer, they said they wouldn't stay out too late tonight. The meeting is just two blocks away. Y'all better be going or I'll be worried about you if you're out on the highway too late. They're still spotting lots of guerillas in the area."

They kissed me good-bye and assured me of the help and prayers of all of our friends at Nasuli. I was happy to count on their prayers. I longed to be able to call on our friends at home, our families, to feel their love and support. I needed love and support so badly.

I cuddled little Simon-Peter in my arms. I rocked back and forth on the foot of my bed, sobbing softly. It seemed like forever until Frank and Beau got home. Frank was totally taken aback to arrive and find my face swollen from crying.

"What's wrong? The baby's still not nursing?"

I burst into tears again. It was all I could do to tell him the details of Steve's visit and the examination he had given the baby. "Dr. Lynip says that the baby has some serious problems. These problems have nothing to do with a difficult birth; in fact, maybe the birth was more difficult because the baby was so weak!" I cried some more, "He says that it is likely to be something that happened in the womb, or his problems could be genetic. He says if the baby is not nursing by thirty-six hours, we should admit him into the Baptist Hospital and begin feeding him by a gastro-intestinal tube. Thirty-six hours will be at eight-thirty tomorrow morning. Let's pray for his healing. I know

God can heal him!"

By now, Frank, Beau and I were cuddling together, the baby in the middle of us. "Lord Jesus, we have seen you do so much healing. We have been healed countless times. We know you can heal our Simon-Peter. Pour out your spirit upon him and make him whole. Help him to nurse normally tonight, so that we won't have to go back into the hospital tomorrow. Give us your peace and protection, Lord. Please Jesus, calm the storm in our hearts. Give us your love for our tiny baby, Lord. Send your Holy Spirit, Father, to strengthen us and unite us in this crisis. Come, Lord Jesus. Amen." I felt a little better after I prayed.

I awakened all through the night, trying to coax the baby to nurse, but to no avail. Finally, the dawn came and I felt like I was sitting on a time bomb. It was almost thirty-six hours, and our newborn baby had received no nourishment. One of the greatest joys in my life had been nursing my babies. I was stifling and battling panic that welled up inside of me.

Frank and I always react very differently in medical emergencies, and it had been a source of tension before. This time it was different. I was utterly helpless before the problem at hand. I needed to be one with Frank and one with God or I didn't think I could have survived. Frank wanted to check one more time with our doctor from town; her diagnosis of the problem had seemed so much easier to hear. He hadn't been there to talk to Steve, and I know he thought I was overreacting. He got up early and asked Dr. de la Cerna to come over to look at the baby, and to give her assessment of his problems.

It was sheer torture for me to wait for their arrival. Second by second, I agonized as those thirty-six hours ticked away. She brought a pediatrician from the hospital with her. Our Filipino doctor said, "I have no sense that he won't be alright later on. Still, I agree that, because the baby has taken no nourishment, he should be admitted to a hospital for tube feeding."

So thirty-six hours after Simon was born, I got dressed and was up and on my feet. I would have to dedicate myself to his constant care. He was admitted into Baptist Hospital, and a tube was installed for his feeding. They began by feeding him one ounce of breast milk every two hours together with fluids in an IV, which they inserted into his little leg to prevent him from becoming dehydrated. He didn't cry at all. He squeaked a little in pain, but he never cried. As the news of Simon's condition and our heartbreak spread, many, many of our friends came by to pray with us. Our helper and our friends in the Servants of the Lord took over our children and our home. Beau was in the middle of getting ready for the Youth Conference.

Simon's left arm and leg didn't move much at all. Tony and Ligaya, and Tita and Rudy and others were in our hospital room, which contained the incubator. We sang, "What a mighty God we serve, Oh what a mighty God we serve." Miraculously, Simon's left arm and leg starting moving to the rhythm of the music. We all praised God and thanked Him for this little sign that He was, indeed, a mighty God and in full control!

The nurse and I settled Simon in his incubator so that I could make a quick trip home. As I left Frank in charge, I said, "Frank, stay with him, I'm going home to get clothes for us and food, and the rest of the baby clothes. I also want to check on the children."

I hailed a motorella, and as I nimbly jumped up into the cab of it, I thought to myself, "It hasn't even been forty hours since I gave birth; taking care of me is the last thing on my mind." It was reassuring to see that the house was in good order. My good friend, Mer, was there. "Don't worry about home," she said confidently, "I'll see to Beau and the little girls."

I sobbed in her arms and felt sure of her motherly care for my family, "I praise Jesus for you, Mer. You are my true sister in the Lord!"

We were not in this alone. God had his saints and angels watching over us. In a most tangible way, His people, whom we had helped to form in His ways, were rallying to our side.

When I arrived back at the hospital, I was alarmed to find Simon beet-red in his incubator with his infusion infiltrating into his leg. "Frank, look how red he is. Look, the thermometer says 110 degrees Fahrenheit. Let's get him out of there!!" I flipped up the top of the incubator and picked up the baby. While I was gone, Frank admitted to calling the nurse because he was worried about Simon staying so warm, so the nurse suggested that a pencil be used to prop the incubator open. We called her back in and showed her how hot it had gotten.

She exclaimed, "It must be broken!"

There was too much happening at once; I didn't think it was medical incompetence. It was the devil who was attacking our baby, and time and time again, the Lord Jesus pulled him through.

Frank had recently written in our newsletter, "God ordains that we shall receive new life, and the servants of the Lord humbly accept the privilege of bearing that new life...So Satan opposes children: *'The dragon stood before the woman about to give birth, ready to devour her child when it should be born.'*" Frank's article continued, "'Behold, sons are a gift from the Lord; the fruit of the womb is a reward.' 'Whoever welcomes one such child for my sake welcomes me.'" (Rev. 12:4b; Psalm 127:3; Matt 18:5).

One woman had read that issue of our newsletter while she was *on the way to be sterilized* and had a change of heart. Others had also decided to be more open to receive children as blessings from the Lord. Our trial with Simon underscored our belief in these truths; no matter what, our baby was a blessing.

I had written in the same issue of *Resounding Praise*, "Sometimes I think children of missionaries are 'over-privileged' by the Lord. Their walk with Jesus begins when they are in the womb. Even in the womb our children experience the joys and trials of our life in mission. I can feel that the child I am expecting (to be born any day now – in this special season) is a child of Love – our love and God's love." How true those words turned out to be. If there is one word to describe Simon's mission and gift in life, it is the word "LOVE". His crisis and his life had already started to bind people together in the Love of God. Our tiny baby was prayed for and ministered to by scores of people, including three priests and the Bishop whose concerns for Simon were real.

However, on December 28, Simon was still not responding well to treatment. He had contracted pneumonia. Our friends, the Weins, came to check on the baby again while Dr. Lynip was out of town. He had advised the Weins to share his concern with us about the baby. Steve felt it would be wise to fly the baby to Cagayan de Oro, where Simon could be treated by a specialist. Our friends at Nasuli were offering the airlift free of charge. We prayed about it, and felt that we should go.

158

The Weins offered to take care of our other children, and the missionary plane picked us up right behind the hospital. As we were flying to the port city I said, "Frank, our God does supply all of our needs. I have often wondered what we would do in a terrible medical crisis."

"I think this qualifies as a crisis," Frank responded. I added, "Can you imagine, even an airplane is loaned to us."

The stay in the hospital in Cagayan was blessed but difficult. Although they did a great job there of caring for Simon, we were separated from Beau and the girls. Frank was able to go back to Malaybalay to check on the children and to participate in the youth conference with Beau. The conference was a great success. Frank was pleased.

Simon seemed to be getting a little stronger. Tube-fed with breast milk, he was gaining weight, and moving about a little more. He was also being healed of pneumonia. Our doctor, Doctor Kho, had studied medicine in the States. She advised, "You can take him home when we get two ounces of milk down him every two hours with an eyedropper or with a bottle." He still didn't have enough strength to suck at the breast.

The most difficult part of our trial was the mental anguish. We asked ourselves, "Why?" "What could have happened in the womb?" "What caused this?" "What is God saying in this?" "What does all this mean for our lives, for our mission?"

One unforgettable spiritual experience for me during our trial was the night we prayed the repentance rosary. Frank and I prayed a rosary, repenting of our every sin, our every faulty attitude, our every omission – all sin that we could possibly think of. On every bead, Frank said, "Heavenly Father, wash us whiter than snow."

I was never closer to Jesus than I was during the first few months of Simon's life. St. Peter says in his epistle, "He who has suffered in the flesh has broken with sin." In my suffering, I said to Jesus, "I have to cling very close to You, Lord. I want to avoid sin at all costs. I want to be near You and dialogue with You with a clear conscience." So, our repentance Rosary served to center us in the Lord.

Finally, we were able to bring Simon home. He never cried from hunger, so I had to set the alarm to wake up every two hours around the clock to try to get him to eat two ounces. The doctor told me to try to encourage him to suck from the bottle to develop his sucking, and then to feed him by medicine dropper what he wouldn't take from the bottle. He barely sucked a half-ounce. It was a time-consuming process. I was still expressing breast milk, then sterilizing the pump and the droppers and the bottles and the utensils to handle them with; the whole procedure took me about an hour and a half. Improper sterilizing risked amoebas. I was walking around utterly exhausted physically, emotionally battered, but leaning on Jesus.

The community continued to rally around us, and one of my sisters in the Lord said to me, "Your ability to keep on proclaiming the goodness of God, your joy and smiles, even when you are suffering, has taken away any doubt about the genuineness of your faith. I believe Simon-Peter's birth is building us into that community you've been talking about."

Bishop Rosales kept reminding us that the Lord had a plan, that it was no coincidence that Simon was born on Christmas day. Our flight out with him to save his life had been an opportunity to share in the mystery of the Holy Family's flight during the infancy of Jesus. Bishop Rosales honored us by baptizing Simon-Peter on January 9th in San Isidro Cathedral; this was the feast of the Baptism of the Lord, and his Daddy's birthday! Hundreds of people came to congratulate us, and it was truly a day of joy.

The trials were not over yet; Simon had several more setbacks. We fought desperately for his life, day in and day out for weeks. Then we had another emergency airlift out of Malaybalay. Finally, the specialist we were seeing talked honestly to us, "There are three possibilities: one – Simon has a condition which, once diagnosed, can be helped with treatment, and the sooner he begins, the better; two – Simon has an untreatable condition that, even if diagnosed, nothing can be done about it; three – Simon has a benign hypotonia which he will eventually outgrow. I cannot diagnose his condition, and the Philippines just does not have available the diagnostic tests you have available to you in the States. If you were Filipinos, I would tell you just to wait and see; but if I was you, and I had the resources to take my baby home to run tests, I would do it. In the case of possibility number one, if something could have been done, and you learned of it later, you'd always regret it."

It was a very convincing argument, and we entered into another family retreat to hear what the Lord wanted us to do. We had recently received a letter from our friend, Dr. Butch Bercier and his wife, Pat. They were keeping us, and Simon, in their daily prayers. Butch's letter encouraged us, "Keep up your faith and hope in the Lord, and trust in the motherly love of our Blessed Mother Mary. Simon-Peter Emmanuel Summers' initials, S.P.E.S., spell the Latin word for *hope*." We hadn't thought of that.

Beau said, "Hope was God's word to us. Simon comes to us as a harbinger of hope."

"This decision is mind boggling. I feel like my heart is being ravaged," I shared in our prayer.

"Me too," Frank said, "I love the work the Lord has given us here. But what's best for Simon? What is the Lord saying?"

Soon, we heard the Lord say, "For Simon's sake, give up this mission until I call you again."

Of course, the health and life of our baby was the most important thing. Still, it hurt us tremendously to give up a mission that was flourishing. Thinking of heading home, I was comforted to know that our families and friends were waiting.

In Manila, we readied to leave. Imagining arriving in Abbeville, with a *seriously ill baby*, Beau, and three young children, I panicked, "I don't think I can live in the abandoned school again, Frank. Simon needs so much care."

"Okay, let's phone Vince," he suggested. Calling from halfway around the world was a real challenge. Our night was their day. Frank got Vince at his house in the evening.

"Man, I'm glad you are coming home," Vince said, "And, by God's providence, we are fixing up a rent house right across the street from Open Door. We're working on it right now."

"No way," Frank said, "That's almost too good to be true."

"It's not big, very simple, but it'll be great for y'all."

S.P.E.S. – HOPE! With our biggest cross ever facing us, we would return to our friends and loved ones in Open Door Community with our precious Simon Peter in a spirit of hope.

161

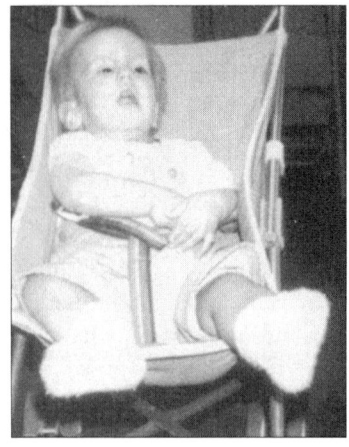

Simon-Peter has Prader-Wili Syndrome. He was born on the birthday of Jesus and has grown up loving Jesus and praying for the healing of others. He is almost thirty. He loves family, especially his god-children, Naomi and Michael.

Our prayer supporters with us and baby Simon while he was treated in Cagayan de Oro, Philippines. We were soon advised to return to the USA to seek a diagnosis.

Chapter Ten

Adding to Our Numbers

We had been so intent on our travel plans and getting Simon home to see the doctors that we boarded the flight unaware of the hurricane that was playing in the Pacific. We'd be in the air for almost a day before realizing we had to fly around and over the hurricane. Others had been aware of it and changed their flight plans, so our flight was under-booked. It was as though the plane had been cleared out for us. Each one of us got to stretch out in the empty seats on the airplane. Our mighty God was taking good care of us.

Our families met us at the airport. They were so excited to see us after our years away! They loved our sweet little Simon, and were happy to see Beau and the girls looking so well. We had gone forth strong, two years before. We were coming back to be strengthened by their love and care.

The new rent house near Open Door was simple and clean, newly renovated with surplus materials. Mom and Dad came to the rescue again with a houseful of furniture from their warehouse. The only thing we didn't have was a refrigerator. I desperately needed one. Simon never could nurse so he was on formula. He was three months old and still being fed with an eyedropper, but the milk had to be sterilized and put into baby bottles. I needed a refrigerator to keep the bottles.

My grandmother called me on the telephone, "Genie, I'm getting ready to buy a new refrigerator because my old one has been giving me trouble for years. It constantly leaks, and forms ice around the light bulb. I have to keep a mop near the refrigerator door. I feel bad about offering mine to you, but maybe you can find someone to fix it."

"I'll take it, Mommee. Thanks. Maybe the Lord will give me another one later."

Once the refrigerator was in our house, it really did keep

the milk cold, but Mommee had been right. "Look, this fridge is both a blessing and a nuisance. The water pours out onto the floor every time the door is opened," I said to Kay, when I showed her the old fridge.

"Vince says he's keeping his eye out for one arriving at the Christian Service Center, he gets one from time to time," she said hopefully.

One day I got desperate, and I laid hands on the refrigerator and prayed, "Lord Jesus, you've healed things for me before, please heal this refrigerator. I need to do so many things for Your glory, other than constantly mopping up after a leaky refrigerator. Thank you, Lord. Amen."

The refrigerator never leaked again, and didn't frost up on the inside again. My grandmother couldn't believe it. My Uncle Walter, who sometimes lived with her, couldn't believe it, either. Every time either one of them came by the house; they walked straight to the refrigerator to see the miracle again.

We took Simon to our family pediatrician, Dr. Ray Nunez. We decided to submit his case to our trusted family doctor first. He prescribed a barrage of tests. I remember the day I was on my knees in the blood lab of the Abbeville General Hospital unashamedly begging the Lord, "Jesus, help the technicians find Simon's veins." Simon's weak muscles made it difficult to find a vein. Once the tests were in, Dr. Nunez called Dr. Tardo, a pediatric neurosurgeon at Oschner Clinic in New Orleans. He described Simon's symptoms and conditions to her on the telephone.

Dr. Tardo immediately informed him, "Dr. Nunez, he has the classic symptoms of Prader-Wili Syndrome." Dr. Nunez answered, "I am not familiar with this diagnosis, can you fax me some information?"

As I read the faxed diagnosis complete with pictures of how Prader-Wili patients looked when they grew up, I was devastated. These precious children of God were short of stature, obese with an oddly shaped body, had slightly crossed eyes, domed shape heads, tented upper lips, small hands and feet, and a far off look. Our baby was a "floppy" baby, with no muscle tone. I could see that Simon had all of these traits, but he was still so tiny and new that they were not pronounced. Frank and I both had difficulty processing the path our boy would have to walk. I couldn't help but cry out to the Lord, "Oh please, Jesus, don't let it be that!"

This syndrome was manifested in two phases: in the first phase, the baby was hypotonic (very weak muscles) and not eating well, and in the second phase, the child never has the sense of being full, so he battles with constant hunger, will hide and scavenge for food, and with weak muscles cannot exercise well. Prader-Wili children become obese and suffer mental retardation, ranging from mild to severe. Simon is moderately retarded. The up side is that these kids are very friendly, and Simon-Peter today is a joyful lover of the people of God. Life without Simon would certainly be less full and happy. God has healed Simon of many problems; time and again we have seen Jesus take care of his special needs in a very special way, but He did not heal him of Prader-Wili. He did not heal him of the obsessive-compulsive behavior and intermittent episodes of aggression and temper. He has shown Frank and me that it doesn't matter what package our children are wrapped in; they are all unequivocal blessings.

While back in Abbeville seeking diagnosis and treatment for Simon, the Summers and the Listis seized an opportunity to visit the Alleluia Community in Augusta. Frank, the kids, and I were used to being off and running in an instant; however, Vince didn't like traveling much at all. We had an adventurous trip and arrived in the midst of a vibrant Covenant Community. The Lord had a lot to say to us, and we had come to listen. Once more, Frank and I felt the grace of God come upon us. We attended a community recreation evening. Families meandered over the grounds at Faith Village; having a lot of well ordered, good Christian fun – Christian community is not all work!

At Alleluia, prayer for Simon's healing was offered to us constantly. "Frank, I am really hoping for a miracle here," I said, "We've seen God heal Beau's broken arm in an instant here in Faith Village, Jennifer (my niece) was healed during noon prayer here."

"That's all true, but not all anointed places have a one hundred percent miracle quotient," Frank hugged me and smiled.

A question had been nagging me in the back of my mind. I found myself wondering as I flew back from the Philippines, "Would this have happened to Simon if we had not

165

been on mission in a developing nation? Was it the environment there in the Philippines that caused his problem?" On this visit to Alleluia, we met parents of children, about Simon's age, who had also suffered similar trials and difficulties.

Some of their handicaps were more serious than Simon's. The answer to my own question was that if we had lived, and delivered Simon in the United States, it would not have been necessarily a safer place for our baby than mission.

"Kay, the Lord is showing me that even in America and in a place where God's grace is working in such a remarkable way, there is no escaping the cross."

"I agree with that," she answered.

I continued, "He calls us to suffer. We just have to know that the cross is a blessing. No matter where we go, we must take up our cross!"

We gave our testimony on Sunday afternoon at the general community gathering. Our sharing was more powerful because of Simon's condition. Afterwards, the whole community prayed over us in tongues. God's Holy Spirit mystically healed and restored *me*. I had come to one of our family's fountains of grace, Alleluia Community, and I drank and was filled. The Listis went on to Florida and the Summers family returned to Abbeville.

Robert and Lorrie Fontana were living in the Open Door Community at that time, and Robert was serving as the youth director of St. Mary Magdalen Church. He invited Beau to be on the staff of the confirmation retreats, and there Beau became reacquainted with several young men. Some of his old friends from Abbeville were in the group, so Beau had preceded us on the bus from Alleluia Community to return for the activities of the group.

Modeling on the youth work he'd done in the Philippines, Beau invited these young men to participate in the Brotherhood of the Cross — a Christian fraternal organization he founded. He began by giving them a series of teachings, and encouraged them to share their lives socially, do service projects, and occasionally, celebrate the Lord's Day Meal. The Lord moved powerfully in their lives, and they began to evangelize others, too. The Brotherhood made a difference while it lasted. These guys would later serve in a variety of church ministries, as well as human endeavors in Up With People! The young men in the group were also generally successful in college, and in careers where they have become influential in Abbeville as well as the region. Doctors, lawyers, bank officers, account executives, and historians came out of their ranks.

Beau had long wanted to attend the local university. We could see that he was truly gifted as a missionary; we thought he would continue to love and serve in that ministry. He had explored the seminary in the Philippines, and we had thought he might attend the university in Cagayan de Oro with some of his Filipino buddies. Once he demonstrated a real desire to enroll in college, we fostered his desire, and advised him of risks and advantages, which would be somewhat different for him than they had been for us. Beau's decision to enter college at the University of Southwestern Louisiana was made about a week before the fall semester began. He had no high school diploma, and had received no real formal education since junior high. Essentially, he had no papers to hand in to the admissions office.

My friend, and former professor, Dr. Paul Nolan, told me, "Take Beau to see Pam Stroup in the office of the Dean of Humanities. Pam will be very helpful."

Pam has reminded me that our arrival was one of her first tasks in her new job. She visited with us, then said, "Obviously Beau is capable of college, but with no papers you are making a rather unique request. Beau will be admitted if he scores high enough on the ACT exam. The Admissions Department will be offering the ACT in a few days."

We left her office thinking, "The Lord will have to work fast!"

When we got home from our interview with Pam, Beau went to the library and took out a book on how to pass the ACT. We panicked when we saw the math, because Beau hadn't taken, or studied math since seventh grade, except for a single self directed foray into geometry. A junior high math teacher agreed to tutor Beau who has always learned quickly. He went into the ACT exam a little worried, but praying and trusting in the power of God. The Lord had shown, repeatedly, that we didn't need to worry about Beau's education. He, Himself, promised to educate Beau. We had trusted, now we would see. And see we did!

With the exception of math, Beau scored high enough for honors classes in all his subjects. Beau was exceptionally well prepared through his reading and mission life. His grades in college would vindicate him. He also took the advanced placement test in Spanish, and earned fifteen hours of credit through advanced placement. With an A in the next level course, he earned a minor in Spanish. We were truly grateful for his academic success, and felt upheld by the Lord. We had endured a lot of criticism for taking Beau out of school. My Daddy said he went to the country club one evening shortly after Beau started college to share Beau's high test scores.

Alvin, one of Dad's friends, said, "My grandson skipped a grade in school this year."

Daddy beamed proudly, "My grandson, Beau, just skipped ALL of high school! He just started USL without ever having *been* to high school! Bev and I are really proud of him."

The week after we got back from Alleluia, it was the feast of St. Clare. At Open Door, one of the members gave a beautiful teaching on the life of St. Clare, whose spirituality echoed with me. Later that night, I heard God say to me as I meditated on the life of St. Clare, "Surrender and trust."

I told Frank, "Jesus is planning something for us and he wants me to trustfully surrender."

"Then do it. He will show you what it is. Don't worry."

God didn't take long to answer the prayer of surrender. A few weeks later, I discovered that I was pregnant for our sixth child! Simon was only eight months old; these two would be the closest babies we'd had so far. I remembered my desire to have faith and trust! The girls were excited, and Beau always loved kids. We would be eight missionaries!

Right away, Frank said, "This is God's plan. This new baby will be a tremendous blessing and healing for us. I am going to pray for a strong healthy brother for Simon."

"I'm happy deep inside, but I am a little worried about being able to handle two babies at once," I said.

Simon made some progress, he was rolling across the floor, able to sit up if propped, saying a few words. His first words were, "Ah wah oo! – I love you." He still says those beautiful words to everyone he meets, and to *all of us, all day long*!

I was pondering the challenge of our growing family. I wanted to be up for the challenge, to be a good wife, a good mom, a good sister in the Lord to our friends, all the while hoping we could get back to the missions soon. "Lord, is our growing family a sign that we should abandon our call to mission? I know you would get me through another crisis with another baby; help me to be faithful. I'm not usually scared, but this time I am."

Shortly after I finished that prayer, a visitor arrived. A new friend of ours from New Iberia, Louisiana, Terry Boudreaux, was standing on our doorstep wearing cowboy boots and a million dollar smile. And was he animated! When we gave our testimony at the General Community gathering in Georgia, Terry just happened to be visiting too. He had taped our testimony on an audiocassette.

"Man," he told Frank, "it was so weird; here I am in Augusta, eight hundred miles from my home, and I was hit between the eyes with the testimony of a couple that lives twenty-six miles from my house!" Terry continued, "I told the Lord, 'You really blow my mind, Jesus. I gotta get to know that guy (Frank) better.' So here I am, and I brought the tape of your testimony. Y'all want to hear it?"

Frank and Terry listened to the tape while I did housework and stayed in hearing distance of the cassette recorder. When our testimony was over, they were about to turn off the tape. Suddenly, Dennis McBride's voice came on, asking the community to pray for us. From the tape, praises rang out! There in my humble home in Abbeville, listening to the Alleluia Community's prayers for us on the tape, a new anointing more powerful than I had experienced there in Augusta came over me. I felt like Jesus was behind me, pouring out His Holy Spirit on me and filling me with joy and peace. Tears of comfort and love spilled down my face. In that moment, I knew that this new child in my womb was a wondrous gift of love, not only for Frank and me and the older children, but especially for Simon-Peter. With spiritual insight, I knew that it was going to be a boy – a brother and companion for him.

"Genie, this son will be a strength for you," the Lord practically shouted at me, "He's my gift to you and to my Kingdom."

That fall, Frank and I and our children left Abbeville, visited and revisited Christian communities around the country, desiring to find a community that would accept us and nurture us in the call to missions. Open Door was clearly not being called to focus solely on mission support; God was calling them to serve the parish and Acadiana. While we pursued foreign missions, Open Door concentrated on parish families with a common goal – living by gospel values. Their vision was a good one and a gift to the local church.

In our heart of hearts, the Summers family still needed both – community and foreign lay missionary evangelization. As we set out on another cross country road trip, we had carefully considered our options and we really laid it all on the line – "Jesus, we need community in mission; we've been knocking, knocking, and knocking!"

We fully expected the door to open somewhere along the way in our planned trip AND it did! But not in the way we expected.

The Word of God Catholic Charismatic Covenant Community in Ann Arbor was our final planned destination. We had lots of friends there. In Ann Arbor, the Lord revealed to us what our next step would be. We met with our friend Ralph Martin, whom we had kept in contact with since first meeting him in Fiji. Ralph is a prophetic voice in the Church, an evangelist, and popular author. Frank and I recounted to him the marvelous ways the Lord had worked through us in the Philippines. Our mission had been proof of the efficacy of lay mission work.

Ralph listened intently and then suggested we consider going back to the Philippines, "Why not work toward the *building of community*, instead of searching for an existing one? It seems to me that you were already building community in the Philippines. By the way, did you all know that Fr. Herb Schneider, overall coordinator of the Ang Ligaya community in Manila, is here in Ann Arbor?"

"Fr. Herb – in Ann Arbor at the same time we are? That is not a coincidence. This sounds like Jesus has his hand in this," I said.

"Maybe we can talk with him," Frank offered.

"I'll try to put you in touch with each other. He will

170

have some insight to share with you," Ralph answered.

Fr. Herb advised us at a meeting later, "I feel strongly that Malaybalay is the place for you. You should return and continue the work you have begun there."

"Well, we do need community and Malaybalay needs and wants community," Frank said, "And Malaybalay has been our most blessed mission post."

"The youth conference that your son, Beau, produced there has been much talked about by Mike Joseph and Gil Galeste to others in the Ang Ligaya Community."

"I was caring for little Simon during the conference, Fr. Herb, but Beau told me how impressed Mike and Gil were with the couples' groups and evangelization teams in Bukidnon that have emerged from our ministry," I said.

"You see what one family can do. Filipino families in mission to Asia would be awesome. If we can do it, others can too," Frank continued, "I got the feeling when we first passed through the *Ang Ligaya Community* on our way to Malaybalay two years ago, that the community worried that we were heading out to frontier territory. Several people warned me that I was taking my family into a dangerous situation."

"We are still alive," I laughed. "Jesus sent us and He took care of us. We probably never would have left there if Simon had not needed medical attention."

"If the Lord calls you back, is Simon okay for the trip? How about your present pregnancy?" Father Herb asked.

"Father," Frank answered for me, "You can see in Genie's eyes a readiness to go back to the Philippines. She loves it there. I feel the same way. We will say 'Yes!' if we hear the Lord. If we do go, we will go out expecting great things."

"We have initiated a program that we developed called *'Couples for Christ'*. CFC is aimed at bringing the strength of the covenant communities to the parish level," Fr. Herb said.

"Yes, we've heard about it. It seems like a very good vehicle for community building," Frank said, "That program is already being exported with success to other nations. When we visited Akron, Ohio, CFC was getting started there."

Fr. Herb's proposition that we return to Malaybalay and build community seemed right; now we needed to bring that suggestion to prayer.

171

"Wouldn't it be great, Genie, to bring this CFC program, which has such good structure and format, to our friends who are hungering for community in Malaybalay?" Frank asked.

"I am ready if this is God's plan. Our mission there was so good," I answered, "So many people came to know Jesus, because He allowed us to be used as a family."

"When we left, I was content with what the Lord had done in our mission, but I had the thought that we could do more," Frank said.

Frank, the three girls, Simon and I drove back to Abbeville. I was five months pregnant, sleeping in the back of our station wagon at campgrounds, and cooking on our camp stove. Although our nights were crowded, our days were filled with fun. We had an eight track in the station wagon and it was new for us to have praise music in our vehicle. One of our favorite tapes was from the Maranatha singers. I loved their version of "In His Time." As I sang along I asked myself, "Is this God's time for us to go back to the Philippines?"

Just to show us that this was His time, God had a surprise waiting for us in Abbeville. When we returned from our trip, in our mailbox was a big envelope from the Philippines – an 8x10 photo of the Jesus in the Mountains evangelization team. It was so affirming to see them happily going out to spread God's word. The photo evoked in us a real homesickness – we were homesick for Malaybalay. Also, our small group, Servants of the Lord, had written with glowing reports of evangelizing more couples into their prayer community. All the groups we had initiated were still meeting regularly. Our work in Malaybalay had not just continued, but it had grown.

"It seems the Lord is quickly confirming the excitement we feel at the possibility of returning to missions and to hopefully build a community in Malaybalay that can serve as our mission home," I shared with our friends and families.

"It seems the Lord *is* calling you back, but we will miss you," one of the ladies in my Louisiana Our Lady's Group shared.

"Y'all just keep meeting, even if I am away. Remember where two or more of you are gathered in His name, Jesus is always there, too," I encouraged her.

We wrote to Bishop Rosales, asking him if he would like for us to come back to his diocese and serve the Lord using the Couples for Christ program. The Bishop's letter entreating us to return arrived in record time!

"I will be delighted to have you back. Your coming will be timely. The need for building community among families is pressing," he wrote.

Good-byes were harder this time. Our families and friends at home were concerned about my returning to the Philippines pregnant. We assured them, "We will be in Manila for our baby's birth – O negative blood is available there, just in case."

"There are lots of Americans and Europeans there, so there are people with Genie's blood type. We'll be cautious," Frank said, hugging my dad goodbye.

Beau would have to discontinue his studies at U S L if he wanted to accompany us. It was a hard decision for him, but he decided to come with us. Maybe he would study in the Philippines. Beau expressed it well in our December 1983 *Resounding Praise* newsletter, published right before we went back to the Philippines:

> *"Now, as we prepare to leave, I have mixed feelings: sorrow and sacrifice at leaving relatives, friends in Christ, a familiar campus, my beloved country, our active church parish, the gorgeous fields, marshes, swamps and towns of Louisiana, the 'Cajun' heritage which I enjoy and take pride in. That feeling is mixed with the joy and excitement of seeing again our brothers and sisters in the Philippines, the mighty blessing of Missionary Evangelism, the attraction of the Filipino people, their country and culture, and that certain assurance of God's grace and blessing, as we follow HIS PLAN and WILL. Yes, the events and circumstances of life vary, but Jesus is always faithful, just and true, and He loves us!"*

In no time at all, we were landing in Manila. As we deplaned, Sarah, Susanna and Mary looked like living porcelain dolls in a sea of Asians. My olive skin didn't set me apart so much, and being short with dark brown eyes and brown hair, I was often mistaken for a Filipina, a mistake I took as a compliment. Frank was tall and thin with a salt and pepper beard. All the children were strikingly blonde; Beau was clean cut and handsome. Sarah, at age eight, was my right hand girl. She was bright and energetic and took "charge" of keeping an eye on the rest of the kids. Susanna was bubbly, bouncy and determined. She and Sarah both have blue eyes. Mary has big, dreamy brown eyes (I call them calf eyes); she was quieter, more serious, but always loads of fun. Simon's blond hair was almost transparent, and he was beautiful. You had to look closely to see the traits of Prader-Wili syndrome; his handicap would definitely show more later in life. When we traveled together, wearing our wooden crosses, there was no doubt about our purpose. We were there in the name of Jesus.

The name of Jesus was being lifted up more and more in our adopted country. "Glory to God!" and "Jesus is Lord!" Neon signs atop two Filipino skyscrapers greeted us. Benito Aquino had been assassinated here in Manila since we flew out nine and a half months earlier. We didn't know how bad the conflict and guerilla war might be. We were happy to see that whatever the problems were, Filipinos were looking to Jesus Christ – that's the right place for solutions to these problems. We spent two weeks in Manila. The girls renewed acquaintances with their friends there and Beau restored his ties with Emmanuel House, the single men's brotherhood. Frank and my focus were on our preparation for a new stage of ministry. Leaders in The Ang Ligaya ng Panginoon Catholic Charismatic Covenant Community, developers of the Couples for Christ outreaches, enthusiastically shared with us the scope of the program. We met them in their offices, read over the materials, attended the Basic Christian Teaching Series in Manila, and visited established CFC household meetings. None of it was new to us. In fact, early on in our mission life we had outlined essentials for our family life together. Back when Sarah was a baby, we had decided we always wanted to:

1. Proclaim the Gospel boldly.
2. Build Christian Community.
3. Serve the Poor.

4. Live a radical Gospel life, trusting God to provide all of our needs – Gospel Poverty.
5. Live this life as faithful Catholics with our worship centered in the Eucharist.

By the grace of God, we had found success in living these principles and seeing them at work in our evangelistic missionary efforts. Couples for Christ incorporated these same essentials, and placed a great emphasis on evangelizing the whole family.

Our ministry's intrinsic power emerged from our own family life. In Malaybalay, and in all the places we have ministered, we saw the incredible impact of the work of a missionary family. Other families seriously wanted what we had.

Already, in the name of Jesus, in Tonga, in Samoa, in Mexico, in Colombia, in the USA, Canada, New Zealand and recently in Malaybalay, we had built couples groups, basic home groups, and fanned the small flame of the charismatic renewal into a roaring fire. Armed with zeal and hope, we boarded a flight from Manila to Cagayan de Oro. The Messinas, our Kahayag sa Dios brothers and sisters, met us at the airport. The next day, in two cars, we drove up to Malaybalay. The highway from Cagayan had been drastically improved, and we made good time. We piled out of the cars at Tita's store, and hugged her until I thought we might break her.

Several friends had offered to house us, and as Tita rattled off the list, she mentioned that Tony and Ligaya were inviting us to stay at La Montana, a small resort hotel that the Evangelista family owned and operated. La Montana was often the site of beautiful prayer meetings. We knew we would be at home with our dear friends. We stayed at the hotel ten days while we hunted daily for a house. According to some of our old neighbors, the house we had rented before wasn't available. We looked and looked for a house and were getting desperate. One day, Tony was driving us around on our house hunt, and we neared our old house.

Sarah said, "Let's drive by our old house just to see it. Maybe we'll see our best friend, Crackers."

Susanna piped in, "Yeah, I sure would like to see Crackers and our Tambis tree." (Tambis is a fruit tree common to the area that grows an unusual Filipino fruit.)

175

We spotted Crackers and got out of the car to talk to her. Our ex-landlord, Roly, came up to us and asked, "Don't you want to rent my house?" We were surprised.

"We heard it wasn't for rent," Frank said.

Roly responded, smiling, "Someone told my wife that you didn't want to rent it unless we put in automatic flush toilets."

"That's ridiculous," Frank answered, laughing, "We were very happy with the house as it was. Can we rent it?"

"It's yours!" Roly said, offering his hand to Frank.

I whirled Simon around and the girls jumped up and down for joy; so did Crackers.

Once we were back at the hotel that afternoon, Sarah said excitedly, "Since we landed in Manila, I have been asking Jesus to make our same house available! At first, I thought He was saying no, but He wasn't. He answered my prayer!"

Our story talks a lot about prayer; Our God is so busy answering our prayers that we saw our kids come to rely on answered prayer. Now their kids do, too.

Our old house became our home again. We were still across from the police station, still had a small yard and the Tambis tree. Our neighbors were glad that we had come back. A lot of the old ministry came right back, too. Frank was put in charge of the spiritual direction of sixteen seminarians and taught a class on Spiritual formation in the minor seminary. Again we were called on for prayers of healing, wakes, and special celebrations. Frank led a weekly Bible study for the leaders of the core group in the charismatic renewal. Our continued fellowship with the Vine and the Branches, and other small prayer communities was rewarding. We still grew in love with and ministered to the MCM sisters. Beau got right back into youth ministry with many opportunities to give days of recollection to college students and annual retreats for the seminarians and religious education majors. The girls went back into school at Nasuli, which was basically home schooling with one day a week in classroom studies.

Beau was so glad to see his friend, Fr. Joseph Stoeffel, a Jesuit, who was a fiery champion of the poor against an unjust political system, and one of his elderly confidants and role models. Beau so enjoyed Father Stoeffel's stories of the early years in Malaybalay. They both had such inquisitive minds. Father had translated large parts of the Bible and the liturgy into Chabacano, the Southernmost Filipino language group. He had founded several free newspapers and a radio station that were later shut down by the government because he used it to champion the cause of the poor. He also managed the recreational library for the Jesuit community. Fr. Stoeffel had celebrated the First Communion Masses of Susanna and Sarah. On his return Beau helped Fr. Stoffel in his battle with arthritis.

Fr. Stoeffel was an excellent sounding board for Beau who was trying to decide whether or not to return to the US to study. Beau was so close to all of us but especially felt the girls relied on him. He stayed focused on his ministry, but continued to feel the tug to study in the U.S.

The new parish priest, Fr. Dards, loved and supported our ministry. Fr. Pacana had been placed in charge of the Jesuit retreat house. He invited us to give talks to the retreatants from all over the diocese. Doors were still opened wide for the Lord's Word to go forth in power and we got really busy doing God's work right away.

Our main interest, however, was the introduction of the Couples for Christ program to the Servants of the Lord community. The Christian Life Program began with an introductory series called the Basic Christian Teaching Series. It was a thirteen-week course. We called the group together and explained the program; they were eager to begin. Rene and Mer, our dear friends and companions in the Lord, said, "Let's get started. We want to do this. We want to complete the series before you leave for the baby's birth in Manila."

Mer was so encouraging, she said, "Ever since we began to meet with y'all in the beginning, we all started living as a community. We love it. Now, with the Couples for Christ program, we will have tools to keep on. We don't want to lose this gift."

Our first series of talks were incredible. Frank gave a lot of prayer and time in preparation of the talks. He used the basic outline of the Couples for Christ program but enriched it with added insights from the scriptures, our personal experiences, and the teachings of the Church. I usually gave a testimony, using stories of God's power and endless miracles in my life. Of course, because we were who we were, evangelism and mission-mindedness were woven into the fabric of the newly formed CFC program from the outset.

Because I have a very rare blood type, O-negative, we went to Manila for two months to have the baby. Mac Bradshaw, a director in World Vision, and his wife, Rhoda, befriended us and helped us to find an apartment in their area. We had a lot in common; Mac and Rhoda were missionaries. Called by the Lord to the Ang Ligaya community, they decided to make their home in the Philippines. They had children Beau's age and two little adopted daughters, Marie and Michelle, who were the same age as our little girls. Not only that; their daughter, Jessie, had married another community member and they were expecting a baby about the same time we were. Rhoda drove Jessie and me to our OB-GYN appointments together because we shared the same doctor.

Daily Mass at the Carmelite Monastery, just a few blocks from our rented apartment in Manila, was a special treat for us. We had often wished to have a monastery of nuns praying for us, and once we were in their midst, they took our prayer needs to the Lord every day. Sr. Pastora, the external sister, became our close friend.

On the feast of St. Joseph the Worker, the priest who said Mass at the Monastery prayed the blessing for expectant mothers over me. When he asked what name we had chosen, we said "Joseph or Joanna."

"He's a boy, and I think he will be named Joseph and he will be the Pope one day!" I gushed. The baby felt like a boy, and the "Pope" part just made me smile.

I was worried that I would have to drive through Manila's intense traffic to get to the hospital, and I especially worried that I might be in labor for hours in Manila's infamous five o'clock traffic. Sure enough, it was five o'clock in the afternoon when we had to cross Manila to go to the hospital. I still can't explain it, but angels must have cleared the way; we arrived in record time. Our doctor was a wonderful Christian, but was not too supportive of allowing Dads in the delivery room. Frank had been with me at all of the children's births since Sarah, and I needed his confidence.

I prayed silently as I was about to deliver, "Please, Lord, let Dr. Neng change her mind and allow Frank in."

Frank didn't wait to be allowed in the delivery room, because he had convinced a nurse to let him don some scrubs and a surgical mask. I opened my eyes and looked up after I had a particularly strong contraction. There was Frank, his beard poking our from under the mask and his hands on my shoulders. He squeezed me and prayed, "Lord Jesus, let this baby be healthy and strong and keep up Genie's courage. Bless Neng, Lord, and all the staff attending us. Amen."

In a few minutes, our bouncing baby boy was born. As the doctor held him up, he was so gorgeous and fat. He had a beautiful nose and Frank's full lips. I sobbed with delight. He was perfect – Joseph Anthony weighed nine pounds and six ounces. He opened up his big eyes, and then opened his lungs with a healthy yell. They let me cuddle him awhile. After Simon's inability to cry, his baby yell was music to my ears. In two days we took him home. God had added a strong son and another little missionary to our numbers.

Three little faces were poking out of the apartment as we drove up with Joseph. This baby, like all of our babies, was the greatest event of the year. Sarah was such a great big sister; she inspired the others in their big sisterly role. All the girls had long hair and wore two ponytails, which always made them stand out at Mass. This day, their ponytails bobbed up and down as they ran to the car to greet us. The joy of Joseph's healthy birth was wonderful.

Beau saw him actually turn his head vigorously the day he was born. However, Beau would leave soon after we got home with Joseph. He had decided to study at the Franciscan University of Steubenville, which meant that he had to be back in Abbeville before the summer ended to procure many documents and take the high school equivalency test. Although USL had waived it, the University of Steubenville required it. He passed with flying colors. Before leaving us, he splurged with the last of his savings on ice cream outings for each member of the family and taught the girls and Simon to make tape-recorded "letters". He had stayed past his visa and past his exit visa window (which were usually frowned on by the Philippines immigration agents) while waiting for Joseph to be born.

179

As he walked out of the door with his bags packed, we all knew a new season had begun for him and for us. The thought of the vastness of our separation brought us all to tears. The wailing of the little girls was really heart wrenching. We entrusted Beau, our soldier for Christ, and his future to the Lord. The concern of his expired visa was not to be an issue. Beau used his charm and his faith in the Lord to whiz through immigration and fly away.

In June, we left Manila and retuned with our new baby to Malaybalay. The flight was uneventful. By now, the ride from the coast in Cagayan to the mountains had gotten even smoother; roads were paved and vehicles were better. The views on the drive up the mountains were breathtaking; I can never get enough of them. Our mountain home awaited us. What a blessing.

It was a few days before the feast of St. Anthony. Sarah and Susanna had both made their First Communion on the feast of St. Anthony; we wanted our little Joseph Anthony to be baptized on this feast, too. Our wish was granted. After the church ceremony, our home was filled with friends helping us to celebrate Joseph's Baptism; we had the opportunity to tell them about our time in Manila. Some stayed late and we shared news with them.

"Guess what? Vic and Agnes Gutierrez as Couples for Christ leaders have agreed to come and give the Marriage Enrichment Retreat. They hope that we can invite other couples."

There were about twenty couples on the marriage enrichment retreat, a great turnout for a first run. The Servants of the Lord were all present; we nicknamed ourselves Ben's Household and were the foundation of Couples for Christ in Mindanao. Later the Ang Buhing Pulong Covenant Community would be forged from these committed couples.

One day shortly after the retreat, Tita and I were having a coke together at our friend Pompey's snack shop.

"I know God wants us to build community in Malaybalay. I wish all of our friends would join," I said.

"If this is God's will," Tita said, "He will send others to join. Remember how small *Our Lady's Group* was when we started? Now we have so many faithful ladies."

She had hardly finished her comment, when a friend of hers walked in and asked, "Hey, Genie, when are you all going to start up another one of those couple teachings? My husband and I are really interested. Can anyone join?"

Tita was right; the Lord was in charge. After all, it was His work, not ours. "*Unless the Lord builds the house, they labor in vain who build it.*"

Frank and I still hoped that an identifiable missionary community would be the by-product of our time here. When that eluded us, we saw that God was saturating His work in Malaybalay with a missionary spirit. (Malaybalay today is a true hub of evangelistic outreaches of every sort.)

As soon as we surrendered the idea that the community we built would have to be labeled "missionary community", we realized that *all of it* was His work, not ours, and all heaven broke loose. Part of the dynamic of the Couples for Christ program was that each couple takes upon itself the responsibility for evangelizing another couple for the next teaching series. Our next series found seven more couples formally committing to building family in CFC. Our core couples joined their lives in a covenant relationship with one another and the Lord. Soon, there were thirteen couples in two households, Ben's household and Vic's household. In the next teaching series, fourteen more couples joined those thirteen! *Twenty-seven families!* The Holy Spirit was on the move. The subsequent series *doubled* the twenty-seven. As Dada and I looked on the new couples from the back of the room, we started counting.

"Can you believe it," I said, "This group is amazing."

She smiled warmly, "I know it Genie. God is moving so fast!"

The scripture verse that most characterizes what I saw happening in those days is, "*This is how all will know you are my disciples: your love for one another.*" We did love one another! From the outset, Ben's household loved being together in a deep walk with the Lord. All of the households reveled in committed Christian love.

"Frank, our core group is so phenomenal. When we present the teachings on hard gospel truths, they just feel called to greater fidelity," I said one Saturday after our Lord's Day Meal.

181

He responded, "I know. I am encouraged by the way we want to meet each other's needs – both spiritual and material. One of the things I marvel at is that we are able to offer and receive correction without bitterness. That's real unity."

Excitement permeated the spiritual atmosphere in Malaybalay. We prayed together; we played together; we reached out together. The men in one household united to build an outdoor bathroom for a family of ten who didn't have one! Generally, we were not a group that was rich in the things of this world, but we were rich people in the work of the Lord.

Our pastoral team grew to five exciting couples – Frank and Genie, Ben and Dada, Vic and Liza, Rene and Mer, and Max and Perry. We were accountable to the bishop and parish priests. We kept in touch with the CFC national pastoral team in Manila. Each small community had its own household head or leader. Besides meeting weekly in the homes of its members, the small households also gathered together regularly for teachings, days of recollection and retreats. Frank and I always made a strong point, as we taught, of reordering our priorities. Couples for Christ Community became our priority – its activities, meetings, and life-style all came under the Lordship of Jesus Christ. Strong Christian families embraced daily personal prayer, family prayer, and Scripture reading, husband-wife dialogue, Christian training of children, loyalty to the community, full participation in the life of the church parish, and the evangelization of other couples.

Most social and family events turned into community gatherings. If we adults loved each other, the children loved each other more. Their enthusiasm kept us faithful. Our children's ministry was beautiful. Birthdays and anniversaries and baptisms and weddings found the people of God celebrating. CFC sports days were great fun and geared to the whole family. Easter and Christmas festivities found us rejoicing together. The more we had of community, the more we wanted.

A lot of the activities took place in our home or in the homes of other members who lived nearby. Cracker's mom and dad, Melvin and Belen Valcorza, were our next-door neighbors. Not only did Crackers bring home daily reports of our family prayers, which she participated in, but she told her parents about some of the fun things we did, too.

Our casual friendship with Melvin Velcorza, a policeman, increased as the years wore on. Our girls were such good friends with his daughter, Crackers, that we celebrated with each other for the children's sake socially once in awhile. Finally, one day Frank asked Melvin to attend the Christian Life Program.

Today, when Melvin gives his testimony, he recalls, "I didn't want to accept, because I thought of myself as a 'bad boy', but I didn't know how to say 'no' to Frank. Besides I didn't know how to make up an excuse in English. I thought we were going to a birthday party and much to my surprise, I found myself saying 'yes!' But, it turns out that although I didn't know it, it was the Lord that had invited me through Frank."

What a thrill it was to me, one Saturday night a month after they attended the series, when I walked over to borrow something from the Valcorzas, they were happily having their Lord's Day Meal. It warmed my heart and I smiled to myself at the thought of how the Lord had worked in Melvin's life. He couldn't say "no," so the Lord had accepted his reluctant "yes" and blessed his family abundantly.

I recall saying "yes," the first time, which was tough. Psalm 127 says, "Behold, sons are a gift from the Lord; the fruit of the womb is a reward!" I remembered the concerns I had when I got pregnant for Joseph, but I needn't have worried. The Lord's plan is always perfect. Once Joseph and Simon began to relate to one another, I realized how meticulously well He had planned our family. Joseph's vigor and strength was an example and a challenge to Simon-Peter. Joseph crawled gingerly along. Simon tried hard to follow him. Simon would scrape and scoot, pausing intermittently to rest his head on the floor because his neck muscles were too weak to hold up his head for a long period of time. Joseph really loved Simon and kept urging him to join in the fun of moving around in the house. Because of Joseph, Simon gained strength and stayed more alert. I know Simon's life would have been very different if Joseph hadn't come along to call him on to victory over his serious physical weaknesses.

One day, our friends, the Benedictines, were having coffee with us in our living room. I put Joseph down outside on the back patio with his sisters and the helpers, kissed Simon on the forehead and went back into the house to attend to our guests. Suddenly from outside, I heard squeals of delight and shouts of joy, followed by a great round of applause. I ran to the back to find out what the rejoicing was all about. The little girls and the helpers had just seen Joseph walk for the first time. He walked back across the patio to me, and as I scooped him up into my arms, another round of applause broke out. As I hugged Joseph, I glanced down and saw in Simon's eyes the look that often wrenched my soul. It was a longing to be "one of the kids," to be able to do what everyone else could do. I returned to my guests.

In just minutes, there was another round of screaming, giggling and clapping. This time it rang out wildly from the back! I thought everyone out there had gone crazy. I rushed out and discovered that Simon-Peter had started walking, too! He and Joseph walked on the same day! Tears of happiness streamed down my face as I watched him walk to me. "Don't cry, Mom!" Simon said, as he flopped into my arms. We had been begging the Lord for Simon to walk. He was two-and-a-half. Miracles never cease; Simon and Joseph walked on the same day!!

The Lord kept surprising me with His ways of doing things. A charismatic religious nun, Sr. Annunciata, was stationed in Cagayan de Oro. We had invited her to come to Malaybalay to give a retreat to our community women on "The Call to Holiness." There was an unexplainable mix-up in the mail. Sr. Annunciata arrived to give our women their retreat on the *same day*, in the *same place*, and at the *same time* that I was scheduled to give a retreat on "The Call to Holiness" to a group of the novices and postulants of the Missionary Congregation of Mary. At first, it seemed as though one or other of the two retreats would need to be called off. Instead, Sr. Annunciata and I prayed about it and felt the Lord telling us that the two retreats could easily be combined.

In our prayer, Jesus said, "These talks will strengthen the faith of the religious sisters when they hear a nun teach wives and mothers about holiness and it will strengthen the wives and mothers to hear a wife and mother teach nuns about the call to holiness. I, Jesus, was not *mixed up* about the retreat. I have planned it this way all along."

184

God moved at that retreat among us in an unforgettable way. We held discussions after each talk in small groups in our distinctive communities. Then we gathered at the end of the day to share our experience of God's love.

One of the postulants shared powerfully, "It makes no difference if you are a wife or a nun. The true Christian vocation is holiness!"

A wife and mom commented, "Women of different vocations are called to the same holiness – we find it in submission of our lives to the Lord in the authority He has designated for each of us. We can submit to the Divine Plan, eagerly partaking of His grace as He pours out on us a 'hunger and thirst' for holiness."

Wives and nuns, filled with the Holy Spirit at the same exact retreat. Only the Lord would plan that.

Perhaps the most wonderful way the Lord "built His house" for us in Malaybalay was the effect of our mission in the whole life of the diocese. When the laity get their act together enough to live the gospel in community, when the laity decide that they want holiness – be they many or few – it will make an immeasurable difference. Bishop Claver's invitation to us to be instruments of spiritual renewal had borne fruit abundantly. The Diocese of Malaybalay in those days was pulsating with evangelistic zeal. The tension and desire to "take up arms" had faded away. Instead, the faithful of the diocese, clergy and laity, wanted to "take up" holiness.

Beau leading the girls on a Caribou ride in 1981. Children make the best missionaries and the life of a child missionary is filled with opportunities to share Jesus, to love others, and to experience God's delight in treating us to the wonders of the culture where we bring His light to a world that waits.

Beau, in his Sophomore year at FUS in Ohio. (Right) Beau with Genie in front of our home in the Philippines in May of 1985. He had come home for a visit and spent a busy month preaching and sharing God's Word and enjoying his younger brothers and sisters.

Chapter Eleven

Unless The Grain of Wheat Falls

The women of *Kahayag sa Dios* Community had invited me to be the speaker at retreat in Cagayan de Oro, which means the city of Golden Friendship. It was a rare time for me to get away and enjoy the fellowship of these wonderful sisters in the Lord. While I was down the mountain and close to a telephone, I called my mother in the United States. About halfway through the conversation, she said, "You must be so happy that Beau's coming to visit you in the Philippines."

I could hardly believe my ears. I burst into tears.

"You didn't know?" my mom inquired.

"No! We hadn't received any word at all. Are you sure?" I replied.

"I think he already has his ticket. He'll be coming down at the end of May and staying about a month. I'm sure that's what he told me, but I'm not sure if those are still his plans."

I was deliriously happy! I couldn't wait to get back up to Malaybalay to tell Frank and the children. Frank and I were so excited; it had been over a year since we had seen him.

His little sisters almost drove me crazy in the weeks before his arrival, counting not only days, but the hours as well. "Beau'll be here in just six days and eight and a half hours.... Right, Mom?"

At the Cagayan airport, Beau gingerly loped off his

flight and hurried over to the biggest family hug imaginable. We had a lot of catching up to do. We didn't want to share Beau with anyone at first, so we planned a family vacation on another island for the first week or so of his visit. Camiguin Island was known as the "Paradise Island." An active volcano, which had last erupted in the 1960's, sat in the middle of the island. The trip took us about ten hours: by bus, by jeepney, and then by boat. My friend, Merced, had arranged for us to meet Fr. Tex. He was the pastor of the principal church on Camiguin. He wasn't there when we arrived, so Beau and the two helpers, Tessie and Inday, stayed with the children at the rectory while Frank and I set out and found hotel accommodations.

In Malaybalay, before our vacation began, while we prayed about where to go, I had had a vision of a place on the beach with a number of flagpoles, flying unfamiliar flags. I wondered if this was a symbolic vision – God letting me know we would find the place He had in mind. In those days, there were no cell phones, faxes, or email. We arrived at a "hotel". The setting was perfect, it was right for our budget, and it was primitive and native. We decided to take two bamboo huts, on a grassy lawn under some coconut trees, right on the beach. The small huts each had two bedrooms, bath, kitchenette, and a front porch.

Lula, the hotel owner said, "This price is especially *reasonable* for you. I am giving you a good deal because you are missionaries in the Catholic Church. I always have Protestant missionaries staying with me, but not Catholic missionary families. I'm Catholic, so I want to take good care of your family."

Frank and I smiled and thanked her profusely. "You will like it here," she said, "Included in the price, are five meals a day for each person and two snacks a day will be served to you in your huts."

"We'll go get the kids at church and be back soon. Thank you," I said. It couldn't have been a more beautiful setting, totally fulfilling our desire to be able to enjoy God's creation and one another.

As the owner walked us over to the dining room to show us the facilities, I stopped **DEAD IN MY TRACKS!!** There in front of the dining room were numerous flagpoles, placed exactly the way I'd seen them in the vision. "What are all those flagpoles used for?" I almost gasped.

"We have a Boy Scout convention here every year for the troops from all over Mindanao, and each troop brings its Provincial flag."

Frank looked at me and I asked him, "Do you remember the vision?"

"Yes, I do," he said, squeezing my hand, "I guess the Lord wanted us to know that this was the place He had prepared for us. With the Lord as our travel agent we can't go wrong!"

Everyone in the family loved our vacation home. We unpacked just in time to watch a spectacular sunset from our porch before heading over to the dining room for a nice meal of exceptionally fresh fish.

It was a once-in-a-lifetime vacation. We couldn't thank the Lord enough. We decided to have a family retreat. We had longed to be united again in prayer and to hear Jesus while we were together. Some think that a vacation is a time to pray less, but we've found just the opposite to be true. Dedicating yourself to more prayer lets the Lord in on the fun; that way it's more fun than ever!

Camiguin Island deserved its nickname – it was truly a "Paradise Island." We were together again and blessed by the sun, the water, the comfort of the bamboo huts, the food, the coconuts, the fresh fish, the colorful fishing boats, the peaceful water buffalos working the rice fields in the distance, the magnificent sunsets, the balmy nights with moonlight reflecting on the water, and a constant refreshing sea breeze rustling the glossy leaves of the palm trees.

We had hours and hours of good, quality family time. We heard the Lord encourage us. At the same time, a very strong word came to us that was puzzling and even upsetting to Frank. It came to us over and over again in various ways. I had so often jokingly fantasized about God calling us to the beach in mission, that when I suggested that maybe the Lord was calling us to start a Couples for Christ Chapter on Camiguin, Beau quipped, "Oh sure, Mom, it wouldn't be hard for you to hear God call you to do that, would it?"

We laughed. Still, the word was unsettling and we interpreted it to mean various things. If God was going to do

189

something new, then the old had to fall into the ground and die. Beau suggested it might mean God would build a new base of support from the States, because he hoped to eventually gather people interested in mission on his return.

I reflected a bit, "I don't want to lose our precious days, worrying about what God wants to do later. Our whole family is together now. Let's enjoy it!"

Five days flew by. It was Sunday. We went into town for Mass. The old church was enormous, and it started filling up five minutes before Mass began. With our helpers, we occupied two pews. Fr. Tex was preaching a very inspiring homily when in the middle of everything, he began talking about us! "I want you all to notice the family that is here with us. They are lay apostles and missionaries. They dedicate their lives to the spreading of the Gospel, the building of God's kingdom, and serving families."

We were baffled; we went to Mass expecting none of this. Beau could see our surprise and whispered; "I forgot to tell y'all that I spent about an hour with Father telling him about our mission."

Father motioned to us, saying, "Mr. Summers, please, come forward and give your testimony. Share a few words with the congregation."

This was certainly something new; we had never been called out of the congregation at Sunday Mass before, without any notice, to address those present. Frank's testimony went very well and the people were open and even touched as he told of God's power to save marriages, and to restore them to fullness of life and love.

After Mass, Father Tex invited us over to the rectory for a snack. He then said, "Come and stay here for the remaining days of your visit here. You wouldn't have to pay for a hotel. We'd give you free room and board. Also, could you give some of your marriage courses to several couples I am working with?"

"Thank you, Father. But, none of us want to cut our vacation short. Our time in Malaybalay has been really intense. We truly need a few more days of just plain rest," Frank answered.

Father Tex was so insistent, that we finally agreed to add two more days to our planned vacation. "That way we can give a short marriage course to the couples you have in mind, and to any others you care to invite," we told him.

Our two days in the rectory were fun, too. We met lots of good Christians who visited Fr. Tex on Camiguin. The course was well attended and well received. We ended the course with a covered dish Lord's Day Meal. At our last meal with him, Father said, "I am inviting you to seriously consider living and ministering in my parish. Some of the couples are already looking for housing for you. Everyone hopes that your family will come back to stay."

When we got back home to Malaybalay, Rene said half teasing, "We have been praying that you would come back. We were afraid that you would like Camiguin and stay!"

Frank laughed and said, "You just don't know how close we came to staying there, preaching the Gospel, eating all the coconuts we wanted and swimming every day. But we came back because we love you too much to leave you!"

Pablo laughed so hard it was contagious. Pablo loved the beach and knew that Frank's joke had a lot of truth in it!

Beau had always been mature for his age, but he had grown into a full-fledged man in the year away from us. He celebrated his twenty-first birthday with us during that visit. We were glad we had taken the time to be together at the beach because Beau's calendar really began to fill up! He had decided, however, that his main priority was to spend time with us and to minister in whatever way we desired to use him in the community. I don't think I ever saw Frank and Beau happier together than the time Beau preached the principal address at the Community's Men's Breakfast.

Beau was then invited to the different households, where he taught on the importance of vigorous praise and worship. Praising Jesus is essential to achieving fruitful household meetings. Newcomers to the community were set on fire in their praise and worship after he shared his teachings.

Before he left again to return to the United States, Beau told us, "Dad and Mom, it's easier to leave because I can see how happy you are. In so many places, we've laid the foundation, but here the Lord has built the house. God has used you to build a real community. I think God's work among His people here in the community is as good as I've seen anywhere. They are

191

committed, faithful and eager to abandon themselves to Jesus, and you've got such a wonderful cross-section of people. I am very impressed at how much the Lord has done in a year. It's truly amazing."

It was hard to let him go again, but I didn't want to be selfish. I had begged the Lord to send Beau to us on a visit, and He had. I was determined to be grateful and satisfied. Our good-byes were calmer – we would trust God, even if we were apart.

Several months earlier, Frank had been invited to fly to Manila to discuss, in conjunction with another missionary organization, the possibility of building a school of evangelization in or near Malaybalay. They were considering funding such a project. During his visit to Manila, Frank also reported to Fr. Herb, Vic Gutierrez and Raul Sarceda, then the national director of Couples for Christ, about the growth and progress of the Couples for Christ community in Malaybalay. He tried to encourage them to become more involved with the work in Bukidnon.

As he explored the prospect of this school of evangelism, Frank made several trips to Manila.

On one of these trips, he visited again with Raul. Raul told Frank, "Ang Ligaya Community was prayerfully and seriously considering sending a mission team to Malaybalay to be with you and Genie. Vic Guiterrez would oversee it. We have made tentative outreaches to Mindanao, looking for places to be "in mission". It seems they are considering your invitation, Frank, to come to where Couples for Christ is thriving."

"That would be wonderful, I know we would love to have other missionaries in our community," Frank said.

When Frank got back home to Malaybalay, he received a letter from the Ang Ligaya Community, "Frank would you talk with Bishop Rosales about the possibility of the mission team coming to Malaybalay? Could Genie start looking at the possible housing situation? We hope the two families and single men can live within walking distance of one another."

"What do you think, Babe? Is Ang Ligaya making quick plans to send missionaries to Malaybalay because others are considering setting up a school of evangelism here?"

"Let's hope it is more about God igniting a fire for

mission," he replied.

I took the news of the coming missionaries to the Lord in prayer, "Lord, is this the something new you told us about in Camiguin? Being in community with other missionaries would be an enormous extra in our lives."

Ang Ligaya's team would have a true mission experience. They would be going out from a home base to live for Jesus in mission in a place they considered to be a frontier. Surely, they would soon learn the other side of mission life, too. They would come to understand the dying, the cross, and the "good news" experience. Jesus had died, He had to die! He understood what the world does not understand: "Unless the grain of wheat falls into the ground, it remains but a grain of wheat, but if it dies it will bear much fruit." Jesus told his followers that it was good that He return to the Father, so that the Holy Spirit would come down upon them. And come He did! Like a mighty wind, the Holy Spirit came, adding to the numbers of believers by the thousands on the first day of His coming. These believers would follow the apostles' instruction, live in community, and share all of their things in common. That's fruit – borne out of the dying of Jesus! Two thousand years later, we are still enjoying the good fruit of His ultimate sacrifice on the cross.

Frank made another visit to Manila; he had some exciting news to share with Vic and Raul about the preparations we had made for the coming of the mission team back in Malaybalay.

"Raul, my conversation with Bishop Rosales went very well. He had a few reservations, but after I reassured him that you intend to stick around, he ended up accepting my recommendation. He has agreed to receive you and hear what you are offering if you send a mission team. Also CFC has been scouting out the situation and we have houses lined up for the missionary team."

The Bishop and Frank received the leaders from Manila when they arrived in Malaybalay a few weeks later. After they spoke with the Bishop, they rented the houses that we and the CFC Community had found and returned to Manila to make further arrangements.

Later, Frank had a meeting with the leaders of the

proposed mission team. Up until then, the unity of the mission effort seemed like a wonderful thing. At this, the final meeting before the team moved down to Mindanao, Frank sensed something was amiss. He couldn't seem to shake the very uneasy feeling. He wasn't clear about the nature of the problem, but it worried him. The enemy of God's plan was opposed to this venture.

Frank's trip home from Manila showed palpable evidence that the enemy, Satan, was waging spiritual battle with us. One of the brothers from CFC in Malaybalay, Pompey Labaria, boarded the flight with Frank bound for Cagayan. After they were airbound, they suddenly heard a very loud thumping noise. The pilots couldn't retract the landing gear, nor could they stabilize it in landing position. They couldn't proceed to Cagayan with that problem, so they had to return to Manila. They circled and circled the airfield – thumping and bumping. The pilots did a fly-by and asked ground control to tell them if the landing gear was safely in place. Ground control said they could see the landing gear bumping back and forth. Frank and Pompey both say that they thought the possibility of a crash was very real. They prayed and prepared! Finally, the thumping stopped, the ground crew called the pilots and reported that the landing gear was now stabilized, and the plane touched down safely. As it landed, Frank shouted, "Praise the Lord!"

Lively applause broke out among the passengers, and many followed with "Praise the Lord!"

In Cagayan, because of the delay of the flight, Frank and Pompey missed the last bus up the mountain to Malabalay. At our house, where we expected Frank to arrive by early evening, our friends from Nasuli, Pat and Joanne Cocharan, were visiting. They were having dinner with me and the children. Frank had planned to be home in time to spend the evening with our guests. At about nine o' clock, I was beginning to worry. About nine-thirty, five hours later than he planned to arrive, Frank walked in the door, dazed and bleeding from a cut on his forehead. "What happened?" I shouted, rushing to him.

"Pompey asked his in-laws' chauffeur to drive us from Cagayan to Malaybalay. We got in the car, and it wasn't until we were on the way that we realized our driver was drunk. He took us on a hair-raising ride, speeding like a madman up that curving mountain road. We finally crashed into a mountain. And as bad as that was, it was better than careening off the other side."

"Praise Jesus. At least you are back safely," I said.

"How did you get back here from the wreck?" Pat asked.

"I was dazed and shaken up. We flagged down a truck and rode into town with a trucker and his armed guard, who was looking out for guerillas," Frank replied, "Praise God we made it home safely." The Lord had saved Frank from the devil's plan.

Frank lightened the mood when he said, "Pompey told me that he said his Act of Contrition three times today!"

The next day, he shared with me the details of his trip. It was the first time we began to understand that the coming of the mission team might not be everything we hoped for. We were apprehensive. We never mentioned our uneasiness to our friends in Couples for Christ. The preparations for the coming of the mission team continued as planned. Mer, Dada, Aida, and I organized a special welcome for them. We cleaned the houses, put fresh linens on the beds and stocked the refrigerators with the bare essentials. We also organized our CFC households into teams and brought them several days of complete meals, main course through dessert, so that they wouldn't have to worry about cooking while they unpacked and got settled.

I had moved so many times, I knew some of the hardships they would have to face, and we hoped to spare them those difficulties. I think the missionaries felt very welcome in their new home, and it gave the CFC community a chance to accept the presence and ministry of the new team in a concrete way. The team consisted of Arben and Armi, a couple with three little children, Raul and Hedy, who had been the national directors of the Couple for Christ movement, who also had two children, and two young single men, Rey and Isban, who would be living in a household with Arben and Armi. They had all taken a big step in faith, and arrived full of hope and enthusiasm. Frank and I were happy to see such promising young people willing to risk it all for the gospel.

Since Frank had invited their participation in our work in Malaybalay several months earlier, our hopes and expectations were that we could work side by side, evaluating and finding direction for the mission together. Ang Ligaya on arrival, set out

195

the proposition that the Summers family should meet weekly with the team to discuss the dynamics of the ministry. They further suggested that we meet socially once a week. Vic Gutierrez, overseer in charge of the outreach to Mindanao, expressed gratitude that we would be there to encourage and help the new missionaries to learn the ropes of mission life.

Even in the initial stages of the mission team's ministry, we could see good fruit. Raul and Hedy added a lot to the Couples for Christ community. The membership of CFC was encouraged by their presence to continue in enthusiasm and zeal. Raul and Hedy were impressed with the extent of the commitment and dedication of the Couples in Malaybalay. The new missionaries adjusted to their surroundings. They tried to move slowly, sensing the Lord's leading. They had arrived with a preconceived plan to guide them as they built the outreach. At first, our weekly meeting with the team went well. The Lord's work was first and foremost in all of our hearts. Arben and Armi had been assigned the job of trying to build *Covenant Community* as a separate entity from *the Couples for Christ Community*. Rey and Isban had been designated to find a way to evangelize the youth and lead them into community. The challenge they had ahead was a big one!

After our three years of working in the diocese, we were insistent that if a covenant community, solemnly committed, was built there, it would be built with the people in the existing Couples for Christ Community.

Frank held fast to his understanding of this truth as he shared with the team and its leadership, "The *only* people in this area who are interested in deeper community are the members of Couples for Christ. They have been primed by us and, recently, by their Couples for Christ experience. CFC is ready and waiting to embrace the next step of covenant community!"

"Yes, that's true," I said, "The other groups are lively, but not nearly approaching the desire that Couples for Christ has to build deep, structured community."

Vic was not convinced. He hoped that Arben might have more success in the charismatic renewal than Frank had. The Sword of the Spirit, an International federation of communities that Ang Ligaya was a part of, espoused the opinion that professionals in any location were the first building blocks of a covenant community. Our Couples for Christ group had some professionals, but generally it was a cross-section of the population. Vic Gutierrez held to the thought Arben was more equipped with cultural insight than we were. He felt Arben could more easily seek out those with leadership potential.

Frank and I remembered that Jesus had called fishermen; He saw their hearts, rather than their professions. The important distinction in leadership emphasis was a line drawn in the sand. We loved the Couples for Christ groups that had grown out of our work and felt that, if anyone deserved the extra attention and teachings it would take to build covenant community, it was these couples and families.

It soon became apparent, that our weekly meetings with the Manila team were not the meetings of a decision making body, in regards to a joint mission. Real decisions for direction were being made at a meeting to which we were not invited. Obviously, this was a takeover of our work. Frank and I realized we had been mistaken to think that Ang Ligaya's intentions in choosing Malaybalay had been to work with the Summers Family. Their mission, according to their leadership, was much *bigger* and more important than Frank and Genie's *small work* in Couples for Christ.

Although we were disconcerted over the attitude of Ang Ligaya's mission leadership, we knew that God knew better, but we felt hurt and confused!

The Lord was my only refuge. The pain of our situation weighed me down. I went to Him in my personal prayer time. "Lord Jesus, what are you doing in all of this? We have been begging you for two years to send the members of the Ang Ligaya Community to bring the riches of its life and experience to the CFC. We have encouraged the couples to welcome them into their hearts and lives as Your gift to us. They have so much to give. They are such dedicated young disciples of Yours!" I could feel Him by my side as I sobbed uncontrollably, "Thank you for answering our prayers, Lord, but now we are suffering. My cross feels extra heavy. Thank you for counting me worthy to carry this cross. You know Lord, that the very last thing we want to do is endanger the work you have done in the hearts and lives of your faithful ones. Show us Your will! You build UNITY! We're feeling *'squeezed out'* of this mission, Lord

Jesus. Are You applying some of the pressure of the *'squeeze?'* Is our time here in our precious Malaybalay at an end? Is it time for us to move on – to go?"

In our many years of being itinerant missionaries, it had never been easy to hear God tell us that our time at any post was at an end. But every other place had been easier than this. Previously, the calling to "Go forth" – the understanding and conviction that others waited to hear the gospel – made the transition from one mission to another mission easier. This time, it was so hard, so incredibly hard. We had reached the point where Malaybalay wasn't merely a *mission*, it was a true *home*. Leaving is like dying, and it is always painful. It sometimes seems unfair, even wrong. Many times in our missionary life, we've had to die to our plans, our hopes, our vision, and our love relationships with those we have evangelized. That's what Jesus meant when He told the parable about the dying of the grain of wheat; unless it dies, it will bear no fruit.

The Lord works all things to the good of those who are called according to His plan. We had to seek the Lord in retreat in order to meet the challenge of finding His will for our future. If He was allowing us to be squeezed out, then He had a better plan. Somewhere in our hearts we knew it was time to go, but we couldn't face leaving. Maybe if we went to Him in retreat, He would tell us to stay and show us a way to do it. The first thing we heard in the retreat was that familiar scripture from Habbakuk, *"Write the vision clearly upon the tablets."*

We set aside quality time to carefully think through all the possibilities that lay before us. We considered the following factors: First, could we continue as the Missionary Family of Jesus, Mary and Joseph? Moving about had been a part of our special charisma! On the positive side, God had called us to the itinerant life – the first vision we received, showed us moving about. We had been commissioned by our church and diocese. We had the experience of our last ten years as a missionary family and the Lord had blessed us in it. Our family lived a special life style. We tried not to be of this world – the way we dressed, the poverty we aspired to, the love of prayer and holiness we fought so hard to incorporate and maintain knowing we were citizens of another world – the Kingdom of Heaven. There were difficulties to consider if we chose to continue in the

198

itinerant life. One was the strain – could we go on alone, without others to live this life with us? What about the ridicule, persecution and rejection that we experienced because of our "littleness"? Was the itinerant life the best thing for our children? Was it right to take our family back into the midst of so many uncertainties? If we decided on this first possibility, when would be a good time to leave? We would have to entrust our future to the Lord. The building of a missionary community would have to wait. The Lord would have to give us contentment in moving about.

The second possibility we considered was whether we could become permanent residents of Malaybalay. Other missionaries had given their whole lives to one place. Covenant community *was* going to happen here, among our loved ones in Couples for Christ, whether Vic could see it or not. Our work in the Church overall was rewarding and satisfying. We had a comfortable living situation; the girls were doing so well in their schooling; our friends and acquaintances at Nasuli were a great support to us. Bishop Rosales was a holy man and a wonderful friend to us; and many of the clergy, the Jesuits, the Benedictines and the religious sisters loved and respected us. Had God's provident plan brought us to the Philippines where there was so much openness and need? Here we could give witness to the usefulness of lay families in mission to a nation that had great potential as evangelizers in Asia. The greatest positive consideration for remaining in the Philippines was our Couples for Christ Community, here in Malaybalay. It was more than a movement; it was a great work of God. It seemed impossible that we could ever love or be loved more.

If God indicated the permanent resident possibility, we'd have to think of ourselves in a new way, as founders and leaders of the actual community among our Couples for Christ members. We'd have to find a way to relate to the mission team in a status as residents instead of missionaries. We'd have to review our life-style and adopt a way of life more suited to the community here. We'd have to learn the language.

On the negative side, we thought that perhaps continuing on as leaders of the community was not the best use of the spiritual talents that the Lord had given us. Not too many families were willing to move about for the Lord. Would it be

199

the highest and best use of our lives in His service to remain in one place? Was this the place that currently needed us most, or had we already given all we could here? Were there other places awaiting that initial thrust of evangelization? Really, the Couples for Christ community was very strong, and if the mission team stayed on, we weren't really needed; they could make it on their own. Our going would free the mission team to proceed without reference to us, and God might have something better in store for the community than we could see. Frank attempted, but hadn't learned, the language of the people; we could only minister in English, their second language. Beau had preached in very limited Visayan, but he had already returned to the United States. I could converse, shop, and read a little bit in Visayan, but was not able to teach in their language.

The third possibility was the one that I could not feel at peace about, yet, but was open to exploring it. Frank was insistent that we lay before the Lord the possibility of returning to the United States and abandoning the missionary life. Surely, there were needs we could serve in the United States, working at a secular job. Our families and friends would rejoice at our being closer. We could be more available to Beau and to our parents. Maybe our children needed to experience a more stable life in the American culture.

On the negative side of the third possibility, first and foremost, was the tremendous need in the world today for missionaries. We had seen it. We had seen the fruits of our labors, some small and insignificant, others foundational as a sea change. One thing was certain, the Lord Jesus had poured out His Holy Spirit on the people we served. Could we find happiness and fulfillment if we gave up our call? All of us found our identity as missionaries and we loved our life! With all of its sufferings and hardships, we were what we were, not by our willing it, but by the call and election of God. Could we survive as ordinary lay people under the pressure of the American way of life? We had been out of the swing of things for so long; could we remain faithful to the spiritual life that we held dear?

If the third possibility was the one God said "yes" to, we'd have to begin now to pray and prepare ourselves for re-entry into American culture. We would have to advise our friends and loved ones that Frank would need a job. Would we live in Abbeville, where Frank could more easily find work? Abbeville was where so many of our loved ones lived. At the same time, we needed strong community in order to live a radical Christian life. We considered moving to Alleluia in Augusta. As the retreat progressed, we had laid out before the Lord, these various possibilities for our future.

The Lord began to speak to us in a clear way, using the scriptures, prophetic words and visions. He told us: "Seek and you will find ... Trust, don't be frantic in your seeking. Wait. Listen in peace and I will guide you... I love you ... I know what you need before you ask."

Frank had a vision of a heavy iron bar, pointed on the end, a sort of pick, used for digging. The Lord showed Frank that he was like that instrument, good for digging and the building of foundations. Then the bar in the vision was fashioned by the hand of the Lord into a sickle for the harvesting of grain. Next the vision focused on many bundles of grain, already cut and bound. The Lord indicated to Frank that he was also that sickle, and that the bundles of grain were souls won for the Lord and bound into small communities. The grain was not quite dry; the bundles were standing in the sunny weather waiting for the sun to dry them. Frank asked the Lord, "Where will I work in the harvest, Lord? Who will hire me to harvest their grain? Who will collect the bundles into their barns?"

The Lord answered, "You must pray, and wait, and stand ready to serve. Remember, cutting grain is a steady, monotonous, seemingly endless work. Once it starts, there is no time to loll until the work is finished. You must 'make hay while the sun shines'. You must pray for strength and stamina; be lighthearted in the labor. You must remain sharpened by a life of holiness to be my instrument. You will harvest what you did not sow, like a migrant laborer. The harvest is great, but the laborers are few. You will follow the harvest, as a family. Others will work beside you. You will be happy, because the work I am giving you is good work, clean work, and hard work. You are needed. Go. Go where you are called. Go where you are invited."

These words blessed and encouraged us. We were walking hand in hand with the Harvest Master, and we were able to abandon ourselves to His direction. I heard Him say to me, "I told you in Camiguin, trust Me! I am doing something new!! Take up your mission life again; be willing to go where I lead you. You will not be disappointed. I, myself, will be before you. I will remain behind you, here with your brothers and sisters. They are My children. Do not worry."

The more we thought and prayed, the more we felt that our next mission might be in Mexico again. Maybe we could find a place somewhere in the north, about a days driving distance from the U.S. border. We could have a home base in Abbeville. Our whole future was in God's hands again. At least we were at peace. Bishop Rosales listened carefully as we informed him of our decision to go. It was hard to tell him good-bye and he was sorry to see us go, even though he understood. He gave us his blessing and assured us of his prayers.

Our time in Malaybalay had come to an end. We had played our part in the work of the Lord here. Now others would bring to completion what we had begun. The Lord worked in the hearts of our brothers and sisters to accept our decision to leave.

We told them that it was an opportune time for our Lord to move us to another place, because the mission team would be there for them and that was a gift from God. It was even hard to leave the mission team. We hoped that in no way would our going dampen the zeal and courage they were displaying as missionaries.

When we arrived in Manila, we were prepared for a long wait. Ordinarily, we would spend an agonizing two weeks trying to cancel our visas and get exit permits. We had always stayed in the Ang Ligaya Community during those preparations. But this time, we chose to stay in the Summer Institute of Linguistics' guesthouse, which was about a half block from the apartment we rented when Joseph was born. I needed a place with some conveniences. Readying the girls and two small babies for the long trip home was a big job. We didn't have Beau travelling with us to help with some of the burden. Frank went down to the S.I.L. offices and spoke to someone who handles all of their travel arrangements. We got reservations and exit permits in two days!! The Lord whisked us out of the Philippines!

As it turned out, as the Ang Ligaya mission team attempted to move forward with its plan, they soon discovered that Frank and Genie's assessment of the spiritual climate in

Malaybalay had been correct. Arben was totally unable to generate interest among professionals to build community. He, Armi, their family, and Isban eventually returned to Manila. Raul, Hedy and Rey stayed on. Covenant community was God's plan, and it did evolve from the community the Summers family built, which began with our core couples of CFC. When they became a covenant community, they chose the name Ang Buhing Pulong, which means, "The Living Word" in Visayan. We felt honored by that name. We lived the Word in Malaybalay, and our dear friends and loved ones in Couples for Christ had come to see the glory in that.

Being away from our home in the Philippines was a long and trying adjustment for me. We kept up our correspondence with our brothers and sisters in Malaybalay. We missed them so much, and they missed us. Almost four years after we came back to the States, I was still crying, off and on, about our leaving Malaybalay. Finally, I wrote my sisters in the community in Malaybalay and said, "You have to help me with your prayers. I'm still suffering from the pain of leaving you."

Suddenly, it got easier. The Lord heard their prayers on my behalf.

A letter Mer wrote us from the Philippines, dated October 25, 1989 says: "We just finished a week-long celebration of our third anniversary as The Living Word covenant community.... In our assembly and program, two of the presentations mentioned the beginnings of the community, and of course, they told the story of the Summers family, God's instruments in our formation.... During the Thanksgiving prayer at the assembly, we thanked the Lord for sending you to us. So expect more blessings from the Lord because you have been such an important part of the community, which involves 132 adult members and almost 500 in its outreaches! Praise God!"

On several of my visits to Malaybalay since that time, I have been extremely blessed to see the enormous growth of God's work there. We had died to our beautiful life in mission there.

But one of the fruits of that dying is that we produced more missionaries. It was such a joy to see Joseph, my son, and his mission partner, David, serve in that sacred place. Joseph was privileged to go back to the land of his birth and see that God's mighty work still continues. And by God's providence, our mission company, Family Missions Company, sends missionary teams of families and singles to participate and encourage our beloved Filipino brothers and sisters.

One of the highlights of Joseph and David's mission in 2003 was the opportunity to catechize and baptize an entire mountain tribe. Working with Fr. Rueben of the Diocese of Malabalay, they went weekly to preach the gospel to them. After their Catechesis had finished, one of the tribal leaders said to them with much emotion, "We will never forget you brothers, for the Spirit and all you have shared with us!" At the Baptism, seventeen families were welcomed into the Kingdom – about one hundred people from grandmothers to infants. David was the godfather of the Chief. I visited this beautiful mountain tribe in 2007 and they begged us to send to them more Josephs and Davids, "We want to know more! Don't forget us!"

When we set out to love and serve the Lord as missionaries in 1975, we could not have foreseen that our children and grandchildren would be proclaiming the Word to those who have not heard!

Joseph and David with their FMC Mission Intake Group, 2002, just before they left for the Philippines. This group was sent out in mission across the globe: one team went to Malaysia, one went to St. Vincent and the Grenadines in the Caribbean, one team was osted in Northern Mexico, one team went to Coazacoalcos, Mexico. Some stayed in Stateside Mission.

Chapter Twelve

From the Bayou to the Desert

Like a sponge soaking up water, I felt strength returning to my soul as I watched the kids play in the colorful, crunching, fallen leaves at Kisnoaks, my childhood home. Back at home, after my "lifetime" in the Philippines, I was sitting on a swing and admiring the view of the bayou. I mused on its faithfulness. It moved along with the tides and the seasons, fast or slow, depending on a force greater than itself to move it. It sometimes flooded the land with the overabundance of water. Sometimes, it barely moseyed along, looking hot and murky and still.

The bayou did its duty of keeping the people, towns, and cities along its banks supplied with the life-giving water they needed. People had fun on the bayou, too. They water skied and boated. Frank and his brothers used to have a rope swing in their back yard that swung out over the bayou; it provided untold hours of good, clean entertainment as they dropped off of the swing into the water. Some fishermen earned their livelihood off the bayou, following it out into the bay, catching fish near its mouth. Sparkling clean tugboats still ply the waterway with barges of fuel for energy, and sand and shell for building roadways.

Missionary life can be like a river or a bayou. Missionaries must go and come as the Lord our God directs. At times, we must be still and know that He is God. We must be faithful to give as much of the "living water" of the Holy Spirit as God is giving to us, even to the point of flooding others with His love. We must provide those we evangelize with recreation that gives them real respite and refreshment from the cares and

205

troubles that the daily duties of life impose. They must be "re-created" by God's word. Missionaries must bring fuel and energy from one community of God's people to another. Frank and I felt that we had so much fuel for gospel living to bring to our Church at home. Missionaries must supply those waiting in bondage and darkness with materials for building the roads that lead to freedom and light. Our lifestyle should console those who look upon it, as they notice us faithfully running our course.

Sometimes after a drought, people standing on the banks of the bayou shake their heads, saying, "Look how low the bayou is!" Missionary life has its droughts, too. That's when we need to pray for rain, for a new filling of God's Holy Spirit. Sometimes, we have to go home to the people – family and friends – who love us unconditionally, to feel the power of our prayer together. The Summers family came back from four years of mission in the Philippines needing a refreshing rain to fill us anew. Our resources were depleted. We needed the filling of the Holy Spirit. We needed a game plan. We were ready to keep serving. Jesus had to show us what His priorities were for our immediate future.

Right off the bat, the word that came to us was, "Don't look back, keep your hands to the plow." "Trust Me!" "I am doing something new!"

Then, more specifically, He began to tell us to build a **Home Base**. After much consideration and prayer, Frank decided to do legal research as a means of supporting our family while we were in the United States. The Lord was going to give us a season of being still and knowing He is God! Like the bayou at times, the coming year would be a year of moseying along.

Our time at home was to be a mission, too. We had thought of going to Mexico right away, but the Lord had things for us to do in Acadiana. To console us in our waiting and our eagerness for the opportunities to go to all nations, the Lord gave me a vision of a monorail train that had one station in Abbeville and the other in Northern Mexico. The train came and went, bringing passengers and supplies – both spiritual and material. That mission to Mexico would surely develop, but we were just going to have to trust Him on the timing.

Part of "being still" for a missionary on a "home

mission" is to have *a home*. My Daddy, as a realtor, was handling a house for sale. He insisted that a house on Third Street was a very good buy for us. It was simple, sturdy, but in need of a few repairs, and in a good safe neighborhood for the children. Frank's parents were in total agreement, and his dad offered to hold the mortgage on that simple house. His parents were happy that the house we had in mind was right across the park from their colonial home. We didn't have a stick of furniture, dishes, pots, pans, or anything.

I had a few objections to the house at first, but the greatest obstacle to our buying the house was my fantasy about having a simple, rustic house in the country, at Big Woods, where Frank's parents had a farm. I was the *only* one sold on the Big Woods idea at the time, but Frank was willing to explore the idea.

It was November of 1985, my birthday. Frank asked me what I would like to do. "Let's pick up a bucket of chicken and go out to Big Woods to show the children the spot we've picked for our house."

In my fantasy, once we lived out there, Vince and Kay, Cheryl and Donald and other friends would spend lots of time with us getting away from the more complicated life that living in our little town brought. I thought we could invite people to camp out with us on the weekends where we could praise the Lord and fellowship. It was such a good idea; I couldn't understand why the Lord wasn't supplying a house to be moved onto the farm. The kids had their hopes, too; different hopes than I had. They liked the house on Third Street. The thought of being so close to grandparents and friends thrilled them.

"Never mind," I thought to myself, "they will all fall in love with Big Woods, and then the Lord will supply a house to be moved there."

We drove out into the country. The smell of the fields, the feeling of the freedom of the open spaces, the tranquility of cattle grazing contentedly in the pastures – I loved it all. We drove up to our property at Big Woods. Beau, who was celebrating my birthday with us, got out of the car to open the gate that led into the main pasture, not too far from the spot we had picked out for our new home. He hadn't even gotten the gate open when we could see his clothes turning black before our very eyes. Opening the gate, he began to swat at his clothes wildly. The black dots were mosquitoes!! Millions of them!!

"Are those mosquitoes on Beau's clothes?" Susanna asked in a horrified whisper.

"Yes, they are. Wow, it's a plague. We won't be able to have a picnic out here. What do you want to do?" Frank asked me.

"Let's just go quickly to the spot where I want to put the house, show the children, and then we can leave," I said. Beau got back into the car, and we drove a short distance. His clothes were full of mosquitoes, and now they were biting the other children. It was chaos! The kids didn't want to walk over to the site; they just wanted to get away from the mosquitoes!

"Why would anyone want to live out here with all these mosquitoes?" Mary asked innocently.

"There weren't any last week when we came; the hurricane probably blew them inland and they took shelter at Big Woods. It's not always like that out here!" I said insistently.

We had to drive about a half a mile with the car doors wide open, madly shooing the mosquitoes out of the car. On our way back to Abbeville, the family in a unanimous voice totally disagreed with my Big Woods idea. I began talking to the Lord silently in my heart, "Really, Lord, did you have to send a plague of mosquitoes? Okay, okay, I do get the message. I guess the house in town is the place you've prepared for us. Give me grace to love that idea. Amen."

We signed the papers for the purchase of the house in early December. The former owners were an older couple who had passed away. Their children lived far from Abbeville, and had no need of the furnishings already in the house. They were willing to sell the house fully furnished for a small additional sum. God provided us with a house *and* furniture. In the "package deal," we got beds, appliances, living room furniture, porch furniture, kitchen furniture, dining room furniture, chests of drawers and vanities. The house had everything else, too: linens, pillows, tablecloths, china, pots, pans, small appliances, silverware, flower arrangements, bobby pins, band-aids, liniment, old luggage, and other knick-knacks. It wasn't the rough and rustic, simple, artsy house of my fantasy; it was a throwback to the nineteen-thirties and forties. Yet countless people walked in, felt welcome and at ease, and said, "This reminds me of my grandmother's house."

The first day Beau sat on the old Duncan Phyfe love seat, he said, "Mom, I don't know why you objected to this house in the first place. I think Pops had trouble selling this house before we got here because the Lord had OUR name on it!"

That night, as I began to clean out the linen closet, I found some monogrammed hand towels. The beautifully embroidered initial on them was the letter "S"! The previous family had been the Smiths. Jesus HAD found us a house with our name on it.

When summertime rolled around, we found that the Lord had prepared a swimming pool for our use, too. Our next-door neighbors generously gave us permission to use their pool anytime we liked, provided that the children were supervised by an adult. Claude and Autherine Sirmon had built the pool for their children, who had grown up and moved away. Their grandchildren came often for the weekends, but generally the pool was not being used. This was a great blessing for Simon and for all of us because Louisiana summers are relentlessly HOT. We beat the heat with nice long swims. It was like having our own pool without the worry of upkeep.

Part of home mission for most missionaries is to find a vehicle, especially in a small bayou town that has no public transportation. We were in the market for a vehicle that could make it on the rough roads in Mexico for our future mission; it had to be large enough to accommodate our family, and it had to be cheap. Frank thought the perfect vehicle for our family at that time would be a crew cab pickup truck. We searched everywhere! The Lord was bound to have a vehicle for us. One day, we had all the children piled in the car that Frank's Dad was lending us. We were at the end of a long afternoon, going from one used car lot to another. Finally, we were driving down an expressway, and we passed a white crew cab truck. It was hooked up to a wrecker. It kind of looked like a pinto pony because there were big black repair spots on it.

"There's our truck!" I shouted as we whizzed passed it.

Frank had only seen it out of the corner of his eye, and he asked, "You mean the truck on the wrecker hook?"

All of a sudden, how unreasonable it was to buy a truck

off of a wrecker hook seeped into my head. I answered, sheepishly, "Yeah, maybe it's for sale. We could probably get it cheap if it runs, and we haven't found anything else."

"Let's go look at it," Frank said, looking for the next U-turn in the highway.

"Does it run?" Frank asked the wrecker driver, and owner of the vehicle.

"Sure does. It runs well!" he said confidently.

Our family piled into that pinto crew cab truck, we took it for a test drive, and it kept killing on us. Finally, it stalled, died, and wouldn't start up again. The owner came looking for us on the highway. It still amazes me that we bought that truck! We just knew in our hearts that it was the truck for us. Poor Frank went through three weeks of waiting in agony as the seller promised to have the truck ready tomorrow, then tomorrow, then tomorrow. Every once in a while, the promise of tomorrow was accompanied by the news that an additional part was needed and the price increased, too. Finally, Frank and Beau went for the truck. On the way home, it started killing again.

Frank was desperate! "Lord, please heal our truck; we will use it to serve You and Your glory."

God moved our friend, Tippy Guidry, to offer to help Frank with the truck.

"All that's wrong with that truck is that it has water in the gas tanks," Tippy said.

He was right and we were happy. They worked all morning, draining the gas tanks. After it had clean gas, the truck ran like a dream. Another friend painted it. A different friend gave us a camper top. Frank built a cozy living area in the camper for the children, and it turned out to be one of the most wonderful, practical vehicles we've ever had.

I remember our rousing prayer session when we finally got the truck in good order. We loudly called out, "Jesus! Thanks for having us at home again."

"Thank You, Jesus, that we live across the street from Gammie's and the park." little Mary said.

"Thank you for our big truck," Joseph added.

"Thank you that we have friends in the neighborhood," Sarah added.

"We do thank You, Lord, that we have a vehicle and a

home!" Susanna summed up our prayer.

In order to finish moving, and to buy supplies for the work Frank was doing in the house, I went to the drive through window at the bank to cash a check. I had my old friend, Tiny, with me. At first, I was going to write a small check. Then I decided to write a larger one for two hundred and fifty dollars. Tiny and I were chatting away as I took the capsule, which held the cash, into the car and withdrew the envelope containing the money, then replaced the capsule into its box. The automatic door closed on the box, and I drove away. I put the bank envelope on the seat of the car and took out a twenty dollar bill. I ran into the store to buy brooms, mops, and things.

We met Frank at the house as he was heading to the paint store. He asked me for some money. When I looked into the envelope that should have contained two hundred thirty dollars, there were only forty dollars! "I can't believe it!" I gasped, "One hundred ninety dollars are missing! What could've happened?"

I rushed out to the car to see if any money had fallen out in the car. I called out to Tiny to see if she had any idea about what could have happened; she had no idea. We prayed in a huddle, begging the Lord to help us find the missing money.

"Maybe I only wrote the check for sixty dollars. I was debating about the amount. Let's go to the bank and find out."

Tiny was really upset; she was worried that we might think she had the money. I would trust her with my last penny, and it really saddened me to think that she thought that I didn't trust her. She and I walked into the bank. I asked the teller to find my check and tell me the amount I had written on it.

"Two hundred fifty dollars," she announced. We told the whole story to the tellers, and there were several other people who were listening attentively.

"I don't know what could've possibly happened to my money," I ended my tale of woe sadly.

"What lane were you in?" the teller asked.

"I was in lane three."

She pressed the button that automatically brings the capsule into the bank. When she opened the drawer containing the capsule, she whipped it out of the drawer and held it high in the air, victoriously, "Here's your money!!" We had been gone

211

over a half-hour, and my money was still there! Tiny and I hugged each other, praying, "Thank God; and praise the Lord!"

The teller explained, "Sometimes money slips out of the envelope and people replace the tube without noticing. Always double check your tube."

A stranger who had witnessed the whole event couldn't help but speak out, "Lady, you must surely live right. I think it's a miracle that your money was still there. It's Christmas time. I don't know if the Lord himself could have looked at one hundred ninety dollars and resisted the temptation to drive off with it!"

I smiled, "I think it is a miracle. I asked the Lord to help me find my money, and I'm sure he posted an angel in lane three to keep people from driving through."

One of the first families to visit us in our new home was the Touchet family. Doug and Imelda were old friends of ours from the early days of the charismatic renewal. They were the Family Life Ministers in Fatima parish in Lafayette, and leaders in the Couple to Couple League, which is a natural family planning apostolate in Acadiana. We shared our Lord's Day meal with them.

"This is a wonderful celebration, Frank," Doug commented, " Did you say that all the couples in that community in the Philippines are doing this as a regularly scheduled thing? That sounds like a great program. I sure wish you could give us a year to get that type of program off the ground. Fatima, all of Acadiana, for that matter, could use a boost in building community."

"Well, Doug, we're still waiting on the Lord's direction. We feel sure He's saying `Go to Mexico - but not yet.' I don't know exactly what he has in store for us here."

"We've just moved into the house. Frank is doing legal research in one of the law firms here in town. But the desire to be in mission `burns in our bones.' Maybe the Lord wants to use us here. We can pray about committing for a year. We still haven't gotten the *go* signal from the Lord," I said tentatively.

Mission life is very demanding, unrelentingly demanding at times. When we, as missionaries, come back to our home base, some think that we're on vacation. The truth is life back home is often harder, a lot more expensive, and affords less spiritual support for living a strong Christian family life. We had also become aware that I was expecting our seventh child in September.

As soon as I realized I was pregnant, I told the Lord, "This time I am going to praise you for this baby from the first moment. I have a feeling this is my last one and I plan to really enjoy this pregnancy. I want him to be a happy baby."

It was only January. It might be nice to be settled in Abbeville for our new baby. We hadn't had much time to spend with our parents in the last several years. Beau was in a time of transition in his life. There were a lot of good reasons to make Acadiana our mission field for a year. After prayer, we decided to accept Doug's proposition that we give a year to community building in Acadiana. We could be like the bayou; we could bring building materials needed for the building of roads to community. We had long hoped, along with our brothers and sisters in the Open Door, to see many families involved in Christian relationships. If we could serve the Lord in doing that, we'd be happy.

The telephone rang a few days later; it was Vince. "Frank, I just talked to Doug. Are y'all really going to commit a year to teaching the Couples for Christ program in Lafayette?"

"We just decided to do that. The Lord hasn't showed us not to, and Doug is excited about it," Frank answered.

"I need to talk to Monsignor Mouton before we decide, but it would be great if y'all could do the program here in St. Mary Magdalen, too. We'd probably want to modify it some, to try to incorporate the existing Catholic Life communities. What do you think?"

"Well Vince, I like the program just the way it is, but being that we're going to be here anyway, we'd be happy to work with y'all, too. Let me know when you know something."

It was a challenge, but we gave two Basic Teaching Series simultaneously. We'd give one in the afternoon at Fatima, and one in the evening in Abbeville. Thirteen weeks really stretched out to almost four months. Couples and families saw the Lord working powerfully in their homes and marriages. Both programs bore great fruit. In Abbeville, the Family Life Program still exists; giving families the opportunity to live committed Christian lives in community.

When we began to feel that we had "moseyed" long

213

enough, Jesus finally directed us to begin seeking our next mission! In June, the small groups in both Fatima and St. Mary Magdalen Parishes arrived at a place where we, as presenters, could take three weeks off. We packed up our five little ones, and headed for Mexico on what we called a "reconnaissance" trip.

Frank felt inspired by the Lord to look first to the Saltillo Diocese. We knew the bishop. We knew the need; it was real and urgent. Geographically, it seemed perfect for our vision of encouraging interchange between Acadiana and the missions. In land area, Saltillo was the largest Diocese in Mexico. There are a few cities, but the majority of the residents live in small towns, villages, or "ranchos" scattered about in the desert. It had been almost six years since we had talked to our Saltillo friends, but we took the chance, and tried Rogelio Salas's old telephone number. We wondered if they would remember us and be as happy about our coming as we were. Rogelio answered the phone; the international operator asked for him by name, and connected us.

"Rogelio?" I said questioningly.

"Hermana Genie! Hermana Genie!!!!" (Sister Genie! Sister Genie!!) his warm, enthusiastic voice replied; he had instantly recognized my accent.

Rogelio and Isabel had moved into a new larger house since we last saw them, and they were happy to have us stay with them during our visit to Saltillo. Our children took to each other like ducks to water. It was fun to watch our kids taking their "baby steps" in learning a language.

Isabel and Rogelio were on the Diocesan Steering committee for the charismatic renewal, and, if we had given them the opportunity, they would have kept us busy ministering from the first moment we stepped in the door. Our old friends couldn't get over how our girls had grown, and how cute our little boys were. Simon's handicaps were almost an advantage among the simple, unaffected people of Mexico. Mexicans are willing to look past outward appearances and look into the heart, and they genuinely loved Simon.

Being back in the missions blessed Frank from the inside out. The grace of foreign missions can't really be explained, it has to be experienced. Going out in mission can be compared to

214

being sent with a banquet to a group of people who are starving. They would easily be satisfied with a meager meal. Instead, the Lord sends a banquet. We were only there a few days, and already a young priest in the Holy Spirit Parish was asking us to work with him. We made an appointment with the bishop to formalize our offer to serve. We hoped to receive his instructions and blessing for our ministry. We remembered the occasion when Fr. Cardona had invited us to serve with him in the town of General Cepeda. We prayed, "Please, Lord, let that invitation still be open."

General Cepeda, Coahuila, nicknamed the "Emerald of the Desert," is an old colonial town characterized by a special timeless charm. Stately old pecan trees, apricot, quince trees and mesquite bushes keep it very green. It seemed like it would be a good place for us, a family in mission. Even Sarah remembered General Cepeda from her few visits when she was almost four. People were friendly and open to us.

Fifty-four ranchos were part of the municipality of General Cepeda. These villages were also outreaches of St. Francis of Assisi Parish. The people of the ranchos were in dire need of the ministry of the church. One priest for 54 villages was absolutely not enough. Frank always felt the needs of the ranchos; they tugged at his soul.

The mother of two priests is a friend of ours. She told me her story. She and her husband had lived on a rancho, trying to raise their three little children. Her husband had been killed accidentally while her babies were young. She felt so helpless without the breadwinner. In her agony and grief, she turned to the Lord. She was consoled and helped by the presence of Jesus through her struggle of caring for her family alone. Finally, she felt led to leave the rancho and move to a bigger city. She said, "In the ranchos, we lived like little animals, busy about life, but without really knowing God. Oh, we knew God existed, but we didn't know we could have a relationship with Him. We thought He was unreachable and distant. I went to live in the city where I could hear God's word at Mass and receive Him in the Eucharist every day, and my life became happy." She continued, "We were still poor, very, very poor! I took in washing and made tortillas by hand to sustain us, but we were happy because we had the Lord. I remember when my oldest son made his First

Communion; I had no money for extras. One of the ladies I washed for gave him a new shirt, another lady I washed for gave him a pair of pants; but I didn't have any money for his shoes. I suggested he wait to make his Communion when we could afford shoes. He wouldn't hear of it. He said he was ready to receive Jesus into his heart. When the children lined up for the celebration of the Mass, the priest and the catechist told the children that those who were better dressed should be at the front of the line; those less well-dressed or without shoes should be at the back of the line. My son was the last one in line. It really grieved me, but looking into his face as he walked up to receive Jesus, took away all of my pain. His little face was all lit up with the love of the Lord. Just think, now he is a priest!" Tears streamed down my cheeks as she finished her story.

"No wonder Frank loves the ranchos," I thought, "the very poor are last in line, and yet there are those whom God can use in His high service, waiting to hear the good news." I was reminded again: "The last shall be first and the first shall be last."

Trying to be of help to us as we sought a place to serve, Isabel had done some investigating. She told us that our friend, Fr. Cardona, had been transferred from General Cepeda, after almost twenty years there. The new priest was Fr. Manuel Pachicano. We decided to drive over to General Cepeda and pay him a personal visit. When we drove up to the rectory, he was outside closing a garage door; he had just parked his pickup truck.

"Where can we find Fr. Pachicano?" I called out in Spanish.

"At your service," he said smiling. He was friendly and open. He invited us into the rectory. Eloy, Rogelio and Isabel and their children were with us. He showed no shock at being invaded by nine children and five adults. We were bursting with energy and ready to talk to him.

Frank told him about our time in General Cepeda, several years ago, and Fr. Cardona's invitation. "We're very interested in serving your parish in evangelization, Father, if you would like to use us."

"The need is overwhelming! I surely can use some help. There is so much to do!" he responded, "You are invited."

He and Frank knew that, of course, it all depended on

the bishop and the Lord. Fr. Pachicano was one hundred percent in favor of evangelism, and worked tirelessly bringing the Holy Mass to as many of the ranchos as he possibly could. We left him to prayerfully consider our desire to serve. We wanted him to feel free to change his mind if God showed him otherwise.

The next day, we were walking up the steps, about to enter the Bishop's house for our appointment, when Frank stopped me and said, "I feel like we shouldn't go in there already determined to be in the place we wish we could serve. I think we should offer the bishop the chance to place us *wherever* he decides to put us."

I agreed with Frank. God would surely place us where He planned to use us. The bishop would indicate the Lord's choice. I liked Bishop Francisco Villalobos. He's a very personable man who wears his authority well. He's very much at ease with the humble and with children. His teachings are usually packed with good, solid gospel truths. Our meeting went extremely well. We told him about the different types of ministries we had been involved in.

Frank said, "Bishop, we are willing to serve without expecting monetary support from the people or the diocese."

He replied quickly and wholeheartedly, "I am happy to accept your offer. Family life and evangelization are priorities in our pastoral plan. The diocese is being invaded by Jehovah Witnesses. It is likely that your coming is part of an answer to that problem."

"We will give ourselves completely to this mission," I said.

"I am encouraged that the U. S. is sending Catholics to a Christian Catholic nation", the Bishop added, smiling.

I thought to myself, "*Jesus* is sending out *these* U.S. Catholics. I hope others will be sent out soon."

Toward the end of our interview, he said, "There are two places most in need of ministry in my diocese – the first is General Cepeda. The other is San Jose' de Aura, near Barroteran."

Our mighty God did have a place prepared for us – General Cepeda! After visiting San Jose' on the way home, we realized that other Mexican lay ministers in Barroteran were already providing evangelization and small group ministry. Our reconnaissance trip had been successful. We drove into Abbeville thinking about Mexico. It might be really hard to wait five more months to go!

In Our Lady of Fatima Parish, very few couples finished the Basic Christian Teaching Series. That did not discourage us, because we had seen the work of grace begin in a small and humble way in the Philippines. The Fatima Family Life Program participants came through the series seeking a deeper experience of full covenant. We saw good fruit in their midst, even though they were a small group. They were zealous and totally committed. The Lord confirmed their fidelity with signs and wonders.

Donna and Graham Smith, overseers in the community, were the proud parents of two lovely adopted daughters, Sarah and Ellen. They had been married seventeen years. They had suffered miscarriages. God showed them that even in the midst of "reworking" and "renewing" their marriage, He was also giving them "new life". Donna bore their first natural child at the age of forty-one. Andrew is still a living sign of God's faithful love. He ministers music in God's service.

In Abbeville, the group was using the term "solemn commitment"; they didn't want to use the word "covenant." Frank and I participated in the Fatima community, and in one of the household groups in Abbeville. We gave the Marriage Enrichment Retreats and Days of Recollection. Counseling individual families kept us busy in our Acadiana mission field.

Our household group, the *Salt of the Earth*, grew strong. Judge and Elizabeth Edwards became a strength for us. The McCrorys, Bourgeois, and Leges supported us in mission with prayer and fasting, and made a difference for our lives. One family we fellowshipped with at that time would become our "real family". Donald and Cheryl Romero, their daughter Sarah and son, Sammy, began to be a significant part of our lives. The Romeros were so genuine, so open to the Spirit of God. They would always be our friends when we needed someone to lean on. Our girls loved each other; I was able to relax in Cheryl's easygoing presence; Frank and Donald became best friends and our boys were like brothers. (Now our married children still pray together.)

Beau had his usual complicated schedule with several

jobs and ministry obligations that summer. One day he said, "Mom, I think I am ready for a serious relationship. The woman for me will need to be someone who can understand me and my background." I began a Novena to St. Therese for him to find a wife. In the middle of the Novena, he met a girl named Michelle Denise Broussard, who was a native Abbevillian and a fellow honors student at USL. Beau had had other girlfriends in college and in the places where we served. Michelle was unique. She immediately joined him in daily prayer and Bible reading, as they commuted to USL in his old T-Bird every day. We wished she understood his missionary background better. His former life was an obstacle to their relationship from time to time. Michelle had scars from hurtful childhood experiences, and had said she would never marry. As she and Beau fell in love, she rethought her position on marriage; she was in love. Beau was very serious, and we were happy to see him content.

Our family had been strengthened and solidified by being "still" for over a year. We realized how good it was to have a home base. Knowing Jesus at home in Abbeville helped us to know Him in Mexico. In early January of 1987, the time to go to Mexico had finally come. Leaving behind Cajun country, the land of majestic oak trees draped in moss, lush green growth, and bayous running their course, was easier this year. A life in mission in the desert intrigued us.

We had less than a month. We needed funds for essentials – our truck needed to be capable of making the long trip; our house in Abbeville needed repairs - it would be uninhabited for an extended period of time; we needed to assist Beau with his education; and get settled in Mexico.

I asked the Lord, "Jesus, please send us ten thousand dollars. What we don't use for necessities, we will give to the poor, and You know that."

Within a week, we received a check for two thousand five hundred dollars, and the rest came in quick succession. Now we could leave; the pipes were fixed; Beau could go to school; we had painted the peeling parts of the house; the truck would have new tires; and we could begin our mission in Mexico and not have to worry. The Lord had supplied all of our needs!

A mission about to go forth must expect that the enemy will usually try to force us to stay put. The Lord often allows our decision to be tested by unexpected events. He calls us to be faithful to our "Yes, Lord!" Sometimes, the world, the flesh, and the devil tell us to change our minds and we say "Not now, Lord!" Ten days before we were ready to leave for Mexico, Sarah needed emergency surgery for a ruptured appendix.

Days before our scheduled departure we were sitting in Sarah's hospital room. "Gosh, Frank the enemy doesn't fight fair at all; he'll come against the children first," I commented in frustration, "We will probably have to delay our plans to leave for Mexico."

"God, we beg for Sarah's total and rapid recuperation. Please, Lord, work all things to her good," Frank prayed and God answered. Sarah's recovery was miraculously fast.

"At least Sarah had her surgery *here*," my Mom said.

"You're right, Mom, it would be tough to start our new ministry with an appendectomy in Mexico," I replied.

It was very difficult to leave the bayou, the people God had formed into community, and our beloved Beau. Yet, we were on fire to go, eager to bring living water to a desert land. It had been over a year since we lived in the foreign missions. Sarah, ten years old, wrote in our December 1986 Newsletter:

"BEING A MISSIONARY KID"
"I wonder how many of you are 'missionary'. Some people wonder how we bear it coming and going all the time. Sometimes it's hard; but most of the time it's lots of fun being a missionary kid."
"I like going places, seeing communities being built and people being helped, making friends and learning about their way of life (and living it with them while we're there). I think being a missionary is the best thing I could be. It's a way to be near Jesus a lot and share with other people about Him The only hard thing is leaving and missing people. By the way, in this New Year pray for missionaries who are leaving the people they love."

Chapter Thirteen

Something New in General Cepeda

There are two ways to drive from Saltillo to General Cepeda; both routes are beautiful; panoramic views surround you. Vignettes of oxen plowing, burros almost invisible under a great load of cornstalks, a peaceful shepherd tending his flock, women carrying wet clothes in a bundle on their heads, and vigorous young cowboys racing their horses for the sheer pleasure of it, animate the vast landscape. Living cactus fences ten feet tall guard pigs and poultry. Crosses on the roadside pay homage and indicate the spot where someone's beloved family member was accidentally killed. A steeple of the church in each village marks the center of activity. Tiers of mountains stretch across a landscape peppered with outhouses, pecan orchards, rocks and more rocks, a splash of brilliant green where the irrigation wheels are spinning. Beautiful children peeking out of adobe houses drew us in to a world that was so old and yet so totally new.

When Jesus told us to go to all nations, it wasn't just for *them*. It was for *us*, too, to be confronted and challenged. The new things we see and the new people we meet are supposed to do something new in our lives. We must become a new creation, a real part of them, and yet still be us!

We were bringing "something new" with us to Mexico. We had a four and a half month old missionary, John Paul, who would be called by his name in Spanish, Juan Pablo.

Back in Abbeville, before he was born, the Lord was fitting into His timetable the birth of our baby. Our schedule was completely filled in August and September of 1986. We gave a Marriage Enrichment retreat only days before he was born. I let this pregnancy be fun for me. He was a little early, but my

221

nesting instincts had kicked in and I was ready. Joseph was out of diapers and easy to handle, Simon had made strides in independence. The girls, Sarah, now ten, Susanna eight, and Mary, just six, were very helpful. Our family was a "mission team", and our team was ready for the next player.

Early Sunday morning, on August 31, my membranes ruptured. This was the *one and only* Sunday we had off from ministry – God's timing! We arrived at Abbeville General and were quickly placed in the hospital's new birthing room. It was brand new and perfect.

"Frank," I said, "I am so happy. This room is really comfortable. I don't even mind that my doctor won't be here. Doctor Foreman, his replacement, is really nice. And this time, you get to stay with me. This baby has been the Lord's gift all along."

"God wanted us here in Abbeville, this time, just for this moment. You will have a smooth delivery. I sense it," Frank said, patting my hand.

John Paul was born on Sunday, August 31 at 7:00 pm. As I held him in my arms, I knew this was my last baby. I was two months shy of my forty-third birthday. I would relish this season, and not let a minute of the joys of motherhood escape me. His role was being the baby of the family. We let ourselves be blessed by this bundle of joy. Jokingly I had said, "This baby is going to be a tie-breaker. I already have three boys, and three girls. Three of my children have a unique kind of hair – we call it fuzzy hair. Three have straight hair. What'll it be – boy or girl, fuzzy or straight? Anyway, he broke the tie in favor of the boys and the fuzzies. John Paul had handsome features, even as a newborn, and he was a happy baby. He ran with the pack at an early age, fitting into the family like fitting that final piece into a puzzle. The picture of our family of missionaries was complete – until the next generation.

While I recovered from his birth, God blessed us through the couples of the Family Life Community. I didn't have to cook a main dish for our family for almost six weeks after John Paul's birth. When he was only one week old, he and I made it to the introductory talk of the Basic Christian Teaching Series of Abbeville's Family Life Program. I gave a testimony holding my newborn in my arms. Even before he was baptized, Jesus used him to be a witness of the joy of new life. Now, he was just four months old and off to his first mission! Our new mission in General Cepeda, Mexico would become home to him. Nothing says to the people a missionary hopes to evangelize "I trust your culture" better than bringing a newborn into it. It is a tool for instant enculturation.

I often say jokingly, "I have a Ph.D. in packing!" In the weeks before our departure for Mexico, I had been home schooling the girls, caring for our boys Simon, Joseph and our newborn, ministering in the communities in Lafayette and Abbeville, relating to the Gremillion Clan, visiting with my ninety year old grandmother, participating in "Our Lady's Group," and getting to know Beau's future wife. Getting ready to go on a mission trip when the Lord says go, is a cross that's inevitable in missionary life. If we do get stars in our crown in heaven, I know one of mine will be shaped like a suitcase.

Once we hit the road for Mexico, the baby and I rested well in the cozy camper Frank had set-up on the truck. I had spent three or four days packing luggage, and three hours in the middle of the night, packing the truck. All the while, we trusted that the Lord had a home picked out for us in Mexico. In General Cepeda, Father Pachicano had a few houses lined up for us to look at. There was very little choice. Someone had a key to an abandoned house owned by a doctor who lived away. Rogelio and Isabel were with us when we decided to rent it. "This will be fine, the price can't be beat - fifteen dollars a month," I declared enthusiastically.

"But it's in ruins. Ruins! How are you going to live in it?" Rogelio asked.

Isabel squeezed my arm, "You have to have a **lot** of imagination."

In my years of serving Jesus in the missions and in the States, I have had to meet the challenge of starting anew in making a home many, many times! The scary thing is that it is a time when we are vulnerable to the attack of the enemy in our personal relationships. As a missionary wife, I feel I owe my family an environment that is conducive to prayer, service and family living. As a missionary husband, Frank feels we need order, peace and acceptance of whatever the Lord provides, and he shares the responsibility in helping me make our house a true

223

home. Settling in to General Cepeda was a challenge for us.

After we decided to rent the abandoned house, we searched for the landlady to clench the deal. "La doctora is very difficult," our new Mexican friends warned.

Within a few weeks, Frank said, "Manuel was right. She is not easy to deal with."

"Even if we have to pay for repairs, with the rent being fifteen dollars a month, it is worth it," I decided. Eventually, we moved into the house, but the walls were literally crumbling; that's what happens to neglected adobe walls. We had to have a construction man come in and cement and plaster the walls, and replace all of the windowpanes because there wasn't one in the entire house. Moreover, Frank didn't want to paint without getting approval from the landlady, all of which led to one delay after another. We were able to repair and refurbish one of the bedrooms, and someone came over that very night with beds, cots, and mattresses. We had a table and some chairs, and a stove and a tank of gas. Our outside bathroom had a flush toilet and a shower, but neither of them worked. A hot water heater needed to be installed before the plumbing could function. To make things worse, one of the walls of the bathroom inclined at about a seventy-degree angle.

Getting things done in developing nations, especially rural settings, is one of the greatest trials of mission life. Americans are accustomed to going out to buy the things we need. That's not the way it is in Mexico, certainly not for a missionary. Trying to make our home presentable is such a strong drive in me. I found the interminable waiting on house repairs in General Cepeda very frustrating. At the same time, I knew I had to "overcome evil with good." Deep in my heart, I knew our home would take shape. The evil that most threatens me in mission is not the "Mexican Way" or the "Tongan Way" or the "Filipino Way", but my stubborn insistence on *my way*! I need to keep reminding myself that "efficient" and "good" are not synonyms. "Good" overcomes evil when love wins out. A loving heart, a patient mother, a smiling servant of God is infinitely more valuable to the Lord than efficiently accomplished projects bought at the cost of disunity and complaining.

Building a new ministry always challenges us as we

enter each new mission. The only way we've ever been able to begin is in prayer. We had been praying since our previous trip to General Cepeda, for the Lord to prepare us to serve His people there and to prepare them to receive us. From the start, Frank had an excellent working relationship with Fr. Pachicano.

Father, who did not know Frank or his abilities as a missionary, said to him after Mass the first Sunday, "I'm assigning you to a few ranchos to begin evangelization courses. Then I will take you with me out to the ranchos when I celebrate Mass, and introduce you to the people."

At the ranchos, Fr. Pachicano announced, "Frank will be coming to begin meeting with you regularly for songs, prayer and God's word."

Very, very seldom does Frank go out evangelizing all alone. He prefers to go out with others, and to get them involved and praying for the success of the ministry. At first, we didn't know anyone who would accompany Frank to the ranchos, so our girls and I took turns going with him. Mary Magdalen went to the rancho of La Rosa; she was responsible for keeping the people of La Rosa in her prayers. Susanna and I went to Hedionda, and we prayed for its people. Sarah went to La Parrita; she prayed for the mission to La Parrita.

Later, as we knew more of the townspeople of General Cepeda, a team evolved: catechists, guitar players, an extraordinary minister of the Eucharist, and lots of just simple prayer supporters. The townspeople were passionate about rancho ministry when they saw the openness and dire need of the isolated villages.

Another facet of ministry in most mission territories is that the people place little importance on being timely. Frank and the team would arrive at a rancho, drive up to the chapel, and ring the bell. The villagers don't even get dressed and ready for the service until the truck drives up. After a few minutes, Frank rings the bell again and goes in to start singing. It may not be logical, singing in an empty chapel, but that's how the villagers know that the service is about to begin. Frank says when they gather, "Let's open our time tonight with prayer and songs. Lord Jesus, we invoke your name, send your Holy Spirit. Renew, inspire, and heal everyone present. Don't leave anyone out."

Several lively faith filled songs follow. Frank reminds

225

them that Jesus said, "Where two or more are gathered in My name, I am present in the midst of them." St. Augustine tells us "to sing is to pray twice". During the first sessions, he shows the newcomers how to thank the Lord in a spontaneous, spoken prayer. When he starts, he encourages each one to pray in turn. After they've been doing it awhile, they pray spontaneously. More songs follow and then Frank shares a message from God's Word. Then there's another song, followed by a time for testimonies. Usually the team members give testimonies and stories of God's work, encouraging others to share, too. Eventually, the people of these small communities learn to give testimonies about how God has been answering their prayers through healings, God's providence, restored relationships, and any and everything the Lord is doing in their midst. The meeting ends with petitions, a closing prayer, and brotherly hugs or handshakes all around, otherwise known as the sign of peace, finally closing with more songs. After the meeting, the sick who want to stay for healing prayers may do so. Healing attracts many, and signs and wonders confirm God's word.

It never fails to amaze me seeing these simple, hardworking folks responding to the Gospel preached in power. In such a short time, individuals and the whole villages are completely transformed.

In one of the villages where we first began, a man was healed instantly of alcoholism. When he gave his testimony, he said, "I have been a hopeless drunk. I have caused my family suffering and untold misery." He looked tenderly over at his wife who was shedding tears of release; "I know my poor wife wondered where they would find me when I left the house drinking. The Lord gave me a new life. My family is transformed, too." He was too choked up to continue. His wife was glowing with happiness and the presence of the Spirit and the whole village took notice of his newfound faith.

Generally as the life of faith in the small communities begins to grow, all things start getting better; the physical appearance of the chapel improves. Family, personal and community lives are all radically changed. Jesus takes good care of His friends! The villagers grow in self-esteem. Life becomes more than a mere daily struggle; it becomes meaningful. They notice God's hand in so many things they hadn't noticed before.

They become grateful for who they are and for their relationship with the Lord.

One of the village leaders told me, "We are happy with our life now. We used to want only electricity, television and other conveniences. Now we are content with having the Lord and one another. We don't want to lose the most important thing we've ever had. God is so good to us. We want to be faithful. We wonder if electricity will distract us from the Lord?"

The first time we went to La Parrita, which is Spanish for little grapevine, the chapel was one tiny, unpainted, adobe room. There was a simple wooden cross on the outside to distinguish it from the surrounding adobe houses, which adjoined one another by connecting walls. The "altar" was a simple table with fresh and plastic flowers and a few holy pictures. There was no electricity in La Parrita, so the chapel was dimly lit and Frank read his notes by the light of a kerosene lantern. Children's school desks, which had certainly seen better days, stood starkly on the dirt floors, but the people filled the chapel and were very receptive to God's Word. The women and children were seated and the men, who turned out in good numbers, stood at the rear. Don Carlos, the manager of the village, came faithfully to the evangelization. Soon, he and Don Lorenzo joined Frank in playing the music, and before long there was a full-fledged music ministry with Don Carlos playing the guitar and Don Lorenzo playing the fiddle.

People participated from surrounding villages, too. Juan Antonio, his parents, and his entire family, which consisted of a wife and six little children, walked over the mountain in the dark to be at the meeting. From the village of Orartorio, several families piled into one small pickup truck and drove over to the evangelization course.

The effects of the evangelization showed in the constant improvement of the chapel. Each time we went, something new had been added. First the inside walls were painted white, then the outside walls were painted white. Plastic curtains were replaced by real ones. The wall to an adjoining room was knocked down, and the chapel grew to twice its size. A concrete floor was put in, and a bell tower with a bigger sturdier cross was installed. When we first drove in to La Parrita, it was hard to distinguish the chapel from the other homes; later, it became the prettiest thing in the rancho!! Now in 2011, La Parrita has a beautiful new church, a real sign of their love for God.

The renovation of the chapel absolutely paralleled the renewal of the village's spiritual life. It blossomed into a wonderful, worshipping community. Fr. Pachicano told Frank one day, "The villagers of La Parrita have grown in their ability to respond to the Gospel. Their leaders are trained and confident; the people submit to them. Because of their good response, the bishop is allowing them to have a tabernacle with the Eucharist reserved and the Sacrament of Communion on Sunday. Jesus in the Eucharist will always be available."

As we drove from the rancho, after the installation of the tabernacle and the reservation of the Eucharist, I commented, "A peace settled on me tonight, Frank. It is so precious when Jesus let's us see the fruit of our labor."

Men that once accompanied Frank as part of the team, later evangelized on their own. One of them is named Manuel; he calls himself Gallo, which means the rooster. Gallo is an expert carpenter, whose work is in constant demand in General Cepeda, and even in the nearby cities of Saltillo and Monterrey. We first met him when we lived near his carpenter shop. We needed work done on some old furniture. Gallo was genuinely interested in what we had to say about the Lord, but also very openly attached to his vice of drinking and sleeping late in the morning. I really felt the Holy Spirit lead me to pray continuously for him, and to witness my faith to him whenever I had the opportunity.

Before we left Abbeville to head to Mexico, Frank had taught my nephews to play the guitar. Unknown to us, my Dad, who's a pretty good "fix-it" man, bought a twelve-string guitar, with a broken neck, for twenty dollars. We told Daddy that it was useless; the boys could not play a broken guitar. Our tradition was to have breakfast at Mom and Dad's before we left on our missions. I had packed practically all night. Every available inch of the truck was packed neatly, leaving room only for sleeping and making sandwiches.

After our second round of good-bye kisses at Mom and Dad's, and after someone had run in for one last trip to the bathroom, we were ready to go. We piled in the truck. As we were about to drive out of the driveway, Daddy comes out with that twelve-string guitar! "I feel like the Lord wants someone in Mexico to have this guitar," he said, handing it to me through the camper door.

"I don't know if Daddy really heard You say that, Lord," I said to Him in my heart, "I don't feel like taking the guitar. It probably can't be fixed. How aggravating! I just finished straightening out the back of the truck and I know there is not a single spot for it." But I thanked my Dad anyway, blowing him a kiss as we drove off. About a mile down the road, I called to Frank through the sliding door window in the back of the truck, "Frank, what are we going to do with this guitar? It's ruined. Why don't we just throw it out?"

"Can't you find some place for it?" Frank called back, "Your Dad said he thought the Lord wanted someone in Mexico to have it. He's often right when he says the Lord has told him something." I heaved a sigh, and managed to tie it out of the way by one of its broken strings.

When we moved into our house in Mexico, we stood it up behind the sofa, waiting for the Lord to show us what to do with it. After Gallo was finished reupholstering our dilapidated sofa and returned it, he inquired about the guitar standing alone in the living room.

"Whose guitar is that?" he asked.

"It's not any good, the neck is broken. My father made me take it over here. He said the Lord told him He wanted someone in Mexico to have it," I answered.

Gallo smiled confidently, "I can fix it. Maybe it is a guitar for me."

"Do you know how to play the guitar?" I asked. "No, but I can learn," was his happy reply, "Frank can teach me!"

"I'll have to ask Frank about the guitar and I'll let you know."

We gave the guitar to Gallo. In no time at all, Gallo had fixed the guitar, and done a fine job too. We had to send for strings in the U.S. Just about the time the strings arrived, our friend from Mexico City, Eloy, came to minister with us for a month. He's an expert guitarist. Eloy and Frank taught Gallo to play.

At first, Gallo would play only if Frank were playing;

229

however, after he gained self-confidence, he is now playing and evangelizing by himself. Gallo's coming to "new life" has been very slow, with frequent falls, but he has come to know Jesus and he loves to sing his praises. He told me not too long ago, "I'm not the same Gallo. I'm a new one, a new me."

Daddy was right. The Lord did want someone in Mexico to have that guitar. Gallo is like a favorite uncle around our house and our children love him. Anytime something was broken, John Paul was quick to say, "Don't worry, Gallo can fix it."

While the villages were being steeped in God's love, and our rancho ministry was flourishing, we had a different response in General Cepeda. We had never lived in a small rural Mexican town before; this was another "something new" the Lord was doing in our lives. It is hard to be accepted in small towns, and General Cepeda was no different. The missionary usually has an initial period of grace, where people will listen to them; even if just out of curiosity, but General Cepeda was difficult even with that grace. We had to learn the weaknesses and strengths of the place, the culture and ways, to bring "Christian culture and tradition" to displace a "tradition" that led to perdition.

"I love this work, Frank, but never have so many attacks of Satan come against our mission," I confessed one day.

"Let's focus our family prayer on praying for deliverance," Frank responded.

One day Sarah shared a very disturbing vision she was having as we prayed, "I see legions of demons hiding behind rocks in the desert and around the General Cepeda area." She took a deep breath and continued, saying, "Praise You, Lord. I see Jesus and his angels defeating the demons." We hugged her and called on Jesus.

The place was plagued with superstition and spiritism. My friend, Maria Louisa, commented one day, "Before your family first arrived in General Cepeda, the talk of the town was always about witchcraft and spiritism. Now that the Lord Jesus is changing hearts, the talk of the town is about prayer meetings and church activities. Thank the good Lord that you came! The witches and warlocks are moving away."

A spiritual battle raged, but the Lord always has the

230

victory! We were finally planning an evangelization series in town when suddenly Frank's back went out again, as bad as it had at Damascus Ranch several years before. He was bedridden for several weeks. During the struggle with his back, we read the Scripture that says, "Jesus called out to the Father with loud cries and supplications."

The children and I were so tired of not having Frank at our mealtimes. We wearied of his being down, and so did he. Obeying the scriptures, we started shouting to the Lord at the top of our voices. "Please, Lord Jesus! Hear our LOUD cries and supplications. Heal Frank!"

Then we turned the volume of our supplications up even more. There's no half-heartedness when you cry out to the Lord with as loud a voice as you possibly can. We screamed again, "Heal him, Jesus!! Pulheeze, please heal him! Heal his back, God, heal his back!!"

A little while later, Frank came walking into the dining room, "The pain is gone. While y'all were shouting, I saw a hand come down and touch my back!" This time we shouted for joy, "Praise you, Lord Jesus!"

The next serious attack was also against Frank. Satan did not want Frank preaching God's Word! Barely up and around from his bout with the back injury, he came down with high fever. After two days of fever, I was concerned. "It must be the flu or something," I thought to myself, "What is this? He just got healed of his back problem, and now this new thing hits us." Our doctor in General Cepeda started him on medication. Fever reducing medication didn't have *any* effect; nothing seemed to help! I had no idea what it was. He was severely weak, too weak to do anything but lay there. Sitting up for a couple of hours utterly exhausted him. After four days, I tried to get hold of my doctor in Abbeville. I left a message, but he never called me back. Finally, I called our local doctor, "Is it normal for a grown man to have a fever of one hundred and four, for four days?"

Dr. Quintanilla, the president of the parish counsel and one of our new friends, is a very calm and collected man; nothing seems to rile him. Cholie, his wife, is a nurse who helped him on his rounds.

"Yes," he said calmly, "in this kind of fever, it is very

231

normal."

"In what kind of fever?" I asked.

"In typhoid fever. You can't just make typhoid fever go away. It has to run its course. Cholie and I will be there to change his medication. We'll start an intravenous infusion on him in a little while."

"Typhoid fever? Are you sure? How long does Typhoid fever take to run its course?" I asked, trembling on my end of the phone.

"Twenty-one to thirty days," he briefly replied.

I couldn't believe my ears. I hung up the phone, terrified. I had studied about Typhoid fever, and knew it is serious business. Frank suffered with high fever, day in and day out, for almost a month. He'd feel a little better and try to do something, and then he'd be right back in bed shivering with chills, burning with fever, and as weak and limp as a wet strand of spaghetti. Toward the end of four weeks, I noticed that his skin was beginning to look yellow. I really panicked.

We'd been praying and praying to the Lord, and Frank's condition remained the same. Even on his sick bed, Frank was constantly ministering; weak and feverish, he would counsel and pray with the steady stream of visitors. "Frank, I'm really concerned. I'm really worried because it looks like your skin is turning yellow. That could mean all kinds of things. Can I call a specialist in Saltillo?"

He agreed, and I started packing for all of us. I wanted to be prepared, in case Frank had to be hospitalized. I had not yet driven our truck to Saltillo and I knew that would be hard. Frank was going to have to lie down in the back while I drove. I packed enough clothes for two weeks. We'd drive to Isabel and Rogelio's house, drop off the helpers and the kids, and go by taxi to our appointment with the specialist.

I packed late that night, and into the wee hours of the morning, and began talking to the Lord.

"What's wrong, Lord? I know you're allowing this for my good. What lesson do I have to learn before you can heal Frank?"

"No greater love than this, that one lay down one's life for one's friends," was His answer.

It took me awhile of silent meditation to hear what the

Lord was saying to me. I knew what I had done wrong. I had not come to General Cepeda really ready to lay down my life for these people in this place. "If something bad happens, we can be at the border in a few hours," was what I had been counting on. What a terrible mistake. I prayed, "Lord, I'm sorry I let myself think that my security and safety is on the other side of the Rio Grande River. My security and safety are in YOUR hands. Frank is so weak that it will be a great feat to get him to Saltillo. There was no way in the world that I can drive to the border with Frank sick and six little children! Jesus, I need You. I need your help."

I had certainly been willing to lay down my life for the people in the Philippines, in Tonga, and in Colombia. What was it about being so close to home that had blurred my understanding of this essential missionary truth? In tears, I continued to ask God to forgive me, "Lord Jesus, I've been selfish and blind. Please forgive me. I know you're concerned for Frank, but I also know that you're concerned for my wholehearted commitment to your humble poor. Help me to have that commitment. Let me accept my own death and even my family's, for the building of your kingdom."

I was crying harder as I finished my prayer, "I do lay down my life. Being a widow would truly be much harder for me than accepting my own death because I really can't wait to get to heaven." Feeling "right" with the Lord, I called on the Holy Spirit. I asked for Frank's healing. I had been strained to the breaking point. I would accept it, but I wasn't ready for widowhood. I needed a miracle.

In Saltillo, the specialist changed Frank's medications and the yellowness completely disappeared from his appearance. We came home, and Frank had a steady, slow recuperation. I worried a little until the incubation period of Typhoid fever had passed; no one else in the family had contracted the disease.

Adjusting to a new germ environment was always a challenge for us. New places brought new health problems. Never have we been so sick as in our first six months in General Cepeda. The baby had measles, amoebiasis, and an allergic reaction to the amoebiasis medication. Frank's back went out on him, which left him flat on his back for three weeks. Sarah's health deteriorated from constant tonsilitis. Susanna and Mary suffered from flu and infections. I was greatly discouraged, and then Frank got Typhoid fever. Since we've been in the missions, we have had to treat our water by boiling or by chlorinating it. More recently we have had the luxury of buying purified water. Without telling me, Frank had decided he would *adjust* to the water by drinking a little bit of the village water each time he visited. Water that generally does not sicken the natives can be like poison to us. Taking precautions is a lesson we've had to learn. The hardest part about avoiding the water is that we're not always able to partake of the hospitality our new friends offer, and being ambassadors for Christ, we didn't want to offend anyone.

Sickness is part of our carrying the cross in the missions. We do take it to the Lord in prayer and he heals us, instantly, miraculously, or slowly with treatment, but our life is always in His hands. Three times in our first six months, I had decided to leave, give up General Cepeda, sure that I couldn't take it any more. I wanted to find another mission. I foolishly thought that maybe the Lord wasn't pouring out His grace, and without that grace of mission, I couldn't stay! Each time, I took my decision to the Lord. I told Him, "I'm sorry, truly sorry, but my resources have run out. I can't walk on the stormy sea any longer."

Each time, He reproached me, "Oh you of little faith!"

Each time, He had calmed the storm, and I stayed.

And it was so good that I did stay. A new chapter was about to unfold in General Cepeda for the Summers family.

Tejocote, a typical *rancho*, (village), in Northern Mexico.

Chapter Fourteen

There's Room at the Inn

"What do you mean, the toilet tank exploded?" I asked Susanna.

"It almost burned me, the water was so hot!" she answered.

"Hot water in the toilet tank? How can that be?" I asked, almost yelling.

"Gallo's here and he said someone must have run the hot water pipe to fill up the toilet and then he laughed," Sarah said.

The doctor's house we rented in General Cepeda for fifteen dollars a month was starting to fall apart. The tank of the toilet exploded because the hot water heater had backed up!?! The walls were leaning more than before. Our landlady opposed the renovations we wanted to do, which left us little doubt that we needed a new house. There was a small inn in General Cepeda called the Casa de Viajeros, which means house of the travelers. We had heard about it and toyed with the idea of buying it when we first arrived. At that time we didn't have the ten thousand dollars it would have cost.

I had begged the Lord, "Please, supply the finances we would need to purchase or rent an accommodating home for our family. We need one that serves us and our many ministries. I am trying not to worry, and to put all my trust in you."

Shortly, in direct response to my prayers, we received a generous donation.

I strolled John Paul around General Cepeda looking at houses that might be for sale. We strolled around the central plaza and passed by the inn. The massive front doors were still locked from the outside, but the wind had made a little opening where I could peer in. It wasn't what I saw that impressed me, but a little peek at the patio tile had magnetically drawn me to the place. I experienced a cool breeze of the Holy Spirit who whispered to me, "*This* is the place for your ministry, your family and your community."

Frank was at a rancho, so I strolled over to my friend Lucy's house. I had started another "Our Lady's Group" in General Cepeda, and Lucy was one of the founding members. She was the niece of the owner of the abandoned inn. "Lucy, is the inn still for sale? Really? Can you get in touch with your aunt? Can you tell her to call me?" I excitedly inquired.

Lucy was answering with her darling smile and a half of dozen head shakes indicating, "Yes!"

She could tell I was interested, and she gladly took my phone number. Phones were rare in General Cepeda but it just so happened that our rent house already had one installed.

Frank came home that evening and as I served him his supper, I said, "I went house hunting this afternoon. I strolled John Paul all over town and we stopped at the inn."

Frank interrupted, "Did you get in to see it on the inside?"

"No, but I got a good peek. But beyond that, the Holy Spirit inspired me to believe this was our house. I felt Him tell me in a strong way, that we are supposed to have the inn."

"Did the Holy Spirit tell you how much it costs now?" he laughed.

"No. I went to visit Lucy because the lady who owns it is her aunt. I told her to have her aunt call me."

Frank asked, getting a little more interested, "Will Lucy tell her aunt?"

"It sounded like she would call her this afternoon."

"We'll just have to wait and see, and most of all pray to make the right decision - if we could afford it, which I seriously doubt," Frank said, and then added, "I don't remember who told me that house will never sell because the people are convinced it is haunted. They say the Marquess de Aguayo's wife walks the patios at night."

"Yeah, I heard that too. So much the better if no one has bought it. Maybe God is saving it for us."

"Don't get too excited. I don't want you to be disappointed. If it is not that house, He has another house for

236

us," Frank assured me.

While we were still in the rent house, God was using us powerfully – all of us, even Simon. It had not been too long since we made the move to General Cepeda. I really had my hands full and very little help. Frank would often bring Joseph along to Saltillo or on other errands, not because he was showing favoritism, but because removing the three year old from the situation lightened my load. One day, Frank had taken Joseph to Saltillo. The house had painters in it, our kitchen was moved to the other end of the house, and I had no one to help me with the children. The older girls stayed behind. They felt that Simon being left behind made him a victim of injustice. They challenged me on the issue.

"Why does Joseph always get to go? Simon never gets to go."

"First of all," I told them firmly, "It isn't true that Simon never gets to go. Simon is so happy around here, that sometimes it's a help to me for Dad to take Joseph, who is so active. When Simon stays he falls asleep more easily. Girls, even if Mom and Dad aren't perfect, *Jesus* treats us all fairly. He cares for all of his little sheep and Simon's not losing out!"

As we prepared lunch, we began making up a song to the tune of the song "Hey, Hey, We're the Monkies." That theme song from an old television show has a catchy tune. We were singing "Hey, Hey, we're for Jesus, some people say we're out of bounds, but we're too busy praying, to put anybody down!"

Simon was really getting into it, he was bouncing around to the music, and able to sing the "Hey, Hey we're for Jesus..." and mumble the rest. We sang our new song and praised God again at our grace before meals, just as we've always done when we sit for each meal.

As I prayed the grace before the meal, Simon kept tugging at my arm, saying, "Mama, Mama, Mama, Mama." I quickly ended the grace to ask Simon what he wanted.

He answered, very excitedly – "Mama, Jesus shook my hand!! He shook my hand, Mom!"

He was beaming, his little face aglow as he kept looking up at the ceiling and repeating his statement. Next to hugging, handshaking is Simon's favorite thing in the world. He couldn't have been happier.

The girls were happy, too. I told them, "See, girls, Jesus will never leave Simon out."

After grace, I served the four children and nursed the baby. But later, Simon accompanied me to the laundry patio. As I washed our dishcloths on the washboard, I asked him some questions about his encounter with Jesus. "Simon, were Jesus's clothes shiny?"

He smiled from ear to ear, "Mmmhmm.... shiny, very shiny." He looked pensive, and then sad. "But Mama, poor Jesus had a bloody 'booboo' (sore) on his hand." Simon pointed sadly to the palm of his hand.

Joseph got to go to Saltillo, but Simon got to shake Jesus' hand.

Rogelio had been right; our rent house was practically in ruins. The more our house fell down around us, the more I had the abandoned inn on my mind. Finally, one afternoon, I knelt and prayed, "Lord Jesus, I don't want to be thinking constantly of that inn. Help me to trust you. But, please, let me hear one way or another. If the answer is no, I will completely surrender to any other house you might have for us. Also, Lord Jesus, we have seven thousand dollars in savings right now. I know it could not possibly be that cheap, but I am begging you to let us buy it with what we have and have money left over for the minor details. Amen."

We got very few phone calls in those days; almost no one in General Cepeda had phones, so they usually came over if they needed to talk to you. No sooner than I had gotten off of my knees, than the phone rang. It happened so fast that there was no doubt in my mind that this call would be the answer to my prayer.

"*Buenas tardes*. Is this Genie?" a genteel voice on the other end of the line asked, "Lucy called me the other day and told me you all might be interested in the inn. Is that right?"

I was surprisingly calm, "Yes, that's right, if the price is in our budget."

"I talked it over with my family, we are ready to sell, and so we have reduced the price to fifteen million pesos."

"Fifteen million pesos? Wow! Well, thank you for calling. Can I have your number? After I talk to my husband, we will call you back."

238

"I'm not trying to rush you, but we think it will sell fast at this price, and it is fully furnished. Would you like to see it?" she asked.

"Of course," I laughed, "We don't want to buy a house sight unseen."

The owner lived in Saltillo, so she continued to explain the arrangements; "One of my nephews has the key so I'll send the key to Lucy today or tomorrow."

"That sounds wonderful! God bless you."

After nursing the baby, I fell asleep. He was so precious, his perfect features, olive skin, hazel brown eyes and stark white-blonde, almost luminescent, hair caused him to be the hit of every gathering. Praise the Lord; he was a friendly, relaxed baby. He also loved his mom, and never strayed very far from me. He still remembers being carried in my front kangaroo pack, with his little head poking out of the V-neck of my poncho.

When Frank and Susanna walked through the door, I got up to serve them some coffee milk and bread. Susanna's pretty, big blue eyes, sparkled with joy, "There were lots of kids at Hedionda. I gave my testimony about Simon shaking hands with Jesus. The ladies loved it."

I smiled and gave her bouncy, blonde ponytail a gentle tug. She and Frank had enjoyed their rancho ministry. As we sat down to share, I said, "Frank, Lucy's aunt called me today. She says the Inn is for sale, they are in a hurry to sell it."

"Did you ask how much they wanted for it?' Frank asked

"Fifteen million pesos. That's a big discount, though I'm not sure I figured out the exchange properly. God decided this price and whispered it in the ear of the family," I said excitedly.

"The recent peso devaluation....hmmm. The price would be about $6,500.00, exactly what we could afford, and still have some left for the attorneys and the closing of the sale. Call her first thing in the morning, and tell her we are interested. When can we see it?" Frank queried.

"I already told her we were *interested*. She's sending the key to Lucy tomorrow. I am so anxious to go and see it on the inside," I said.

A series of minor miracles, the counsel and advice of Bishop Villalobos, as well as the expertise of his diocesan attorney enabled us to purchase our new place. To this day, entering the ancient, enormous entrance doors is a spiritual experience. As we walk into twenty thousand square feet of enclosed house and garden, with its graceful archways, sunny yellow patio tile, walls two feet thick, and wood-beamed ceilings twenty feet high, a sense of history descends on us. The front of the house opens on the principal plaza with its abundance of stately old trees and green shrubbery. It was, and still is, an amazing house that sits directly across from the ancient historical church. Our house was standing in 1735 when a Franciscan Friar stayed there, and he wrote to his superiors about it. That Friar's letter is in a museum in Mexico City.

The inn was fully furnished in simple Mexican style, with absolutely everything from linens to band-aids. We knew that such a spacious house with so much potential for ministry was part of the Master's plan. He would surely use this house and use us, his humble servants, who made it our home.

The townspeople were so glad the missionaries bought the house. They figured we'd have it blessed and it would stay blessed. If anyone could drive out evil, they figured we could. They knew it would no longer remain haunted after we prayed with holy water and vigorous praise. Soon after, the haunting stories were replaced by stories of magnificent signs and wonders.

Since it had been a hotel, with only three bathrooms, everybody and his brother, had eaten or slept, or worked there before. Be they rich or poor, they felt right at home. The travelers, who had found refuge in the town of General Cepeda's inn, were not rich American tourists, but the folks from the nearby towns and ranchos, who came to see the doctor, go to weddings and to buy their meager supplies.

After only one night in the house, we still had our things scattered all over the place, as we began the process of settling into our new home. I looked at the disarray, all the re-arranging we'd have to do, combined with all of the cleaning we'd have to do, and it was formidable. After my prayer time that night, I fell into bed exhausted.

Frank had just joined me when there was a knock on the door. It was a seminarian who lived at the rectory. We didn't have a telephone in this new place. Frank answered the door.

"There's a phone call for you. An *Americano* left his number for you to call him right back," the seminarian reported. In the rent house, we had a phone, but phones in our homes in mission have been rare indeed. Today, Casa de Misiones has one, but for many years we used the phone at the church office or the rectory. Of course, cell phones and email have further transformed communication for missionaries.

Frank went over to the rectory and answered the call. Almost an hour later, he came back and happily reported, "That was a young man from Lubbock, Texas. His name is Chet Marko. He and his wife are the young couple Catherine asked us to pray for last year. He's the youth director at St. John Newmann Parish, and wants to bring a group down here on a short-term mission this summer. They'll be coming down this Monday from Lubbock to scope it out. He and Valerie are interested in Missions. I felt great about our talk!"

I could tell that Frank had really been blessed by his conversation. Because I had been moving from and cleaning out our rent house, and settling the children in, I was almost comatose from sheer weariness. I sleepily gave him a big hug and a kiss, and promptly dozed off.

The next morning I awoke with a start, suddenly realizing that we would be receiving visitors from the states in two days hit me full force. "Frank, we are going to have to pray for some organizational and cleaning angels to help us to be ready to receive them on Monday," I said, trying not to panic.

"Their coming to visit us so soon can be a blessing. We will all have to pitch in," he said. Everyone got busy: we prayed, sang, cooperated and put out a lot of "elbow-grease."

When they walked in the door on Monday, we had just put the last few things in place. God's timing is perfect.

God sent easy visitors first. Our children climbed up into their arms like they were long lost relatives. Chet and Val were Beau's age and it was good to be around youthful, vigorous Christians again. They loved Mexico; it was a great trip. Valerie and I remember the time of sharing late one evening in the car, talking about life in mission for families.

Val said, "Before coming, I had been concerned that missionaries wouldn't have a nice family life. Here, with all of you, my eyes are being opened. I can see the joy and peace on

241

your children's faces. They obviously have a good life!"

"Val, it's the best life! We're not settling for less. We're getting more. Missionary activity is the greatest and holiest duty of the Church. One thing I've learned as a mother in a missionary family is that whatever is good for adult Christians is good for children Christians, even including the cross. 'Let the little children come to me,' Jesus said. There is no better place to bring your children to Jesus than on the mission field!"

The Markos left our home in Mexico with a decision to bring their youth group down in the summer, and with an even more exciting decision; they had decided to seriously consider *joining us* in mission! The Lord had first given us the perfect environment to receive mission groups. Our home had an open courtyard with many rooms opening out on to it. Now He had given us the ministry and lots of visitors! We prayed, and prayed, and prayed for the Lord to send our friends and loved ones to visit us. Until this mission, one of our greatest sadnesses was that no one knew what we were talking about when we tried to tell them about our life in Mission. Things would be different now. In a little over a year and a half the Lord sent over one hundred-sixty visitors to share life with us in the missions.

The Romeros were the first family from home to visit with us. We had begged them to come but their reason had been, "No funds for the trip."

"We do want to experience the mission life that means so much to y'all," Cheryl said. "The kids are now asking to go, but we don't have the finances."

"Just say to the Lord, 'Yes, we will go to visit the Summers', and He will get you here," I wrote Cheryl; I was so lonesome for them.

Cheryl and Donald said, "Yes!"

Much to their surprise and even mine, young Sarah Romero won a drawing at her school's festival and the cash was exactly what they needed to ready their car and come. Video cameras were new then, but they were able to borrow a video camera and their videos plainly show the love between our families and the scope of our mission. I know heaven was tuned into that scene when they drove up to the historic house in General Cepeda.

Dennis and Florence Crain were some of our other

favorite visitors. They loved missions from the first moment they set foot in General Cepeda! They came more frequently than anyone and brought us blessings each time, except the time they brought us the chicken pox. It didn't matter, when the Crains were there, they were missionaries.

Dennis and Florence were chaperones with the St. Mary Magdalen youth group, when they first made a trip to be with us in Mexico. Their children, Katie, Lisa and David were with them. We took the whole group out to a beautiful cavern in the desert. The place is called the *Oratorio*, a place for prayer. This cave had been a secret hideout for Catholics to celebrate Mass for many years. The altar crafted from stone used for these secret Masses was high up in the cave near the mouth of a spring. A terrible persecution had been inflicted on the Catholic faithful in the *Guerra Cristera*, from 1926, lasting three long years, and the faithful had taken refuge at *Oratorio*.

There is about a fifty-five foot drop from the top of the ledge of the cavern. There is, however, one fairly safe climb up to the very top on the right side of the cave. There at the mouth of the spring, the water begins to run down, out of the cavern, creating pleasant pools surrounded by lush green grass at the bottom. Frank had taken four-year-old Joseph to the mouth of the spring early in the morning. Later, around lunchtime, Joseph asked permission to hike with Sarah and about fifteen other teenage girls and go up to the altar again. I was lying on a boulder in the sun taking care of John Paul and Simon, out of view of the mouth of the cavern.

Suddenly, I heard several voices. Sarah, Andrea Listi, and others started calling out in loud voices. "Come back, Joseph, come back!"

The urgency alarmed me, and as I was coming down from the boulder, I heard them scream even louder, "Joseph, come down. Ooooh Joseph, watch out, Joseph!!!"

The next thing I knew, pandemonium erupted. Bloodcurdling screams exploded from fifteen young girls and other onlookers. I turned to see Rick DeHart, one of the youth leaders, take off running, stepping across rocks and streams like a gazelle toward the mouth of the cave. I knew I could never get close enough in time to help, so I threw myself prostrate on the ground. I cried out, "Save him Jesus, Oh God, save him!!"

Joseph had followed close behind the girls all the way to the top, and sat quietly for a while as the girls prayed and talked. Soon he got restless and decided to head back down. He slipped away from the girls and got distracted by Rick's older boys. The older boys were standing on the ledge right near the dangerous fifty-five foot drop overlooking the face of the cliff. Joseph started scaling the face of the cliff where it was steep and risky, to try and reach the older boys. They had moved over a bit to the ledge they were on; Joseph was *going up* from midway. Scaling the face was almost certain death for a four year old, but he made it almost to Cody's reach and Cody bent down to extend his hand to Joseph so he wouldn't fall. It was too late; Joseph reached up to grab his hand, but grabbed only dirt, and started freefalling dangerously to what seemed like certain death. He kept grabbing for the face of the cliff and not throwing himself backwards, sort of like a cat sliding down against a wall.

The bloodcurdling screams had come when a huge boulder broke loose from the mountain and started falling over Joseph's head just inches away from him as he fell. As he landed at the bottom of the cliff, the huge boulder was seconds away from landing on top of him. Inexplicably, the boulder "exploded." The boulder turned into a huge, dense cloud of pure ashen dust. It looked like a giant bag of flour from heaven had been shaken out all over Joseph. The *whole youth group* insisted that when they saw the <u>boulder</u> falling, it was a <u>boulder</u>! They can't explain how it happened that when it almost landed on Joseph, it was exploded into dust! Inexplicably, the boulder *exploded and became dust*!

Frank was closer than I was to Joseph, and when he got there and picked him up, he was unharmed, but looking like an ashen, beige snowman. It was hard to see his hair or his eyes.

Frank brought him to my arms and I clutched him crying, "Oh, Joseph, I'm so happy Jesus saved you!"

He bear hugged me back.

"Mama, my angel saved me. My angel saved me. My angel told me, 'Don't panic. Be calm and you will get a big surprise.' "

Being calm, not looking back or reaching out had *saved* Joseph. His calm leaning in towards the cliff had saved him from a fifty-foot free fall and his angel's caution to remain calm had kept him safe. If he had panicked, and leaned outward, he would surely have been killed.

When we agreed to let Joseph bathe in one of the pools, which he had been begging to do all day, he felt that this was his reward for remaining calm. At four, he figured out that the "big surprise" the angel promised was that, because he was so dirty, we allowed him to wash off and splash in the stream fed pool.

It was one of the most exciting, most profound, and most witnessed miracles we experienced as a family on mission. Joseph's best friend, David Crain, who was also four at the time, was on the trip. Later, David's parents were talking to me about the miracle. Florence told me that much earlier in the day, she had taken David up to the spring. Frank and Joseph had been following behind at a distance. When the Crains turned around to look down, David pointed down at Frank and Joseph and said excitedly to her, "Look, Mom, there's Joseph's angel!"

"Where, David?" she asked.

"Right there, next to Joseph" he replied.

David pointed to the spot where Joseph and Frank were. Florence didn't see anything and didn't pursue it. She thought maybe David mistook Frank for Joseph's angel. It wasn't until she listened to me recounting the part of the story where Joseph told me it was his angel who saved him, that she remembered that David had seen Joseph's angel earlier in the morning.

Just as we were discussing David's sighting of Joseph's angel, the boys walked by.

We called them to come over to meet us where we were sitting under the trees. Dennis asked David, "Did you see Joseph's angel this morning?"

David nodded his head vigorously in agreement.

"How did you know it was an angel?" Dennis queried.

Very simply, but very assertively, David replied, "By his wings!!"

For several years, Joseph and David would discuss seeing their angels. On one such occasion, I had heard the two of them talking about their angels. So when David was gone, I asked Joseph, "Do you know your angel's name?"

He didn't skip a beat; he said matter-of-factly, "*Golden Crest of God.*"

It was one of those moments when time stands still for a

few nano-seconds. "Golden Crest of God," I said, stunned. "That's a great name for an angel, Joseph."

"Yup," he said, "and he's really, really strong."

I knew that was a genuine response. I hadn't expected such a clear, appropriate name for his angel.

Youth groups came to our new mission house; families came, singles came, priests came, and our relatives came. Fr. Randy Moreau was stationed in Abbeville at the time and he was one of our first visitors in 1987. He had spent six weeks in mission as a seminarian and he knew how great the need was. To date, he has been one of our greatest supporters and believes wholeheartedly in mission. If every priest did what Fr. Randy has done, the world would be teeming with lay missionaries.

The first summer we received three youth groups, with their adult leaders, from different cities. As we planned and scheduled for their arrival, we readied the house. We put our schedule on a big poster board calendar that covered the two months of youth groups. It all looked so neat and manageable on paper, it was our first time to minister to American groups in the foreign missions. I still laugh when I think of that calendar. The plan looked so "do-able" on paper. Living it out was another matter. It was intense; we were all just learning the dynamics of short-term mission trips. So much got done in such a short time. We were just a family, not an organization. Only the Holy Spirit could have "pulled it off."

One night late, one of the adult leaders and her daughter were praying over me because I was so tired. I fell asleep with my head in my hands. I guess I was subconsciously listening to the prayer, and when she got around to closing her prayer with an Our Father, I prayed instead, "Bless us, Oh, Lord, and these thy gifts, which we are about to receive...."

I had prayed the blessing before meals, instead! Laughing and smiling I went to bed and crashed. During another youth group visit, I was walking into my bedroom at about 1:15 a.m., and I had been up since 5:30 a.m. the previous morning. A young girl came up to me and asked, "Miss Genie, can I talk to you?"

It was way past lights out, but she wanted to talk. I had talked with her the night before about her problems and concerns, and told her that the only way she would find true joy and happiness was to give her life fully to Jesus Christ.

"Okay, honey, I said, "but I can only give you a few minutes, I'm so tired."

"Yes ma'am, I don't think this will take too long. God has spoken to me so much through my mission. Remember what we were talking about last night? I want to give my life to Jesus, what must I do?"

The Lord worked signs and wonders before our very eyes. The groups built bonds of love and respect between themselves and those Mexicans in the villages who attended the evangelization. We were worn out by our summer schedule but, it was all worth it - the Lord was calling these young people to Himself.

Gary Guidry, director of Abbeville's youth group had prepared a beautiful journal for each youth group member so that the kids could record the workings of God during their mission to Mexico. Many of the kids did keep the journal faithfully. Here are a few excerpts:

"I wrote this down after reading a story about St. Francis of Assisi: Sitting on this cliff, the wind is blowing so hard. I feel that God is blowing through me with the wind. I have chills all over, and the Lord is everywhere. Right now, He is talking to me. I know the Lord has so much in store for me, and I don't want to let Him down. I am filled with so much courage right now. I know that God is with me. I never thought I would receive so much by giving to others. I have the strength now to carry my own cross, because God is with me now. It's almost like He is saying, "Come follow Me!' And I say, `Yes Lord, I will'."

Although the short-term missions had taken much of our time, we had also been the catalyst of the Holy Spirit in the parish of St. Francis of Assisi and its fifty-four ranchos. We had suffered, carried the cross, and laid down our lives for the Gospel. We had seen the Lord renew the land with water, making streams run in the desert, literally and spiritually. The people prayed for rain, and the rain came. The Abbeville youth group prayed for rain in one rancho, and two weeks later, a small lake that had been bone dry was filled with water!

In a similar incident, we were praying in a rancho chapel for rain. Frank pleaded in faith, and a very loud voice, "Lord

God, please send rain to the people of La Parrita. They have been asking you so faithfully, hear their prayer. Water the dry land, Lord, I beg you!"

As soon as the words were out of his mouth, the sky exploded with thunder and lightning. It had been cloudless and starry minutes before. But within seconds of his prayer, huge drops of rain pounded the chapel. A full-fledged rainstorm followed. It was awesome. The people of La Parrita still love to tell the story to our grandchildren about when their grandfather, Francisco, prayed for rain.

When we share with others about missions, we always emphasize the effective and essential work of prayer. I say, "A paraplegic could be an effective missionary. He could go into the new environment in mission lands and pray with faith for their needs. Praying is the first thing, and a continuous service to the building of the Kingdom."

Living in that two hundred fifty year old "Inn" was the Lord's plan for us. The monorail vision I had seen earlier was fulfilled. That vision has proven true for the coming and going of thousands of people mainly from the USA, but also from Canada, Europe, Latin America India, Malaysia and the Islands, to General Cepeda through our mission. The Lord Jesus has kept that *spiritual monorail* faithful to its purpose, putting missions on display for those who don't know the urgency, and bringing the riches of mission back to home churches.

In Scripture, Jesus says, *"My Mother, brothers and relatives are those who hear the word of God and keep it."* He is not denying his mother. No one knows better than Jesus, how many times His Blessed Mother died to her personal hopes and dreams, paying the price to truly hear God's word and to keep it. He owed his human life, as he knew it to her excellent faithfulness in keeping the Word of God. I believe that Jesus was demonstrating a new, real level of kinship. He was saying that special blood relationships can be achieved, not only by being born into the same family, but by hearing and keeping God's Word together.

That's why it was such a blessing for us to have our families visit us in General Cepeda. We had often prayed, "Lord, let them understand that when we feel called to 'go', we 'go' to obey and share Your Word." Frank and I longed for them to have a better understanding of our call. Frank's parents came first. "This is much better than we expected!" they commented, happily surprised.

"I am so impressed with how much love these people have for you and the children," Frank's mom said.

His dad visited with our friends, and our kids interpreted. He told me, "It was a wonderful experience to attend a rancho evangelization outreach and see the hunger in those villages. They do need the things of God. I am seeing the value of your work, and why you answered God's call. I can see so much happiness in our grandchildren on the mission field. Their lives are full, having all their little friends over, and loving Jesus in a dedicated way."

Frank's Mom told me one day after a visit to La Rosa, "I was blessed to carry on my lap the ciborium for the Communion Service. I didn't feel worthy but I was so blessed to be holding the real presence of Jesus and bringing Him to a rancho."

Frank's Dad wanted to treat the family to a meal in a restaurant. Restaurant Josefina was the closest one to our home in General Cepeda. A family that had been very good to us owned it. The grandmother, Doña Ninfa, said that she had been praying for years for a missionary to come to La Rosa. The restaurant was a family style restaurant, but very clean and the food was delicious. Doña Ninfa came by to visit with us while we ate our dessert; she was honored and blessed to have Frank's parents with her, in her restaurant. When it came time to pay the bill - Doña Ninfa refused to accept payment.

"Missionaries don't pay!"

Frank's Dad was in shock, and said teasingly, "I think they love y'all too much around here, that would never happen in Abbeville."

A small sign that Jesus had worked in their hearts, and that they accepted our ministry in their hearts, was the first letter we received from Frank's Dad after he got back home. It was addressed to "Don Francisco Summers," the title of respect that our Mexican friends had given Frank.

Several months later, my parents and my nephews, Robin and Gabriel, came to Mexico, too! My sister and her family accompanied my parents. When Rachel called long distance to notify me of their intentions to visit us, I was so happy I almost couldn't contain my joy!

Rachel explained, "Jude and I went to visit Mom and Dad, we joked with them, I said `We're going to take Joshua and Jennifer and go to Mexico to visit Genie and Frank. Jude's got a vacation in two weeks. Do y'all want to come along?' Genie, I nearly flipped when they agreed to come."

The telephone was wet with tears of happiness and I said, "I don't know if I can wait two weeks!"

They made the trip faster than any of our other visitors. I was amazed. I asked Rachel, "Didn't y'all have any delays going through customs?"

"We did it in fifteen minutes," she said.

"I can't believe it," I told her, "How did y'all do that?"

"Daddy just kept smiling at everyone and handing out finger rosaries."

Mom got sick right before they left, but that didn't stop them. My valiant mother came even with fever. The fever slowed her down a bit, but the grace that God was pouring out on our families together in mission perked her up again.

It was a spiritual pilgrimage for them. They worried a little at first that four teenagers would get bored – they needn't have, the teenagers had lots of fun! They joined in our family prayers, we sang to the Lord together in rousing praise; we went out to the ranchos together; we toured General Cepeda; they rode on a burro; we went on a picnic and we explored beautiful Saltillo together. God exposed them to the full Mexican experience.

"I am so deeply happy," I told Frank, one night after everyone had gone to bed, "I can't thank the Lord enough for bringing them, but most of all, I'm so happy with the way they are giving themselves to this time with us and our work."

He pulled me close to him, "I'm so happy for you too. They would make good full-time missionaries, your dad gave a great message at the rancho tonight."

Mom and I were in the kitchen; a friend came to visit, and to ask for a donation. Genoveva and her husband are caretakers of a large summer home owned by friends of ours from Monterrey. Their weekly pay was late. Genoveva was part of Frank's evangelization team, she knew Jesus. I translated for Mom. Genoveva was saying, "All we've had to eat today is salt and tortillas! But that's okay, we are happy to have our good health and the Lord. It's just a little difficult for my husband and my sons to work all day on tortillas and salt. I'm not worried, I know the Lord will provide."

Just prior to that another friend, Lucita, an eighty-four year old lady was visiting, and as I unpacked my groceries, she spied my four-roll pack of toilet tissue. "Oh, could I have one roll?" she asked longingly, "I haven't been able to afford a roll of tissue in a long time."

Mom is tenderhearted – she had to walk out of the room choked with tears. The thought that a roll of toilet tissue could mean so much to that sweet old lady was more than she could take. Rachel and Jude visited several more times, they loved mission.

I recall how my father encouraged me after reading a draft of **Go! You Are Sent** that he found in my office. My busy schedule in Mexico at that time had forced me to put my writing on hold. He told me one day, "I want you to finish the book."

"I'd love to finish, Daddy," I said close to tears, "but I don't know how I'll ever find the time."

The next day he told me, "I walked across the Plaza with your manuscript, and I went into Church and laid it on the altar. I asked the Lord, 'Please, Jesus, let Genie finish the book, through the intercession of Your Blessed Mother.' I think you're going to finish it."

Their visit ended on the First Friday healing Mass in the parish in General Cepeda. It was a beautiful finale of our time together. My joy knew no bounds, as we lined up by twos into three healing teams – Michelle Slate and I, Mom and Dad, and Rachel and Jude. Frank and Susanna played music while we prayed. Hundreds came up for prayers. Many were healed! Others were touched by our loved ones, who came from so far away, speaking another language, to bring God's tender mercy and concern. My family, Mom and Dad, spoke the finest of all languages to my "brothers and sisters" from Mexico – the universal language of God's love.

251

Beau and Pops
(my dad) at a
bonfire on the
bayou in 1972,
before we left
for missions.

General Cepeda,
Casa de Misiones
1987
Frank's Mom and
Dad visited and
finally understood
our mission call.

Both Frank's mom and my mom
were named Beverlee (Beverly).
(R) My mom and (L) Frank's mom
celebrating Mother's day in 2007.

Chapter Fifteen

Chickens, Trumpets and Kingdom Building

"Does anyone have a Bible reading to share?" Frank asked in our morning prayer.

"I do," little Mary Magdalen stood up with her Bible, it almost looked too big for her. But it wasn't. She opened her Bible and read, "Enlarge the place of your tent, and let the curtains of your habitations be stretched out; hold not back, lengthen your cords and strengthen your stakes."

Our children from any early age were disciplined into having a daily personal prayer time with Scripture. Each child had read the Bible all the way through before they made their confirmation at about sixteen (Simon would be the exception). Our family made its home in God's Word. All of us understood that this was our handbook, our blueprint, our "Manufacturer's Manual." If something was broken, we knew where to find the instructions on how to fix it. Scripture was a light for our path, our daily portion of food for the soul, and an anchor for our faith.

Mary, at eight, was experiencing this reality. Sharing a passage from the Bible was as natural for her as breathing in and breathing out. She looked extra cute this day, with her dirty blonde ponytails, exquisite, delicate nose and her favorite red t-shirt. As Mary read the passage from the Bible, the Lord was speaking. We could feel His presence pulsating in the room. We had often received this reading right before a new baby arrived on the scene. We had stretched out our tent pegs to receive each new life the Lord sent us. But we knew our family was complete.

This time, Jesus was saying something different, "The Lord surely means visitors, we have to enlarge our 'tents' to receive all of the visitors. But that's not all, I think He also means we should prepare for *future missionaries* who might

253

want to join us," I commented, "More people than ever are interested in our family life in mission."

Frank paused pensively, and then said, "I think we should hold another family retreat. Do you think we could find a retreat facility nearby? We will never escape the constant demand at the door and the needs of the ranchos for a retreat, if we don't get away."

"Sure, Frank, I'll find Lauro today and ask him," I said, truly excited. How wonderful it would be to get away as a family.

Lauro is a fixture in the church in General Cepeda. He has been the church secretary, bookkeeper, assistant, maintenance supervisor, driver, and liaison with the Diocese for years. He knows all the spiritual movements, clergy, religious sites, retreat houses and events of the diocese. He could be on a commercial for Mexican coffee, neatly dressed, sporting a disarming smile from under his well-trimmed moustache. And he was our friend. He went with Frank and later with all of our missionaries to the ranchos at night; he made tabernacles by hand for the village chapels. Lauro was a fount of information for us. He did know a place! He generously called, reserved the place, and recommended us to the nuns who ran it.

We were the only retreatants in a facility that could house one hundred fifty persons. The peace and quiet was immediately soothing. The nuns were so kind. In the chapel, soaring over the altar was the most inspiring image of the resurrected Jesus! It was the *first* time our family had held our family retreat in a real retreat house!! This was a milestone. Using the same format we always followed put us at ease. Three sessions a day of assigned Bible readings, were allotted to Frank, myself, and the girls. Our two live-in helpers, Angelica and Lupe, were included. Because we were free from the time consuming duties of our daily routine, we had time to add a daily family rosary, and the "joyful noise session" (all three of our little boys had a percussion instrument). With Mass every day, and a time for confession, we were totally blessed.

We filled the spare hours with happy leisure activities. The kids loved our newly invented sport – family "volleyball-soccer- kickball." This sport, we made up as we went along, and specifically designed it to include the athletic abilities of all of

254

us, including Simon's semi-stable running ability. We luxuriated in the luscious green lawn, a rarity in the arid desert region of Northern Mexico. The purple mountaintops of the nearby Sierra Madres provided a beautiful backdrop for the awesome sunsets that the Lord thrilled us with each evening. Fatigue and flagging spirits faded away.

The Lord spoke to us about preparedness, that He was preparing our lives for His work. He spoke to us about **community**. We had been praying all of our missionary lives for the Lord to build community – a community of itinerant missionaries, who would be ready to receive marching orders from the Holy Spirit, and hold to the Gospel values we held dear.

My first reading was from Ecclesiastes. It spoke to me about seasons in life, I understood the Lord say to me, "The season has come, I want you to share with others the wondrous riches of the missionary life you have lived, the easy times and the hard times, the mountains and the valleys, the agony and the ecstasy."

Frank felt He was saying, "I will send families to share life with you in mission, but you need to change some ways of thinking. *Start thinking in terms of a family.* Your kids are your kids, little or grown, you love them no matter what. In family, you bear with their weaknesses and they bear with yours. Even when you're apart – you are still family!"

After the kids were in bed that night, Frank and I revisited the Word we heard that day. Frank said, "The missionary *family of families* would have to differ from community a little. Sometimes communities set up their structures very tightly – and that's necessary for their care and shepherding. I have noticed that in community, it is hard for someone who is hearing God's call to 'go' – to get up and 'go'."

"That's true, Frank. It is different in a *family*. A *family* rears children, and then lets them '*go!*' We, in our missionary family, would have to be able to do that too!"

"The new missionaries won't 'belong' to us, they will belong to the family of families, together we will belong to the Lord," Frank continued, "We need to be of one mind and one heart."

Our family of families needs dedication, holiness, and commitment. We would have to disciple and pastor and train –

255

like parents do with children. This was radically new thinking for us. We didn't have a model for that kind of thinking. How could we build a family of families? The answer was simple, we couldn't. God would have to do it. Who would become a part of our family of families? This shift in perspective, from building a community of missionaries to the idea of a family of families in mission was one of the major shifts in our lives. However, we didn't know how long we still had to continue laboring in prayer. When, in 1996, Family Missions Company was founded, it was the fulfillment of decades of prayer. We had been asking in Faith and Hoping in things not seen. Jesus still says, "The harvest is plenty but the laborers are few."

Our get away retreat had been for us a "big success", we had a lot to think and pray about. We had ended the retreat with a prayer for a new "in-filling" of the Holy Spirit. The Holy Spirit never disappoints. We came home to the Casa de Misiones, our home in General Cepeda, full of zeal to serve the Lord by receiving the "short-term" missionaries from America. *He* was sending them to *His* Mexican poor as our visitors: families, friends, and youth groups.

In the full bloom of his young manhood, Beau had entered into a "Holy Struggle" encountering many challenges and many victories. He would at times find himself in locked battle with the enemy. He and Michelle became engaged and they travelled to Mexico to announce it to us. We begged God for a beautiful life for them, and hoped mission would one day be a part of it.

Chet and Val Marko, the former youth leaders from Lubbock, came to live with us and train for full-time missions. We gave them a basic Christian teaching series, geared to missionaries. Then we invited them to enter a year of spiritual formation, to imbibe the way of life we had lived in mission. They dedicated themselves to prayer and the study of God's Word. We provided them with pastoral guidance. The year we spent together was a foretaste of the family of families in mission. They wanted to raise a family in mission. "What are some of the essentials that make family 'work' in the missions?" Val asked as we visited over coffee.

I took this question to the Lord in prayer, I heard him say, "Missionary families are the salt of the Earth. Your family has found its 'saltiness' in the life You live for Me."

I responded to Jesus in my heart, "We love our life, we love being missionaries. We love You, Jesus, our friend. We love Your Holy Spirit. Thanks for empowering us to keep 'salt' in our hearts, and not to let it lose its flavor."

As I continued meditating on this word, I also thought, "Saltiness does immunize us from crosses to carry, trials to endure, and our own discouraging failures which weigh us down at times. This business of loving and appreciating our life is not an effortless accomplishment; we need God's grace. If we want to be salty, if we want to be His instruments, we must remember the price. *All it costs is everything*."

Over and over and over again, we go to the Lord in prayer, each one personally, and all together as a family, empty handed. We are beggars, thirsting at the fountain of grace. We have no flavor, unless the Lord allows us to dip into the Divine salt cellar for our daily portion of life giving salt.

Over the years, our family gathered traditions that strengthen us. We honor one another on our special occasions, we play together, we go on outings together, and we serve the Lord together. Visitors to our home are served in the name of Jesus. When we do our chores and daily duties in the name and power of Jesus, it has great value and merit. We sing a lot, and we laugh a lot. We remember, too, that just *being a Christian* makes us salty. Salt doesn't go around looking for a cooking pot to jump into. The *chef* adds the salt to whatever he wishes, and by its very nature, it makes the food taste better.

Sure, our children were growing up as one hundred percent, bona fide children. They squabbled over toys; they got revved up and played hard. They spilled their milk, and had to be reminded to clean their rooms. They played jokes on one another, and tattle-taled. Neighborhood kids were always in and out of our houses. They occupied imaginary worlds for hours. Our kids enjoyed one another, and supported each other. If they hurt one another, we insisted that they repent, ask for and grant forgiveness, and hug till they meant it. I had a technique called the "rerun." If they said or did something that was unacceptable, they would have to do a rerun – leave the room and walk back

257

in, then say or do it over again, properly. For us as parents, it was an effort, well worth it, to consistently, insistently, train them in desirable virtues – "the spirit is willing, but the flesh is weak!"

In 1989, Frank and I were in our mid-forties, when we began planting the "seeds" of a family of families in mission. Frank, my "knight in shining armor", wore a full beard, gold-rimmed glasses and looked slender and fit in his simple, Sears working man's clothing. He seldom left his guitar at home and never left his Bible. He preached like a prophet, studied like a scholar, and mostly loved us and the people to whom he went. In his ministry, mountains were moved and a "straight way" in the desert was made for the Lord. The kids always had access to their dad, and our family prayer times and meal times cemented us as a mission team. I was still *in love* with him.

In the "saltiness" of life as family, we take some world issues very seriously – there are many things happening in the world today that concern our family very much. Even though, we are often far from the scene, these problems disturb the rhythm in our lives. So we do what we can.

I remember the day, Mary Magdalen, who was nine years old, came to me with tears streaming down her face. "Come quickly, Mama," she said, "Susanna's crying."

"Why is she crying?" I asked, hugging her.

"We saw those pictures of the aborted babies." (A friend had mailed me a packet of pro-life materials, I put them aside in my office.) I went into the bedroom of my eleven year old and found her sobbing her heart out.

We all hugged, cried and prayed for a long while. "Please, please, Jesus, save the babies!" they wailed with real grief.

My three year old, John Paul, said, "I want to go to church to save the babies!"

Mary Magdalen put her arm around him and said, "Prayers do help, John Paul, if you pray, you *can* help to save the babies."

"Why do they *KILL babies*?" he asked horrified.

"Their daddies and moms don't want babies, I guess," Susanna replied.

"Mary, some people don't know Jesus the way we do,

and they make awful mistakes," I interjected.

"Mom, why doesn't the Pope stop them, or the President?" she asked, throwing her hands up, desperately.

"Baby, God wants this horror to stop. We have to help! We have to pray and sacrifice; we have to do our part," I said, "God will help us to help the babies."

God is pro-family, pro-life! Preaching that truth has earned for our family much persecution and disdain over the years. Children, for us, are a "blessing from the Lord," not a curse. There is absolutely no place in Scripture that quotes the Lord saying, "I will curse you with children." The Lord delights in the children of men. Contraception and abortion prevent and kill God's delight. In the years before my conversion, I had made a foray into Women's Liberation. Since my conversion, I have found that my truest freedom lies in living out my call to raise a family according to Gospel principles, and that means being open to life. I'd hate to think of what I would have missed if I had not been open to receive all of my children, every single one. I lived through a crisis pregnancy, I missed the child I surrendered for adoption every day, but I shudder to think of the suffering I would have had to endure if that pregnancy had ended in abortion. I know Jesus loves the second victims of abortion, the moms and dads of the babies. He has the answers for them. They just have to ask Him.

Our own involvement in the pro-life movement goes back to the time when we stopped practicing artificial contraception. We have prayed, and given sacrificially – living in poverty ourselves, using as much as we could for the building of God's Kingdom, a Pro-Life Kingdom. More importantly, we have borne seven children, six of them since I was thirty-two years old (just about the age when some doctors recommend that you stop having children). And, as we live the pro-life witness, we have seen hearts touched and lives changed. Babies by the hundreds have been brought into the world that might otherwise have been prevented or aborted. We have also seen God use us to pray in faith for couples who want to conceive – dozens of little ones were welcomed into the homes of "childless couples".

During our "furloughs" in the U.S., we had several occasions to pray in front of abortion clinics. On one occasion, we were the only family doing a prayer watch. It was drizzling slightly, I was holding toddler, John Paul, in my arms, Joseph, with his strong faith, sandy hair and big hazel eyes was a young boy. He knelt on the public sidewalk outside the building with his dad, holding his own rosary in his little hands. The three girls and Simon knelt too and prayed fervently. Frank had on a brown quilted jacket with a hood. When he pulled the hood over his head to stop the drizzle, he looked like St. Francis. After we finished the first decade we could see a shuffle inside the building. The staff was moving those in the waiting room to another location, away from that powerful scene of our kids, crying and praying for the lives at stake. Shortly, an enraged man, someone on staff, came out and told us we could not be on the sidewalk. We knew he was incorrect, the sidewalk was not off limits at the time, but we moved to the street and finished our rosary on our knees. I hope babies were saved that day.

Many years ago, Fr. Randy Moreau, assistant pastor at St. Mary Magdalen Church in Abbeville, gave a sermon against abortion, "Believe me people, we can *do* SOMETHING. It is not enough just to lament the abominable reality of abortion."

My Susanna, then ten years old, came home and declared, "I'm going to give up candy for the rest of my life (except on my birthday, Christmas and Easter) as a penance and fasting to stop abortion." She has made that sacrifice a permanent part of her life. So have some of our other children.

One day, I ran to locate the sound of crying. It was Joseph. "Are you hurt, my man?" I asked.

"I smashed my finger in the closet!" he said. The finger was turning red and blue. I prayed over it and ran cold water over it.

"Does it still hurt?" I asked.

"I'm offering it up for abortion, Mom," he answered, holding his wound.

In that same season, Susanna heard the terribly sad news that Mexico's president was about to legalize abortion in Mexico. She had met the President of the Republic, Carlos Salinas de Gortari, on two occasions. Once she had breakfast in the Presidential Palace – a privilege she earned as an outstanding scholar in the sixth grade. She ranked first in the state. She was heartbroken that *her* president might sign a bill that legalized abortion.

"Mom, what can we do? Can I write to him?"

I answered, "Let's do it right now, Sweetie, I'll help you."

She reinforced her letter, which begged for the life of the babies, with a picture she and President Gortari had taken together. She was easy to spot, standing right next to him with her flowing blonde hair. She also sent some pamphlets with the graphic pictures of aborted babies. We prayed harder than ever as we slipped the envelope in the mail. Until April of 2007, abortion was still illegal in Mexico, now it is allowed in an early term, and only in Mexico City.

When I give teachings to women on womanhood and motherhood, I always remind them, "Your children's walk with the Lord is important, not only for the child, but for your whole family. Each family has a mission, and all of you in the family are a mission team. Christian families living out their call in an ordinary way, and in an ordinary environment, need to live *extraordinary* lives. Your families must evangelize your neighbors, friends, and churches! Programs and outreaches are good, but 'bold,' faith-filled Christian children, who love and serve the Lord, are better. In the missions, our children often opened doors that would otherwise have stayed shut. So many mothers have told me, "Your children have made a difference in our family. Since they play with your children, our kids want to pray, go to church, and sing praise songs."

The Church teaches that parents are the first and principal educators of their children. Proverbs says, "Train up a child in the way that he should go." Because we lived such an itinerant life, educating our children at home was part of the process of building the Kingdom of God. I believe that if our family had done nothing else for their education but share, read and live God's word; they would have had a super education. Of course, they would have lacked math skills, but they could have caught up. Their very identity as missionaries, as God's servants, educated them. Very early on, they began giving their testimonies, playing Praise music, and organizing children's prayer meetings.

Once, I shared with another Catholic mom who was on a short-term mission, "Missionary children have a world view which acknowledges the Lord as the center and author of life.

For them, Jesus *is* the answer, they know Him personally. They choose the narrow way. Serving affirms their purpose in life; they understand that He sends them to share Good News with a world that is groping in the dark. Having a mission, being commissioned by Jesus and His Church, endows them with powerful tools for living and for success."

I commented further, "We homeschooled our kids most of the time. Sometimes we felt the Lord wanted them in school, but even as they attended schools, public and private, the identity of missionary filtered out the bad stuff. Our kids often had a transforming effect on their schools. When the Scripture says, 'Do all things for the glory of God', it doesn't leave out educating our children."

Rachel, another mom, said to me, "I want that for my children, I want them to be Kingdom builders. I can see how confident your kids are, but I feel like I lack confidence."

"Honestly," I said, "It's like everything we do in mission, we do our best and let God do the rest. Seek first His kingdom, and all else will be added. But most of all, relax, enjoy serving with them, make them part of your mission team."

She asked, "Isn't the concept of service over their heads?"

I answered, "The Word of God is not really over anyone's head. 'Out of the mouths of babes and sucklings, I have formed perfect praise.'"

"I know that's true," she said, "The local people can hardly keep their hands off of my little one. (She was holding a precious, golden haired three-month old.) He just smiles and is touching hearts."

"For, example, Rachel, when we built community in the Philippines, Sarah, Susanna and Mary were essential. There were so many young families that we started a children's ministry. Sarah shared her testimonies with the children almost every week, picked out teachings and games along with the adult leaders. Our younger children have followed her strong faith, and now she is witnessing in school."

When I had finished speaking, Sarah walked in. She had caught the tail end of my comment. She was a pre-teen, with the promise of a cute figure. She wore her full blonde hair in two barrettes. Her glasses accentuated her tiny nose and full lips. I thought, "She's as pretty as a picture."

She plopped her books down, she was mastering sixth grade in a second language. "Mom, my teacher said that he and his wife are going to come to your couples' seminar. He told me I had convinced him, 'cause I don't give up!'" We laughed, and sure enough, her teacher and his wife were at our next seminar.

One time we were in Abbeville, Frank walked into the store of a young businessman, he said, "Hey Frank, did you know we have recently entered the Family Life Program?"

"You look like something good has been happening, tell me about it." Frank answered.

"Our family is really being blessed by the teachings and the prayer. We are walking with the Lord with other families now and it is keeping us strong as a Catholic family."

As Frank was leaving, he called out "Come back here, Frank, I want to show you something."

Tacked up on the wall of his office was a poem that Sarah had written for our newsletter, *Resounding Praise*, when she was eleven, "I read it every day as a prayer. It has really ministered to me," the businessman smiled and tapped the poem on his wall.

A TALK WITH GOD
By Sarah Summers

God, just calling to say `Hi',
Cause you know me.
You know I'm happy.
I don't need to explain.

Well, it's a nice day you've made.
I wonder how it's going to end?
You know,
You have it all planned.
God, how do you know everything?
You know about me
And everyone else
And you understand.
God, when I try to be good
How come I so often fail?

Why?
Well, you understand that, too.
I love you, God -
You know that -
Cause you're 'great'
I know that.

God can use his young servants to build the Kingdom.

God used our family in General Cepeda for the healing of many. Our missionary kids did not doubt for a moment that the Lord Jesus heals others through their prayers. They also knew it was His work and not theirs. The Holy Spirit blows where He wills. Susanna, when she was eleven told me that she couldn't understand why people are afraid to be missionaries, "Cause missionary life is fun." Susanna's heart always went out to the suffering, she wrote an article about a little boy named Angel.

ANGEL EDUARDO
By Susanna Summers

"There's a farmer, Don Trinidad, and his wife, Senora Maria Louisa; they have a grandchild named Angel Eduardo.

"Angel Eduardo suffered brain damage in heart surgery when he was a year old. His mother abandoned him and left him with his father's parents. Since the surgery, he was bedridden until he was four-and-a-half years old! Then Dad prayed for him and a few days later he started to crawl. The other day, we girls and Mom prayed for him and that very night he took **two steps**. Praise the Lord! Alleluia! He is five years old and taking his first steps.

"When Mom told me that news, I felt real happy. **God heals!** I always feel happy when others do."

God wants to build up our children's faith. It is very hard to have pets in the missions. We hardly ever had pets. One of our family's favorite miracle stories is the story of Joseph's chicken.

A family came over with a baby chick, and said it was a gift for Joseph.

It was too late for me to say, "No" because Joseph was running all over the patio, declaring, "I've got a new pet! A new pet!! I've got a chicken for a pet!" The chicken was there to stay; they had even brought cracked corn for it. After the chicken was a juvenile, almost grown, our family went on an outing. Simon was not feeling well so he stayed behind with our helper. The chicken also stayed behind on a freezing cold January day. Simon bathed the chicken in ice-cold tap water. The helper said the bath probably drowned and froze it. Several hours later, when we got back, the chicken was lying limp on a bench in the patio with its head hanging off the edge. It was dead. Frank examined it and so did I. We were planning to comfort Joseph by allowing him to plan an elaborate funeral. Mary tells the story in an article she wrote for our newsletter, *Resounding Praise*:

THE FAITH OF A CHILD
By Mary Magdalen Summers

"My brother Joseph was four; our helper gave him a baby chicken. One day we went on an outing and when we came back my brother Simon had bathed the chicken (!) and it froze to death.

"Joseph was crying; then he knelt down in the patio and grabbed the chicken in his hands, and he started to pray. He shouted, '**Jesus, save my chicken - please save my chicken Please bring my chicken back to life!!!**'

"Then he brought the chicken to my Dad, and he said, 'Dad, my chicken is moving.' But Dad said, 'it still looks dead.' My brother Joseph shook his head. And he screamed again, **"Jesus, please let my chicken be alive!" Then he showed it to dad and said, 'It is alive, Dad; it is!'**

"And the chicken jumped out of Joseph's hands and ran about in the patio. And my Dad was amazed at how much faith children have. Joseph thanked the Lord for the miracle."

Our trip home for the Christmas holidays in 1987 had

265

been centered around Beau's wedding. Beau and Michelle had a beautiful, traditional Catholic wedding on December 19th. They were so obviously in love. We had a very memorable rehearsal supper for them. Beau serenaded Michelle with a song called "Darling, Let Me Be Your Servant..." They had received good instruction, but issues that arose for them in their Engaged Encounter never finally got resolved. They were madly in love and felt ready to live the vows that they themselves had written.

The wedding was wonderful. As they recessed down the aisle, the wedding guests stood up and gave a spontaneous round of applause, a standing ovation!

The marriage strained to the breaking point in seven years. One of the great heartbreaks of my life was to watch Beau's suffering through a divorce and annulment.

In the beginning of our walk with Jesus, the Bordelon family meant so much to us (Ch. 10 of *Go! You Are Sent*). I often talk about our "Heavenly Board of Directors". Our friends who have graduated to our eternal home can assist us with our mission. Of course, Jesus is the only mediator between the Father and God's people. But, He's not the only intercessor. Jesus' heart was moved by the people who interceded for others – the parents of the dead girl; the friends of the paralytic who opened a way in the roof; the official who pleaded for his servant. Jesus is still moved when we intercede for each other.

Several of our close friends have gone on, passed through the gates of death, and are now with the Lord. I have experienced the effectiveness of their prayers for me. I feel sure their perspective is perfect; they know *exactly* how to pray. I think Barry Bordelon must be on our "Heavenly Board". I recall his last visit with us the week before he died. We were home in Abbeville preparing for Beau's wedding. Barry had been serving the Lord in another Diocese, not far away, as a permanent deacon, working full-time for the church.

One Monday, he and Diane came to Abbeville to visit, and to bring Beau's wedding gift. We had a wonderful visit, just like old times. Barry told us that he had recently retired, due to his health. He had undergone a quadruple bypass surgery on his heart. "The doctors don't give me five years to live," he told us.

What he was telling me just wouldn't register, "Oh come on, Barry, I'm sure the Lord still has things for you to do around here. Or better yet, why not come to Mexico? You don't know how to speak Spanish, that ought to slow you down somewhat, and we'd make you take a `siesta' every day."

He and Diane laughed, but he asserted, "We might just take you up on that; but I have some things, I need to do just in case – like get my social security lined up and everything for Diane and the children."

It was a great afternoon, and I began to pray that day that they would come to Mexico and let us help him get stronger. Barry was like a bulldozer for Jesus – determined and unstoppable. He had his failures and weaknesses, but I believe he was like King David: a man after God's own heart. He loved the poor and the downtrodden. He loved the Lord; he loved his family; he loved the Church - even in its imperfections (which he readily saw); he loved his friends; and he loved us.

Barry and Diane had nine children. He was on the move, often a thorn in the flesh of both liberal and reactionary Catholics. He was devoted to old people and to new converts. He and Diane took care of his dying father, and his mother with Alzheimer's disease. We didn't see each other as much as we wanted to because our individual lives were so full. We promised to call more often.

I had been overwhelmingly busy with wedding preparations. To top things off, I had three sick children. In the middle of the night, I awakened to give them their medicine. Even though I was really tired, I could not go back to sleep. I tossed and turned for a half-hour and then I got up. I realized that I had been so occupied that I neglected my personal prayer time for two days.

"Maybe that's why I can't sleep," I said to myself, "I've missed my appointment with the Lord!"

I went into the living room, and grabbed my Bible. I quieted myself for a few minutes to enter into the presence of the Lord. It was about 1:00 am. Suddenly, I heard the sound of *trumpets*! I could physically hear them loud and clear, the music was beautiful. I leaned over in the chair, to see if the music was waking up Frank.

I wondered, "Won't the police come to get these trumpet players, whoever they are, for playing music at these early hours?" I was just about to go and wake up Frank, to see what he

267

thought. Then I heard the Lord tell me, "Sit back, these are heavenly trumpets!!"

So I sat back. The music was so exquisite – beautiful and clear. Then the music stopped. I read the scriptures; I couldn't imagine why the Lord had allowed me to hear the heavenly trumpets. My readings focused on "going" and "mission". I thought, "Maybe the Lord is admonishing me for not being more attentive to my personal prayer-time and my mission call as I rush about preparing for the wedding. But why the trumpets?" I asked myself.

Early the next morning, the phone rang. It was Kay Listi. "Barry Bordelon died last night," she said. I was too struck with grief to think of anything about the trumpets at first. I ran to Frank – we held each other and wept. We called little Sarah in, and told her that her Godfather had died. Then I got up to telephone Diane. As I walked into the living room toward the phone, I remembered the trumpets!!

As I told Diane the whole story of my hearing the heavenly trumpets, she said, choked with emotion, "Genie, do you remember that Barry played the trumpet?"

"Now that you say it, I do," I smiled up to heaven, and wiped tears off of my face.

With a tremble in her voice, she said, "Tell Frank that I'd like for him to talk at the funeral, no one loved Barry as Frank did."

When we drove up to the church on the day of the funeral, there were two huge Christmas decorations in front that had been there since after Thanksgiving, big, shiny, golden angels – blowing trumpets!!

Barry donated his body to science – Medical Technology had been his first career. It was a beautiful funeral. In some way his body's absence reminded all of us of the Empty Tomb of the Master that Barry had served on Earth. There was an arrangement on the altar containing his personal effects. It depicted all the services he had rendered to the Church. The family had chosen his deacon's stole, a food basket for the poor, his Bible, his guitar, his campground shovel, and gracing the top, was his *trumpet*!

Barry had continuously taken youth to the missions in New Mexico in the summertime. Putting on Vacation Bible

School for the Navajo Indians was the focus of these missions. Young people enjoyed the camping, really roughing it. Barry played "Reveille" and "Taps" on his trumpet during mission camp trips.

Frank gave the Eulogy, and Fr. Calais gave the Homily. Diane wore Barry's favorite of her dresses. It was white – a sign of celebration for Barry's ultimate victory. As Frank began his talk, he said, "This reminds me of the time we sent Barry and his family off to the missions in New Mexico. Fr. Calais and I both talked at that Mass, thirteen years ago."

Diane interrupted him in an audible voice from the front pew, "It was *thirteen years ago, today*, Frank!" Barry had gone out to the missions with a big send-off. We celebrated his decision to answer to the call to "go", to take his family to serve the Lord among the Navajos. Thirteen years later to the day, he was having another kind of send-off, and the angels had heralded his "going". When I opened the Bible later that evening, it gently opened to a passage about silver trumpets. Silver trumpets were used by the chosen people to break camp. Tears of gratitude flowed freely; the Lord had allowed me to be a part of Barry's "breaking camp". I had heard the heavenly reveille.

Our children and grandchildren in mission – Pictures here are from the slums in India, the Amazon in Ecuador, the mountains in Mexico, and the coast in Veracruz. We are zealous to bring the Good News and to BE the Good News. Like St. Paul, we are little known, but well known by those we serve all over the globe. We do medical missions, visit the homebound and sick, meet with leaders, travel by horseback, lead short term missions, play games with the children, and love our life in Jesus.

Chapter Sixteen

Follow the Butterflies

Frank and Father Pachicano sat at his dining table in the simple St. Francis of Assisi rectory. They each had a cup of coffee, their planning calendars, and a pad and pen. "Frank," Father began, "One of our major priorities in this work is to raise up lay leaders in the villages who could become Eucharistic ministers, and prayer service leaders. What we need are laymen who are surrendered to Jesus, faithful, committed and trained."

Frank agreed, "Most of the men I have met in the ranchos have a hunger to be closer to God. But you are right, Father, they have no training, and because of that they lack self-confidence. I would love to evangelize and train them."

"Yes, once they are trained we can obtain permission for them to have a tabernacle in their ranchos, and Communion Services on Sunday," Father looked hopeful as they mapped out a plan to bring training to Eucharistic Ministers.

"Frank, Mexico is so in need of evangelists. My pastoral responsibility for fifty-four ranchos is overwhelming. The need is urgent. I can't express how happy I am that you and Genie have brought your family here to help," Father commented as they closed their meeting.

Mexico at the time had the worst priest to Catholic ratio in the Church. There was one priest for every fifteen thousand Catholics. The needs were staggering. When we first arrived in General Cepeda, only a couple of the fifty-four ranchos had tabernacles, and therefore infrequently received the Eucharist. A yearly visit by the priest on the Chapel's Feast day (for example, St. Joseph's Feast Day, or The Feast of the Immaculate Conception) was their only scheduled contact with the Church. The majority of people from the ranchos would try to get to General Cepeda a few times a year on a Sunday to attend Mass.

271

Baptisms and Weddings rarely took place in their rancho chapels. Faith was kept alive by celebrating at community events and holiday traditions, which all originated in the Christian tradition. They prayed the rosary, letting the mysteries teach the highlights of the life of Christ. Each village had at least one Catholic who taught Catechism to the children.

"How are we going to help the ranchos to have more access to the Sacraments?" I asked Frank one morning at breakfast.

"First, you have to evangelize the whole rancho. Once the love of the Lord takes root, leaders will rise up," he answered. "We will be there to help them learn all that they can. Later, they will have the tabernacle installed in their rancho. I have total confidence that they will be faithful to the sacraments once they have access."

Our General Cepeda brothers and sisters in the Lord, those that belonged to our evangelism groups, realized that the Summers vehicle left from the front of the Casa de Misiones almost every night. They were ready and waiting on park benches in the plaza across from our door. The evangelization team, often including some of the Summers kids, headed out to two, sometimes three, ranchos every evening. The team was being spiritually fed by Frank's preaching of the Word. They swayed and clapped to joyful songs in vigorous praise of Jesus. Their own testimonies, and the testimonies in the ranchos of miracles, large and small, were a sign of His approval of their weekly meetings. God's word in Scripture excited them. We found donors of Bibles and reading glasses. Women Catechists from General Cepeda took the children aside in the ranchos after the praise and testimonies part of the prayer meetings, and taught them Catechism. The villagers were so surrendered to God's work among them; they were hungry for this spiritual food! And He was satisfying that hunger. When Frank and the crew drove up and rang the bell at the rancho chapel, people readied themselves for the best night of the week – the night they spent with each other, with Jesus and with His servants.

At the time, there were so few vehicles available in the whole region. Our friends and the *campesinos* (our friends who worked the land in the ranchos), seldom had transportation, other than their donkeys. Our missionary trucks or vans were often pressed into service as ambulances to drive the sick to Saltillo or Ramos Arizpe. Sometimes the vehicles we drove were burgeoning with wedding guests and the bride and groom. Our white crew cab pick up truck was on the verge of giving out.

One night Frank came home from the Ranchos past midnight.

'What happened, Frank?" I asked.

"We limped home with one of the front wheels chained to the frame!! The holding arm was broken."

We made a long distance call to our Mission Council back in Abbeville. Our Mission Council consisted of friends and supporters who believed in our work and prayed for us. It was vital to our life to have the Council to report to. Not only that, but we sought their advice, and relied on their prayers. We asked our Council to pray and start looking around for a new (used) vehicle for us. We thought our crew cab was ideal; another one might be a good idea.

Several of the men investigated tirelessly, asking everywhere about a vehicle for our mission; but more than that, they faithfully prayed. One council member, Wayne Broussard, jogged by a crew cab owner's home. They hadn't met before, and he kept asking the owner if he didn't want to donate the truck to the missions. Other mission council members stopped drivers on the street asking them to consider donating their truck to the missions. They were bold in an effort to support our needs. Suddenly, in a glorious way, our storming of heaven paid off. A brand new van was donated to our mission.

Frank's parents had substantial means, and used to make generous donations to all of their children and grandchildren. They always included us in these gifts. But while they gave funds to other family members marked as "for your law practice", "for school", or in some other way recognizing their particular work and way of life, they had never included our *missionary* work.

They experienced a change of heart after visiting our base in General Cepeda. We were so grateful that now we had the freedom to be *us, their missionary children,* when we visited with them in Abbeville. Frank received a call from their house one day, then reported to me, "Be prepared to be amazed, Dad and Mom want to buy us a brand new van!"

I *was* amazed, "Frank, that's so wild. What a sign!"

I smiled at his joy when he said; "They said they want us to use it for our mission."

When we called the Council to report the good news about our new van, they all rejoiced. "God answers prayer!"

Donald asked, "Is it a 'super-maxi' van?"

"Yes, it seats fifteen – fifteen average Americans. It will hold a lot more in Mexico," Frank said, and he was right. Christian brothers and sisters didn't mind piling in, either. We joked, "This van could be called the 'Holy Roamin' Catholic Church."

When we took it for a short ride in Abbeville the first night we received it, twenty-five singing, praising, friends and Mission Council members squeezed in. We were happy even sitting on laps.

One night back in Mexico, Frank got thirty-four villagers into our van, coming to the rescue when a passenger bus broke down in one of the ranchos. The van really was a blessing to the rancho ministry. I rested better on the nights he had to be out late at the ranchos. I knew that he, and whichever of our children whose turn it was to go with him, could count on a reliable vehicle for their trip.

Just as Frank had predicted, men and women in well-established weekly prayer meetings were emerging in the role of leadership. The women came forth to be trained as Catechists for the children of the rancho. Families were bolder about arranging prayer gatherings in the Chapels, even when it wasn't one of Frank's visits. The older ones loved their reading glasses and became faithful to a personal daily prayer time. The transformation showed in everyone in the Rancho's faces, their dress, and the orderliness found in their homes.

Many of the men played the guitar; they began to play praise songs with relish. We trained the leaders in the villages and set up training weekends for them in General Cepeda. They matured as Christian husbands and fathers, and leaders in their communities. I believe that it was a missionary "show and tell". They were nourished by the words Frank spoke to them as he evangelized, but they saw and touched and became friends with a man who walked the walk. They loved this man's man who introduced them to their Savior. They followed him, and learned to follow Christ through his example. Soon Chapels were having tabernacles installed by the dozens, with Eucharistic ministers conducting Communion Services. Where Jesus' sacramental presence had been totally lacking, the people of the ranchos prayed in their chapels, and received their Eucharistic Lord once a week.

Bishop Villalobos became aware of the spiritual awakening in the ranchos of General Cepeda, so he initiated a campaign to ensure that these Catholics in the ranchos received the Sacrament of Confirmation. His delegate went from rancho to rancho, hearing confessions and questioning candidates. He found them well prepared, and conducted Confirmations for all.

I was visiting with Lauro on the steps of the historic St. Francis of Assisi church in town. He flashed me a wonderful grin and said, "I counted over one thousand people that have received Confirmation through the Bishop's campaign. A lot has happened since your family got here."

"Frank told me I should have been with him at Jalpa last night. He said almost the whole village received the sacrament of confirmation," Lauro continued, "What was so beautiful about it was that the candidates spanned all the ages. There was a very old couple, middle aged people, young married couples, and the youth."

I said, "I'll bet Father is happy."

"Yes, he is, but now that everyone is so much more involved with their faith, everyone wants more ministry from the Church. I think the Bishop is going to assign an associate to this Parish."

As I walked back across the abundantly green plaza, passing by the picturesque gazebo in the center, I thanked the Lord for being able to see the fruit of our ministry. "Lord Jesus, thanks for sending us to your people here in Northern Mexico. If we had never left the Philippines, we never would have come here. You really do have '*plans for our welfare and not for our woe!*'"

Well, the very morning I visited with Lauro, I was walking on the side of the plaza, headed for the general store. One of the ladies in a kiosk that sold candy, chips and sodas flagged me down. We were acquaintances. I visited with her from time to time, and her twin girls were Mary's age, they played together. "Pssst, pssst," she said motioning vigorously, "I hate to ask you this, but when are you going to pay your bill? Something has come up and I need the money."

"Bill, what bill? How? I don't know anything about a bill," I answered, cocking my eyebrows in surprise.

"Simon's bill," she said sheepishly, realizing I hadn't authorized Simon's purchases, "Simon comes almost everyday and gets snacks in the afternoon. He never has any money, so he says, 'Charge it!'"

I burst out laughing, and so did she. Simon loved General Cepeda; the life was simple and accommodating for him. The bill was only about three dollars, but I hated to be the one who had to reign in one of Simon's pleasures and cut off his "Charge account."

Simon was waiting for me in the open door of the casa.

"Hey, Mom," he bear hugged me. "Where have you been?"

"Simon, Simon, Simon," I said. By then the other kids had gathered around. "I've been paying your bill at the kiosk on the plaza, you monkey," I said tickling him gently.

Handling of Prader-Wili syndrome requires us to help Simon restrict his consumption of food. We made certain rules in the house about meals and snacks, trying not to make it too hard on him. But, as the Kiosk lady story demonstrated, our Mexican friends totally disagreed with us about Simon's eating. They surely did not think that we should monitor Simon's eating. Next door to our Casa, a kind lady that Simon called Tia (aunt) Tila, fed him an "extra" breakfast every day. He quietly left the house at mid-morning and walked into her restaurant. She and her staff, sat him down, put a cloth napkin in front of him and let him order anything he wanted for breakfast, as though he were a paying customer. All this was unbeknownst to us. We thought he was playing in the back yard or in his room. Healthy children, in the minds of Mexican mamas, were "well filled out" and they loved to feed Simon, he was such a good eater. A few weeks before the kiosk incident, I discovered Simon in the restaurant, having his "secret" second breakfast.

I was visibly alarmed, "Simon Peter Emmanuel Summers, what ARE you doing? You have already eaten your breakfast, you *know* you must not eat too much," I exclaimed loudly as I unseated him and made him follow me out.

I looked at them apologetically, "I'm sorry that I have to take Simon now, thank you, Tila, for being so kind to him," I said, "It is very harmful for Simon to eat too much, you can see that his muscles are really weak and extra weight is hard on his heart. How often does he come in here?"

She answered, "*De diario, (*everyday). I want to feed him; he's always so hungry. I don't mind at all. Besides, he's so cute and so sweet. He loves my cooking."

Simon grabbed her hand and said in Spanish, in his most sincere, charming voice, "I love Tia Tila too, she's my *best friend*."

Prader-Wili patients are super friendly and they have tons of best friends. I wanted to impress on Tila that I didn't approve of Simon coming in for breakfast, or any meal for that matter, unless I gave him permission. "Please don't feed Simon anymore unless I say it's alright," I pleaded.

She begrudgingly nodded, "Yes." But the *looks* that she and her nephew gave me were saying what I'm sure their minds were thinking, "It's too bad that Simon has such a *mean* mother! Sadly, she must not know that a *fat* child is a happy child."

A group of families from Abbeville came for Thanksgiving one year. The Crain family made it easy when they brought visitors. They were our Mission Council coordinators. The Dubois family remembers fondly that special week when we ministered in mission together. The Millers were real troopers and took the Mexican life in stride. We had our Thanksgiving dinner on the courtyard patio, and invited many of the locals. Our photos from that Thanksgiving look almost like a reenactment of the First Thanksgiving.

Fr. Pachicano was transferred to teach in the Seminary, a new pastor was assigned to St. Francis Parish. In 1980, in Saltillo Fr. Feliciano had been a friend of ours. He was one of the original twelve that prayed on that New Years Day with Fr. Burciaga at the Sanctuario. His younger brother, Adolfo, was also a priest. Now Feliciano was assigned to General Cepeda! He really understood our call. He affirmed our hope of a family of families in mission.

The winters are often so bitterly cold in the high mountains. It is a hardship to expect the folks of the ranchos to come out to the sparse chapels that have no heating. So, our family took the opportunity to head back home for a short stay. Because Chet and Val were expecting a baby in February, we planned to meet again when the baby was old enough to travel. So we sought the Lord about when and where and how to take up our ministry in the early spring.

The Lord surprised me by what He spoke to us on retreat before we left the Casa de Misones. Frank brought to our prayer a recent sense he had about God's plan for our future. On two separate occasions, and at two different locations, once in a canyon and once atop a mountain ridge, thousands of Monarch Butterflies made their way past him. These fragile butterflies were on a journey, confidently headed south. Frank sensed God's directions in this display of His creation. Was the Lord alerting us to a future time of movement? Would we be headed south, too?

"Gosh, Frank, this is a surprise. I am finally getting so comfortable here in General Cepeda."

Val agreed, "We all are, I'm looking forward to seeing our baby grow here."

"This Word has troubled me for a couple of weeks now. But as I share it this morning, I feel God's anointing. He almost insisted I bring it to our prayer."

Sarah said, "But, Daddy, if the Lord wants us to go, we will listen, won't we?"

"Sure, Sarah," he said, and then closed his eyes and raised his hands to the Lord, "Jesus, we are ready to go wherever you send us. But please speak very clearly. Our plan was to stay here a while longer. People are writing to us trying to schedule youth groups here this summer. It doesn't seem like the time to become itinerant again. And yet, Lord, we want to surrender completely to Your will. Speak to us Lord!" We held hands as we prayed, and felt His peace descend upon us.

The Lord didn't delay in speaking to us again about "going". We had called a pre-furlough retreat about our schedule for the coming year, but He had other things to say first. Jesus talked with us about His very important command to missionaries, the command to Go!

As our retreat began, Chet received a vision; "I see a bucket with a faucet over it." He said, "Drops of water fall into

278

the bucket one by one. Each drop lights up and then falls into the bucket."

The significance of this vision was unclear until Susanna (ten years old) was directed to a Scripture reading that said, "The nations are but a drop in a bucket."

A number of references to "nations" and "many nations" went along with other things the Lord was telling us. Valerie had a vision, too. "The Lord is showing me that all of us are skipping happily alongside a long line of people of different nationalities; these people are holding hands. We are making forward progress along the line. As we move ahead, some of the people break rank and follow behind us, smiling, skipping, happily. God is saying He will use us to call others."

We received one vision after another. We saw coastlands. We saw people waiting to catch blossoms blown by the wind – the blossoms represented the Gospel, and the wind was the Holy Spirit. We were there to help them catch the blossoms. In our reading of God's Word there were passages that stirred up in us a zeal to go forth in mission and to go south. Susanna kept getting the reading called "The Sacred Way!" The Holy Spirit wanted us to travel on a Holy way, a way consecrated to Jesus.

Yes, there were readings that kept saying "South!" One night during the retreat, little Joseph came in to our prayer session and said, "I have a reading. I can't read, but Jesus gave it to me. Maybe Mama can read it." Joseph's Bible was opened to a passage that said only those who were unafraid should go into battle. We were being called to renounce our fear.

We let the retreat and its words from the Lord settle into our spirits. Frank and I went out to pray and have our weekly "pastoral session." In these sessions we together examined our lives, our marriage, our call, our children's needs, and our schedule. As we parked on a hill, overlooking the distant mountains, the colorful Mexican cemetery and the expansive desert, we reviewed the message the Lord spoke to us in the retreat.

"God's plan is beginning to make so much sense. We want to train Chet and Val in our way of life. One of the elements they will need to learn is to live the itinerant life," Frank said.

279

"Yes. I had not thought of that. What surprises me is how excited our kids are about going forth with the Gospel again," I said, "Moving about is beginning to sound better to me, but we have a lot to do before we move ahead with this guidance."

"The Markos will need a vehicle, and some sort of camping trailer and so do we," Frank mused. Within seconds of Frank's remark, something popped into my mind. It was a "mini" camper van; and if I remembered correctly, it had been on a camper lot in Abbeville for a long time. It was still there the last time we visited. Its owner was a good Catholic. We prayed that Mr. Benny would give it to Chet and Valerie for our trek to the South – and he did!! A widow from a nearby town gave Frank and me a sixteen-foot camping trailer. We were really great at fitting our family into small spaces, so all eight of us managed to sleep in that compact area.

One of our major concerns was a surgery Simon needed. It had been put off as long as possible and would have to be taken care of before we went south. We'd been praying for years that Simon's testicles would descend from the abdominal cavity. If they remained undescended they could become a risk for cancer. Most doctors had been able, with a degree of difficulty to find one of the testicles, but the second one had never been palpable. Since he was three, doctors had recommended that he have the surgery; and they said it would have to be done before he was seven. He was just seven. Now, in light of our plan to go south in Mexico, we decided that the second week after Christmas was the time, and Abbeville was the place for the surgery. We couldn't put it off any longer.

Each time we went to schedule the surgery, each time we almost agreed on a date with the surgeons, I was anxious and afraid. Earlier it had been said that Simon was a high risk for anesthesia. His muscles were weak. The heart is a muscle, and under anesthesia there was danger of heart failure. I couldn't be at peace about it. In Abbeville, we had a perpetual adoration chapel, where Jesus was adored twenty-four hours a day. Someone was always present in the chapel praying. We posted a notice on the bulletin board, and asked the people to pray before the Blessed Sacrament for Simon's healing.

Frank took an afternoon off work to take Simon to the

doctor to schedule his surgery. Dr. Weston Miller is a cousin of Frank's and a well-respected surgeon. After examining Simon, he had some wonderful news.

"Simon doesn't need surgery, Frank, I can palpate both of his testicles." Frank could hardly believe his ears, "Really!!?" He asked surprised, "Are you sure??"

Wes examined him again, for Frank's sake, and said, "I'm sure, but if you want to you can come back in a year to check him again!!"

On the way home from the doctor's office, Simon said to Frank, "The Lord told me."

"The Lord told you what, Simon?" Frank asked him.

"The Lord told me that He was going to heal me. On the sofa, I was sleeping on the sofa in our house, and He came to me in my sleep and told me that I wouldn't have to go to the hospital, He told me He was going to heal me."

When the notice first went up on the prayer bulletin board, a lot of people had telephoned me. They were concerned for Simon and asking about his upcoming surgery. Many more calls came in when we gratefully put up the *thanksgiving notice* on the board: "Thanks for the prayers, Simon's been healed without surgery. Let's offer a week's worth of prayers of thanksgiving!"

Simon still needs lots of healing, but we've seen the Lord's faithfulness to him. Simon is a good witness. It's not harder to "go out" with a special child like Simon, it's easier! He and Jesus have something special going on!

"Frank, I felt like we'd go forth better prepared if Simon's surgery was behind us. Now that he has had this healing, I'm going out with a greater trust in our Savior!"

Frank said, "The world would be a better place if everyone had the faith of Simon."

Another thing would have to fall into place before we could take a long leave from General Cepeda - we needed caretakers for the house in General Cepeda. One day, I went into the meat market and talked with the butcher, Raul. For three years I had been witnessing to Raul, and he had responded, truly responded, little by little. First, he and his wife, Marta, began reading the Bible, and then she started going to Mass. They were already married civilly, had three precious little daughters, but had never been married in the Church. Goodness followed upon goodness as they believed God`s Word together. They became fully active Catholics. Marta was Confirmed.

And after receiving our instruction, they had a wonderful church wedding. Frank and I sponsored them, and gave them a lovely reception in our home. In the Mexican tradition, we were their *Padrinos*, Godparents. (This relationship with Raul and Marta has deepened and borne so much fruit for the building of the Kingdom across the years; they are now, (2011), full-time Family Missions Company missionaries in their own right.)

That day in the meat market, Raul looked a bit burdened. He took me aside, and asked me if I had any advice for them. They were living very near to their relatives. He wished he and Marta could move, but they didn't have any money. The house they were living in had no lights and no water. It was a roof over their heads and nothing more. I told Raul I would get back to him after I talked to Frank. Frank and I felt that we could entrust our mission base into their care.

"It is so typical of you, Lord, to work things out so well," I said to Him in prayer, "You know how to meet the needs of your children by having them help one another."

Raul and Marta became our new caretakers. They moved in way back in 1990, and always care for our house while we are away.

Butterflies are changed from confined, crawling creatures whose world is small, into wonderful, winged wanderers. Their task it is to pollinate the flowers that burst into bloom. Butterflies empower the flowers to grow and gladden the world with beauty. Somehow, in the cocoon a marvelous transformation takes place. The drama of the butterflies has always spoken to Frank and me of our own life – a life transformed from brokenness and strife into something meaningful and filled with beauty!

Thousands of migrating Monarchs now spoke to us again, about "going". This time Chet and Valerie and their new baby would "test their wings" with the Summers family. We would obey our calling together - we would go south in the mighty name of Jesus.

From the very first moments of Christianity, families with a mission were part of God's plan. Remember the lives of

Jesus, Mary and Joseph; Zechariah, Elizabeth, and John - two little families. But God's great plan was much, much bigger than their littleness. The Holy Family obeyed God's directive. When He said, "go", they went! The Savior's family traveled, bringing the Gospel, the "Good News Personified", from Nazareth to Bethlehem, then to Egypt, and back again.

Our family had heard the Lord say, "Go south! Make yourself ready. Start planning to go!" His clear voice was igniting my heart of hearts. The grace to go to the ends of the earth again was being poured out on me. Jesus spoke and I listened, He said, "Your itinerant mission to the south should be called Southreach. You, all of you, will reach out to those who wait in the south."

Frank, Beau, Simon, Joseph and John Paul in Micronesia.
Genie, Sarah, Susanna and Mary in our chapel at Big
Woods Mission in Abbeville, Louisiana.

Chapter Seventeen

The Garbage Dump to Sea Island

"Guadalajara? Yes, Father, we can be there in about four days," Frank spoke enthusiastically into the phone, "Yes, we do have our trailers and campers, but if your friends will let us park them in front of their home, it would be a blessing. Goodbye, God bless you."

I walked into the room at the very end of his conversation. "Who was that, Frank? Father who?"

"Father Burciaga. I knew he was ministering in Guadalajara. Rogelio and Isabel want to visit him, so they suggested we begin our Southreach by calling him and offering to work in his apostolate," Frank replied.

"It is a wonder that you got him on the phone. He is always so busy."

"Babe," Frank said, "He was genuinely happy that we are available. He already has things lined up for us. There is a youth event planned. He wants Chet, Val, Sarah and Susanna to give some talks and lead share groups. A couples retreat is coming up, too, and he wants you and me to give several of the talks."

As we ate lunch, we told the family and the Markos that we were headed for Guadalajara. It certainly was south of us, not due south, but south nonetheless, and God was already opening the doors for our proclaiming Him as we went along.

Of course, there were huge hugs, waves, and tears as we drove away from General Cepeda starting our Southreach. Our convoy consisted of the big, blue fifteen-passenger van with a large top carrier that was home built and painted blue. The van was pulling a sixteen-foot camper trailer with a newly painted blue stripe on it. Next in line was Chet and Val's recently donated mini camper. We had eight Summerses and three Markos. Their newborn daughter, little Hannah, was only about six-weeks old. We also had one of our helpers, Hilda, and her baby daughter. Hilda loved the kids so much; she couldn't bear to see us take off without her. She insisted she and the baby could sleep in the van at night.

When I prayed about taking Hilda, the Lord answered loudly, "Yes!"

Guadalajara is an absolutely beautiful city, much larger than I had expected. Picturesque neighborhoods boasted ancient trees. The Cathedral was comparable to European cathedrals; the central area of the city was very continental. Fr. Burciaga's apostolate offered us a really special opportunity to minister, and it was good to be in the Lord's service with him again. We were received like a band of celebrities, but our "lead guitarist" was Jesus. Our host family allowed us to park in front of their home and in their drive. They took all of us into their spacious home and the food was excellent, fresh, and abundant. God was taking good care of us on our first leg of the journey.

It was Good Friday; our hosts took us to a nearby town that was enacting the passion of Christ. Crowds filled the cobblestone streets and we followed the actor who was portraying Jesus. The costumes were pretty authentic and the anger of the guards as they beat "Jesus" was compelling. The whips had been soaked in dye and makeup artists did a good job on his back. Sarah held Joseph's hand, Frank held Simon's hand and I was holding John Paul's hand.

After a few lashes by those soldiers with the whip, John Paul crawled into my arms. "Mom, why are they hurting Jesus? Why, Mom?" he said crying.

"John Paul, that's not the real Jesus. It is an actor who is trying to remind us that Jesus died for our sins."

"But you told Susanna that Jesus died on Good Friday, today is Good Friday."

"I know, but this is not the real Jesus."

"He looks like Jesus. Why did Jesus die anyway?"

"Jesus died so that we can go to heaven and not live in sin," I said, trying to placate his anxiety. It didn't work. "Mom, tell them to stop. Let's don't sin anymore, so Jesus won't have to die. Tell them to stop! Please, tell them to stop!" he cried in anguish.

I knew that this was too graphic for him, so I left the crowd and crossed the plaza. I prayed that he would be consoled. He played a little on the swings, and I thought we'd walk a bit and "window shop". Suddenly, the crowd rounded the corner on the street where we were. I had inadvertently picked the very spot where they actually set up the crucifixion scene. I was standing in an interesting archway. John Paul could barely see over the crowd, but as they started nailing Jesus to the cross, artificial blood gushed from his hands. John Paul started screaming, first in English, and then in Spanish, "Don't kill Jesus!! He's my friend! Don't kill him, He's so good!!"

I picked him up and made him bury his head in my shoulder. He soaked my dress with his tears, but a wave of total reverence shot through the crowd around us. The impact of the death of Jesus on our four year old, and his anguish over the supreme sacrifice, hushed the crowd around us. It made them ponder deeply how important this event really was. Our friend and Savior - this totally innocent, completely superior, God-man - had laid down His life for us.

Southreach had no real day-by-day plan. We did know we were moving toward Coatzacoalcos in the state of Vera Cruz. Our friend, Bishop Carlos Talavera, had recently been appointed the first Bishop of the new Diocese of Coatzacoalcos. We were going where we felt the leading of the Holy Spirit – pilgrims, missionaries, families on the move, telling the Good News to everyone we met. We didn't have a plan, but as we moved, we discovered He had one.

Our new friends in Guadalajara sent us to their friends a day's drive away. On our arrival, we realized they had already set up an opportunity after the healing Mass for us to preach in their church, and lead the prayer meeting. The church was packed. Two American families on mission in a simple Mexican city painted a picture of zeal for the Lord. We were like a new species to them. Catholic Families in mission – they had never imagined something so wonderful even existed. People came to us after, testifying to healings that Jesus had done while we prayed. Just as it was for Jesus, when we went home at night after these talks, a small crowd would find the place we were staying and come to that place for more.

We next stayed at the Benedictine Monastery in Cuernavaca. Again, old friends and new ones invited us to talk. Then moving on, we stopped at a plaza in a small town to park our vehicles for the night and to cook on a park table. We usually picked a plaza near a church where we could attend weekday mass if possible. The parish priest saw us at mass and invited us to give a talk and prayer session in his parish. He made the rectory bathing and cooking facilities available to us.

When we got to Coatzacoalcos, we knew we had about five to six weeks to spend. Frank's parents were going to celebrate their fiftieth anniversary with a weeklong event, inviting their children and grandchildren to join them. Frank's dad was battling cancer, so we knew the Lord wanted us to go and be at the anniversary. The plan that evolved, in light of having to return for the anniversary, was that after a month in Coatza the Summers would join the fiftieth anniversary celebration in Sea Island, Georgia. Chet and Val would visit with Chet's family in Texas, and then we would all rendezvous in Augusta, so that Chet and Val could experience the Alleluia community with us. After Alleluia, we would travel back to General Cepeda, spend a little time there, and head out for some more Southreach, hoping to get as far as Guatemala.

We did have a month to give, and the first thing we did when we arrived in Coatza was to present ourselves to Bishop Talavera, offering to spend a month or so in his diocese.

"*Francisco, Maria como estan*? (Frank, Genie, how are you?)" he said, opening his arms to embrace Frank. We kissed his ring and then each got a hug. The last baby he had met was Susanna at the Puebla Conference. Now she was now almost twelve and we had four more children.

"Look how many little missionaries you have now, all beautiful," he exclaimed.

"Thank you, Bishop. You are looking well yourself," I said, "How's your mother? Is she well?"

"She was here not long ago. She is still doing well, traveling at ninety-two. How is Beau?"

"Married and studying," I replied, "He and his wife recently visited us in General Cepeda."

"What brings you here?"

"God has directed us to set out on a Southreach mission," Frank explained, "With guidance, we hope to reach South America." Bishop Talavera had been long involved in the Holy Spirit Renewal, and he easily understood the visions and the signs we had received. Frank continued, "Monsignor, the joy we have in arriving here with you confirms our whole plan."

"I am happy that your Southreach has led you here. You offered to serve where the need is greatest. The whole diocese has so many great needs. I will pray about it and get back to you in a day or two," he said.

Then he turned to Chet and Val, "Are you happy to be missionaries, bringing with you your new baby?"

"Yes, Monsignor, we are. We need to adjust to our baby anyway. Why not adjust to her as we travel and evangelize?" Valerie said.

"Good, I have arranged for you to stay in the backyard of some friends of mine until I decide where to use you," the Bishop explained, "Let's go. I'll drive you to their place and you can safely park your trailers there."

Once again, the Lord made a way for us. The backyard that accommodated us was perfect. Surrounded by a high fence, it had green grass and some trees, mostly coconut palms and the kids had plenty of space to play. There were servant's quarters equipped with laundry facilities, which we were able to use, and which were a real luxury. We also had use of the bathroom and the shower. It was nice to *land* for several days.

Finally, Bishop Talavera showed up one day with Father Manuel. Father Manuel was recently ordained and had been appointed pastor of the Parish of San Felipe de Jesus. Bishop Talavera was offering our service to him. With our hosts and the whole mission team, we went out to look at San Felipe.

"Disadvantaged" is not nearly an adequate word to describe what we found. We drove around potholes in the streets big enough to hide a submarine and some streets were small, impassable canals. The whole area was reclaimed from the swamp. It literally was built on sand. There was row after row of makeshift one-room houses filled block after block of squatter neighborhoods. Some houses were made of black corrugated roofing paper – in the southern Mexican heat. And what a heat!

Coatza in April and May is very hot. San Felipe de Jesus Church was on one edge of this new settlement, only a few hundred yards from the garbage dump. Marsh grasses mostly hid the dump from view, but when the wind blew from that direction, there was no stopping the stench. The "church" was a former brick-manufacturing site. It consisted of a large tin roof, covering an expanse of sand, held up by rebar posts and trusses. One small section near the front had a concrete floor and a half wall of cinder block. The simple table-altar faced the backless, rustic benches that the congregation sat on. A nice crucifix hung over the altar but inside this structure, there was no place for a tabernacle.

Adjoining the "church," was a small three-room structure, made of cinderblock, still under construction. The one room that was finished held the tabernacle, which was locked away. Father Manuel didn't live there because the plumbing had not been installed and there were no screens on the windows. He had no car and lived at the Bishop's house. He commuted each day on a public bus, carrying his heavy vestments and mass kit to the sixteen chapels and the church under his care. I could sense Bishop and Father thought we would panic and say, "No, not this."

Our kindly, wealthy Mexican hosts said to us, "You don't have to *move your trailers* there. You won't be safe at night. It's only about a month before you leave. Stay at our house and come every day like Father does."

Honestly, in my flesh, I was tempted to take them up on their offer, but at their house, our ministry had been so limited by our enclosure in the back yard. We all looked at each other and could sense agreement. God had led us here - here to edge of the garbage dump, here to the poorest neighborhood I had ever seen, here to the people that, even as we spoke, were already surrounding us. Blond hair, and tall "giants", like Chet, Val and Frank attracted them like moths to the light. While the others towered over the parishioners, Sarah, Hilda and I, all nearly five feet tall, fit right in.

These people were of tribal descent. They had left their mountain homes and villages to come to the big city, seeking an easier way of life. I thought, "If it were me, I'd scurry back up to the mountains, leave these living conditions behind and live off of the land."

That afternoon we moved our trailers and our tent to the sandy land in front of the church. Electricity was available, but not enough to run air conditioners. Our kids loved the big roofed "playground", the rest of the concrete slab that the church was built on. As they ran around and explored their new surroundings, many, many neighborhood children joined them. In no time, a squealing, giggling, lively game of freeze tag was in progress. If you want to start a youth group in a strange place, bring a newborn baby. Squads of teenage girls which were followed closely by teen-age boys, hung around us, wanting to hold our babies, bombarding Sarah with questions and listening to Chet play the guitar.

By the end of the evening, one neighbor across the street ran a hose from his house to our trailers, filled them up, and brought extra barrels for water telling us, "It is very humble, but anytime you need a bath, please feel free to use ours." Bathrooms were almost always separate from the houses in these neighborhoods, and we used his shower without disturbing him.

After we got set up, I made one room of the cinderblock building a "kitchen". I put out my Coleman camping stove, large basins for dishwashing, got a colorful oilcloth table cover for a table in there, some artificial greens in a vase, and brought in a few benches from church that we returned when mass was celebrated. Our family had a favorite, portable image of our Blessed Mother and a sturdy crucifix that made our temporary homes feel familiar. The camper trailer had an awning that provided shade, and we had some folding chairs. One afternoon, we were honored with a visit from Father after saying mass at one of the chapels. I cooked fajitas and soup and he stayed for dinner. "I am so surprised at how fast you have made a home here," he happily shared, "I can hardly wait to introduce you all at mass tomorrow."

"We are happy to be here, Father."

"Your coming here is a miracle for me. Imagine. I am recently ordained, only two months. The bishop appoints me pastor of San Felipe," he smiled, "I have fifty thousand Catholics in my parish, no real church; about half of the chapels are tiny and are made of tin. The people themselves are very poor and have no extra money for building expenses."

As we looked at this brave young man, who had dedicated his life to serve Jesus and His Church, our hearts broke with pity. How could he do it? He was facing a monumental challenge.

Father went on, "I just kept begging the Lord, 'Please, Jesus, send me some help. Send me a way to break through and bring some life to this place. I can't do it alone. Please send me someone.'" He teared up a little, and waved his hand toward us in a sweeping motion.

Smiling, he continued. "A few days ago, when the bishop told me that a *chorro,* a big group, of lay missionaries wanted to give me a month, I could not stop praising God. You came *straight from heaven* out of the sky for me. We can cover speaking in all of my chapels and start a youth group. This is truly amazing."

That month we spent at San Felipe, the garbage dump and the squatter village, was one of the busiest and most eventful months of our missionary life. Sarah, a beautiful teenager, celebrated her fourteenth birthday while we were in San Felipe, but celebrating her birthday in that poverty was a catalyst to her making a serious, lifelong surrender to Jesus.

On Joseph's sixth birthday, we saw the Pope in nearby Vera Cruz. We slept in the car the night before to be sure to get a spot. Frank's daily pocket planner was totally full of ministry appointments; we gave retreats, Life in the Spirit seminars, talks at chapels, healing services, Bible studies, home visits. Families had us over for meals in their humble homes. The youth group met regularly; Val and I prayed and studied scriptures with some ladies of the parish. Apart from the ministry, it was just plain hard work to maintain ourselves with meals, going to the market, washing clothes and our daily prayer times.

Our girls slept in a tent right outside our camper door. Tropical, coastal rains similar to a monsoon would blow in and the girls often woke up commenting that their sleeping bags were floating in the water, so Frank and I switched places with them. They slept in the trailer. Lo and behold, rain never got into the tent after the switch; maybe God moved them out and us into the tent because they were safer in the trailer.

Because of the physical hardships, less time to enjoy community and the oppressive heat we had a few "family of families" skirmishes. Chet and Val realized that the Southreach mission was vastly different from the General Cepeda lifestyle they had committed to. While God was so effectively using Frank in this ministry, Chet felt at times that his gifts were underused, although he had work assigned to him, it was not the work he longed to do.

Chet was Beau's age, so I felt like his mom. I know I hurt his feelings once by correcting him in front of our kids and Val missed ministering to the poor at the door of the mission house and her elderly shut-ins in General Cepeda. The enemy was after us. The Holy Spirit was at work everywhere else. The breakthrough that Father had prayed for was happening. San Felipe Parish, in the main church, and in the chapels, was coming to life.

Sacred Heart Chapel, an older area of the parish experienced a great deliverance. Electric red votive lights flickered, and a large statue of the Sacred Heart of Jesus took up a good portion of the sanctuary of the chapel. This chapel was a good size, had nicer benches, and fans. It was made of that black corrugated material with a tin roof, but they painted it barn red on the outside and fluorescent blue on the inside. As we knelt there before starting our first healing service in that place, I felt a nagging uneasiness, an annoying oppression. "Frank, something is not right in here. Is the Blessed Sacrament in here?" I asked.

"Father told me that he wants to have a tabernacle here, but he needs some Eucharistic ministers first. But I feel what you're talking about."

"Do you want the Holy Water and the Holy Salt out of your bag?"

"Yes, let's walk through and pray over the chapel."

As Frank preached that night, he was led to spend more time talking about deliverance from evil spirits and the hold of Satan. He denounced evil practices, "Witchcraft, superstitions, and horoscopes do not honor God, nor do they recognize Jesus, the Son of the Living God as the One who has power to save."

He encouraged them further, "Trust Jesus. He can and does break the bonds that Satan has on you. No curse placed on

293

you or anyone else is ever bigger than our Lord. That's the truth. Jesus said, 'The truth will set you free.'"

As he preached in power, a few members of the congregation started trembling uncontrollably, others swooned and fell to the floor, still others began to weep.

One young woman screamed out in an eerie shrill voice, "Cristo, ayudame!" (Christ help me.)

Those who were not manifesting signs of deliverance seemed concerned. Frank reassured them, "Keep singing. Jesus is setting these people free. He is here. His power is at work."

One layman took over the guitar and Frank and I went down the rows praying over the people with Holy oil. After we prayed over them and sang a few more praise songs, the oppression completely lifted. The aspect of most faces was one of peaceful joy. Many faces were covered with tearstains and they looked consoled as well.

The next week, when we arrived at that Chapel for the second service, several people were already there. Señora Conchis, an elderly lady, came over to me and said, "Thank you for the prayer last week. I did not know how to feel peace and joy. The Lord set me free from Satan. I am so happy now."

Others had similar testimonies; the news of the deliverance had spread. The chapel filled up quickly – standing room only. By the end of our four-week series, people were lined up outside, singing, praying and basking in the freedom of the Holy Spirit. The Truth did *set them free*!!

After our month was up, we drove away from San Felipe and Padre Manuel. He could not have extended a more heartfelt, insistent invitation to us. "Come back," he pleaded, shaking Chet's and Frank's hands, "Come for a year or forever."

We knew we were not coming back soon, but we diligently kept the people of San Felipe and Padre Manuel in our daily prayers for a long, long time. Our caravan left San Felipe after Mass on Sunday. We bought the makings for sandwiches, but we needn't have bothered. Our new friends showered us with gifts of food for the journey.

"Here, take this mango cake. Your little girls love it," Senora Louisa said.

"Thank you so much," little Mary answered.

"These are my wife's best tamales," Señor Alberto said, handing me a plastic sack of warm, savory smelling tamales.

"We will have a great lunch today," Frank said, shaking Doctor Santos' hand. The girls' friends exchanged addresses with them, and we wanted to keep in touch. However, in Coatzacoalcos, there are no mailboxes and no real mail delivery system. We had to use the name of the Parish Church as our address and contact place. We left resolved to raise money for San Felipe Church, and to buy Fr. Manuel a car. As soon as we got home, by God's grace, we were able to send him $5000.00 dollars and he was able to buy a car. Padre Manuel no longer had to lug his vestments, mass kit and lectionaries with him each day from the center of town to his parish.

The scenery along the coastal ride in the state of Vera Cruz is spectacular. The highway winds along the mountains, with occasional views of the shore, of lakes and of miles and miles of lush coconut groves. Pineapples grow in perfect rows and plentiful profusion. Picturesque towns and the stately city of Vera Cruz add history and interest. We stopped at the principal plazas in the middle of towns to cook or prepare our lunch. This route along the east coast seemed to have more campgrounds available than other drives we've found on similar Mexican highways. We stayed in them whenever it was possible. Always when we traveled, we kept up our daily routine of prayer as a community, as a family, and our individual prayer times. We always sang praise songs before our meals, and during our longer prayer sessions. This common prayer was very evangelistic. When we were among Mexicans, we sang and prayed in Spanish. I can't remember a single incidence when we didn't attract at least one person to be with us in prayer. The onlookers would soon start asking questions, and we jumped at the opportunity to talk to them about Jesus.

Even the campgrounds, whose restrooms were primitive, were a step up from the austere circumstances of San Felipe in Coatza.

"It's good to be moving again," Sarah said one night after swimming in the Gulf of Mexico.

"I think so too, sweetheart," I answered, "Mama knows that 'going' is always part of our growing."

My Mom had suffered a mild stroke while we were driving along the Gulf of Mexico on the way home. Something told me as we travelled that I should find a telephone and call Louisiana. The news of Mom's stroke unnerved me. There was no way I could get to her sooner than we had planned. The biggest danger, according to my sister, Rachel, was that she could have a more serious stroke. We prayed and sang, pleading with God to heal and protect my mother.

When I did get home, I went straight to her house, "Mom, that night after I called home and learned about your stroke, I sat on the beach praying a rosary for you. I prayed 'Lord, Jesus, please heal my mom; please give me peace as we make our way home. Keep her well. Lord show me Your will.'"

"Well, He heard you, because I am a lot better," Mom smiled, "I still have trouble pinching these two fingers together, though." She indicated her left index finger and her left thumb.

"Right after I prayed, Mom, I saw a glowing 'V' on the water just past the surf. I wondered what it could mean. I felt like God said, 'V is for victory. Your prayers will be answered and your Mom will have the Victory over this stroke.' When I got a chance to call Rachel the next day, she told me you were so much better and out of danger. Praise the Lord!" I shared.

"Well, I'm glad you're here now. We also had Mommee in the hospital not long ago. It's hard to reach you when you are on those long trips so far away," she shared, trying not to sound too reproachful that I hadn't been there for my aging grandmother.

"I guess it is hard on the Moms of missionaries too. We'll be leaving in a couple of weeks again; this time we're headed to Sea Island, Georgia to celebrate my in-laws fiftieth wedding anniversary. They are taking all of us."

"I'd like to come too," she laughed, "Are you looking forward to it?"

"I'm happy to go and I'm rushed," I answered honestly, "Our family has not been to a resort in years. I have to get the children clothes, dressy and casual, clothes for myself, and for Frank. We need bathing suits, beach towels and shoes. I am going shopping at the local second hand clothing store; run by some really cool Christians. You know, The Refinery?"

"Yes, you ought to find some great bargains there. Here,

take this little gift to get a few new things," she said, stuffing a one hundred dollar bill in my purse. Mom always loved to treat her kids to little extras.

The fiftieth wedding anniversary celebration for Frank's parents was just a few weeks away. God blessed my shopping for our family. At The Refinery, I was able to buy Frank the first suit he owned since we set out for the missions, and it was almost exactly what he would have bought in an expensive retail store.

The humble house on Third Street in Abbeville seemed like a palace after our trek to the south. Although it was not air-conditioned, we had plenty of fans, two full working bathrooms, a screened porch that overlooked the park, and our neighbor's, Ms. Authorine's, swimming pool. Beau and Michelle cleaned our house and stocked the fridge. We caught up with the communities in Abbeville and Lafayette. We had dinner with our mission council, and we enjoyed being in our own hometown and in our own culture.

After our short respite, we headed for Sea Island in our big blue van, also pulling our small travel trailer. We hoped to visit our nation's capital after the anniversary celebration, to visit Jim and Cathy in Charlottesville, and then to rendezvous with Chet and Valerie in Augusta. We wanted them to love Augusta the way we did. I assessed the season of our lives, and I thought it was time for our kids to "be Americans".

I relaxed and commented as miles of interstate slipped by, "Frank, I couldn't be happier with the life we live, but I know that there is a place where the children have to connect with the best America has to offer. I am so glad we will be able to go to Washington, D. C. after Sea Island."

"Sea Island is going to be an American experience too," Frank explained, "My Mom said that we were going on the 'American Plan', which includes all of our meals, snacks and use of their exclusive facilities."

"Well, we could never have afforded it, but being it is a gift, let's enjoy it," I smiled, "I want the kids to absorb as much of this experience as possible. If we continue the Southreach in August, they will be headed out as 'American' missionaries."

Frank and I had crossed the Atlantic on the S.S. France and the Q. E. II when it was brand new. We had been on a

Caribbean Cruise, eaten at Maxim's in Paris, at the 21 Club in New York City, dined often at Antoine's in New Orleans, been to the Opera House in Vienna, Covent Garden in London, and stayed in many fine hotels and establishments. Most of our kids had dined in style, stayed in nice hotels, and visited with prominent leaders from other countries. But, by our choice, we had clung to the ideal of living in gospel poverty – trusting in the Lord to provide all of our needs and keeping those needs as best we could on a level with those we served.

Even after all the fine places we had stayed, we were still unprepared for the luxury of The Cloister at Sea Island. The suite of rooms reserved for us was extra roomy and boasted every imaginable convenience.

"Can you believe this place, Mom?" Sarah asked, "It is bigger than our whole house in Abbeville. *And* they put chocolates on our pillows at night."

"Cousin Leah says they have a train that takes the children everywhere and there are ice sculptures at all the meals," Susanna added.

"I saw three swimming pools and the beach," Joseph said, jumping on the overstuffed couch. Mary added, amazed, "We have three TV's, one in each room and cartoons on a lot of channels!"

"Can we live here?" Simon asked, as everyone laughed.

As we got dressed up for the anniversary meal, I asked Frank, "Do you have any idea of how much our accommodations cost?"

"Babe, we could live in mission for a couple of months on what it costs for *one* night, and for a whole year for what is going to cost for the week."

I felt God saying, "Honor your Father and Mother," so I said aloud, "I think Jesus wants us to put that out of our minds and just be here for your parents. They could have spent this money on a lot of other things, but they wanted their family to have a wonderful week rejoicing in their fifty years together."

"Good, because I'm hungry and looking forward to roast beef au jus and cherries jubilee tonight," he said squeezing my hand as we walked out of the door.

I love the water, being in it or being near it – the ocean, a swimming pool, a lake, a pond, or a crystal stream. I got up early every morning to walk on the beach saying a rosary. It was an unusual opportunity for me. I didn't have to cook breakfast, lunch, or dinner, wash clothes, or entertain the children. A sand dune stood between our room and the beach.

The first morning, as I reached the top of the dune and the Atlantic Ocean glistened in the sunrise before me, I closed my eyes and prayed out of sheer thankfulness, "Jesus, help me to be worthy of all that you do for me. I am so blessed." As I began my rosary walk, I spotted something not too far away in the surf. Swimming just about a hundred yards from the water's edge were two dolphins. They were swimming even with me, at about the pace I was walking. I was totally delighted. "Thank you, Jesus, for the dolphins," I said silently.

I turned around to come back in the middle of the third decade, half way through the rosary. I was blown away when the dolphins turned around, too, and swam back to my beginning spot and then submerged and swam away. I don't know how a marine biologist would explain that behavior, but, to me, it was a sign! Jesus was showering me with spiritual luxuries as well as material ones. He was there – with me – sending his graceful creatures to keep me company. Even more amazing was that the dolphin came every day that I prayed the rosary on the beach. And every day they repeated that same pattern of accompanying me on my prayer walk!

Above:
     Frank and Genie at Susanna's wedding in General Cepeda, 2001.

Although we don't have that many occasions to enjoy dancing, Frank and I love to dance. Here, we are celebrating the 25th Anniversary of the Ang Buhing Pulong Community in Malaybalay, but we are celebrating with their members who live now in New York City.
  September 2011

300

Chapter Eighteen

Being Americans

We left Sea Island and meandered up the east coast to Washington, D. C. Beau had seen Washington, but the younger children had not. We first drove around the center of the city, visited the National Shrine, and moved on to the Capitol. We parked at a distance and moved at a slow pace because of Simon and John Paul. First, we went to pray on the sidewalk of the Supreme Court, begging the Lord to have mercy on America, especially the unborn.

"Is this where they said it is okay to kill babies?" little Joseph asked.

"Yes, Joseph, it is," I answered, "But there is nothing more powerful than prayer. We will keep praying."

The children folded their little hands and closed their eyes. No one around made fun of us; those beautiful children in prayer were a Gospel message.

Next, we moved on to the Capitol. As we rounded the side of the Capitol to climb the stairs, we were greeted by strains of the powerful Alleluias of Handel's Messiah. It was actually like a scene in a movie. I have always said the Lord is the greatest dramatist. The Alleluia Chorus belted out as the Summers family started to climb the stairs. The music was so familiar, and yet it seemed unusual to encounter this beautiful music on the Capital steps. We looked up and saw a very life-like manikin of Jesus as the Good Shepherd, carrying one lamb in His arms, and one on His shoulders. Hidden behind the lambs at his feet was the portable stereo, *"Alleluia, Alleluia…."*

I could not believe my eyes. Of course, it was just a representation of Jesus, which was obvious. But I have known Jesus too long to think that He wasn't arranging this scene for us.

301

This event, although artificial, had a huge impact on me. This beautiful Holy "greeting" waiting for our family, on the Capitol steps, was most certainly a "God-incidence".

I wondered, "Wow, Lord, this is an awesome welcome; but, is this allowed? I did not know they allowed this kind of display on the Capitol steps."

Simon tugged at me and said, "Mom, is this where Jesus belongs?"

"Look at the Good Shepherd," the little boys exclaimed, "Is he real?"

Frank and I exchanged puzzled, but happy, looks.

Suddenly, we saw a couple of men running up to the, grabbing it together with the lambs and the stereo, taking off in another direction. They practically "threw" it all in a waiting van and sped off. We turned around and saw a small group of police officers running after them. I don't know how long this manikin had been there before we arrived, but in all these years, I haven't met another family of Capitol visitors who were greeted by the "Good Shepherd" and blaring "Alleluias".

I instantly knew my desire to "Americanize" my children was "alright" with my Lord. I also understood more than I ever had before, in a heartfelt way, that Jesus *loves* America even more than we do.

Jim and Cathy, Frank's brother and his wife, had a lovely summer home on the James River in Virginia. It was not too far from Washington, D.C. It would be a week or so before Chet and Val could meet us in Augusta, so we asked Jim if we could stay at their summer place. As usual, they were so gracious. We heaved a sigh of relief as we unpacked the van for a stay of a week or more in Virginia. An ideal house in an idyllic setting afforded a much-needed rest.

During that week, we received a phone call from Chet and Val. It was a surprising phone call. "Sorry y'all, we are phoning you today because we've had a change of plans," Chet said, "I am only one semester away from my college diploma and all I have left to do is to write my senior thesis. My parents are offering to help us, and I don't know if that offer will be open to us later. So for now, we won't be going back into missions."

302

Val continued, "We'll let you know what our future plans are when he finishes his thesis."

Both Frank and I knew that Chet and Val would not be back. This decision certainly affected our plans to continue our Southreach. The Markos had been such an important element in the concept of families in mission, traveling together to proclaim the Gospel. We would miss them.

"What does this mean?" I asked Frank later that evening.

"It means *our* plans have to be changed," Frank replied, "It also means we need to seek the Lord again about what He has for us next."

"Well, Frank, here we are, alone for the first time in over a year," I pointed out, "We couldn't be in a better situation to have a family retreat to hear what the Lord's plan is."

"Let's start tomorrow," he agreed, "Tonight when you pray, ask God to give you a scripture for our first session in the morning."

I snuggled up to him, and he gathered me in his arms. This news marked another painful disappointment in our search for a family in mission. Sure, we had to trust God, but it still hurt. We understood the Marko's decision. We were not angry, and sent them our blessings and prayed for the best future for them.

The next morning, I woke the kids up with a rousing rendition of "*Rise and Shine and Give God the Glory, Glory....*" We had a hearty country breakfast, and sat down for our everyday morning prayers. Frank announced the turn of events to the kids. They were crushed. They, too, wanted to hear from the Lord, "What's next?"

They entered enthusiastically into our retreat.

Our opening prayer was offered by Frank, as was his usual practice. He began, "Lord, Jesus, we need to hear your voice. Please shed some light on what you are doing now. What do you want us to do? We will go wherever you want us to go and whatever you want us to do. Amen"

The rest of us chimed in with, "Amen, Alleluia, Glory!" Then we sang our special song for guidance, "*Lead us on, Oh Lord, Lead us on, Lead us where we dare not go....*" After we sang a few songs, we settled in to the presence of the Lord.

The first one to share was Sarah, now fourteen, "I'll go first, Daddy. I had a wonderful vision. It was a clear vision of the steeple at St. Mary Magdalen Church in Abbeville. The sky was blue and we were happily going into church. I think God is saying we should be at home in Abbeville for awhile."

Frank breathed in heavily. Shifting gears from being in the foreign mission to being in a stateside mission was always a hard word for him and me to accept. We thrive in foreign mission, living simply on small oil checks and occasional donations. That all changed when we had to live stateside. Those checks didn't support us with the demands of stateside living – utilities, insurance, groceries, social obligations, the children's education, etc. With our bigger family, Frank would have to again engage in his "tent-making" occupation, practicing law.

Although, I sensed that this new direction was smashing in to the walls of Frank's heart, I had to say, "That's what my reading for this morning says too. It's from Jeremiah 29, verses 11 – 14. This is one of my favorites about a future full of hope. But it was verse fourteen that struck me as guidance today, '...I will restore your fortunes and gather you from all the nations and all the places where I have driven you says the Lord, and I will bring you back to the place from which I sent you into exile.' I agree with Sarah that I hear the Lord saying Abbeville for a season; however, I feel strongly that the Lord wants us to accept His direction as good news. He wants us to know He has a plan for our welfare and not for our woe."

We continued our retreat for a day or so more, but each Word from the Lord unmistakably confirmed that His plan for the immediate future was a season in Abbeville.

We stopped at Alleluia in Georgia on the way home to Louisiana; it was their Fourth of July celebration. Again, the time among these wonderful brothers and sisters blessed and strengthened us. Someone in the Alleluia community gave me Frank Peretti's books, *This Present Darkness* and *Piercing the Darkness*. As we traveled home, I read these life-changing volumes. These fictional accounts of the spiritual battle that is always pitched against us reinforced so many things I already knew. The message was powerfully presented, renewing my zeal. The daily skirmishes didn't defeat me. I gave my all to the fight at hand, knowing that I was not alone. It also showed that faithfulness is an indispensable element for the Lord's warriors. Our side wins in the end, and we have powerful partners in the epic confrontation. Jesus set my soul on fire, and I was ready for our season at home. God was not finished Americanizing our family, but He was the magnificent General, and I could have confidence in His commands.

When we returned to Abbeville and settled in to life on Third Street, Terry Boudreaux showed up for a visit. He noticed right away the flame of zeal for the Lord burning in my heart. Terry had married a wonderful woman, Anne, and Jesus led them to each other with their own miracle story.

"What's going on?" Terry asked. "You look all fired up. Is it your visit to Alleluia?"

"Well, it's super to visit Alleluia, but actually I am on fire again with the Holy Spirit since I read these books by Frank Peretti."

Terry responded, "Maybe we ought to read them too."

"I definitely recommend them, Terry. Frank hardly reads any fiction, but when he saw how renewed I was, he read them, too, and Sarah has just finished reading them. Our family's praise and worship is off the charts now!"

Terry and Anne read the books and passed them on to our friends, Graham and Donna Smith, leaders of the small Good Shepherd Community. Soon all three of our families were ablaze with the desire to worship and praise God with all of our strength. We had all been immersed in many different ministries, but we yearned to enter into the High Praise of God. The first time we met to praise God together as three families, was on January 1, 1990. What a way to start the New Year! It was the inspiration of our mutual reading of the Peretti books, but it was far more than that. We began to praise God vigorously and Jesus *showed up*. The Holy Spirit infused us with inspiration, supernatural gifts, and an overwhelming awareness of His love. Angels surrounded our house, we didn't see them, but we could feel them. All of our children were close to the same age and they loved gathering for these praise evenings. We praised God for hours, thanking Him for the privilege of being His servants, praying, interceding, dancing in the Spirit, and finding a freedom to abandon ourselves completely to Him.

Two o'clock in the morning, January 2nd rolled around, and we were hugging good-bye. Sleeping children were bundled up and carried to the car. "When do you want to get together again?" Frank asked.

"How about Saturday night?" Terry answered.

"Sounds good to me," I added, "Tonight has been so wonderful. This is an answer to a prayer I prayed a few Sundays back. I remember asking the Lord, 'Jesus, I am drowning in a sea of longing for you. Please, throw me a spirit filled life preserver. This evening has been just that, now I am bobbing on the waves of High Praise.'"

Everyone agreed to meet the following Saturday. That was the beginning of the Saturday night prayer meeting. For the first eight months, we did not feel any need to open up these high praise and intercession sessions to others. Whatever was happening was completely marvelous. We did not want to change anything. Miracles, signs, and wonders fell to us from the Hand of God. Later on, we began to share the joy of these meetings with a few of our good friends. Soon the Romeros were regulars. The Borbas family, the Dunbars, the Sampeys, the Leonards, the Touchets, the Gardiners, the Leleuxs, the Keefes, their full households, and scores of others participated in this life giving event each Saturday.

As the years progressed, and the children became teenagers, they still wanted to be there on Saturday night. Their friends might arrive late, but as the hour reached midnight, the room was filled with youth, praising God with all of their might.

A tradition from the beginning was a super-strong intercessory time. We began to sing, "Our God is an awesome God, He reigns from heaven above, with wisdom, power and love, our God is an awesome God."

Then someone in the group would offer a petition out loud, "Lord, Jesus, for anyone who is contemplating suicide tonight."

We would sing again, "Our God is an awesome God...."

Another petition, "Lord, Jesus, for the healing of my aunt. Heal her cancer." "Our God is an awesome God...."

Another petition, "Lord, for a good job for Godfrey." "Our God...."

We really did have so many answered prayers. That meeting became a fountain of spiritual strength for many in the Acadiana region. It lasted for ten full years, we celebrated our tenth anniversary of the existence of this meeting, and almost as quickly as it had begun it was over. God spun off from that meeting so many ministries and evangelization efforts; it bore fruit one hundred fold.

After we got back from Virginia in the fall of 1989, and settled in, we were at a prayer meeting in the home of the Gardiners in Crowley, Louisiana, with Terry Boudreaux. As we prayed for what God would have us do in the Acadiana region, I had a vision and shared it with the group.

"I had a vision of God the Father with a big chef's hat on and a white apron. He was cooking in a big iron gumbo pot, stirring briskly. Suddenly he picked up a saltshaker to season the pot and as He shook it, students came out of the holes instead of salt. In the vision, I could see several different types of school uniforms."

Terry asked me, "Do you understand what the Lord is saying?"

"I am not sure exactly what the Lord is trying to say to me in this vision," I admitted, "Let's ask Him."

Frank prayed, "Father God, what are you trying to say to us? What is the message for us?"

I heard him answer in my heart, "I am cooking up something important in Acadiana, and the youth are going to be the seasoning."

Our family came to understand that the Lord had a purpose in our life in Louisiana, and that it included our children's witness in the school systems. He wanted to season Acadiana with some missionary kids who loved and served Jesus. For the most part, that vision has been constantly fulfilled in the following years until now.

While the Saturday night prayer meeting was in full swing, Frank got a job practicing law in Lafayette, Louisiana about twenty miles from Abbeville. Beau taught at St. Thomas More High School, and Sarah enrolled there too. They commuted from Abbeville everyday for a year. Our other children were homeschooled. With Sarah's school activities, Frank's job, the prayer meeting, and the need for a bigger house, we decided to move to Lafayette. House hunting for a home in our price range was an arduous process. The good side of that was getting to really know Lafayette. We had hoped to find a house in Donna and Graham's neighborhood. When we didn't find one there, we were really waiting for the Lord to indicate the right house for us.

Finally, we bought a house two doors down and across the street from St. Pius X Church Parish facilities. Monsignor Richard Mouton, former pastor from St. Mary Magdalen Parish during the years that we lived there, was the recently appointed pastor of St. Pius X Parish. Now he would be our pastor again. His rectory was across a playing field from our house; I could see him walking to his office every day. One day, when he came over for a visit, he, Frank, the kids and I sat in front of my picture window, having lemonade.

"Look, Monsignor, I can see your house from here. You'd better behave yourself!" (I was teasing him because he is a *super dedicated* pastor and priest.)

A lot of folks think Msgr. Mouton is very serious, but he has a charming, dry wit. He answered my comment by saying, "That view works both ways, Mrs. Summers!"

The life on Lippi Street Americanized us more than we had imagined. We walked to church, became ministers of communion, lectors, and active parishioners. The Saturday night meeting met in our house on a rotating basis. My boys lived a thousand adventures in their tree house in the big back yard, and neighborhood kids played basketball and built forts in our backyard. Our boys went to the public school nearby, Plantation Elementary School. The principal there was a daily communicant at St. Pius. After school, they played on soccer teams and rode bikes and skateboards in the subdivision.

Mary Magdalen went to Paul Breaux Junior High, ranked first in her class, and became a cheerleader. She had her little posse of friends and countless opportunities for sleepovers, socializing, and retreats.

Susanna and Sarah went to St. Thomas More High School, recognized nationally for its academics and extracurricular activities. They excelled there. In fact, at an awards ceremony at the end of one school year, I overheard someone say, "They should have called it the Summers Girls awards ceremony." I'm sure my girls would want me to delete that comment, but by the awards they received, it was obvious that God demonstrated that mission life does not give you less preparedness for the academic world. They had not lost out by living their mission lives. In fact, He educated and gifted them with discipline and virtue to meet the challenges of a challenging American Catholic high school.

The most important part of our life was testifying to the wonders of our life in mission. Our children struggled to live in Lafayette with the same dedication to Jesus they had lived in mission. Others noticed they were fervent and wanted the zeal that they had; not by the thousands, but God slowly added to their numbers. Beau, a teacher, and Sarah, a sophomore, arrived at STM early each day. He taught Theology after studying Theology at Franciscan University. Every morning they had Mr. Dan Jurek, the new campus minister, initiate Morning. In the school chapel, they gathered for about ten minutes every morning. Beau attended when he didn't have too much preparation for his classes, but Sarah and Mr. Jurek attended every day. The vast majority of the time during that first year, they were the only ones present at Morning Prayer, sometimes a handful of teachers came, and usually Sarah was the only student. However, by the next year there were fifteen to twenty students who went almost every day. In a few years, the school chapel would be enlarged and it was generally *full* of faculty, students, and some parents gathered for Morning Prayer.

Beau loved teaching, but wanted to continue his education. He received a Board of Regents Fellowship at the graduate level at Louisiana State University. He and Michelle moved to Baton Rouge where he studied for two years, completing his Master's degree in History.

Sarah called me one day from school at the end of the 1991-92 school year, "Mom, Mr. Keefe told me they need a religion teacher for next year. He wonders if you are interested. You could go and talk to Dr. Bollich."

"Tell him thanks for thinking of me. That's really nice. I haven't taught in a good while, besides I'm still a semester away from my degree, but tell him I will pray about it, and I'll talk to Dad about it. We'll see."

I hung up the phone and began to think about Sarah's proposition. I remembered the vision of the Father in the chef's hat. "Am I being called to minister to these young people, Lord? Is it possible to evangelize by teaching religion? Maybe if Sarah, Susanna and I are there together, we can make a positive difference in the spiritual environment of STM."

When Frank got home from the office, we sat down and chatted about our respective days. I said, "Sarah called me today and suggested I apply for the job of teaching religion at STM next year. What do you think?"

"I know we have to pray about it. Simon, Joseph and John Paul will be in school next year. Maybe God wants you more involved in the life of our girls," Frank suggested, "Even Mary will be at St. Thomas More in a couple of years."

So I sought the leading of the Lord in my prayer time. I was surprised at how fast I sensed that God was saying, "Yes! Genie, trust me. Take this job. I have a plan." I opened the Bible to Psalm 25:4 –5. "Make me know thy ways, O Lord; teach me thy paths. Lead me in thy truth, and teach me for thou are the God of my salvation; for thee I wait all day long." I understood that the position of teaching Church History at STM would be a path for me; I would be learning things the God of my salvation wanted to teach me. I also felt the Lord would allow me to teach the students His way and His path.

We had no idea what it would mean for our family life if I were working outside the home, but as I announced it to my family, they were extremely supportive. I made an appointment to speak with Dr. Bollich, who was head of the Religion Department at STM. "First, I want to tell you that one of your best recommendations came from Beau. I really enjoyed having him here. He is sure you will be great for this job," Dr. Bollich said.

He described the job and I felt an excitement about teaching; a feeling I knew came from the Lord. "You will be teaching Church History to sophomores," he paused, then said, "Ordinarily, new teachers teach five classes, but we really need someone to take six classes."

One of my problems is that I am not very good at saying, "No." So I said, "Okay, I'll teach six classes."

We also discussed my lack of a degree, but because I was certified as a Master Catechist, had been a missionary for so many years, and was a certified evangelist in the diocese, it was sufficient.

"Religion is the only position where we can accept a non-degreed teacher. However, the policy is that our non-degreed teachers must be working toward their degree."

"No problem, Dr. Bollich. I have often wanted to finish that degree. When would I have to enroll in the university?"

Dr. Bollich answered, "Next summer would be soon enough." I went home thinking about what getting my degree might mean. We didn't feel that we were out of the missions permanently. It seemed pursuing my degree and teaching locked us into this season at home for at least a couple of years. As much as we missed the missions, I considered my new job at STM a "mission."

In 1975, when we left for the missions, I was only one semester away from graduation with a degree in English. Frank and I had often disagreed about my returning to college to study and finish those credits that were required to earn a degree, and usually we were almost never in the States long enough for me to enroll. Another important issue was our finances, which could only be stretched so far. But with my new job, finances for college would not be a problem. It had been twenty-two years since I was in college. I was sure that many new classes would be required before I would be allowed to graduate. I wondered how the eighteen hours lacking all those years before would translate in today's university. I hoped it would not mean lots of added years.

I prepared for teaching religion by praying about how the Lord would have me teach Church History. I knew that love for the Church would only come if students grew in love for the *Founder of the Church, Jesus Christ.* The church doesn't make any sense at all apart from its founder. Jesus is the groom of the Church; He describes His relationship with us as a love affair.

I decided to be true to the teachings I knew from experience on how to be effective in bringing young people to love Jesus. I kicked off my curriculum with a modified Life in the Spirit seminar as we had taught it in the missions. The topics: God is Love; The Problem of Sin; Who is Jesus Christ;

311

Repentance and Salvation; The Holy Spirit; Growing as a Christian; and Suffering.

I was so pleased with my students' response. They were hungry, and this was real. Not everyone, but generally most of the sophomores I taught were enriched by that Holy Spirit beginning.

We began each class with deep prayer. I announced the first day; "We are going to meet Jesus everyday in this prayer time. He promised that where *two* or more are gathered in His name, He will be there. I know His promises are true. Therefore, I am *one* gathered in His name, and I know that in this Catholic school that there is at least *one more person* in this room who will join me in Jesus' name, so that makes *two*. He is here and He will be here every day. In the coming months you will learn about so many miracles that I have seen Jesus work in my life. When we gather in His name each day, you can ask for miracles and then you will be able to tell us all about your answered prayers."

And I shut my eyes and prayed. "Lord, Jesus, I thank You that I am here in your name. I thank You for the others who are also here in your name. I thank You that I know You are here according to your promise. I can feel Your presence," I continued, (and I could), "Please, Lord, accept our prayers of thanksgiving as well as our petitions. Hear and answer us."

At this point, I would allow each student to offer first a thanksgiving prayer and then their petitions. Sometimes I made them go row by row. Soon the thanksgivings and petitions were spontaneous. God was answering their prayers. They knew He showed up every day, and many began to enter into a personal relationship with Jesus. STM was an elite school in many ways. A percentage of them were from working class or underprivileged families, but the majority came from affluent backgrounds. But I reminded myself that this was a *mission field*. They were all needy, they all needed to know Jesus better.

They kept a prayer journal. I asked them to write ten prayer requests. Then they scratched off the prayers and added new ones as the prayers were answered. I could see transformation in a lot of the kids. The Church History book I used followed Avery Dulles's teaching on the Church. He considers that there are five models of the Church: Church as

Herald (of the Gospel), Church as Institution, Church as Sacrament, Church as Community, and Church as Servant. Nothing could have better fit my ability to bring our witness to bear on the subject. I personally had lived all of those aspects of Church, and had the life experiences and stories that made them understand Church.

Two things were important to me. First, I wanted them to know the Lord of the Church, Jesus the Incarnate Word, Son of the Father, and sender of the Holy Spirit. Secondly, I wanted them to know that *WE ARE THE CHURCH.*

It was a question on every test. "Who is the Church?"

The correct answer for extra points was always, "*We are the Church.*"

I insisted that they acknowledge that if the Church needs to be renewed, WE need to be renewed. If the Church needs to be more faithful, WE need to be more faithful. If the Church needs to be Holy, WE need to be Holy, and that we can never leave the Church, because WE ARE THE CHURCH.

Once a month we had chapel time. We played beautiful, inspiring songs in the background, gave thanks, discussed the day's Mass readings, and then we had a prayer warrior session. This consisted of two kneelers in front of the altar and two chairs facing forward on either side of the altar. It was in those chairs that the prayer warriors sat. They held their hands and arms aloft, doing battle in prayer for the two who knelt in front of the altar. The warriors did spiritual battle with the students who were kneeling, for the additional strength they needed for their prayers. We did this exercise after teaching about how Aaron and Hur held up Moses' arms and the Israelites won the battle. Prayer warriors loved the story in Exodus 17: 10-12. Volunteers came up to kneel or take a prayer warrior chair. I was always amazed at the reverence and order that prevailed in our sessions. The Spirit moved them and they followed suit. The Holy Spirit never failed to show up and anoint our chapel time.

I did not teach 210 teenaged angels. I taught 210 sophomores in high school. At times, the classes were unruly and other times were easily distracted. However, each time they heard a story, a true recounting of the miracles and signs and wonders I had experienced, or miracles that had happened to my loved ones, they were unwavering in their attention. Pencils went down; other homework hidden behind their textbooks got shut away, and note passing came to an immediate halt. I remember one student I'll call Zeke. He was in his first year at STM, and one of the most difficult students in my class. He never seemed to be on the right wavelength with me, or the class; he talked and made fun of serious stuff; and even fell asleep from time to time. Zeke just seemed to have slipped through the cracks. The day before school ended, I asked him to stay after class for a few minutes.

I said to him, "Zeke, you make good grades in this class but I feel that you haven't gotten as much as I wished you would. Is there anything I can do for you?"

"Sure, you can pray for me. I'm going to be okay though," he flashed me a mischievous, confident smile.

On the first day of school of the following year, I was walking to my classroom before the first bell sounded. I was laden with my books for the new school year when someone came up behind me and picked me up from the back by both of my hands. In order not to drop my books, I stiffened. The strong young man behind me, whom I could not see, carried me along for three or four yards. When he set me back down, he ran in front of me. It was Zeke. He looked like a new creation. I hardly recognized the boy that I thought had gotten nothing out of my class.

"Even though I am a junior this year, can I join your class for opening prayer? My religion class is right next to yours. They say my teacher is always late. I can stand at the doorway of your classroom and join the prayer until my teacher shows up," Zeke asked, "Please? I have a lot to pray about."

"Of course you can if it's okay with your teacher. I am so pleased that you want to. Gosh, Zeke, you look terrific. What happened to you this summer?" I marveled.

"I went to a Young Life Camp and I got to know the Lord like you said to do last year. I have been so happy. Maybe I can come to your class sometime this year and tell them not to waste the year like I did."

"I would love that. Thank you." I answered.

Not only had my young student found the Lord, but he had become willing to evangelize others. I was very encouraged by his change of heart as I began my second year.

The summer between my two years of teaching, I enrolled in the University of Louisiana at Lafayette. I went into the office of the English Department where Dr. Meriwether was the Dean. She had taught me when I was there twenty-two years before. She was also a great cheerleader for Beau when he won the Outstanding Graduate Award at the University's 100th commencement. She walked through the lobby while I was waiting to be advised by one of the professors.

I greeted her, "Hi, Dr. Meriwether. I'm Genie Summers, Frank (Beau) Summers' mom."

"Hi, Genie," she responded, "I remember you. How's Frank? He's in grad school at LSU right?"

"Yes, he is," I said, "He's enjoying his studies."

"Good. What brings you up here to the English Department?"

"I am waiting for my advisor. Years ago, I left college with one semester left to complete my degree. Now, I want to finally complete my studies and get that English degree," I explained, "I'm teaching at STM and they require you to work on your degree."

"Well, welcome back," she said kindly, "I hope it all works out well for you."

"Thanks. I'm praying it will."

She walked into her office, while I continued to wait in the lobby for my advisor. Even the secretaries there felt bad that my advisor had not shown up. I clearly had an appointment.

I turned to the Lord in prayer, "Jesus, I wasn't too nervous until I started waiting. What if this whole degree thing turns into a big ordeal? Please, send me Your peace, and provide my need to get advised by someone who will *understand my situation.* Thank You in advance, Lord, for Your help."

I sat there for about fifteen more minutes before one of the secretaries asked me, "It looks like he's not coming. Would you like to reschedule for another time?"

"If I must, then I will, but I took the Spanish advanced placement test and the Spanish department is waiting to hear from my advisor. I'm pretty sure I have to be advised soon," I answered, hesitantly.

Suddenly, Dr. Meriwether came to her office door and caught sight of me, "Your advisor has not come yet?"

315

"No, he hasn't," I answered, "They are trying to reschedule my appointment."

"Come on in to my office," she said, "I can help you."

I walked in thanking her profusely. It was certainly an opportunity not offered to most people. I was going to be advised by the *head* of the department. We took out my old transcript and she explained some of the new requirements for an English degree. Miraculously, and because she had the *authority to do so*, she plugged *all* of my old credits into the new degree program form while I sat there, absolutely amazed.

When that was done, she said, "Well Genie, this looks like a good plan. You lack an earth science, a basic computer class, an upper level fine arts class, and one upper level English class. I think the few extra hours can be filled by your credits in Spanish from advanced placement."

"Dr. Meriwether, this is such a blessing. I don't know how to thank you enough," I said as the reality of what had just transpired hit me.

This was unequivocally a "red tape" miracle. *Only* Dr. Meriwether could have expedited my degree program in that way.

Many naysayers had painted a bleak picture of returning to school after so many years. I had been warned by friends, "You will have years ahead of catching up to do. Don't expect to get your degree anytime soon."

So, that summer, I studied advanced Spanish, Creative Writing, and Broadway and Lyric Theater. We had two cars, so Frank would drop me off at UL while my girls watched the little boys, took them swimming and entertained them. Someone came for me after one o'clock and I was Mom the rest of the day. I was totally blessed in my classes. Each class afforded an opportunity to witness to the Lord and the life He allowed me to live as His missionary.

I capitalized on my missionary attitude of gratitude and almost had to pinch myself. I told my friend, Jesus, "How awesome you are, God. I love learning, my classes challenge and interest me, and my professors are superior. What have I done to deserve this blessing? Thank you for my supportive family that is taking up the slack."

In the fall, I taught only five classes and scheduled my two planning periods first thing in the morning. At eight am on Monday, Wednesday, and Friday, I studied Louisiana History, which I loved and had already studied quite a bit by independent reading. On Tuesday and Thursday evenings at five pm, I studied Geology, and on Wednesday nights at eight pm, I studied Computer Basics. When I got home from teaching and the little boys got off the bus in the afternoon, I was bushed. I lay on the living room floor and they would sit on my tummy, forcing open my eyelids from time to time, and tell me their stories.

After twenty minutes of rest, the kids and I came together like a well-oiled machine and made the rest of our day work. Our past life as a mission team, the reality we had lived as Kingdom Builders, came in handy and made my going to school and teaching at the same time possible. Being a family and a team is a gift for God. That was probably one of the busiest seasons of my life, but because I had so little free time, I drew very near to the Lord in my personal prayer. I consider it a major miracle that I walked up and received my English degree after only one summer and one semester of study following a twenty-two year hiatus.

Graduation Day came. Some of my fellow "adult learners" were uninterested in participating in the commencement exercises. I was fifty years old. I waited in line with the young graduates and happily walked up on stage. It had been such a long time coming. It was a gift I never expected to receive.

When they handed me my diploma, there was a loud shout from the first balcony, all my children and Frank called out, "THAT'S OUR MOM GO, MOM."

Chapter 19 tells the story of Paul Nicholas Jordan. Here are pictures of our reunion in 1991; his first birthday (I sobbed my heart out when I saw his first birthday pic.); our last visit in San Rafael; a cute head shot; and a photo of him at Kim's house in his final days. *"All who call upon the Lord will be saved."*

A Secret Comes to Light

There was a major compartment of my heart that needed attention. A secret was locked away and its urgency denied for thirty years. In *Go! You Are Sent,* I tell the story of my baby born out of wedlock. I surrendered him for adoption before Frank and I started dating. For thirty years, this had been a well-kept secret. So few people were in on the facts (Maybe a few people suspected, but only my parents, Frank and I knew for sure.) I had often longed for my beautiful son, imagining an age progression, looking in the faces of the boys his age. I was sure he was handsome, but was he happy? How were his holidays? Who were his parents, and did they stay married? If a day passed without my thinking of him, it was rare indeed. I had prayed for him constantly since my conversion and missionary life. In our season of being Americans, the Lord at last allowed me to address that pain.

When we drove home from Mexico for the fiftieth Wedding Anniversary of Frank's parents the year before, we had been traveling late at night. On late night talk radio, a program featured the reunion story of a birth mother with the son she had surrendered for adoption. I didn't have TV, and was not aware that so many of these meetings between birth mothers and their children surrendered for adoption were taking place. It caught me completely off guard. Frank was driving; the children were sleeping in the back. I had a total meltdown. I began to sob uncontrollably. I was shocked at the severity of the pain it caused me, as the adoptees and birth parents shared the details of their first meeting and the events leading up to it. Frank and I did not talk; he just kept rubbing my shoulders that shook from the sobbing.

That night of suffering planted a seed. I decided that one day, I too, would meet my son. So much stuff had to be dealt with before I could search for him. Our children did not know about him. Our social circles and our Christian circles did not know about him. I had a million questions. Who searched? How did they search? Was it legal? My most profound doubt about the process of searching was my son's well being. Did he have any interest in meeting me? Would his adoptive parents be offended and hurt by my coming into his life? Did he know he was adopted? Was he married, and would his wife and children be blessed or harmed by our meeting? Would the revelation of the existence of my son be a cause of scandal for the mission life we lived? So many questions, and I had not a single answer. But, thankfully, I knew *Who* had all the answers. That night on the highway, the Lord said to me in an extra tender way, "This is not the time, suffer a while longer, and offer up this suffering for him."

Once we were settled back in Abbeville, Frank took up the practice of law again. Most states require continuing legal education for lawyers. Frank had to attend such a conference in New Orleans. Our kids didn't have many opportunities to visit New Orleans, so we took advantage of the CLE conference to show the children New Orleans. A friend gave us a room for half-price in the hotel he was managing. It was a precious Boutique hotel with a loft, a bedroom, a sitting area, and a kitchenette. It suited us perfectly. We called some friends we had not seen in years. He was a lawyer; she was a full-time mom.

"I can't believe how alike our lives have been. Y'all are so into the Church, you have six children, we have seven. This is great!" I said. I was feeling a real kinship with our old friends.

"I think this is not just a coincidence," my friend chimed in.

We talked and talked, when it was time for them to leave, I knew God was doing something special in this reunion.

"It's easy for Jesus' friends to get along together. He is in the middle of our conversation," Frank said.

Dale said as he walked out of the room, "Why don't you all come to our house on your way out tomorrow? We can visit some more then."

"Sounds great to me, what do you think, Babe?" Frank asked.

"I'd love to, I'm dying to see the dream house Dale built for Ellen, it must be something, if they gave up the totally neat house uptown," I replied.

The next morning we enjoyed a fabulous breakfast. Dale was the cook, and Ellen and I kept busy serving and cleaning up. As we talked and worked together, she referred several times to a support group that changed her and staved off the depression that threatened her from time to time, especially after childbirth. I asked her about this group, but we got interrupted.

When I got home to Third Street in Abbeville that afternoon, I realized that I had left my purse at Ellen's house. I'd have to call her and ask her to send it. Later that evening, Frank, the kids, and I, were all piled in our king-size bed. We had brought the simple handmade bedframe that Gallo made for us in Mexico to Louisiana, because it was so comfortable. All of my dearest ones were with me. The phone rang. It was Ellen; she was calling about my purse.

"Hi, Genie. We enjoyed your visit today. But you forgot your purse."

"I just realized that a couple of hours ago. I was going to phone you in a little while. Would you mind sending it to me?"

"Not at all, I will box it up and send it tomorrow. Should I send it to the same address you gave me earlier?"

"Yes, that's fine. Thanks a million."

"Genie, you asked about the support group I was mentioning. I prayed about it and I think I should tell you; it is a support group for birth mothers, for women who surrendered their children for adoption. I gave up a son before Dale and I were married, and don't know anything about him. It always hit me really hard after I gave birth again."

I rolled over to my side on the bed, hoping to hide the inevitable impact that these words had on me. It was like the cork on a champagne bottle was shot out of the top and emotions were exploding, bubbling forth. I could not speak for a moment.

"Genie, are you there? Is that a shock to you?"

I managed to speak, trying to hold a calm exterior. My family surrounded me. They were not eavesdropping but they could hear every word, "No, Ellen. I knew that. I knew it when we were law school wives together."

"You knew then? Did Dale tell y'all then?" she asked, sounding worried that Dale had revealed her secret years before.

"No, I knew because it happened to me."

Now she was silent. A moment or two passed.

"Are you alone?" she asked, concerned.

"Actually my whole family is on my bed with me. We are visiting."

"Oh, my. We'll have to talk more later, but are you saying *you* had a child out of wedlock and surrendered it for adoption?"

To say "yes", to bring the hidden secret to light with someone out of my inner circle of secret keepers was an enormous event. I knew it would change me, but in that moment, I felt the nearness of the Lord, and I said a weak, "Yes."

There was another moment of silence on her end. She was trying to absorb this news. Then she asked, "Boy or Girl?"

Another gush of emotion erupted in me. I said the word, "boy!" Rusty, crusty chains fell off the door to that chamber of my heart. I had told *someone else*. Incredibly to me, I was not the only one trying to live for the Lord that had such a tortuous secret in their heart. As I treaded water in a sea of emotion, I knew some things in my life would never be the same.

"Okay, girl, we'll talk again tomorrow, when you don't have an audience. Are you okay?"

"Sure am," I said, trying to regain the normal lilt in my voice, "Thanks for the trouble it will take to mail my purse, I'll call you tomorrow."

We said our goodbyes and I hung up.

Sarah looked at me and said, "What was that call about, are you okay, Mom?"

"It was about my purse, and she was sharing with me about her support group," I said, trying to appear unruffled.

At our family gathering on our bed, we talked and laughed at our little boys' antics for a while more. After the kids were in bed, I shared the conversation with Frank. He asked, "How *did* you know back then, if you never talked about it?"

"Well, for one thing, when we got pregnant, we both knew too much about pregnancy for *first* timers. I wasn't positive, but she had also 'gone away' for a while," I said, "Her excuse for that was almost as lame as mine. I was pretty sure then, but I never asked her."

"Babe, I think this is a good thing for you. The Lord has given you someone to share this with," Frank said gently. He was concerned for me.

I could hardly wait for a decent hour to call Ellen the next morning. Our surrendered sons were almost the same age. Having participated in her support group had given her a knowledgeable perspective. She said, "Dale is not ready for me to search for my son yet. My children do not know about him either."

"I'm sure that is sooo difficult," I said, "My children will be really surprised."

"My friends tell me that this also affects siblings," she offered, "There are even support groups for siblings of children surrendered for adoption."

"There is so much to weigh in this process," I sighed.

She told me success stories and sad stories about women in her group who had searched for their children. She opened a whole world to me.

"Genie, you can call the institution that handled the adoption," she informed me, "You have a right to 'non-indentifying personal information' about your son."

It was hard to go about my daily tasks without thinking of this new development in my life. But I managed. I had written the first volume of my book, I had struggled so much with the first few chapters. It was so hard to tell the story leaving out the birth of my son; I called him, "Jude Gerard." I found a few minutes of privacy, and telephoned Catholic Charities in Kansas City. St. Anthony's Infant Home had closed down. They did have records though, and I did not seem to be the first birth mother to solicit this non-identifying personal information. My social worker years before told me he would be adopted by a doctor who had two other adopted children. That had been a consolation to me, because I could picture a happy, prosperous home with a nice family of five. Perhaps that family had fallen through, or maybe that was a story they told to a lot of girls so they would not exercise their right to reclaim the child in the first year. I didn't know why those details weren't true, it was not important now.

The person on the other end of the line at Catholic Charities related this information. "He left the infant home after two months and was adopted into a family. His adoptive father is a computer specialist and his adoptive mother is a math professor. The grandparents were involved with the family. We heard from them from time to time at first," she continued, "They were so happy with their son, they adopted a little girl two years later. I have a picture here of him at about four years old, would you like to have it?"

"I would be so happy to have it," I answered struggling to breathe.

"By the way, it shows here that when he turned eighteen, he called for information about you. All we could give him was non-identifying information about you. That's the law here."

"He wanted to know about me at eighteen? He knew he was adopted and he knew I existed," I said, still barely breathing. I was so moved, so emotional. I hung up and cried myself to sleep.

These events happened in the couple of weeks before we moved from Third Street in Abbeville to our new home on Lippi Street in Lafayette. With the move and settling in at our new home, I had to put searching for my son on a back burner temporarily.

"Dear Lord," I prayed, "Please be with him, please, please don't let me make any wrong moves in this effort to find him. Please don't let my search be mainly selfish. If it is better for him that his life go on uninterrupted, without meeting me, then help me to keep things at the status quo. But if I can be a blessing to him, let me know when the time comes. And prepare him to respond to this in Your grace. Protect the hearts of my children if they must learn my secret. Give me the courage to break the news when it is necessary. Amen."

After we got settled, I started searching for my son on my own. It was not long before I realized that searching on my own was destined to be a fruitless endeavor. I called Ellen. She found out from some friends the name of an adoption "researcher". It was expensive, and by and large illegal. Computers had made this kind of information more accessible.

Laws were changing almost daily as a surge of birth-moms and adoptees wanted to fill in the blanks about such an important topic.

Frank agreed to let me contact a researcher. We never had much savings after we lived as missionaries, but we happened to have enough for the search. The searching process took about three weeks, she had told me to allow six weeks. It was a roller coaster ride, as she eliminated one lead after another. The full weight of this decision to search crowded my thoughts and prayers. If we get any closer, it will be time to tell the children. It would have to be Beau first, then the girls, then the little boys. I would have to tell my brothers and their wives and my sister and her husband. And I would have to tell my grandmother. It would not be easy. I thought of my ladies group, maybe they would think less of me, but for sure they would support me. They were close to Jesus, but none of them had escaped the cross. As soon as I told the kids, I would tell them, especially I wanted to tell Charlotte who was my 'sister' in suffering.

I drove to Baton Rouge, Beau and Michelle thought it was very strange that I wanted to talk to Beau alone. Normally they were in on everything together. Beau, of course, was surprised. But after his initial shock, he was focused on finding him. The oldest child is usually the one most affected. It affects their birth order most. Still, Beau was the first child of our family; he was Frank's and my firstborn in the truest meaning of the word. He was the apple of everyone's eye. I passed on the report that ordinarily the intensity of reunion is so powerful at first, and later, life returns to normal with one more person to love. The news did affect him deeply though. Later that evening when Michelle came back, I told her. Beau tried searching, also fruitlessly; using the non-identifying information I had been given.

Next, I gathered the girls in my bedroom. Sarah was a senior in High School, blossoming into a beautiful young lady in love with the Lord, and living a truly chaste life. Susanna was a sophomore, full of zeal for the Lord and also maturing into loveliness. Mary Magdalen was in her last year of junior high, precious and close to Jesus. I am sure they had no clue that their mother had such a secret. We started with a prayer. I announced the news to them, "Before Daddy and I were married, I had a son, and I surrendered him to be adopted by another family. Now, I am searching to find him, and we are getting close."

They all burst into tears, and I with them. Their reactions were very different. Sarah was concerned for me, and how awful it must have been to have a baby, be separated from him, and to know nothing at all about his life. Susanna was clearly affected by the thought that she had been deceived all along. Wasn't our family a trusting family? She thought we were one of the few non-blended families, where all the children had the same mother and father. She also thought it would be unfair to contact him and cause any disruption to his adoptive family. Sweet Mary Magdalen was desperate to find him. She wanted to know him. She was totally upset that she had a brother she didn't know.

"Why didn't you tell us?" Sarah asked.

"Dad didn't feel comfortable with me telling you," I explained, "But he is now, and that is very important to me."

We hugged and closed with a prayer. When they went to their rooms, I could hear soft crying. I thought to myself, "How much more pain can my secret cause?"

And I thought of Susanna's concern, "How can I know if this hoped for reunion will be good for him? Only Jesus knows for sure. I'll ask Him again in prayer."

Quietly, I entered into His presence; my heart throbbed with the emotional pain of having revealed this secret to my children, "Jesus, should I just drop this whole thing? Will this be destructive for my son? What should I do?"

The answer also came quietly, "Genie, his well being has to be one of your major concerns. Are you ready to meet him, no matter who he is now? He is an adult, not a child now. What if he wants no part of you, are you prepared? What if he is a homosexual? What if he has AIDS? I know you have loved him, longed for him all these years, but your son is a real person, raised by his adoptive family. Do you love him no matter what? I love him Genie, he is mine. If you find him, remember he is mine first, and no matter what the process, I will be with you."

I was alarmed and consoled by the Lord's response. I shared my sense of what the Lord had said with Frank. He said, "Genie, when you find him, I think you will find an ordinary guy with a family. He will be your son, and you will love him."

I was also consoled by Frank's take on the search. I talked to my researcher. She reported, "We're getting close, I think we'll know something in a week. He was married and living in Michigan last year, I'm pretty sure about that."

The picture of him at age four came in from Catholic Charities. He was gorgeous. He was dressed just the way I dressed Beau in the sixties. I met with Mom and Dad at a restaurant. I told them I was searching.

"I have always been in favor of keeping this adoption as secret as possible, for your sake. But now that you are searching, I am filled with sheer happiness," Mom said.

"You are not the only one who has longed to see him," Daddy said, "Our hearts ache for our 'missing' grandchild."

When I lovingly showed them his picture at four years old, we all let tears stream down our faces. We prayed for a speedy result of the search. "Please get us a copy of that photo," they begged.

In a few days, the researcher called me, "Genie, I have his name, address and telephone number. I am pretty certain that he is married. His name is Paul Nicholas Jordan; he lives in San Rafael, California on Brett Hart Road. Here is his phone number."

My hands shook as I took down this information. In my heart, I was saying, "Thank you, Jesus. Thank you, Lord."

I held the notepad to my chest. I wept. I prayed for Paul Nicholas Jordan. I named him Jude Gerard, but I knew his parents had changed the name. I knew I would never be his "mother". I did not deserve that place, but I hoped against hope that I could come to know him and that he would accept my love.

I decided not to call, I was sure I wouldn't be able to make it through the conversation without tears. So I wrote a letter and sent it by FedEx. It was November 12, 1991. It was the eve of my forty-eighth birthday. Jesus had given me Paul's name and address for my birthday.

November 12, 1991

Dear Paul Nicholas,

Even as I write, tears are streaming down my face. My beautiful son, no matter who you are, you are beautiful to me because in God's eyes in some way you are still mine. Thirty years ago there was no such phrase as "Solo Mom". Today, lots of young women are opting to keep their babies, with the help and support of family, friends and even pro-life supporters. When you were born, I was absolutely convinced that to relinquish you for adoption was the best for you. Truly, the shame of being an unwed mother played a part in it. I was a freshman in college, and had no personal financial resources. Your birthfather was a neat person, a college athlete, but too immature to acknowledge his fatherhood. I do not resent him, we were so young. But our relationship ended soon after I discovered I was pregnant.

I was six months pregnant before I told my parents. I just loved you in my womb in secrecy, and agonized about my situation. The hardest decision I ever made and the one that has cost me the most was to surrender you for adoption. The decision was not made lightly. In the end, the most convincing argument for me was that it was best for you!

I have hoped and prayed all these years that indeed it was best for you. I have prayed that you grew up in a happy family. I have prayed for your parents to remain together in this world where families are torn apart. I have prayed that you be protected from harm. I have prayed that you not die in any wars. But most of all I have prayed that you come to know Jesus Christ. Knowing Him will give you all the things I can never give you.

The memory of holding you in my arms at the hospital and giving you a bottle are still fresh in my mind. They only let me see you once, but I have not forgotten. I rocked you, I kissed you, I whispered, "I love you" in your ear. Your grandmother was there; she held and kissed you, too. She still prays for you.

As the years passed, I imagined you as a little boy, as a teenager and as a young man. I thanked God for the woman who loved you and fed you and wiped your tears, for the father that

328

supported you and cared for you. I never dreamed there would be a possibility of contact until recently when I shared with another birth mother who informed me that others were doing it.

I called Catholic Charities; they told me that when you were eighteen you had written for information about me. My heart was pierced as I thought of you reaching out and my not knowing it. I feel as though the Lord Jesus has led me in this process of contacting you. I hope and pray that we will find one another and that it will be fruitful and good in your life and mine.

Your birth and adoption had been an unbelievably well kept secret between your grandparents, my wonderful supportive husband, and me. I have suffered this incredible pain of separation all these years. When I found that searching and finding you was a possibility, I began the process of telling your SEVEN half-brothers and sisters, and your three uncles and one maternal aunt. They all had the same wonderful response.

They were shocked and surprised. The greatest response was, "Let's find him quickly!" We have prayed and hoped in unified longing that we will have a reunion. There is so much more to say. I want to get this off in overnight mail, so please bear with me. Just a moment ago, my researcher told me that you are married. Our love and hope and prayers, extend to all of your loved ones. I even hope that your parents could find it in their hearts to accept our love and friendship.

I'm enclosing a photo of your family at the wedding of your half-brother, Beau. This was taken three years ago, all the children have grown up a lot since then but it will give you an idea. That's me in the red dress. Frank, my husband, has loved you with me all these years.

The children's names are Sarah Anthea, Susanna Maria, Mary Magdalen, Simon-Peter, Joseph Anthony, and John Paul.

Please call me collect, any time day or night.
My number is 318-235-3718.
I love you,
Your birth mom,
Genie Summers

After sending the letter, the waiting seemed like an eternity. I had traced the FedEx delivery. I knew it was delivered to Brett Hart Road. It was only a few days before he responded, but a hundred questions popped into my head, "Is he not at home? Is he not interested in meeting me? Have I caused a problem with his parents?" My imagination went wild, but I kept praying.

We had just finished Morning Prayer, it was November 15th, and the phone rang. The voice on the other end of the phone said, "May I speak with Genie Summers?"

I knew in my heart it was Paul. I said, holding back tears, "This is she."

"Genie, this is Paul Jordan, I got your letter…."

The rest of the world absolutely ceased to exist for me in those first few minutes of our conversation. His California accent and deep voice immediately confirmed what the Lord had told me to expect. I was not reuniting with a child I had lost. I was reuniting with an adult, whose world I had hurled myself into. I loved him. I loved the adult. The best part was that he was open to loving me.

He told me he was married to a wonderful wife, had two stepchildren, and lived in a separate apartment in his father's house, the house he grew up in. His adoptive mother died of cancer when he was twenty-one. The mother he described to me sounded wonderful. She was Italian, probably a good match for a Cajun blooded boy. His Irish dad was a great provider and a faithful husband. He had an adopted sister, and two younger brothers that came along later as the biological children of his parents. I was consoled that he grew up in such a family atmosphere. He was thirty now, and writing a book.

When he got the non-identifying information twelve years ago, he realized he was from Louisiana. He and his wife, Patricia had taken a trip to New Orleans and Cajun country last spring. He found a real connect with the state of his birth mother. I could not believe he had been so close. Actually, he was near when I first spoke to Ellen. Was that a God-incidence?

I let him lead in the decision about where we would meet. I was so happy he wanted to meet, any arrangements would do. We decided that I would fly to San Francisco and spend the Thanksgiving Holiday with him. Frank was perfect in his support. He had seen my silent suffering over the years and rejoiced with me that we would meet. Frank and the kids spent Thanksgiving with his mother and father, and all the family pitched in to allow me this special time.

DNA is amazing. Like me, Paul was a writer. He and his wife catered. I considered myself a great cook, and loved doing it. He had been brought up Catholic, but wasn't active. He believed in God, and had recently begun to hope for miracles.

When he asked me what I wanted to eat when I got to his home, I said, "Paul, I eat anything. I am an adventurous eater. The only thing I really don't care for is oatmeal. Something about the texture."

He countered, "You don't like oatmeal? I never liked oatmeal and my mom could not understand that. She always said, 'Everyone likes oatmeal!' She didn't take no for an answer, so I ate plenty of oatmeal as a child. Gosh, this reunion explains so many things."

It would take another book to tell the whole story, but our fist meeting thrilled us. He and his family visited Louisiana in January, welcomed by seven brothers and sisters, grandparents, a great-grandparent, uncles, aunts, first cousins, and all of our Christian friends. He absolutely charmed "Our Lady's Group".

It has been twenty years since 1991 and our first meeting. The reunion journey, past the initial year or so, has not always been smooth. At times, we clicked and the love between us was palpable. There were many seasons of silence. He suffered in his life. I'm afraid he inherited the tendency to addictive behavior from my side of the family. He had a hard time with me being "so religious". He told me once, "I have a problem with the three letter word you use too much – G-O-D!"

I have begged the Lord, "I am yours, Jesus. Help me to be me without offending Paul. Use me to attract him to You, and not put him off. Please keep my own sinfulness and failure from interfering with our relationship."

It is G-O-D who helped me to endure the pain of our inability to communicate more effectively. It is the Lord, whether Paul knew it or not, that could give him the best life possible, here and in the afterlife. I was with him in the hospital, in San Rafael, California, when I realized he was taking meds for

AIDS. I loved him more, not less. He was basically a wonderful person. I know that the prayers that I (and his brothers and sisters) have prayed for him all these years have not gone unheard.

In 2007, Paul was already divorced from his wife. He was living in dire straits in California, when his life suddenly got a lot harder. Our relationship had been renewed by my yearly visits to California. He had an apartment fire and then a stroke at the age of forty-five. By God's providence, Paul came to live in our home with us for seven months. It was not an easy adjustment, but the best part of the praise report is that he got to know, really know, our work. He got to celebrate Christmas and Easter with his brothers and sisters, nieces and nephews. He was integrated into our family. He had an intimate personal relationship with each one of his brothers and sisters. He admired and loved them and felt their love.

I worried that he might be moved farther away from God by being so immersed in our home, which Paul called "the most religious environment ever". After the seven months, I helped him move into an apartment in Abbeville, right in the center of town. His AIDS flared up. He had stopped taking his meds, I don't exactly know why. All I knew for sure was that I loved him, and I asked for God's grace. I really wanted to be what Jesus expected me to be for my son.

When folks saw Paul in town, some small town busybodies tried to put the pieces together. My sister told me one day, "I almost hate to go to the health club, there is a nosy lady there that has seen Paul at Robie's (a local grocery store), and she always bugs me about who she thinks Paul's birthfather is."

Because our mission is high profile in Abbeville and this area, my son with AIDS provided some speculation for curious minds.

"Rachel," I answered, "Don't let that lady bully you. Tell her to call me, I'll end up praying with her and she might just be satisfied with my answers." The lady never called.

I trusted in Jesus to bring Paul to Himself. The scriptures tell us that the "Gospel is an indestructible seed". While he lived with us, he heard plenty of the Gospel. I consider the miracle of finding him and the time we spent together as a blessing and a sign of God's love.

I had relatively few years to spend with my beautiful son. Recently, God has taken Paul to be with Him. His final days were so special in many ways. Because Paul's AIDS reached advanced stages in December of 2009, he spent a lot of time in the hospital. I was so busy at home with our missionary works. I was preparing for Sarah's wedding to Kevin Granger, another missionary, and preparing for Christmas. I could only visit with Paul at night, at about eight or nine o'clock. But these visits became precious opportunities to talk and share, and for me to pray. In his need for health, he truly didn't mind my always praying over him when I had to leave. On one occasion, Paul told me, "Mama, you and I have real love in our relationship. I feel that you love me for who I am. And I love you for who you are. I don't think there have been any other Mother/Son relationships finer than ours."

"I do love you so much, Paul," I said, "I am so grateful for these times together. I am still praying that you totally recover, I cherish these visits."

God provided the final, wonderful miracle in a very unusual way. A nurse on Paul's ward said she had put Paul at the end of her list of visits one night. She was a Christian, and felt slightly ashamed of having had the attitude that "Paul chose his illness". She reluctantly went into his room at the end of her rounds that shift. As she walked up to his bed, he turned and flashed her a beautiful and sincere smile.

Kim told me, "I was so struck by the power of God in that room, I was so drawn to him and that smile that I said, 'Excuse me.' And she stepped out into the hall. She said she breathlessly leaned against the wall and prayed, 'Lord, what is going on in there, who is that? And what do you want me to do?'"

She heard the Lord answered her clearly, "Kim, that is my beloved son, I mean for you to treat him as you would treat me."

Awed by the Lord's response, Kim took Paul on as her personal love and service project in the name of Jesus. She treated him with love and respect. She came to see him even when she was off duty. Paul was about to be discharged; there was nothing further to offer in intervention for his health. Kim called me, we hadn't met, but Paul had spoken about her. She asked if she could take Paul into her home until he got stronger. After hearing her story, I was very willing to see Paul go to a loving home. She talked about her Christian commitment, and told me how Jesus had led her to see Paul as a special person in her life. It really wasn't my decision, but Paul had asked her to check with me. He loved her kindness, and that kindness enticed him to accept her invitation.

I had helped Paul find a nice living situation in the middle of Abbeville, where he could easily walk to all the major places, where we could easily pick him up for family events, shopping trips, and dinners. His neighbor and agent of the landlord, Debbie and her husband, Louis had become like an older brother and sister for him. While he was in the hospital for one of the last times, we had his washer and dryer fixed, his whole apartment cleaned, bought new sheets and groceries for when he got home from the hospital. It was clean and welcoming. However, Paul went to Kim's and never made it back home to his spruced up quarters in town.

When I talked to Paul while he was at Kim's and her two teenaged kids home, his voice had a lilt in it that I hadn't heard in a while. He was happy there. She had Christian symbols all around, scriptures written on her mirrors, and prayer with her family. She sincerely *cared* for him. I was happy and at peace for Paul in those weeks.

Paul's birthday was coming up in March on the twenty-sixth. I had planned to take him to visit some antique shops and to have a beautiful meal at a fine restaurant in Washington, La. It would have been a wonderful birthday celebration.

I had to go to Ecuador on a medical mission in late February. I would be back in time for Paul's birthday. Right before I left for Ecuador, he had been rushed to the hospital in Lafayette. Frank and I went to visit him on Sunday and I was to fly out the next day. Paul looked happy and almost healthy; there was a glow about him. Frank even asked him, "Paul, you look so good, are you in love with your nurse?"

Paul laughed and flashed that gorgeous smile, "I don't think so, Frank, but right now I am happy to be going home to Kim's house. Her kids are wonderful and the whole family is so good to me."

In hindsight, I attribute his aspect of well being to being in an environment that exuded the Lord, and he was accepting that.

The night before I was scheduled to come back to the USA, I got a call in Ecuador. It was Frank, and Beau was also on the line.

"Genie, Paul died today at Abbeville General Emergency Room. I am so sorry, babe. Let's pray!"

I was devastated until Frank told me that Kim's daughter had been with him. She said, "Paul kept calling out to the Lord saying, 'God, please help me. Jesus help me.'"

I could hardly believe my ears. My lifelong prayers had been answered. I am sure that in the midst of his coughing and struggling for breath, he had found his God. The scripture says, "*All* who call on the name of the Lord will be saved."

The memorial service we had for Paul at our house was first class and really anointed by the Holy Spirit. His brothers and brother-in-law sang songs Paul had come to enjoy. He loved to hear his brothers play the guitars. The house was full of people that Paul had touched in his year and a half in Abbeville. Lots of people told wonderful Paul stories. I was consoled by the thought of how much he would have enjoyed his impressive sendoff. I know he watched everything from his heavenly vantage point. I still miss him. I look forward to our next reunion, in heaven.

Chapter Twenty

Begins and Ends on a Pacific Island

The Pacific Ocean is indescribably vast. As we approached what first appeared to be a tiny green dot in an endless expanse of water, we simultaneously praised Jesus, each in our own hearts and some of us in an audible voice. As the jet engines roared a little louder and we dropped down under the wispy clouds, a kaleidoscope change happened to the view of the island. The sea that looked almost navy blue from miles high became a thrilling artist's seascape with a dozen shades of blue radiating out from sandy beaches to the deep. The total body reflex of relief as the wheels touch down, and the plane's stop just short of the ocean, never ceases to impress and bless me. It was January of 1995, when we landed in Chuuk of the Federated States of Micronesia. The simple, almost primitive airport immediately drove home the reality of our reason for arriving in Chuuk. We were missionaries again – missionaries on the "continent" of Oceania. We had begun our lives as missionaries in Oceania, the Tonga Islands. Now almost twenty years later we were back in the islands. It had been four long years since we had actually lived full-time in mission in Mexico. My heart was flooded with familiar feelings of being home. Mission was home. We had been traveling for weeks and not without incident. It would be great to be settled in our new post. It was only a speck on the map, just above the equator in the North Pacific.

It had been extra hard to leave Louisiana behind this time. Neither Beau, nor Sarah, was coming on this mission with us. Sarah was married, expecting our first grandchild and in her second year of college. Beau was also married and in law

337

school. There had been many factors to consider in our discernment process this time. We had prayed about it for over a year. I felt Jesus calling us back to serve him full-time again. We desperately wanted our younger sons to be totally immersed in and live the mission life, the total surrender required. Susanna especially, and Mary, too, in their heart of hearts, knew God was calling our family to this time of service.

We were honored to find that Jesus and our friends arranged a going away Mass and reception at St. Thomas More High School. It was a glorious evening. Even though we were only seven heading out this time, a family of seven leaving for mission impacts a faith community. Our friends and supporters promised to pray for us and to write to us. Some made donations for our travel and settling in expenses. Our family once again was going forth with the Good News. Those at home could see for themselves that our sacrifice was real. We had again given up the right home, in the right neighborhood, great schools, good jobs, a thriving prayer group and loved ones. And yet the call was clear.

"Don't cry, Mary," Sarah had said through her own tears at our going away Mass and reception, "We'll be coming to see y'all after our baby is born, as soon as it is old enough to travel." Sarah's in-laws, Jess and Jackie, who are also our friends, wanted to come too.

"That sounds like years away instead of months," Mary answered, trying to control her crying, "I can't believe I won't be there when my first niece or nephew is born."

My colleague, a fellow teacher at STM advised, "I hope you won't regret leaving in the middle of Susanna's senior year at STM. You know, because she was the Homecoming Queen, she would probably be on the Cougar Court and maybe even prom queen, too!" She was unashamedly scolding me, seeming to really hope she could convince me to ditch the whole selfish idea of leaving until Susanna had graduated. Susanna was one of her favorites.

Susanna and Mary both had built up wonderful circles of friends at St. Thomas More. Susanna had been selected in a beauty pageant as Junior Miss of Lafayette (no swimsuit competition), and was on her way to the State of Louisiana

338

Junior Miss pageant. When we left, she had to surrender her title to the first runner up.

Mary's leaving halfway through her sophomore year meant she would probably never have the opportunity to do either one of the things Susanna had done. They were both "A" students.

We had received instructions from the Lord in our family retreat prior to our departure. He addressed with us the following issues:

1. Getting back into mission was absolutely His will for us right now.
2. That now rather than later was the time for the mission to begin.
3. That He would be with our loved ones left behind.
4. New ways of being in mission would work for us.
5. Our children would learn lessons in Chuuk that they wouldn't learn anywhere else.

Both of our adult children planned to come and visit us in Chuuk, but it would be a *long* time to be half a globe away from one another.

The heart-tearing separation anxiety and the pressure of details in preparation for leaving the USA faded into the background as we all literally kissed the earth of our new home in Micronesia. We piled ourselves and our luggage into open-air jeeps. As we drove away from the airport onto the only main highway, I leaned over to Frank and rubbed his neck. I whispered in his ear, "I didn't know just how much I have missed mission."

He reached back and squeezed my hand, "Me too, Babe."

It took two jeeps to transfer us and our luggage from the airport to our new home in Chuuk. Weno was the Capital of Chuuk, which was formerly called Truk. The Truk Lagoon was famous for World War II battles that left over a hundred Japanese ships sunk and dozens of Japanese aircraft buried off its exquisite coastline. The presence of the sunken ships and aircraft attracted a myriad of tropical fish; species by the hundreds made those ships their habitat. This abundance of sea life established

Chuuk (Truk Lagoon) as one of the premier scuba diving locations in the world.

The house that Bishop Amando Samo had rented for us was across the island from the airport on the southernmost tip. Our drive took us across the center of the principal city, Weno, and we began to truly understand the kind of place it was. It was decidedly a developing nation. Chuuk had only recently given up its status as a UN territory, USA protectorate, and was now an independent nation in the Federated States of Micronesia. Remnants of the American protectorate identity were dotted throughout the poor, simple construction styles of the city. Cinderblock, wooden slat, woven bamboo and some stucco buildings lined the streets. The center of Chuuk was a far cry from the picture post card island setting. Still, the coconut studded beaches and the glistening water were never very far off from the road.

"Look at all the palm trees, and coconuts are all over the ground," John Paul exclaimed.

"And the fishing boats out there on the water," Joseph said.

"I like the banana shops and mango shops on the side of the road," Simon chimed in.

Our landlord, Clark Graham, had been there to pick us up. He was an American, a former Peace Corp volunteer, who had fallen in love with a Chukese girl, married her, built her a house on the beach, had a family, and established a successful scuba diving business. We would be renting a house from him that he had built in his backyard. It was intended to be two units, upstairs and downstairs, but our family needed the entire house. It was new, sides made of the native material, large screens of split and woven bamboo, an outside staircase, and a tin roof. The square footage of our new home was only eight hundred, not so much room for our big family, but well laid out, and, on a tropical island the outdoors is your living room. At first the plumbing upstairs was not connected, so we wore our bathing suits and bathed with buckets from the big metal cistern outside. We were fascinated with the new fangled eco friendly septic system.

Two amazing, wonderful features of the house made it great. The first was the fact that it was about one hundred yards from the beach, which made the location absolutely perfect. From our second story landing and a few windows, you could see the aquamarine ocean, its golden sandy shore, waving palms and colorful sailing yachts moored at a distance. We often went down to the little store next door and bought fresh fish. Lobsters were sold for one dollar each. After location, the next amazing thing was that Clark's family had children the ages of our children. A large circle of huts with thatched roofs bordered our back yard, a stone's throw away – and those huts were full of the most beautiful brown-skinned, big-eyed kids. Our kids had instant playmates, and our "in" to the culture was assured. That whole area was called Neauwo. Our new home address was Neauwo, Chuuk.

We had barely driven up to the house, and were still carrying in our luggage, when Simon, our special twelve-year old son who couldn't yet read, whipped out the small Gideons New Testament he had been given before we left. He started walking straight to the cluster of huts and the noisy throng of kids playing there. I called out to him, "Simon, where are you going?"

"I'm going to preach the Gospel," he answered, "That's why we came isn't it?"

We laughed.

Simon said, "I'm serious. You said we came to be missionaries. I'm going into that village to preach the Gospel!!"

I looked over at Clark with a questioning glance, my eyes asking, "Is that safe?"

Clark smiled, "Go on Simon, but don't go past the highway."

So, off he went. He wouldn't have been much help loading and unloading the luggage. The stairs to the children's quarters upstairs were steep and Simon doesn't manage stairs that well, always having to maneuver them with a slow, cautious ascent or descent.

About a half hour later, we were getting things settled in the very sparsely furnished house, when Simon came back. "Dad, you have to come to meet my new friend, 'Joyful'. He was so happy that I came to preach to him. He's so nice. He loves Jesus. He can't get off the floor. He has to lie there, so he told me to come back often. He's older than me. But he wants to be my friend."

Clark explained that Joyful was a quadriplegic, who was well loved by the villagers. He thought that it would be wonderful if Simon visited with Joyful, who was often alone during the day while his family worked. And Simon did visit him often; a real bond of love grew between them. They would sing praise songs, while reciting scriptures they knew, all the while holding the Bible. Sometimes, Simon would bring Joyful a plate of our food, and sometimes Joyful's mom would feed Simon lunch. Simon and Joyful's relationship made it easy for the rest of us to come to know the villagers and the local children.

Chuuk had become our latest mission post; we had asked the Lord to bring us to an English-speaking place, so that both Frank and I could have jobs to support our family and to be in mission at the same time. Micronesian Legal Services Corporation (MLSC) is a non-profit corporation established in 1970 to provide low-income persons in Micronesia with free legal assistance in civil matters. So, Frank's practice of law was in and of itself a mission. Their clientele were the underserved and the poor, a group that included almost everyone in the island nation. He received a salary, and had an office in a very simple missionary style building.

Their mission, as attorneys, was defined by their board of directors "to provide legal assistance to eligible persons on a variety of matters, including family land, job terminations, domestic cases, immigration, and helping those whose lives have been devastated as a result of nuclear development, including the world's first hydrogen bomb. MLSC extends its services to those in the dawn of life, the children; those in the twilight of life, the elderly; and those in the shadows of life, the abused, the disabled, and the neglected."

I was a volunteer, with a small stipend, for the diocese. I worked in the bishop's office. My job description was Public Relations and Media Development. Except for being a wife and mother, I have never had a job that I liked better. The Bishop was delightful, and a joy to work for. Within a short time he became a real friend for our family. We often shared meals at our respective homes. We loved and enjoyed all of the clergy and diocesan workers. I published the first *Caroline Catholic*, a new diocesan magazine. I flew to the Island of Pohnpei to conduct interviews for the magazine. That job was a dream come true, and it allowed me to be home with the children when they were home.

We also put the children in school. There were two Catholic high schools in Chuuk and one elementary school. Xavier High School, run by the Jesuits, was far away from where we lived and worked, and located on the other side of the island. The other one was Saramen Chuuk Academy situated in the center of town near the diocesan offices. Bishop Amando Samo had suggested this would be a great place for our girls. Saramen Chuuk means "the light of Chuuk". We placed Mary and Susanna in this school believing that they could be a *light* to the light of Chuuk.

Simon, Joseph and John Paul were enrolled in the school nearest to our house. The Chuuk Seventh Day Adventist School accepted Simon in a regular class and he was thrilled. Joseph was in seventh grade and John Paul in fourth. The SDA School had mainly teachers from the USA. The whole day was done in English, which was not the case in other elementary schools, most of them taught in Chukese as well. They began each day with assembly where they read the Bible and had devotions. We questioned our boys each day and they kept us abreast of everything they were being taught. We were generally very happy with the school. The academics were excellent; moral standards, discipline requirements, and affirmation for virtuous behavior were part of the fabric of their educational policy. The boys walked to and from school each day, which was a short jaunt through the circle of huts behind the house and just down the street on the main highway.

There were two beaches within five minutes of our house. The Continental Hotel, our neighbor, was a resort hotel which had a lovely, well-kept beach whose nearby coral reef made it perfect for snorkeling. We were granted permission to use the beach as if it were our own; we could see it from our porch landing.

A few days after we settled in, Susanna came back from a run; she was breathless. "Mom," she gushed, "I discovered the beach on the other side of the hotel which would be a perfect place for my taking the kids, you have to come check it out."

I did check it out that very afternoon and came home gushing to Frank, "That beach is every mother's dream beach for a family of small children. The water's so beautiful, clear, warm and very shallow – for a long way out. I know I will feel completely safe letting the kids swim there together without me."

"Don't you like the snorkeling beach? It's much closer," he asked.

"I do like it. Actually I love it. It's great for the time when we all go out as a family. But it is deep, too deep for me to relax while they go alone."

"What do you like especially about the other beach?" Frank queried.

"They can get really wet, float a little, play in the sand, run around and burn energy and not be in danger from deep water, surging waves or, God forbid, sharks. Anyway, I am so happy that they will be able to swim everyday and I won't have to worry. I dreamed of living near a beach that our kids could enjoy, someplace that was unspoiled and not full of bikini-clad tourists. I didn't dare pray for it, but I know the Lord knew my heart and He has provided this for us. It is just so perfect," I sighed happily.

Island life was incredibly simple – one supermarket with limited choices, small fresh produce markets, no television reception, even though someone had given us a set and a VCR player that allowed occasional movie watching. When residents left the island to move on, they held rummage sales. All the little items we needed, we soon acquired. Our house was filled with all of the necessities and no luxuries. The Chukese people were Micronesian with Polynesians as a minority. They were kind, humble, religious, and friendly, and their culture was unique and fascinating.

"I am so impressed at how welcomed I have felt," I said to Susanna one afternoon.

"I feel completely at home here. I'm not as lonesome as I thought I would be. As long as we keep our time filled with mission work, I'm not unhappy," Susanna commented as she moved furniture to make space in our small house for a children's ministry that she and Mary had begun at our home, inviting the village kids. "The kids are going to be here soon for our children's ministry," Susanna said, getting out her guitar.

Joseph, Simon and John Paul walked to the center of the circle of huts to tell the kids that the prayer meeting was happening now.

"Who are you expecting to come this time?" I asked.

Mary started counting on her fingers, "Well, Kimmy, Ketani and Kurtis (the Graham kids) are coming. Kunio said he would be here, Parfin, Sarfin, Jefferson, and Miss Piggy said they would be here, so counting Joseph, John Paul and Simon that will make it eleven. Sarfin said his cousins might come, and a new kid, we don't know his name, is coming."

"That sounds like a great group, I'm going to run to the little store to buy some cookies for refreshments later. Let's pray first," I suggested, "Lord Jesus, thank you for putting us in the middle of your people who need to hear more about you. Thank you for the meeting with the kids. You promised to be with us where two or more are gathered. Be with us this afternoon. Send Your Holy Spirit, inspire us to reach out and fill these kids up to return to their families and spread the joy and light they receive. You are the Alpha and Omega. Anoint Susanna and Mary's music and sharing. Amen."

Within moments of closing our prayer, the children came running up. They were washed up and combed, mostly barefoot, but happy and excited to be with Susanna and Mary. I scurried off to the store. I could hear them singing as I walked away. My girls would play some games and sing songs of praise with them before prayer and teaching from the scriptures. Then they would lead them in sharing about the teaching they heard. I visited with the clerk at the shoreside store, and headed up the trail to our house. As I approached our house, I could hear them singing, "*Eie era ran, kita fur ati...*." They were singing, "This is the Day" in Chukese. God promised his disciples that they didn't have to worry about what they would say. The Holy Spirit would give them what to say. On the first Pentecost, they spoke in languages they did not know. We noticed in our mission travels, the Lord helped us to minister in and learn languages we did not know. The neighborhood kids were already teaching our kids how to speak and sing in Chukese.

So many major events happened while we were in Micronesia. Susanna graduated from Saramen Chuuk Academy. One beautiful Chukese tradition is to cover the graduate with *mwaramwars*, which are floral leis. Susanna's head just poked out over the abundance of beautiful, fragrant flower *mwaramwars* that accented her graduation gown. We could not have been more proud of Susanna. She was ineligible for honor graduate recognition because she had entered at mid-year. Nonetheless, she had inculturated into the land of her mission post and given herself to the Lord in this experience. During her time there, she had also choreographed Saramen Chuuk's musical, GodSpell. She and Mary travelled to Saramen Chuuk Academy each day in a taxi, which was the back of a small pickup truck, and ate chicken and rice for lunch every day. Mary dove into the school experience, made friends, studied hard and helped at home. Her light shone at Saramen Chuuk. We felt the impact that our family had on the academic family at SCA when the theme of the graduation was, "Go! You Are Sent". (That's when I first realized the Lord had given me the real name for my book.) I was close to tears when they passed out the leaflets with "Go! You Are Sent" in large, bold print on the front. I burst into tears when at the offertory the younger students were asked to carry symbols of the graduating class of 1995 and Mary Magdalen came walking down the center aisle carrying the globe.

Susanna also ran the 880 race, and became the State Champion in the competition. Most of the Chukese people thought she didn't have a chance because she was using running shoes instead of running barefooted.

Back in Louisiana, Beau and Michelle were having fatal difficulties in their marriage, so Beau came to Chuuk to join us and to recover from the jolt of their separation. He found the island life to be soothing, and was able to be distracted by snorkeling, fellowshipping with the islanders and living with the family. Shortly after he arrived, he spent a whole day snorkeling, not being mindful that his white skin was unprepared for the intense tropical sun.

"Oh, wow, Beau," I said, later that evening, "I've never seen such a blistered back. You will have to sleep on your stomach. Here, take some Ibuprofen."

346

"I think I am running fever and the pain is almost unbearable," Beau said, as he tried to fall asleep for the night.

Early the next morning, I went up the mountain to the clinic run by the American soldiers. They said they would come to see Beau later that day. We wanted to avoid the hospital, which we had already attempted to use before on two occasions. John Paul had been sick several days with high fever that could not be brought down with fever reducers. The hospital had been designed and built by Americans, but after the personnel of the protectorate left, funding decreased. The conditions had become inadequate and unsanitary. However, the Chukese doctors had prescribed antibiotics and John Paul recovered. On a separate occasion, Simon suffered a broken arm. After the arm was splinted at the hospital, we came home and prayed and had another healing miracle. Simon's arm was healed instantly.

The US military medics came that evening to check on Beau, when they pulled back the sheet covering Beau's back, they gasped audibly. "I have never seen a blister that big in all of my life, it is the size of a grapefruit," the first medic said. "It's too big to lance, it would leave too much exposed skin if we opened it. We will attempt to cover it with Silverdene creme, give him antibiotics, anti-inflammatory capsules, and pain killers. It will just have to heal naturally."

"We'll need to come back in a couple of days to check on him," the other medic said. "Beau, you shouldn't go out in the sun. Keep as cool as possible. You really don't want to get this back infected."

We had already prayed for Beau's quick healing. We resolved to keep up our daily prayer for his healing. Although we had jobs in Chuuk, we remained faithful to our daily personal prayer and daily family prayer, read the scriptures, frequented the sacraments, and gave teaching series to couples and family days of recollection.

Beau walked around only at night with a cane. He walked bent over because his skin blisters kept him from straightening up. Clark's wife saw him and asked to take a look at his back. When he uncovered the back for her to get a look at it, she became dizzy and almost fainted. His pain and injury gave him time for reflection and assessment of his lost marriage. I knew those blisters were symbolic of the severe burned state of

Beau's heart and soul. Instant healing would have been great, but slow, steady healing was better.

In this island mission, God answered so many of my secret desires, but most of all, my longing for my sons to recapture their identities as missionaries. Joseph and John Paul talked unashamedly about their faith, shared scripture with the kids from the kids' prayer meeting, and became altar boys at the Cathedral. They, with us, fellowshipped with the Bishop who invited us all to many occasions where he asked us to give our testimony. He helped us to quickly befriend the active Catholics in his diocese.

Clergy, too, popped in on our house, to share a meal and enjoy animated discussions with our family about evangelization and ministry. One elderly Jesuit, who taught Math at Xavier and visited frequently, was the favorite of the children. He rode a white scooter and always wore his white helmet. He was tall and thin, and so our children endearingly called him "Fr. Lollipop". He chuckled at their nickname.

As we lived simply, our children embraced that simple life. We enjoyed family time and outings. One of John Paul's friend and classmates' parents owned a private island. John Paul had spent the night with him on a few occasions. Their house was built out over the water and they could fish from their back porch. One day he came home saying, "Mom, C.J. wants us to go with him to spend the day on his island. It would be really great. His dad owns a yacht. That's how we get to the island. Can we go this Saturday?"

"I'll have to talk to Dad, but I don't think we have anything planned this Saturday. Sunday we have that retreat, but Saturday is free. Can you tell him tomorrow?" I asked.

"Sure, he said they are going anyway so we can tell him in a few days."

I absolutely loved being on the water and I knew that their private island must be beautiful. I hoped and prayed we could go. Mary overheard the conversation, and was excited about the prospect too. She prayed, "Lord, Jesus, I pray that you allow us to accept this invitation. It would be such a nice opportunity for us."

"Yes, Lord, please let us be able to go and help me not to get seasick," Mary prayed. She had become my homemaking assistant and I don't know what I would have done without her. She and Susanna had to help out a lot. The Laundromat was a good long walk for them – carrying sheets filled with clothes. They needed a break too. A trip to a private island, swimming on a beautiful coral reef would be therapeutic for all of us.

Frank agreed and Saturday morning early we went to the dock and boarded a nice yacht. CJ's dad occasionally used the boat for deep-sea fishing tourists.

I love salt sea air. I love the incredibly beautiful water. I love being on an outing with my family and jovial company. We had good food packed and picnic blankets to sit on. We anchored a few hundred yards from the shore.

A small launch boat was there to ferry the goods and passengers to shore. The kids asked if they could just swim to shore. They handed me their shirts and swam to the shores of a mini paradise. Coconut trees waving in the wind greeted us. They afforded beautiful shade along the sugar sand beaches. Other indigenous scrub trees, and dwarfish oak trees covered the middle of the small island; the underbrush was almost too dense to walk through. With the exception of a small patch of mangrove trees on one side of the island, we were able to walk the sugar sand beaches that made a complete circle around the island in about an hour.

We had become good enough at snorkeling by then to explore the coral reef. Once we donned goggles and snorkels. We entered a wondrous world unseen from the surface.

"Hurry, Mom. You have got to see how beautiful this is," Joseph said, waving me into the ocean.

"Yes, Mom. Hurry! We'll help you set up the food and stuff after awhile," Susanna and Mary both beckoned me into the water.

"Okay. I'm coming. I'm coming," I made our pile of beach and picnic things tidy, and swam out to where they were. We kept surfacing to ask each other, "Did you see that?!"

Sea anemones, coral, sponges, polyps and amazing sea plants in magentas, pinks, metallic blues, lime green, coral and deep purple dotted with yellow were beautiful beyond imagining. God's aquarium was incomparable, and the gentle movement of the water heightened the experience. The variety of fish that swam in exquisitely colorful schools made snorkeling

349

there a once-in-a-lifetime adventure. Again, I felt a gratitude penetrating deep in my heart, as I thought, "Who gets to do this? Lord Jesus, thank you for your constant surprises."

"You are here at the ends of the earth to preach the Gospel" I heard Him say, "But I brought you here for a twofold purpose. Yes, to preach, but I also want to show *my* daughter my handiwork in creation."

Back home in Neauwo, we unpacked our beach things. As we hung out our bathing suits and slathered on the aloe Vera, we all sported happy smiles. It was a blessed day. We were refreshed and ready to continue our mission.

There was a point where life was working so well that we thought we might make Chuuk our permanent home. Frank and I took drives looking at property for sale. Beau had come and gone and I had been back to the states to be with Sarah while she gave birth to our first grandchild, Alyse. So, we could visit and be visited.

Two purchases we made in Chuuk are worth mentioning. I remember tentatively broaching the subject of getting a canoe, "Frank, do you think we could get an outrigger canoe for the boys? I see them out in the lagoon all the time. They look almost impossible to turn over, and the boys could paddle out a ways and fish. They could dive out there too, away from the coral?"

"Well, we can try to find one in our budget. I have no idea how much it would cost us," he answered.

"I'll ask at the Bishop's office to spread the word and you can ask at the law office. That's a good place to start," I mused out loud.

Sure enough, we were able to purchase a bright blue, dugout, outrigger canoe. It was the real deal and truly authentic, and it did expand the boys' world quite a bit. They were excellent swimmers and very responsible. It was a part of mission life they will never forget. All the kids became bronzed by the sun and their hair lightened up. We were all fairly fit with the swimming and the walking.

Taxi trucks weren't always available, so our second purchase was a used Subaru coupe. It was a four/five seater but we piled in, all eight of us, if we had to be at church or an evening event. It was a small miracle that all eight of us could squeeeeeze in. Frank, Beau (when he was there), John Paul and Joseph were in the front seat. John Paul sat on a small pillow on the emergency brake space, Joseph on Beau's lap. Susanna, Mary, Simon, and I squeeeezed into the back seat. We had to carry belongings, packs, and other things in the trunk. We really discourage (almost forbid) our missionaries to complain, but Simon just couldn't refrain from saying over and over again, "I'm sooooo crunchy!"

The Bishop had added on to the diocesan offices, and one of the new offices he built was meant to house my department – PR and media development. The Bishop celebrated a special blessing and a meal in my office. I remember thinking, "How can it get any better? I really love this job, the construction is fine. It will look prettier once I add my own touches."

That night, when we got home from the office blessing, we got a call from Sarah. She had been calling us weekly with an update on Beau and Michelle's situation. The moment I heard her voice, I knew something was wrong, "Mom, things have gotten much worse. Michelle has moved out and Beau is devastated. I think you will regret it if you don't come home to be here for him."

I walked with such a heavy heart to our house from Clark and his family's home, which was our only access to the phone. I knew that call changed everything.

"Frank, Sarah just called...." I told him about our whole conversation, "What should we do? She is worried. It sounds like she is saying come and come now."

"First, we need to gather everyone together to pray," Frank answered with certainty, "If we hear the Lord saying we should go home, we'll go home. Then we have to talk to the Bishop first. Then, I'll have to call my boss. He's off island right now in Guam. Then we'll have to get tickets for all of us out of here. We can ask CJ's dad to help us with that. I hope we don't have to do exit visas like we did in Tonga."

We gathered all of our family in prayer. It had been hard to leave Louisiana, but now Chuuk was home, and it would be hard to leave this blessed mission post. Never have we gotten guidance from the Lord in a quicker, clearer way. All of the scriptures brought to our prayer session spoke about the Lord bringing his people home, retrieving them from where they were scattered, etc. Also, we all had the same spiritual leading. Jesus was saying that He wanted us to go home.

After graduation, Susanna had taken a job teaching at Xavier High School. She wondered if she should stay, and took it to prayer. She also heard God say, "Go Home."

The next thing I thought about was how to get rid of the furniture, appliances, dishes, pots and pans, microwave, stove top, bedding, curtains, etc. that we had accumulated during our stay. Susanna recalled that a family of missionary teachers had arrived at Xavier High School. "Mom, just today, I got to see their accommodations. They have nothing really, just like when we first got here. Maybe they could use our stuff?" she suggested.

"Well, *that* would be a *miracle*, if all of this could go to one place. Another miracle would be if we could get tickets right away and get packed, although we are going to take only the most essential stuff, and as usual, give the rest away. "

"Susanna, you will need to go to your school and tell them about the crisis at home. But didn't you say the family had a girl your age? Maybe she can take your position."

"That's true, Mom," Susanna smiled, "In fact, today when we talked, she said she would love to have a job like mine. So, God is working on that already."

"Mary, you will have to withdraw from Saramen Chuuk and ask them to mail your records to St. Thomas More in Lafayette. I'll give you the address."

"Okay, Mom," she said, sounding resigned to the change, "What about the boys' school?"

"I'll ask Daddy to stop by and talk to them."

"Let's start packing now. We can get a head start," Mary suggested. She tackles her tasks with determined confidence and firm resolve. That day it was contagious. Susanna, Mary and I grabbed bags and started rolling our clothes.

The Bishop had met Beau and liked him. He also knew that although our decision was made quickly, we were not leaving on a whim. He gave us his blessing, which we received with a tone of sadness. His advice was, "You are right. You should always put family first, before your careers or even your mission work. The Lord is teaching you so much, the hard way. I'll be praying for you. Please pray for our diocese."

The Bishop's counsel and his attitude made us realize that we were on track with our discernment. We were headed back to Louisiana.

Leaving Chuuk was certainly a logistics miracle. The Xavier Jesuit volunteers backed up a fairly large truck to our house and took everything we had. They were elated. They had prayed for provision and saw our donation of stuff as an answer to their prayers. They had expected a long slow process of furnishing their quarters. The Lord knows how to match up the needs of His servants. We needed to get rid of our stuff and, praise Jesus, they needed our stuff!

One of our friends was in charge of Continental Airlines Micronesia. He got us tickets at a reasonable price and enough seats for everyone. The Bishop came and gave us a blessing for our journey. Someone had already approached Clark about renting our house, so he generously let us out of our lease. We also gave away the outrigger canoe to some young boys that admired it, and a doctor friend bought our Subaru. We packed all of our clothes. The girls and I had very little sleep, but we packed everything up and were on the plane 24 hours after the Bishop gave his approval.

The boys were experiencing the cross. They were sad about leaving the place they loved. Sarfin, Jefferson, Parfin, and Kimmy were all crying as we waved good-bye. And so were we.

John Paul said as we drove out of sight of the village, "The only thing good about leaving Chuuk is that I am going to get to see my best friend, Sammy Romero."

We all laughed – comic relief.

The family of Jesuit volunteers was at the airport. They had come to tell us good-bye. This was a sign for me. In all of our travels, we hadn't met many Catholic missionary families. And one had arrived just days before we were suddenly called out of there. Bishop Samo had told us often that the witness of a family in mission was having a positive effect on the building of the Kingdom. It was a joy to feel that we were passing on the baton in that witness. There was a good size crowd milling around and joining us in a final song and prayer. We had arrived eight months before as total strangers, and were leaving friends that felt a lot like family.

I prayed in the silence of my heart, "We set out to love and serve You, Lord in Micronesia, Oceania. Bring fruit from the seeds we were able to sow. Thank you for this time and this end of the earth, where we have seen you provide all of our needs. Give us a blessed and safe trip and uphold Your simple family of missionaries. Amen."

Enjoying Mission Life on a Pacific Isle. The beautiful Pacific Ocean was in view of our 800 square foot house (Three adults and five children were housed in it.) in Weno, Chuuk, Micronesia.

As usual, our home was always filled with kids from the adjoining village. Island culture is always inclusive. Some days I found kids napping in my bed, they were irresistible.

Chapter Twenty-One

God Is Not Dead!

Tears, joy, exquisitely long hugs greeted us at the airport in Houston. Sarah and baby Alyse were there to meet us. All of our family was so excited to see the first grandchild, their first niece.

"She is so precious. Can I hold her?" Susanna said, reaching out for the baby, "My pretty little Godchild. Let's see if you look like your nanny."

"I wanted to hold her first," John Paul said.

"Me too!! She's *MY* niece," Simon said, "I'm an uncle."

All hands were reaching out to hold her. "Of course, we all want to hold her. Anyone can see that she's going to be very popular. But let's don't fight over her. We'll all have the chance. Too much handling can upset her," I cautioned.

"Mom, it's okay. You always let us get all passed around a whole bunch. Alyse is not too delicate," Sarah said, moving Alyse from new aunt to new uncle.

"Sarah, she is so fat and healthy. Not only is she pretty, but I think she's very alert for her age," Frank commented when it was finally time for him to hold her.

"Thanks, Dad. She's a good baby, too. I'm so happy to have y'all back," Sarah's heart had so longed to have her family around to share her new experience of motherhood, "How was your trip? I can't wait to hear all about your mission. I'll tell you all about our crisis here later."

It was really good to be back together again. Our generous friends had rented a van to pick us up at the airport. We only had the possessions we carried with us. We had left a box of very precious things to be shipped to us: albums, movies, jewelry, papers, etc. But those things never made it. We arrived at midday on a Saturday. Sarah had arranged it so that we would arrive in Abbeville at the Romeros just in time for the Saturday Night Prayer Meeting. And the best part was that we were going to surprise our friends. Cheryl and Donald did know we were coming, because they were going to house us for a while. Our parents were there in Abbeville, but getting older. The Romeros always made us feel as though having us and all the kids was a gift to them. Being with them, our beloved Romeros, our brothers and sisters in the Lord, was healing and support for us.

Chaos erupted as we walked into the middle of the meeting. The praises went wild. John Paul, Joseph and Sammy excitedly embraced, all of them talking at once; and ran off together to Sammy's room. We had lots of folks to see, housing to find, a crisis to face, but for this night we rejoiced with our faithful prayer warriors and basked in the presence and assurance of the Holy Spirit. We had jet lag but Jesus is stronger than jet lag, and He was ministering to His travel weary, humbled missionaries. Our God is an awesome God!

My Dad was still in real estate; he had just bought a two-bedroom home as a rental property – another miraculous example of God's provision. Again, this house was *fully furnished*. We had nothing at all for setting up a house. So shortly after we visited with all of our families, and connected with Beau, my dad offered to rent us the house on Marmont Street.

We would pay the monthly payments on the note, which was pretty affordable. The older couple had left furnishings, albeit out of date, and a supplied kitchen. We put up a set of bunk beds and a chest of drawers in the oversize laundry room, which served as the quarters for Simon, Joseph and John Paul. Susanna and Mary opened up the sofa bed every night in the living room. Beau had a bedroom, and Frank and I had a bedroom. Our commitment to Gospel poverty came in handy again. Because we were missionaries, we happily lived in the places He provided. We thought this place would be pretty temporary – a few months at most.

Back in Chuuk, we hadn't had time to pray for what was next in our service to Him. We would have been discouraged if we had realized that was the last time all of us as a family would live full-time in the missions.

But the Lord's plan is not to discourage us. One of my very favorite scripture quotes is from Jeremiah 29: 11: "I know well the plans I have for you, says the Lord, plans for your welfare and not for evil, to give you a future and a hope."

We returned to the USA only looking to be there for Beau as he dealt with the dissolution of his marriage, and the tremendous blow that was to him. We soon found that Beau's time with us was a small part of the reason Jesus had sent us home. He had a plan. He had a hope. He had a future. As we resumed our life in Abbeville, He would unravel the mystery and reveal it to us.

The Saturday Night Prayer Group sustained us, our family and private prayer nourished us, receiving the sacraments at St. Mary Magdalen and St. Theresa, our childhood parishes anchored us and consoled us. Frank returned to the practice of law with Charles Sonnier, our lifelong friend. Mary enrolled in STM again, excelled, and gave a strong witness to her classmates. The boys went to the public schools. They, too, were honor students. Susanna heard the Lord Jesus tell her to honor the commitment she made in Chuuk, to give him a year of service before starting college. She served us and different stateside ministries. She founded a Club Life for youth in the Acadiana Area. This would later give birth to Faith Camp, FMC's summer youth camp. Susanna had graduated from High School at sixteen, so she happily dedicated that year to do what the Spirit said, "Do!" She also applied for and received the *Disciple of Christ Scholarship* at Franciscan University of Steubenville. That scholarship, funded by a generous benefactor, paid for all four years of study at Steubenville. Being the Disciple of Christ scholar was an honor that we knew God had bestowed on Susanna. She asked and He provided.

It wasn't long after we arrived that a major event happened for me. While I had been home in the states for Alyse's birth, I had finalized work on my first book, *Go! You Are Sent.* We self published and had ordered 10,000 copies because that made the copies affordable. I was pleased with the shiny red paperback and the semaphore light showing a glowing globe in the green light. Frank's mom allowed us to use a room in Frank's old law office to store the books. Frank and I and Donald and Cheryl were there when the eighteen-wheeler pulled up into the parking lot.

"Well, Miss Genie," Donald teased, "How does it feel to be a famous author?"

"I guess I won't be famous until all these books are sold," I replied, "And remember, Frank always prays for us to live in humble obscurity."

"That's a lot of books, Babe," Frank said, whistling at the sight.

"We prayed about it, and that's the number we felt to order. But it sure looks like a lot of books when they arrive in boxes of forty-eight," I agreed.

"I have a good feeling about this," Cheryl said, "I think God is going to use this book big time for your ministry."

After we had stacked the boxes in the little back office, we prayed. "Jesus, this is our story, but it is Your story. Use these books for Your glory and the building of Your kingdom. You be our distributor. Amen."

Our book was an instant success on a local level. The area media covered its publication and availability. I did most of the distribution at first, mainly book signings, local Christian bookstores, and requests by mail. Later, Beau handled my book, other books and miscellaneous inventory with his business, Resounding Praise Publications. This part-time business for Beau had five thousand invoices, in six countries, and in thirty-two of the states. We heard from so many that they had shared their personal copy of *Go! You Are Sent* with family and friends. Now, in 2011, that storeroom filled with boxes of books has a handful of those boxes left. Praise God, our story has blessed many and built the kingdom of God.

As the book became more widely read, we were invited to speak locally, nationally and internationally. Our testimony of abandoning the familiar world around us and our material goods to head into missions as a family was powerful. People were eager to be inspired by that story. We were guests on **Life on the Rock,** EWTN's guest ministry show, local radio stations, and statewide television stations. We were featured in newspapers, **The National Catholic Register**, various magazines including

The Priest, and **Acadiana Catholic,** and in the newly emerging media source, the internet.

We were speaking at the Annual Charismatic Conference in the Diocese of Lake Charles over the Thanksgiving holiday in 1996. It was an amazing weekend. The anointing of the Holy Spirit flowed through the whole weekend. We were there as a whole family. My daughters remember vividly walking along the sidewalks near the Civic Center where the event was held. A big group was signing at the top of their lungs, "The Lord liveth, and Blessed be my Rock, and let the God of my Salvation be exalted!"

Later, as I was giving my testimony before a large crowd about the miracles I have seen, I said, "I have seen food multiplied, the blind healed, the dead raised, time stand still, gasoline in a tank multiplied, crippled hands stretched out, a paralyzed face released, marriages healed, gifts of speaking in a language we did not know, prophetic visions, broken bones healed instantly, and cancer disappear overnight. We have had our own book of Acts. One thing I have never seen is someone walking on water. I'm still waiting on that one."

The crowd chuckled and applauded. They had all seen miracles, maybe not the same ones I saw. But they believed.

As I stepped down from the stage, I heard Jesus say to me, "I am going to show you a water miracle."

And I smiled up at him and said, "Thank you, Lord. I can't wait."

God had already planned His miracle. Earlier that Fall, the telephone had rung one morning, "Genie, this is Mary Lou McCall, I've read your book, and I'm inviting you to speak at our Family Life Conference in New Orleans in December. Archbishop Hannon and I think your family would be great for this. It will be on the 13th, 14th and 15th. It's going to be held at the Hilton on the Riverwalk. Do you think y'all can come?"

"It is a real honor to be asked, Mary Lou, I'll have to check with Frank, but I'm pretty sure it will be okay. Frank has already scheduled a CLE (Continuing Legal Education) seminar in New Orleans that Thursday, the 12th. We can just check into the Hilton a day earlier."

"Your children are welcomed, too," she added, "We plan to have a children's stream. Oh, and bring your book to sell."

"How about if I accept right now and I'll call you immediately if Frank has another commitment?"

"That sounds fine," she said happily, "Just call me if you need more information, okay?'

"Sure will. And our family will be praying for the success of the conference."

Two weeks after the Lord's promise to me to show me a water miracle, we were staying in the Riverside Hilton for Frank's CLE, and for our talks at the Family Life Conference. Frank had to spend all day in his seminar. The Riverside Hilton opened onto the Mississippi Riverwalk Mall. Simon, Joseph, John Paul and I walked down to the Mall to window-shop and have lunch in the food court. One of the Conference attendees had asked us to pray for New Orleans and its deliverance from violence and drugs (someone she knew had recently been murdered). The boys and I went out onto the open-air veranda near the food court. The "Mighty Mississippi" is a nickname that is not quite big enough or strong enough for the river at the port of New Orleans. The bend in the river at the mall is mesmerizing for its size, the flow of the water, the enormous cruise ships, freighters, ferries, tugboats, Coast Guard vessels, and helicopters patrolling the steady maritime traffic.

I called the boys together at the far corner of the veranda, the breeze blew against our faces, delicious food aromas hung in the air, and the sky was clear and blue. New Orleans is one of the world's most beguiling cities. I am never immune to its charm. I told them, "Ms. Karen asked us to pray for New Orleans, her friend was murdered. Isn't this a beautiful city? Let's ask the Lord to protect New Orleans."

"Let's hold hands," Simon suggested.

"Okay, who wants to start praying?" I asked as we grasped hands. We were off in the corner, but my little guys were not ashamed to bow their heads in prayer.

"Jesus, please protect New Orleans. Lord, help it to be a good place. Don't let the devil mess it up with violence and drugs," Joseph asked.

"Yes, Lord. Let the people of New Orleans have a happy Christmas. Christmas is my birthday, Lord. Let them have a happy Christmas on my birthday," Simon prayed emphatically.

"Bless our sales of rosaries at the Conference, Lord. Let

the people hear Your Word. Bless Mama and Daddy's talk," John Paul said. (He, Sammy, and Joseph had made rope rosaries to sell at the Conference.)

"Yes, Lord Jesus, bless and protect this wonderful place. Let Your word go forth to set the people free from acts of violence. Free them from drugs and alcohol abuse. Let them see your miracles, Lord," I prayed, "Let them see your hand at work. Amen."

Then we went into the food court and had po-boys, a favorite of the locals. We walked around the mall, jam-packed with holiday shoppers. We took crazy pictures, I bought each boy a souvenir, and we went upstairs to our room on the sixteenth floor of the Hilton. I had prayed for a river view. The Family Life Conference was paying for our room, so if we had come on the day of the Conference, instead of a day earlier, we probably would not have gotten a river view. I was really grateful. The kids colored on the floor in front of the glass wall that opened onto the Mighty Mississippi. I had my personal prayer time and started reorganizing my talk for the next day. Soon Frank came in, tired and worn from sitting in lectures all day. The kids told him about our day, and even told him about our prayer. Donald, Cheryl, Sammy and their daughter Sarah were staying in one of our friend's condo a few blocks away, within walking distance of the Hilton. We walked over to meet them and have dinner.

The next afternoon, Friday, the conference began. Meeting the participants and presenters activated our faith. It was a breath of fresh air to be surrounded with God's people who held family life in high esteem. The boys set up their Rosary sales table, my book, and some of our mission literature. They were pleased to see how many other kids were there. They had happy reports of the children's ministry; it was well-planned and not just childcare. Our Sarah and her family were coming the next day, and would meet us in time for our talk, they were going to stay in the condo with the Romeros. Susanna and Mary were not with us.

Saturday morning talks were also inspiring; we networked with family ministry people in the speaker's lounge. Because our boys were selling Rosaries, we met lots of Christian vendors. We began a lifelong relationship with the Yarboroughs,

David and Lisa, and their children. They exuded a zeal for the Lord, which connected us as friends and colleagues in the Lord's service.

Frank's and my talks were scheduled for the four o'clock session. After lunch, around 1:15, I walked the boys to the rooms on the ground floor of the Hilton; they were still attending the children's stream. It was not too far from where we had prayed on Thursday. Then I met Frank in our room where we situated ourselves to put the final touches on our talks. The wall of curtains was open but I sat with my back to the window so I would not be distracted by the expansive view of the busy river.

We had hardly gotten started, when I heard the blaring of a ship's horn. It took a few seconds to let the *mode* of that horn arise from my subconscious to my mind. Suddenly, I got chills. I had lived on a river. Ships horns are normally soothing – deep, resonant and calm. But not this horn – there was a ship in the river sounding a distress signal. Five, short, full out blasts of the horn signaled distress.

I stood up and whirled around to see the freighter, Bright Field, being carried by the current, out of control, headed straight for the shopping mall and the bottom floor of the Hilton. It continuously sounded the terrifying alarm.

My boys were downstairs, the mall was filled with holiday shoppers, Sarah and her family and the Romeros might be walking through that mall right this very minute. I knew I was witnessing a major maritime disaster. The freighter could not slow down. The current was swiftly moving it right into the place we had prayed yesterday – the beginning of the mall and the hotel.

I began to scream with a loud voice as I moved toward the window, *"Stop that ship, Jesus!! Stop that ship, Jesus!! Save Your people, Jesus!!*

I called out to Frank who was putting away his notes and staring at me, *"Frank, come help me pray!! Quickly!! Quickly!!"*

Frank came and he held his hands out with me. We finally placed hands on the window, still crying out with all of our might, *"Stop that ship!! Save your people, Lord Jesus. Help them!!"*

Then we saw the *unthinkable* happen. The ship crashed into some apartments, part of the Hilton, the Riverwalk Mall. Walls, roofs, windows crashed and smashed and looked like a house of cards crumbling down. Electric wires snapped and crackled and sparked. Gas pipes and water pipes were spewing into the air. I couldn't get the images of the happy go lucky shoppers the day before. I felt like we were watching hundreds of people die! We kept screaming, and crying out with loud voices, *"Save Your children, send Your Angels to lead them out of there. Give them light in the darkness, Lord! Save them. Save them!!"*

As our view followed the freighter's destructive path along the riverfront, it seemed powerless to stop, hardly slowing down as it toppled one building and dock after another. We could see the panicked masses rushing out from all the exits; terrifyingly looking for loved ones behind them.

Then we realized the Bright Field was on a collision course with the gambling boat docked at the other end of the wharf. We asked the day before how many people can be on the ship and were told that about eight hundred could be on board at once. I just thought we are going to watch those eight hundred be smashed like flies by the ship that was enormous even compared with the three story casino boat. Even though they were tiny figures from our view on the sixteenth floor, we could see pushing and shoving behind the glass windows, faces with horrified expressions plastered against the glass. We could see a few people jumping off the casino boat. I thought they were jumping to their death. When the freighter was about to slam into the casino boat, I made a fist, closed my eyes, hit one knee and shouted louder than ever, *"Send a mighty angel, Lord. Send a mighty angel, Lord. Jesus stop that ship!!"*

I had closed my eyes to avoid seeing the inevitable crush and destruction of the casino. But when I opened my eyes, the ship had stopped. And I saw *him* standing there. The Mississippi River at the dock only came up to his knees. He was holding a glowing sword in front of him with his forearm outstretched like a crossing guard holds her stop sign. The runaway ship was stopped. Science to this day does not have an explanation for the stop. They know what caused the boat to be powerless and loose, but they have no concrete answer for why it stopped. Frank and I do. We shouted again in pure emotion, *"Thank You, Jesus. Thank You for your angel!"*

The destruction was halted, but panicked people were everywhere. Sirens, sirens, and more sirens jarringly approached the hotel. I could think of nothing more urgent than finding my boys. I was begging God that the children's ministry rooms had been out of harm's way. Frank and I rushed to find them. Praise God, they were alright, but the destruction was just in the next wing of the building. As the sirens squeaked and squealed, first responders were everywhere. Even as I tried to move about the Hotel, along with Hilton employees by the score rushing around assessing damage, I thought fire could break out in the mall where electric wires were snapped. I dreaded hearing the news that night, especially the death toll. We had watched the whole thing. We had prayed for the Lord's help, but the whole area looked like a bomb had gone off. I was really shaken up and really hoarse.

The main assembly hall for the conference had been sheltered away from the collision of the Bright Field with the mall and the Hilton. After we had our boys in tow, we poked our heads into the conference room to see what was going on. Frank and I were supposed to speak at four o'clock, but the participants were just being made aware of the tragic maritime collision. The children's ministry staff was bringing children to their parents; husbands were wondering where their wives were and vice versa. Mary Lou and Archbishop Hannon were quick to make a logistics decision. They decided to postpone our session until five o'clock when everyone should meet and figure out what we would do from then on out.

Because all of the rooms occupied by the attendees, the dining rooms, the hall, and children's room were unharmed, we resumed the conference. Not one family member of those attending the conference had been harmed. As a matter of fact, miraculously, there was no death toll. It was a major miracle, a major *water* miracle.

I couldn't give the talk I planned to give. I had almost completely lost my voice in crying out to the Lord. I told the families the story of the prayers, the ship and the angel in a hoarse, cracking voice:

"God hears our cries for help. I suppose if someone had been filming Frank and me on the sixteenth floor this afternoon, the world could have taken it one of two ways. Either we were stark, raving mad fools who were screaming our guts out for nothing. Or, we were two of God's servants praying the prayers He inspired. We were standing in the gap of intercession, begging God for His angels to save His children. I say that we were those servants. We felt like we were working with Almighty God. His power was displayed moment by moment; I was in awe of that mighty angel."

Frank interrupted, "That's right, Genie. God is not dead!! **Our God is a real God**, who does **real things** for **real people** in the **real world**!"

The audience burst into applause.

Families left that conference with the truth that God is Not Dead! Fixed in their hearts is the truth that He is still in the miracle business!

News reports everywhere used the word "miracle." Some shoppers that escaped from the crumbling mall reported that angels had led them out when it all went black.

The Associated Press released this news:
17 December 1996
Loaded with 56,380 long tons of corn, the ship lost engine power and crashed into the Riverwalk shopping mall and the Riverside Hilton. With its emergency horn wailing and its anchor dropped in a desperate attempt to stop, the freighter narrowly missed hitting two cruise ships holding some 1,700 people. "It is nothing short of a Christmas miracle," Mayor Marc Morial said.

All the local newspapers reported the Miracle as their headlines. Even the New York Times had a huge article on the accident that became a miracle:

NEW ORLEANS, Dec. 14— A 700-foot freighter, moving down the Mississippi River here, went out of control today and plowed into a popular downtown riverfront shopping mall and tourist attraction packed with Christmas shoppers, injuring dozens.

Rescue workers said in the late afternoon that at least six people had been killed in the crash, basing their count on witnesses who reported seeing people disappear under the river or in the debris. But Coast Guard officials said tonight that they could not confirm even a single death. As of 8:30 P.M., no bodies had been reported found, neither was anyone reported missing from the collision.

The Liberian-registered freighter Bright Field slammed into the Riverwalk shopping mall at 2:15 in the afternoon, crushing a 100-yard section of the riverfront structure and sending thousands of shoppers running in panic.

The ship, loaded with grain, had drifted and then, riding the strong currents, bore down on the crowded mall. Shoppers, especially diners in the elevated structure's outdoor food court, looked up from their red beans and rice and shrimp po boy sandwiches to see the massive bow of the ship looming over them, horns and sirens sounding a warning.

As they ran, witnesses said, the freighter plowed deep into the side of the three-story elevated structure and raked its side. Some people did not notice it in time, and they disappeared in the rubble when the ship came crashing in, witnesses said.

Odieen Matthews was working as a saleswoman at Chico's, a clothing store in the Riverwalk, when the vessel pushed into the building. "It felt like an earthquake," she said. "It shook the entire building."

The Coast Guard said the freighter was heading down-river when it lost power and steering and struck the building. The crash, which left the building so unstable that rescue workers could not go into some sections of it, could have been much worse, rescue workers said.

The freighter came within 70 feet of a three-story casino gambling boat crowded with 800 people. As the freighter appeared to be bearing down on them, many on the boat panicked. Israel Perez, 23, an unemployed car salesman, was gambling when an alarm sounded and people shouted, "Abandon ship!"

"It was a mass stampede, and some people jumped into the river," said Mr. Perez, who suffered a dislocated shoulder. "I wouldn't jump in the river. I know how furious it is." In the crush and panic, he said, "people were falling everywhere, into the river, into the side of the deck."

Mr. Perez said he was at the casino because friends convinced him that "it was my lucky day."

While rescue workers picked through the rubble and searched the muddy water for victims this afternoon, workers at hospitals here said that most of the injuries were not life-threatening and that people were generally treated for such conditions as heart attacks, broken bones and bruises, the result of "trampling" as they tried to escape the complex.

A group of Girl Scouts who initially had been reported missing was found safe, but four disabled children could not be located after the accident, the authorities said.

Rescue workers searched the rubble with heat-sensing equipment and used dogs to try and sniff out people who might be trapped in the rubble. Meanwhile, tugboats kept the badly damaged freighter pressed up against the wreckage, to keep it from doing more damage. A hole 15 feet in diameter was gouged into its bow, and wreckage from the shops could be seen inside the hole.

Some city officials said the ship might actually be helping to stabilize part of the surrounding structure, but others said it was in the way of the rescue effort.

"Where there was a wharf there is water now," said Oliver Thomas, a New Orleans City Councilman.

The 180,000-square-foot Riverwalk is the former site of the 1984 Louisiana World Exposition. It has more than 100 shops, restaurants and cafes, some underneath the adjoining Hilton Hotel, the rest built above the wharf. It includes stores such as Abercrombie and Fitch, the Gap, Eddie Bauer, the Sharper Image.

Those stores and others were jammed with shoppers this afternoon, a bright, clear day. Patrons had some warning as the freighter and other boats and ships sounded their horns in warning. Some witnesses said the horns started to sound as much as three minutes before the impact,

367

and some shoppers moved safely away. But when it was clear that freighter was going to strike the building, the crush of bodies and ensuing panic slowed down their retreat,

"It just kept coming," said Chris Storey, who works at Riverwalk. "People started running in a panic."

On impact, concrete, glass and water rained down on them. One witness said he had seen a woman and a child walking along the wharf, and then they just disappeared.

New Orleans is one of the nation's busiest shipping ports, and it is common for freighters to hit wharfs. But that usually happens with much less force, rescue workers said, and in places where there are few people.

The Baltimore Sun reported:
December 17, 1996

A CHRISTMAS MIRACLE is how folks in New Orleans are referring to the weekend accident at the Riverwalk mall there. To understand why is to see the news photos of the fancy shopping complex, crushed like a soda can by a grain freighter run amok, and to learn that no one was killed even though the collision happened in midday as shoppers lunched and browsed at the height of the holiday season. The scenario was dramatic and horrific: A 70,000-ton grain ship, the Bright Field, as long as two football fields, lost power due to an oil pump failure. The rolling current of the Mississippi River swept the ship toward a casino riverboat with 800 passengers and the mall on the site of the former Louisiana World's Fair, filled with 1,000 shoppers and ... (no one was killed.)

When our family, Sarah and her family, and the Romeros gathered together later, we were glued to the news. Not only had the angel stopped the Bright Field freighter, but there had been no serious injuries and NO ONE HAD DIED. Was that accident just a coincidence? Had it happened at the same time as the conference purely by chance? Of course, the Lord knows that renewing families in this culture is a monumental task, and that it takes a monumental miracle to make them aware that He is their rock and their fortress. He is very much alive!

Chapter Twenty-Two

Build the Kingdom and They Will Come

The *few* months of surviving in cramped quarters on Marmont Street, would become a year and two months. When we moved into the house in August, we never thought we would be spending Christmas there. We expected to promptly find a suitable, roomier house. Our girls, ages seventeen and fifteen, didn't have a room other than the sofa bed in our living room. Our boys were in the laundry room. Thank God, they had made lots of neighborhood friends and spent plenty of time outside. One bathroom for eight of us also made things difficult. We had been in the homes of God's wonderful children all over the world. By those standards, we had nothing to complain about. We didn't really complain, but we knew that God wanted us to minister and train others for mission. For that reason, I had set out to spend most of my spare time house hunting.

While we were in Chuuk, I had told myself, "If ever I move back to Louisiana, I want to live near a body of water. That shouldn't be so hard. I had flown at low altitudes in a number of small aircraft, and south Louisiana has water *everywhere*."

I more or less narrowed my search to waterfront properties for sale. That was the first challenge of our house hunt. Of course, the price of waterfront property is very high. However, there were some places that were reasonable. The second challenge of my house hunt was that we were hearing the Lord tell us to teach others what we had learned in the missions. He wanted us to train and receive lay missionaries. He wanted us to give retreats, and to continue the hospitality ministry that He always made happen in our midst. We would need a large house for gatherings, and property to expand on. My brother, Bruce, is

369

a building contractor. He was super patient with me as I asked him to evaluate one big old house after another that might meet our needs.

"Frank, you need to come and see this house on the river. It is in our price range, and it has potential. Bruce and I looked at it, and he says it is solid and the roof still has a lot of life in it," I said before he left for work one day.

"Okay, if you can get an appointment during lunch, we can grab a sandwich and go look at it."

"Great, I think you'll really like this one," I said, putting my arms around his waist and waiting for my goodbye kiss.

He kissed me and said, "Pick me up in front of Charles' office at noon."

"I'll be there."

I had seen the house a few days before and my mind had already started renovating it. We would have to remove a wall in the kitchen and one in between the formal living and dining room. Bruce had said they were not load bearing walls. We'd have to install a half bath under the stairs, and close in part of the back porch. Those changes would not be too expensive and would make the house just perfect.

I picked up Frank at noon, and we drove a short distance to the house. Frank did like the location and the property that could eventually house more living quarters for expanding. He also liked the view of the bayou. But as we moved through the house and started talking about tearing down walls, I could feel his resistance to *the idea* of tearing down walls, and closing in the porch. He thought all of that was more trouble than it was worth. He could not see in his mind's eye, the same thing I could see in my mind's eye.

After we ate our lunch, sitting on the back steps of the house and gazing at the bayou, I drove him back to the office. I was very disappointed.

"We'll never get another house, if he can't see any changes," I thought to myself, "Jesus, he is being too picky, I am about ready to give up."

That was a Wednesday. Saturday afternoon, Joseph came up to me as I was reading in my bedroom, "Mom, when are we going to get another house? I really love playing with

Matt and everybody around here, but I can't breathe when the dryer is running in my room."

Joseph has had upper respiratory problems since early childhood. It broke my heart to have him ask about another house. He was not a grumbler, so I know he must have been suffering.

I went into the living room and found Frank watching television, "Frank, I think we ought to reconsider that house we looked at this week. Another buyer is about to put in a bid. We should act on it now."

"That is not the house for us. It requires too much renovation, and I think it will turn out to be a money pit," he answered decisively.

I made a point of turning on my heels angrily and went back to my room.

We had a Saturday Night meeting that night, I had already fixed our meal to bring, bathed, and dressed. The kids were bathed and dressed. It was in the nearby town of Crowley at the Leleux's house. Frank came to the bedroom door.

"Are you ready, it's time to leave?" he asked.

"I'm not going, but you and the kids should go. Just grab the casserole on the snack bar and take off," I answered sullenly.

"Why aren't you coming? We can all stay home if you like?" He answered.

"No, y'all go. The kids are looking forward to it. And I need some time alone; I'm bummed out with God. He and I have to talk," I said, still pouting.

"Well," he said cautiously, "Let's pray right now that you will feel better.'

"Look, Frank, I don't want to pray with you right now. I want to talk to Him. You can pray for me later, on the way. Y'all are going to be late, so get started."

When I heard the door shut, and the car drove off, I fixed myself a cup of coffee and sat down with my Bible. I sat there quite awhile, just breathing in the peace that comes when you sit down to have a conversation with the Lord.

"Okay, Jesus. I keep wanting to blame this all on Frank. I know that's not the answer. He is really not stubborn; I know that you have a plan and that we just have not discovered it yet. I preached this same truth to thousands of women. I know my

371

enemy is not flesh and blood. It is so obvious that the roaring lion (Satan) is prowling around trying to divide and devour us," I sighed, "Joseph's need for a new room and the girls need to have privacy and a place to bring their friends is real. What should I do?"

"What do you want to do?" I heard him speak into my heart.

"If it gets down to the nitty-gritty, I want to serve You and do what You want me to do."

"Well, that's more like it. What is standing in the way of that in this house hunting?"

I sat there in silence for a while, reflecting back on the time that passed since we came home from Chuuk.

The phone rang.

"Hello," I said.

"Hey girl, I asked Frank why you weren't here and he said you were 'bummed out' with God, are you alright?" Cheryl asked, really surprised and concerned that I had missed the meeting; she knew I was upset.

"I am 'bummed out', but I needed to stay home. The Lord is here with me too. I am going to find out what I'm missing. Y'all just pray for me, okay?"

"Sure thing, I'll see you next week," my sweet friend replied, "God Bless."

"God Bless you too. Love you, Bye."

It was reassuring to know my friends were praying for me. The Saturday Night group's intercessory prayer results were phenomenal. Heaven tuned into the Saturday Night meeting "channel" to watch us pray!

I began to ask myself what I was doing to make finding a house more difficult. The first thing that popped into my head was my insistence on being on the water. That was limiting the hunt. The next thing I thought of was my attraction to big, old houses that needed to be renovated. I needed to be more open to anything. Frank was probably wise in not spending too much money on the charm and personality of a house. Maybe we could do something different. We had looked into moving a house onto our property at Big Woods, which was definitely not on the water. The house that had been such a bargain to move already had a bid on it and the family in line before us bought the house.

I opened the scriptures; Isaiah 65: 21 spoke to me. "They shall build houses and inhabit them.... they shall not labor in vain.... they shall be the offspring of the blessed of the Lord, and their children with them. Before they call I will answer, while they are yet speaking, I will hear."

The word, "build", jumped out at me, so did the part about our children being blessed with us. The promise that we would not labor in vain, I saw as an assurance that we would be engaged in a fruitful ministry. And the part about the Lord answering before we called made me feel like we would have an answer soon. It was the first of March, Louisiana's amazing, springtime, green explosion was about to happen, and maybe we would experience it at Big Woods.

So, I prayed, "Lord Jesus, You win. And when You win, I win. Okay, I give up on being near the water; I surrender the idea of an old fixer upper, rambling, big house. I would go to Big Woods if that's where you are sending us. I'll have to trust You that people will drive that extra fifteen minutes from Abbeville to get there. I'll have to trust that our family will be happy way out there. Jesus, forgive me for blaming Frank for being choosy. Thank You for Your timing and that I feel that we will have an answer soon. I love You, Lord. I only want to do Your will."

The presence of Jesus and the Holy Spirit, the resolution of the conflicts in my heart, and the verses from Isaiah were planting the peace that passes understanding in my heart.

I began to tidy up, put on another load of clothes so that they could dry before Joseph had to go to bed. I could feel a spring in my step that hadn't been there in a while. I thought of the vigorous praise of my brothers and sisters in the Lord at the prayer meeting in Crowley. I began to sing praises in my kitchen as I defrosted things for our Sunday meal, "Thank You, Jesus that You were not *bummed out* with me."

I was already asleep when the crew got in from Crowley. Frank crawled into bed with me and I snuggled up to him, "How was the meeting?"

"It was one of the best ones yet!" he answered, tucking a pillow under his head.

"We say that almost every week," I laughed.

"It's true almost every week," he countered, "How was your night?"

"I'm much better. The Lord and I got it all worked out. I'll share with you tomorrow. For sure, He wants me to give up the idea of being on the water. It was a good night for me."

He squeezed my arm, and said sleepily, "Sounds like a plan."

On Sunday, I shared with Frank about my prayer time with the Lord. He liked the idea of new construction at Big Woods but doubted that we could afford anything substantial. The kids, especially the boys liked the idea of being at Big Woods; it was as much of a woodsy paradise as Chuuk had been an ocean paradise for boys. The wheels started turning in my head. If we built, should it be something we could add on to, should it be like a barn type house? We even drove out to Big Woods to walk around. Not a mosquito in sight, God's favor was on us.

Tuesday morning after all the kids had left for school, Frank and I were in the living room, where we had just had prayer. We had a half hour or so before he had to leave for work.

"You know, Frank, I've been thinking about the kind of house we need. I definitely am not looking for a 'Better Homes and Gardens' type home. We just need room and functionality. It can be rustic, it could have exposed wiring," I paused, "It could be like the center at Holy City."

Immediately, when I said those words, "Holy City", both our hearts leapt within us. Honestly, even as I write this, a chill just went through me remembering the feeling. We knew it! That was the house the Lord had for us! We could *both* envision it. We knew it would work for what we wanted; we had used that center at Holy City (a Catholic Christian Community base in Topsy-Bell, Louisiana not far from Lake Charles) for so many functions. It was perfect.

"Whoa, Babe. That is it! Do you think Paul Thompson would give us the blueprints?" he asked excitedly, "Do you think we could afford it? Would Bruce build it for us?"

"Frank if this is the Lord's answer for us, and I know it is, then the answer to those questions is 'Yes, Yes, Yes.'"

"I'll call Paul and ask him if he would let us use the blueprints. I'll tell him you will go to look at it soon," Frank offered.

374

"I'll call Bruce and ask him when he can go with me. He's super busy, I hope he can take a day off soon," I said.

Paul Thompson was a permanent Deacon and an Architect. He had founded the Catholic Covenant Community called Holy City. Their role in community building and deeply committed Catholic Life was very influential in the Church family of south Louisiana. Their retreat facility was simple, rustic, but charming and functional. The woods and places to romp made it an awesome venue for family retreats. Our Saturday Night group spent several of our Mardi Gras getaways there, and grew in our spiritual lives each time. Paul had also drawn up the plans for the Center at the property. He was honored that Frank wanted to build our place like his. He gladly agreed to donate the plans to us.

It was a week or so before Bruce could accompany me to Holy City to see the place and to get the plans. As we drove along, I filled Bruce in about the history of the building and about the community.

"There are some minor changes I would make in the overall layout, Bruce," I said happily, "But basically we would want to build the exact same structure. I do know that they have three foot high lofts over the wings of the building, but I would want to go at least as high as five feet. (In hindsight, I wish I had gone up to six), then we could use them for children's bedrooms and attic space."

"Yeah, from what you are telling me, it sounds like the roof needs more pitch anyway," Bruce answered.

"I'm not going to talk about the changes I want to make in front of them. I don't want them to think I don't like their place just the way it is. So I'll just emphasize certain areas," I explained, "One thing I want that they have, if I can find one, is an old cast iron commercial stove. Except their two ovens are the same size. I would want the second oven to be ½ the size of the first oven."

"Genie, you can't find those ovens anywhere. I've been looking for one for my camp, and if you do find one, they cost about $5,000.00 dollars," Bruce cautioned, "You would have to give up a room to fit one of those into your budget."

"Well, I'll just have to pray for one then," I smiled confidently.

We drove up into the woodsy setting, and pulled up to the center. The front of the center at Holy City is simple and inviting, but not very impressive. The same is true for our house at Big Woods. But after you cross the front porch and enter the house, it is impressive. It is impressive from a design standpoint. The huge open space you walk into is also impressive. The vaulted ceilings go up fifteen feet. The one open room is 1200 square feet. This "great room" is used for reception, kitchen, and dining. There are four 4x4 posts in the four corners and an 8x8 center post. The house is in the shape of a cross; an aerial photo shows a perfect cross. The chapel is in the top part of the cross and can open onto the dining room, or combine with it to become the size of a small church. It's perfect when priests offer Mass for us.

As we walked into the Holy City center, Paul and Selma Thompson greeted us. They served us coffee, and showed us around the place. I was waiting breathlessly to get Bruce's take on it. I wondered what he was thinking.

A few minutes after we arrived, Bruce and I were alone for a few minutes. "Genie, this place has your name written all over it," Bruce smiled, "This is what you have been looking for. I'm thinking we can build it within your budget. I'll have to put a pencil to it after we get the plans, but I am impressed. I like it a lot."

Tears of joy almost sprang from my eyes, "Wow, that sounds wonderful. And now that I'm here and seeing it as a possibility for our home it feels like an even better idea."

Paul showed us around, pointing out to Bruce essential features of the plans, making suggestions of doing things differently. We went through the whole 4,400 square feet of the building. The last place he showed us was the back porch behind the kitchen.

When we stepped out there, Paul gestured to a big item under several sheets of visqueen. "I have something to give you, if you want it," he said to me, "The Benedictines gave it to us from their kitchen. It is a cast iron stove just like ours, the only difference is that their second oven is ½ the size of their first oven."

As Paul was speaking, Bruce was picking up the layers of plastic film and revealing the old cast iron stove. He turned and looked at me with an incredulous smile, "This whole project is going to be like this, isn't it?"

"I sure hope so, Bruce," I laughed, "Why don't you tell Paul about the conversation we had on the way over here about a cast iron stove?"

Bruce did put the pencil to the project and told me, "If you do most of the procurement and wrangle for cheap prices on materials, we can build this house and remain within your budget. Also, you'd need volunteers to paint, etc. And my contribution to this mission project is that I wouldn't take a contactors fee, I'll only charge you for my labor."

"Thanks so much, Bruce. That is a giant gift. May God repay you," I said.

God had told us back in Saltillo to build a family of families in mission. As we waited for construction on our house to begin, we invited families we knew to come out to the property at Big Woods and pray for the success of our building venture, both of the house and of the mission training. We brought lawn chairs and picnics, and sat in a circle with the kids running, playing games, and swinging on the rope swing Frank had installed.

We signed the contract, and shook hands on the project on March 19, 1996 – the feast day of St. Joseph. We drove the first stakes and officially started building on May 1st, the feast day of St. Joseph, the worker. We call it *Casa San Jose,* in honor of St. Joseph.

On one of those prayer picnics, our daughter, Sarah, shared, "I have just had a vision of the pasture around us. It was filled with families, sprouting up like flowers. They were really happy and were here to live and be missionaries."

"Susanna, you look like you have a reading. Do you?" I asked.

"I do," she affirmed, "My reading speaks of family, like Sarah's vision. It is from Jeremiah 29: 6 'Take wives and have sons and daughters; take wives for your sons and give your daughters in marriage, that they may bear sons and daughters; multiply there and do not decrease.' I think God is saying in this reading that He is going to make Big Woods a place for generations of missionaries. I believe that Jesus expects this work to increase and not to decrease."

"Amen to that, I hear the Lord saying the same thing to me," I said, happily.

Fifteen years later, Sarah's vision has been fulfilled. Family Missions Company was born through the labor and delivery of our twenty-two years of mission life. Our amazing Big Woods home has been filled with a family of families in mission. Our own kids finished growing up here, became missionaries here, married and blessed us with grandchildren here. The missionary community we longed for is all around us, and we see the Glory of the Lord Jesus together. He is reserved in our Chapel. Our beloved Lord in His sacramental presence is in our missionary house, waiting always to receive us in prayer.

I remember when the construction of our house was drawing to a close in September of 1996. I was so happy and excited, "Wow, Frank, I can't believe we're moving in. We never could have finished in record time, five months, if we hadn't had all the volunteers."

"And we stayed in our budget. Now that's an answer to my prayer," he said, smiling.

"And how about the dates? We didn't plan in advance to start construction on the feast of St. Joseph the Worker. And, without planning it, we will move in on the Feast of St. Theresa, patroness of missions!"

As I unpacked the last box of dishes from the little house on Marmont Street, I felt the Spirit of the Lord envelop me.

"Thank you, Lord for leading us on," I prayed, "Thank You for allowing us to go to the ends of the earth with Your Gospel. Thank You, Jesus for the children You gave us. They have made being a family in mission an undiluted joy!"

I was shedding tears of happiness. I knew that the house at Big Woods was the beginning of something new. Joy and suffering would find us here, but we would love and serve Him.

Our own book of Acts was still in progress.

There would be more signs and wonders confirming his Word, and empowering us to love and serve the Lord!

Epilogue

St. Luke's book of Acts begins with these words:

1Chapter 1 In my former book, Theophilus, I wrote about all that Jesus began to do and to teach 2 until the day he was taken up to heaven, after giving instructions through the Holy Spirit to the apostles <u>he had chosen</u>. 3 After his suffering, he presented himself to them and gave <u>many convincing proofs that he was alive</u>. He appeared to them over a period of forty days and spoke about the <u>kingdom of God</u>. 4

On one occasion, while he was eating with them, he gave them this command: "Do not leave Jerusalem, but wait for the gift my Father promised, which you have heard me speak about. 5 For John baptized with water, but in a few days you will <u>be baptized with the Holy Spirit</u>."....

6Then they gathered around him and asked him, "Lord, are you at this time going to restore the kingdom to Israel?" He said to them: "It is <u>not for you to know</u> the times or dates the Father has set by his own authority. 8 But you will receive power when the Holy Spirit comes on you; and you will <u>be my witnesses</u> in Jerusalem, and in all Judea and Samaria, and <u>to the ends of the earth</u>."

In my first book, ***Go! You Are Sent*** I wrote about our incredible odyssey of Faith. Jesus saved our marriage and commissioned us to be missionaries. We had taken our first steps on a lifetime of surrender that built the Kingdom of God. The entire Bible, the sacred scriptures, was our bread for the journey. The book of Acts was in a special way our handbook. **Our Family's Book of Acts** is the second part of the story; the story of one family that <u>was chosen</u> and <u>saw many convincing proofs</u> that <u>Jesus was alive</u>. He made sure that our <u>baptism in the Holy Spirit</u> was a renewable resource for us in building the <u>Kingdom of God</u>. We often <u>did not know</u> what He had for us next but we asked for His guidance and were <u>His witnesses</u> at home and <u>to the ends of the earth.</u> Many beautiful accounts ended up in this book, but I can say with St. John (21: 25), "There were also many other things which Jesus did (in, for and through us); were every one of them to be written, I suppose the world itself could not contain the books that would be written."

Frank and I are putting money in a piggy bank, hoping that we can save enough to have an outing with our whole clan on the occasion of our <u>Fiftieth</u> wedding anniversary, which will be in 2013. Fifty years! We are super busy with Family Missions Company, and our children and grandchildren. When we have a holiday dinner at our house, if everyone is there, there are twenty-eight of us. We have fourteen grandchildren: Alyse, Anika and Soren – Sarah's kids (Kevin's step-kids), Michael, Anthony, Dominic, Thomas, and Marissa – Susanna and Mike's kids, Eli, James, Cecilia, and Naomi – Mary and Chris's kids, Elliot – John Paul and Jill's kid, and Anthony – Joseph and Brooke's kid. Then there are two new additions on the way. Baby Summers, who John Paul and Jill are expecting in April of this coming year, and baby Isaac Granger, who Sarah and Kevin are expecting just one week ahead of baby Summers. We also have ten precious holy innocents in heaven, babies our daughters have lost before their births – who are missed but still loved.

Frank and I have a time of couple's prayer first thing each morning and we bring our family to the Lord, with very grateful hearts, and with detailed attention to what we know their needs are that day. We still see miracles for them and know that Jesus loves them more than we do. We see that He heals them, blesses them, has cars donated to them, gives them success in their studies, helps them find jobs, grants safe deliveries for our grandbabies, helps them with finances, with relationships, sends them on mission, and most importantly keeps them close to Him. And now, we're onto the grandchildren. Life flies by, and suddenly my oldest granddaughter, Alyse, has her driver's liscense. We can't thank the Lord enough for all of their relationships with Him and their fidelity to our Catholic Faith.

Beau lives at Big Woods in our home and helps with logistics. I never have to wash a dish when he is around. Frank never has to take out the trash. Beau, with a Masters Degree in History reads voraciously. He is also a prolific writer, and now with the internet, he has a network of international friends and readers. In the not too distant past, he taught English at a university in Yantai, China. Currently he is looking to teach abroad again. He is a loyal parishioner. He's still my Bible scholar in residence, and his quick answers keep me from having to run to the concordance. He is a dedicated Uncle and never forgets a birthday.

Sarah graduated at the top of her Class at LSU, and received the University Medal. She struggled valiantly for years to preserve her first marriage to the father of her children. After moving 11 times with him in 8 years, she came back from Rome with her children. She embraced the Lord, relying on His mercy, the support of our family, and a wonderful Catholic counselor to help her recover from the heartbreak. Quickly, she threw herself into the missionary life, moving to General Cepeda as a full-time missionary with her children. Fr. Pedro, the priest she worked with in Mexico told me, "Sarah is another Mother Teresa for Mexico." After her divorce, she was quickly granted an annulment. Sarah's was blessed by the comments of the Annulment Tribunal that stated, "This was the clearest case we have ever seen." She always said the Lord would have to provide a husband if she were to remarry. She remained single for seven years, and then He provided a wonderful husband and stepfather for her and the family. Kevin Granger, whom she met on mission in Mexico, is also a missionary, and a talented musician, who loves the Lord. He is completing an intensive RN program; he already had a degree from ULL. They plan to use his nursing expertise to serve the poor, and make Missions their life. Kevin is such a loving stepfather to the kids and now the whole family is blessed by the newest addition, baby Isaac Granger.

Susanna and Mike were both missionaries before they married, working together in Mexico and China on different mission teams. They began their married life on mission in Thailand, Northern Mexico, and the Yucatan Peninsula. After living with their three oldest children in mission, they heard the Lord call them out of missions and have lived in Baton Rouge, Dallas, and now in Lafayette, Louisiana. Susanna and Mike VanVickle both graduated from Franciscan University of Steubenville, and love the Lord and their Catholic faith. Mike is a great provider, an involved father, and loves sales. Susanna loves being a wife and mother to their five beautiful children, doing pro-life work, and other ministries in the United States. God answered Susanna's prayer for a house in walking distance from church. They attend Daily Mass, are faithful to their family prayer and seek opportunities to share their faith with others.

Mary and Chris met and fell in love on a short-term mission to Cuacotla, Veracruz. They were seniors in high school. They dated through college, a holy courtship, and both graduated from ULL. Chris is now a Physicians Assistant and a member of both FMC's Board of Directors, and FMC's Medical Mission Board. Family life is a high priority for Chris and Mary, and they are faithful in passing on their Faith to their four amazing children. Since their college days, where they were members of a Life Teen Core Group, they have fellowshipped with other couples who love and serve the Lord. Mary is a full-time wife and mother, a strong woman of prayer, and a member of Theresian's, an international movement of Women dedicated to following the Lord in Therese's Little Way.

Simon-Peter, an adult now, lives in his own apartment with a personal care attendant. He joins us two to three times each week for mission activities, and all holidays. He still considers himself a missionary and evangelizes the people he deals with on a daily basis. I frequently have clerks and waiters ask me, "Are you Simon's Mom?" When I say, "Yes, I am." They always say, "We love having Simon come in here." Simon is the proud Godfather to Michael, his nephew, and Naomi, his niece. His favorite activity is giving gifts. Because of his handicap, he sometimes misses a beat, but at Mass he sings to the Lord with all of his heart.

Joseph has a degree from ULL in nursing. He chose nursing because it is a profession where he can find employment when he is stateside on furlough from his mission life. He is a dedicated mission leader, a faithful servant of the Lord and his family, and zealous about the spread of the Gospel. Three years ago, I was on a medical mission trip that Joseph was leading. One of the short-term missionaries, Brooke Ortego, was on that trip with us. I was so impressed with her love of mission, her love for the poor and needy, her "can do" attitude hoped and prayed that Joseph would notice all the things I admired about her. He did. They began dating shortly after the trip. Brooke had already made up her mind to become a missionary. They married in March 2010 and have an eighteen month old son, with another one on the way. I love their surrender to Jesus.

My youngest son, John Paul, graduated from ULL in broadcast journalism. His new business, Infinite Focus Video is taking off. He loves performing music, writing, reading and graphics. Our FMC Board Members, Jim Thompson and Denese have been a great advocates for the missions. Their family has been on countless short-term trips. John Paul and their son Jason became inseparable best friends. Jason's younger sister Jill is beautiful, and a lovely person. John Paul fell in love with his best friend's kid sister. They married in June of 2009, and have a twenty-two month old son and a five month old son. John Paul and Jill are great parents. John Paul is the coordinator of Faith Camp, FMC's summer camp for junior high kids, using high school and college-aged kids as counselors. It is a conversion experience for almost everyone, and a huge percentage of the time, the decisions the kids make to follow Jesus are long lasting and authentic. Jill is working on her degree in Photography, finishing slowly, allowing time to be a mommy.

As I try to catch the readers up on our family, one paragraph each for our seven children makes everyone seem so "flat". However, it has been exciting to watch God's plan unfold for our children. They are all strong people with noble desires. And they are fun. At weddings, they are on the dance floor longer and more than anyone else. They love to sing, to cook for others and each other. They love the great outdoors, and are enamored with the beauty of creation. My grandchildren are 100% children, Jesus-centered, academically excellent, and loving. They still squabble occasionally among siblings and cousins. We love life, we believe in miracles, we cultivate an attitude of gratitude, and we are missionaries.

I hope Sarah's new book, *Eat Raw Omelets: And Other Life Lessons I Learned from My Mom* is out soon. It is an easy read and puts life's important faith lessons in a fun format.

When I was looking for old newsletters to jog my memory for the book, I found a card Susanna had written on her last day at Steubenville. Because she uses the phrase, "to love and serve Jesus," I thought it would be a good insight into our family's life:

Dec. 13, 99

Dear Mom & Dad,
*   "Peace and everything good!"*
PRAISE THE LORD!

*   I am done! It's amazing – this morning at 8:45 I turned in my last exam. I went out into the hall and waited a minute for Kiquis, who came running up to me – gave me a big hug – and said, "Watch out world here she comes." So, it's a monumental day, but the biggest thing I feel is a <u>challenge</u> to take all that I have learned in every class, every homily, every conversation, every holy hour, every household function, and every prayer meeting and now go out and LIVE IT!*
*   I have been <u>so</u> blessed here at FUS. God has truly given me more than I ever asked or imagined. God is so good! I want to thank you Mom and Dad for your constant prayer and support for me. I thank you for paying for my incredible college experience – not with big bucks, but with your <u>lives</u>! It's only because of your amazing faithfulness to God and abandonment to His will and His service that I received the Discipleship scholarship to be here. You are the disciples who first taught me how to know, love and serve my beloved Jesus! Thank You!*
*   Truly I have so much more to thank you for. But the biggest thanks is for giving me the gift of my faith. I thank you for teaching me to share, to not complain, to serve, and to live simply. I thank you for fostering in me a total love for the scriptures. I thank you for teaching me about purity, modesty, and chastity. I thank you for teaching me the power of the name of <u>Jesus</u> and the power of praise.*
*   I thank you for being awesome prayer warriors & teaching me to pray with faith. I thank you, Mom, for training me to say, "Praise You Jesus" every time I stub my toe (or get in a wreck). I thank you, Dad, for teaching me to play the guitar & lead others in praise.*
*   I can't thank you enough.*
*   I love you tremendously!*

*   Your Susanna*
384

Go! You Are Sent ended with Frank's song, **Walking with Jesus – a** good theme for where we were then. Our FMC missionaries, led by Kevin Granger, recently put together a CD. **The Ananias Project** offers the listener a musical evening in the missions. The first song on the album is written and sung by Joseph, our son and now, with Brooke, director of FMC. I think this song embodies the depth of our call. It is a challenge for Catholic Lay Evangelists who want to live the book of Acts!

Rise Up

Rise up, Rise up
To say, "Amen" is not enough,
We must fly
To every corner of the earth
'Till every heart has felt his worth
Oh, that tonight, we would rise up

Sons and daughters of the Church
Let us harken to His Word
For the fields are ripe,
With the fruits of the Kingdom
Oh, that tonight
We would go forth to reap them

Holy Spirit, fire fall
We will listen for Your call
Yearn in us, you are our Desire
Burn in us, set our hearts on fire

Chorus:
Rise up, Rise up
To say, "Amen" is not enough,
We must fly
To every corner of the earth
'Till every heart has felt his worth
Oh, that tonight, we would rise up! (x2)

Joseph and Brooke
March 19. 2010

John Paul and Jill
June 19, 2009

Big Woods Mission Community House
We, now (August 14, 2012), have eight houses at our home base,
Big Woods Mission for FMC's family of families in mission. We
are in constant awe the way Jesus grants housing miracles!

Genie Summers Recommends:

Go! You Are Sent
> By Genie Summers

Eat Raw Omelets:
And Other Life Lessons I Learned From My Mom
> By Sarah Summers Granger

For Inspiration and Information:

The Missionary Family Podcast
A Podcast by Genie and John Paul Summers
themissionaryfamily.com

Family Missions Company's Web Site www.fmcmissions.com

Blog by Alyse Spiehler, Genie's Oldest Granddaughter
www.missionaryalyse.blogspot.com

The Ananias Project, Original Music by Missionaries
www.cdbaby/cd/AnaniasProject

The Magnificat Retreat, CD of a women's retreat by Genie and Sarah

SUMMERISE MEDIA PUBLICATION
Genie Summers
12630 Everglade Road
Abbeville, La. 70510
USA

Requests for more copies:

FAMILY MISSIONS COMPANY fmcmissions.com

Contact Genie:
praisingcajun@yahoo.com